PORTRAIT OF AN AGE

Victorian England

ἀρεταὶ δ' αἰεὶ μεγάλαι πολύμυθοι·
βαιὰ δ' ἐν μακροῖσι ποικίλλειν
ἀκοὰ σοφοῖς.

'Great deeds are always the subject of many tales:
but to embroider a few themes in a long story,
that is something for wise men's hearing.' (Pindar,
Pythia, ix 133–5.)

G. M. YOUNG

PORTRAIT OF AN AGE
Victorian England

Servants talk about People: Gentlefolk discuss Things
Victorian Precept

ANNOTATED EDITION
by
GEORGE KITSON CLARK

with a Biographical Memoir
by SIR GEORGE CLARK

LONDON
OXFORD UNIVERSITY PRESS
NEW YORK TORONTO
1977

Oxford University Press

GLASGOW NEW YORK TORONTO MELBOURNE WELLINGTON
CAPE TOWN IBADAN NAIROBI DAR ES SALAAM LUSAKA ADDIS ABABA
DELHI BOMBAY CALCUTTA MADRAS KARACHI LAHORE DACCA
KUALA LUMPUR SINGAPORE HONG KONG TOKYO

ISBN 0 19 212961 9
© Oxford University Press 1977

First published by Oxford University Press, London, 1936
Second edition 1953
First issued as an Oxford University Press paperback, 1960
and reprinted in 1961, 1963, 1964, 1966, 1969, and 1973
This annotated edition first published in 1977

PRINTED IN GREAT BRITAIN
BY RICHARD CLAY (THE CHAUCER PRESS) LTD
BUNGAY, SUFFOLK

CONTENTS

G. M. YOUNG

A Biographical Memoir

by Sir George Clark

On an early page of the present volume a summary of a very large matter begins with the words: 'Anchored to its twofold faith in goodness and progress, the early Victorian mind swung wide to the alternating currents of sentiment and party spite.' This metaphor from the tideway of a river is one of many such in the works of G. M. Young. They may seem to have welled up from unconscious memories of his childhood, but this appearance may be deceptive. He conjured metaphors from many spheres, some of them far outside his own experience. It would be unsafe to draw inferences about his life from his writings, but the course of his life helps to explain his purposes and methods as a writer.

He was born in 1882 at Charlton in Kent, between the Thames and the Dover Road, in Dickens country. His father, who lived to a great age, was faithful to this neighbourhood and made his home for many years at Greenhithe. One of the son's characteristic ideas was that there survived from mid-Victorian days into the eighteen-nineties 'a far more widely diffused interest in the culture-bearers and their doings than we have known before or since'. In one of his essays he illustrates this idea with a personal reminiscence. 'I was standing on a railway platform one day in the summer of 1896 when a man, certainly not of the aesthetic class (I guessed him to be a Gravesend pilot), opened his paper and exclaimed to a friend "Millais is dead".' To make that particular guess at the age of fourteen implied special knowledge, and in fact Young's father was a Thames pilot, a position of skill and responsibility, solid and respected. The belief in the home as the basis of society, which persists all through Young's writings, may well have grown from his early experience of a stable family, not of the aesthetic or the literary class, but sure of its place in the world.

To another early memory, of seeing Queen Victoria driving through the streets of London when he was only ten years old, Young adds that even then he was a Tory and opposed to

Gladstone's second Home Rule Bill. This tells us something about the politics of his home. We do not know when or how he came to be noticed as an exceptionally gifted boy. Some of his qualities must have been inborn, including some which attract the attention of schoolmasters. He had an exceptional power of responding to words, and using them. He also had an exceptional memory. Some of those who read his books or listened to his conversation believed that his apt and unfailingly ready allusions were drawn from unlimited resources, but, wonderful as it was, his memory was not superhuman. The notes in this volume show that he made mistakes, and it may be added that when he was right he did not always rely only on memory. He did not disdain the proper use of books of reference. He wrote a favourable review of Professor Ghose's *Annals of English Literature*, and he kept Mrs. Cowden Clarke's Shakespeare Concordance, as one might say, at his elbow.

When he was almost or quite fifteen, rather above the usual age, he went as a Scholar to St. Paul's School. The High Master, F. W. Walker, early marked him out as likely to sustain the school's outstanding reputation for success in university examinations. This hope was fulfilled. Young rose to be Captain of the school and won a classical scholarship at Balliol College, Oxford. His political ideas seem not to have changed during his schooldays. English literature was one of the subjects in which he won prizes, but the great acquisition of those years was his classical education. It was classical education of that species in which St. Paul's excelled, a firm foundation of pure scholarship, with a liberal superstructure of reading, but reading confined to a limited number of the greatest books. This was the equipment which enabled Young in due time to write, agreeably and persuasively, for a generation which had turned its back on the Greek and Latin classics.

In Oxford he played a normal part in undergraduate life. He even went down to the river and rowed, though with only moderate success: the attempt was the more creditable because he had none of the physical co-ordination that makes the athlete. At that time Balliol was full of vigour, partly because its undergraduates included wider extremes and a greater variety of types than those of any other college. The word 'arrogant' has drifted down in connection with Young, but it seems only to mean that he was shy and diffident, especially in contact with those who had least in common with him intellectually. In his studies he did not, as might have been expected, run straight through the regular course without a check. The classical curriculum included two examinations, of which the first was in principle mainly a continuation of the work he had done at school. In this he duly obtained his first class; but in the final school he was awarded a second. At this distance of time it would be useless to speculate how this came about. It may have been due to some mischance or some misjudgement. Young may not have taken kindly to philosophy, which was an important part of the examination, or his attention may have wandered from the prescribed routine. Perhaps this is the place to mention another unexplained fact. Six years after taking his degree Young competed for the Arnold Essay Prize. The subject set was 'The Road System of Medieval England'. Young did not win the prize; indeed there was no award, but, strange to say, he was specially commended. It is not certain that he submitted an essay on medieval roads, because the regulations allowed a candidate to write on an approved subject chosen by himself. In any case we do see him here definitely interested in modern history, a subject well outside his classical upbringing.

Whether or not there were any setbacks, the Balliol years ended triumphantly with Young's election to a fellowship by examination, a prize-fellowship, at All Souls. Of the forty-four fellows, about half were university teachers in Oxford or elsewhere, the rest followed the law or other professions, if any. They formed a very friendly, though not an unreservedly intimate, society. It preserved something of the ethos of the old aristocratic regime, particularly equality in which the young shared as fully as the most senior. There were no undergraduates, and so a fellow who wished, as Young did, to follow an academic career in Oxford had to find work in one or more of the other colleges. After a probationary year the prize fellow was free to live where he pleased; but Young lived on in college and became a lecturer of St. John's, teaching ancient history to undergraduates. He evidently did it well, for after a year his stipend was increased by £50. All Souls, however, was still entangled in statutes which had been intended to prevent the fellows from enriching themselves from the college endowments. The £50 brought Young within £50 of the maximum income which he was allowed to receive along with the stipend of his fellowship. Regular promotion in Oxford could be had only by migrating from All Souls to a fellowship in another college, and fellowships in ancient history were few. In 1908 Young chose to keep his fellowship and, like a few earlier All Souls prize fellows, to enter the more reasonably organized career of the civil service. His years in All Souls certainly ripened his shrewd, but not uncharitable, insight into the ways of men of thought and men of affairs. Carola Oman, in her book *An Oxford Childhood*, among her pictures of another side of social life, names some members of the college who made friends with the Oman children, ending the list with 'our favourite young Mr. Young'. He might have prolonged his All Souls years, by taking advantage of a statutory provision which meant in practice that, when his term ran out, an unmarried prize fellow might be re-elected with token emoluments. That he did not do so may have been due to the nature of his new work or to some other practical reason: it was not the result of any ill-feeling on his side or on that of his colleagues.

Among the civil service departments he chose the one which imported the least change of direction, the Board of Education. He had the best possible chance of knowing what he would find there: until three years before that date the Warden of All Souls had been Parliamentary Secretary to the department. Under the inspiring leadership of Sir Robert Morant, the permanent head, Young found himself engaged not in pedestrian administration, but in a crusade to promote the capabilities and the culture of the British Isles. To begin with, his work was connected with the universities (not including Oxford and Cambridge, which were still private institutions), and when the financial grants to them needed their own organization, he became the first secretary to the Standing Joint Committee for Universities, the predecessor of the University Grants Committee of the Treasury.

After war broke out in 1914 Young was one of the many able men who were assigned to new duties. He was private secretary to the President of the Board, the labour minister Arthur Henderson. When his master left the department and became a member of the War Cabinet, Young went with him. He even accompanied Henderson on his ill-starred visit to Russia in 1917, after the first revolution and before the second. What he saw on that journey did nothing to fortify his hopes for a better future, but he was still working among the practical idealists when, in the same year, he became one of the two joint secretaries of the Ministry of Reconstruction. This ministry was concerned with domestic affairs, and it was not allowed to make any major contributions to their settlement when peace came; but it did initiate some social and constitutional studies of lasting value. Young, who had been awarded the C.B. for his services, seemed likely to follow the orthodox course of promotions.

No doubt the exertions of war-time, relieved, as far as we know, only by hard reading on such subjects as the French Revolution and the Russian language, had done something to impair his energies; but after the end of hostilities he went abroad again, following up some of his newly acquired interests. On his visit to Russia, at Archangel, he had met Sir Francis Lindley, a diplomatist ten years his senior who became British Minister in Vienna in 1919. There Young joined him, with the temporary rank of Secretary, to administer a special relief fund granted by the Treasury. This led on to other work on the financial problems of what had been the Habsburg lands. As a director of the newly created Anglo-Austrian Bank, Young was active in Vienna, Prague, and elsewhere; but he did not establish happy relations with the professional bankers, who are said, probably enough, not to have appreciated his talents. Like many others he was disillusioned by the realities of European reconstruction, and in the middle nineteen-twenties he left the government service altogether.

For the remainder of his life, more than thirty years, Young devoted himself to literature. He had already many friends among editors and writers. Having belonged in his younger days to the Savile Club, famous for talk, he now became a familiar figure at the Athenaeum. He was slight in build, not below the middle height but stooping slightly, always properly but not smartly dressed, with bright eyes, and what has been called 'a longish, inquisitive nose'. He took a place in the indispensable body of those who man the boards and committees, unseen by the public and seldom noticed by the press, of the great libraries, museums, and galleries of London. His experience and his cast of mind marked him out as fitted for this, and in the nineteen-thirties, in quick succession, he became a Trustee of the National Portrait Gallery, a member of the Standing Commission on Museums and

Galleries, a Trustee of the British Museum, and a member of the Historical Manuscripts Commission. On all these bodies he worked regularly and usefully, always reasonable and well-informed, neither over-emphatic nor undecided. His last appointment of this kind came in 1947, when he was chosen for the laborious Royal Commission on the newspaper press. He never married and his tastes were simple. When he was about sixty he began to share the home of his friend Mona Wilson, at Oare, between Marlborough and Pewsey in Wiltshire. She was a writer of distinction, with tastes and interests near to his own, and a member of a remarkable family. Their home became a place of resort for their wide circle of kindred spirits. Young used all his literary accomplishment to bring the downland landscape in all its significance before his readers, and this was the background of his best creative work.

Much of his writing was done under the limitations of literary journalism, but it brought the appropriate reward of wide reputation, and his books, from the *Gibbon* of 1932, provided the firm connecting tissue. He was much sought after for engagements of a more conspicuous kind, public addresses and lectures. He was invited by one university and one learned society after another and, wherever he went, he charmed his audience with something completely his own and perfectly appropriate to the occasion. He received academic honours which gratified and also reassured him, among them doctorates from Durham and Cambridge, and an honorary fellowship at Balliol.

After the second great war the foundations of his happiness broke away: Miss Wilson died, and the house at Oare was sold. But it was not long before he made fast at an old anchorage: All Souls invited him to return as a fellow. He lived in the college for the last years of his life, surrounded by younger men in whose company he delighted and whom he more than repaid in the same coin. There is, however, a misadventure to record in these years. In 1952 Young published his largest book, the authorized biography of Stanley Baldwin. To undertake this work so soon after Baldwin's death, when his policy was still subject to harsh and sometimes ignorant criticism, seemed a duty, but one surrounded by hazards. Young acceded with reluctance to a request which Baldwin himself had made. The materials proved to be far less in quantity and less informative than had been expected; there were difficulties and delays in making them available; and, worst of all, in the course of his work Young found that his estimate of Baldwin was changing and becoming less appreciative than it had been. The thought and industry that went into making the book were not wasted, but it was not well received and it does not rank as a standard work.

Young's development was unlike that of most historians. He never studied or taught modern history at a university. All his writings grew out of his private reading. No one would mistake them for the work of a dilettante, but his readers may wonder whether his studies of the nineteenth century are the work of a specialist or of a scholar of wider range, who chanced to meet more opportunities of working on this period than on any other. The answer is that he published several highly finished pieces about subjects very remote from his central interest, and he might easily have done the same many times over. It would be rash to set limits to his range of knowledge and interest. No doubt it did not extend far into music or, in general, into sport; and there might seem to be a case for saying that he did not concern himself seriously with natural science. This, however, can scarcely be maintained. He was in the habit of keeping up long exchanges of letters on intellectual topics. After reading one of the excellent books of popular science written by the zoologist Sir Edwin Ray Lankester, whom he did not know, he wrote to the author and so began one of these correspondences. This was relevant to his main interests, because zoology was central in the nineteenth-century revolutions of English thought, but it shows how little Young resembled the mere historical compilers.

The same may be said of his outlying studies. Of these perhaps the most remote from the centre is the lecture on the origin of the West Saxon kingdom. The experts may think it unconventional or even unorthodox; but they do not omit it from their bibliographies. Another is the lecture *Shakespeare and the Termers*. This has been accepted as sound and full of original thought. It is not indeed clear whether Young was aware that some of his suggestions had been anticipated by earlier, not very important, writers, but he does not claim that they were new discoveries. Towards the end of this lecture there is a brilliant and moving passage about *King Lear*, which exemplifies his reluctance to obtrude his own personality. The passage begins abruptly: 'On the stump of Lee

Old Church near Blackheath—where the road to Dover runs—may be seen the monument to Sir Brian Annesley. . . .' Young does not mention that Lee Old Church was within three miles of his birthplace.

Although his mind never ceased to pursue its inquiries it seems that the main structure of his beliefs altered very little after he was forty. He often expressed two opinions which must owe something to his continental travels. The first is the idea that anything Victorian is simply European. The other is a sense of the importance of modern psychology. It will be remembered that Young chanced to live in Vienna at a time when the name of Freud was only beginning to be widely known in England. Although he was genuinely impressed by the importance of these two opinions, he did little to develop or apply them in his historical work. He continued and reanimated the classical and ethical tradition of his early days. His belief in education as the vital principle of society links his writings with his years of office-work; and at the core of his historical interpretation is his conviction, whether just or unacceptable, that Victorian culture was fractured by the failure to carry further the reform of education.

INTRODUCTION TO THIS EDITION

G. M. Young's *Victorian England: Portrait of an Age* was written in two parts. The first part was published in 1934 as the final chapter of a book of studies on *Early Victorian England*, which he had edited. It goes down to the break on page 110, in this book, after the paragraph in which he says 'We are approaching a frontier'. He was then induced to carry the work on till the end of the century, and the whole essay was published as a separate book in 1936. He had conceived *Early Victorian England* as a period which stretched from 1831, the period of the first Reform Bill, down to the death of Palmerston in 1865. The whole book naturally ended with the Queen's death in 1901.

Though he used the word 'Victorian' in his title he did not in fact regard the Queen's reign as a significant period in history, nor did he believe that the people who happened to live in that reign necessarily displayed any common characteristics; indeed, he started his earlier study six years before the Queen came to the throne, and wished afterwards that he had carried his later period up to 1914, twelve to thirteen years after her death. It is, however, likely that whatever name he had chosen for his period would have proved to be unsatisfactory, and that his limiting dates, whatever they were, would have come to seem arbitrary and meaningless. The subject-matter of history is too continuous and too various for it to be neatly divided into periods; before any date which is cited as a beginning there will be anticipations which challenge its claims, and after every suggested end there will be challenging survivals, while the period in between them will soon disclose too many variants and discordances to allow it to be easily acceptable as a unity. Nevertheless to think in periods is probably still the best way of recognizing the historical process, and for this reason it is very well worthwhile to try to recognize the characteristics of the 'Victorian Age' as portrayed by Young, and to consider carefully the various 'frontiers' or lines of division which he marked to chart its course.

For Young's *Portrait* is an historical essay of unique interest and importance. It is not easy to think of another example of historical writing to which it can be satisfactorily compared. In his introduction to the completed volume Young said that at first he took as his model the famous third chapter of Macaulay's *History*, but destroyed the first draft because it seemed to be only a 'flat imitation' of the original. It is impossible to say how far this was true, but in his account of the development of his thought from that point he shows clearly what came to be a critical difference between his own work and that of Macaulay. He says he came to the conclusion that the 'central theme of History is not what happened, but what people felt about it when it was happening'. History should therefore be conceived in the terms in which contemporaries thought and spoke and wrote, and should only attempt a description of what they did or of their environment as realized through the medium of their perceptions. Macaulay was also interested in what people said and wrote and he shared with Young two characteristics which meant that he was unusually well equipped to discuss such matters. He had an extraordinarily comprehensive memory, and he had read the literature of his period avidly, not only the literature of permanent value, but the ephemeral literature and the rubbish. But Macaulay was also concerned to give an account of the physical condition of England in the reign of Charles II as he conceived it to have been. This necessarily occupies a great deal of his canvas. Moreover, brilliant and vivid as is the work of Macaulay, when he comes to deal with men's thoughts he seems to lack the subtlety and flexibility of mind which gives to Young's work its remarkable interpretative power.

There is, however, another, and significant, difference between the work of Macaulay and that of Young. Macaulay described England as it existed at a fixed point of time. It is true that while he was writing, his attention seems to have strayed, at first possibly anxiously, and then with growing confidence, to the progress of human affairs in 1848, and that what he noted caused him to make triumphant comparisons. But it would be wrong to value Macaulay's work by the measure of his rather naïve view of the historical process. On the other hand the value of Young's work lies precisely in his sense of process. His is a picture of intellectual and spiritual change, of the process by which the ways of thought of a society developed by subtle stages from what they were in

1831 to what they were to become in the early years of the next century. It is indeed as a picture of change that Young's work is distinguished from other descriptions of nineteenth-century Britain, from for example Élie Halévy's notable account of Britain in 1815. They are apt to be either descriptions of Britain round and about a particular date, or else histories in which the general description is rightly subordinated to the narrative of the succession of events and the ascription of causes.

But it is as a portrait, not as a history, that Young's essay should be understood and appreciated. As with a portrait, it contains that selection of facts which commended itself to the vision of the artist. As with a portrait, it is the natural product of the personal technique of the artist, with the potentialities and limitations which are peculiar to that technique. As with a portrait, the subject is seen from a particular standpoint and at a particular angle. Young's standpoint was among the highly educated, moderately liberal, professional middle class. This was a most important class. It supplied most of the men in the upper Civil Service, many of the leading figures in academic life, many important lawyers and doctors. Most of those who were eminent in literature became members of it. It was responsible for much of the progress in the nineteenth century. But though its powers of recruitment and absorption were great it was never more than a very small section of the nation. If Young had drawn his portrait from the point of view of another group its perspective, its values, its selection of the objects portrayed, would not have been the same. If he had taken his stand with one section or another of the working class it is possible that harsh economic pressures and such institutions as Trade Unions would have bulked larger. If he had seen England from the point of view of the aristocracy, or of the squires, or of some group of businessmen, or of some religious body, the view of England would in each case have been different. For there are innumerable points of view from which a community can be surveyed and in each case what is seen and what is not seen, and the light and shade in which they are seen, will differ with the standpoint of the viewer. In most cases if the viewer is honest and has some interpretative power his view will be of value and interest. Only it will be of importance to remember who he is and from what point he is looking. This, however, is true of every type of historian.

Young had unusual interpretative powers and an altogether exceptionally extensive view, and his essay is an unusually stimulating and valuable contribution to English nineteenth-century history. Unfortunately it has another characteristic, which is also unusual in historical works of comparable importance. It is practically without references. It contains many quotations; it is full of allusions to men and events, many of them not obvious, some of them obscurely phrased; it deals with subjects with which, often enough, the ordinary reader is not likely to be familiar. But there are singularly few clues which might enable a reader to check, or evaluate, or even in some cases to understand or identify, what is being cited or discussed. A number of reasons have been advanced to explain this, indeed one explanation will be suggested later on; but whatever the explanation there can be little doubt that this omission has affected its usefulness.

It is this fact that may be held to justify the present attempt to supply what Young failed to produce. I have to confess that as far as I am concerned I started it as a game to be pursued by myself and my friends in the intervals of what seemed to be more important work. It was an attractive game. The citations in the text were often very vague, and to follow them up not only required a rough and ready knowledge of the probable sources, but also an attempt to reconstruct the ways in which Young was likely to have thought and the works he was likely to have consulted. Often enough the pursuit of a particular reference led nowhere. When all likely coverts had been beaten the quarry was not to be found. However, even when the end was a blank the pursuit had often carried one into nooks and thickets of nineteenth-century history which were interesting on their own account. And gradually luck and the co-operation of friends began to produce a reasonably large number of attributions.

The desirability of publishing these results was first brought home to me by an experience which I found that I shared with others who were trying to teach nineteenth-century English history in other universities. We had all been anxious to get young men and young women to read *Portrait of an Age*, in order to help them to get nineteenth-century English history into focus; but we all found many of them singularly unwilling to do so. Many of them would not read the book at all, others read it half way through and abandoned it, others read it through and resented it.

I did not understand, I do not now fully understand, the strength and generality of this feeling. They were not after all expected to agree with Young, or to accept his values, or to recognize his quotations or allusions. Many people had enjoyed the book and gained profit from it without doing that. But I believe this dislike had something to do with Young's failure to supply references and to explain himself, that it was felt that the reader was being presented with a number of references and quotations which he could not be expected to recognize and that the object of this parade was to emphasize the superiority of the author. This was no doubt unfair on Young, but if this was what was thought, it seemed possible that to publish as many references as could be identified might restore the essay's usefulness, as it would also be of use as a starting point for research.

Very soon, however, a totally unexpected reason for publication emerged. Many of Young's quotations proved to be inaccurate, some of his facts were mistaken or at least misdated, some of his judgements were clearly perfunctory, for they were not supported by any reasonable interpretation of the documents he cited in their favour. Now it is probable that few people who have tried to write history would wish to adopt too superior an attitude about inaccuracies. We most of us know how easy it is to copy something down wrong, how critical facts slip from our memories when we form our conclusions, how convenient quotations and assertions emerge from our inner consciousness and adorn our arguments until we look at the source that should have supported them, and find something quite different. We know and fear these things, and we know also that they can only be eliminated by that tedious business of checking all that has been written. Indeed most of us know to our cost the filter-passing mistake that finds its way through all checks on to the printed page. But Young's mistakes are more numerous than can be explained by the ordinary incidence of human error. Their number can only mean one thing. He had not checked his references. He had not even returned to many sources after the first swift reading. He had trusted a magnificent memory and an unusually well-stocked mind, and, as is usual in such cases, his memory had on occasion betrayed him, and his imagination had sometimes constructed assertions which he could have realized were not in accordance with the facts, if he had only been prepared to reconsider the facts.

If this was so, one reason why he had cited no references was a simple one: he probably no longer possessed them. If he had ever written them down, he had lost them or not looked at them again.

It would be wrong to exaggerate the extent to which these errors vitiate the value of Young's work. In many cases they are trivial, and on the other side of the balance should be placed the fact that what was presumably his method of work, the consignment of what he read to his memory so that in due course it was fused into a coherent whole by his imagination, was likely to produce a more valuable synthesis than could ever have been achieved by a scrupulous scholar who simply added one carefully established fact or citation to another. Nevertheless corrections must be made: it is necessary to produce corrected versions of the various quotations; it is necessary to suggest another way of looking at things where Young seems to be definitely misleading. It is also desirable on occasions to make suggestions for further reading.

All this enhances the need to supply notes for the essay; but it also adds to the difficulty of the task. The problem is where to stop. It would clearly be impertinent and wrong to rewrite Young's work, or to place alongside it what is in effect another book on the same subject. Yet a mere list of references would not suffice. In many cases I have tried to produce not simply a reference but also a quotation, partly because where there is a mistake a full quotation seems to be the best way of correcting it, and partly because many of the quotations seem to me to be intrinsically interesting. In other cases I have ventured on a longer explanation where a more elaborate elucidation seemed to be necessary, or the point seemed to be important. But in all things I have tried to subordinate the notes to the needs of Young's essay, for it is the object of this work to reproduce his *Portrait of an Age*, not an alternative version. These problems have been complicated by a fact that has become increasingly clear in the course of this work. The staple of knowledge which any educated person may be presumed to possess changes with each generation, and so does their probable range of interest. I have therefore been urged by those who know the minds of the young men and women of today better than I can do to supply notes which I did not consider to be necessary. This in several cases I have done, but I hope that readers will not find it difficult to disregard any notes which they do not need, or which do not interest them.

By no means all Young's references have been traced; a number of them have defied all efforts to pin them down, even after an approach has been made to scholars who are recognized authorities on the subjects to which they refer. A considerable number of people have helped me to find those that have been identified. I have placed the initials of those who have contributed at the end of the appropriate note, and a list of their names on pp. 189-90. I hope none of them will quarrel with the way I have produced their finds and that they will realize how grateful I am to them, as also to many who have helped me whose names are not recorded in this list because what they suggested to me, though it was possibly of great value, did not produce a citation to which their initials could be attached.

There are others to whom my gratitude is due. To the Warden and Fellows of All Souls I owe the fact that I have been permitted to publish this work; I hope it will produce for them some revenue which as we have agreed will be applied to further that research in nineteenth-century history which interested Young. I owe a particular debt to the Warden for the readiness with which he accepted my suggestion of an annotated edition, and commended the idea to his colleagues and to the Oxford University Press. I owe much to Lord Blake who read through many of the typed notes at a fairly early stage, to Sir George Clark for writing his description of Young, and to those working for the Oxford University Press who have found the way through the difficulties the work presented. To all these I owe my gratitude, but my greatest debt is to Dr. D. R. Fisher and Mr. J. M. Collinge. They retyped, checked, and edited all the notes, and in a large number of cases have discovered quotations and references which had eluded me. Their work has been both laborious and skilful; indeed I cannot see how, without their help, this edition could ever have been completed.

Trinity College   G. Kitson Clark
Cambridge
1974

Dr. Kitson Clark died on 8 December 1975 before this book could be printed. It has been seen through the press by Mr. J. M. Collinge, Dr. D. R. Fisher, and Dr. R. Robson.

INTRODUCTION

TO THE SECOND EDITION (1953)

IN the First War, partly from curiosity and partly for comfort, I set myself to study the course and outcome of the great Napoleonic struggle. When Waterloo had been fought and won, I went on to the years of peace and distress which followed, and so to the collapse of Tory domination in 1830, to the Reform Bill and the New Poor Law, to the England of young Gladstone, young Tennyson, young Darwin: of the Oxford Movement: of the Benthamites: of Factory Inspectors and School Inspectors: of Chadwick and Horner: of *Sybil* and the People's Charter. As I read, my picture of Victorian England grew clearer, and it was a very different picture from the one at that time commonly accepted by popular opinion and set out by popular writers. So, in a fit of wrath over what seemed to me a preposterous misreading of the age, I wrote an Essay★ which was intended as a manifesto, or perhaps an outline for others to fill in. I had had little or no experience of writing, and the Essay was in places sadly crude, and in places badly rhetorical. But it did, I found, induce some readers to reconsider their ideas, and re-orientate their attitudes: ideas and attitudes generated rather by an emotional antipathy to the Victorian Age than by any insight into its historic significance. So when Oxford asked me to plan a book on *Early Victorian England*, to match those on *Shakespeare's England* and *Johnson's England*, I felt I was committed to do my best, and I think I can justify my rashness by saying that I persuaded Sir John Clapham to write the chapter on 'Work and Wages'.

For myself I reserved the final, summary chapter, to be called 'Portrait of an Age 1831 to 1865', the Reform Bill and the death of Palmerston being, as it were, the natural limits of the period. In the Essay of which I have spoken, I had, somewhat paternally, exhorted young historians to study the methods of the great

★ Published as 'Victorian History', in *Selected Modern Essays*: Second Series (The World's Classics, No. 406. Oxford University Press, 1932).

masters. I followed my own advice with the result that my first
draft rapidly degenerated into a flat imitation of Macaulay's Third
Chapter. It went into the fire. The second was more promising,
but, as I was thinking it into shape, I found myself asking, what is
this chapter really about? For that matter, what is History about?
And the conclusion I reached was that the real, central theme of
History is not what happened, but what people felt about it when
it was happening: in Philip Sidney's phrase, 'the affects, the
1 whisperings, the motions of the people'; in Maitland's, 'men's
2 common thought of common things'; in mine, 'the conversation
3 of the people who counted.' Who were they? What were the
assumptions behind their talk? And what came of it all? Then 'the
boy born in 1810' offered himself as the interpreter of that talk,
and my first paragraph wrote itself.

I had always been convinced that Victorianism was a myth,
engendered by the long life of the sovereign and of her most illustrious subjects. I was constantly being told that the Victorians did
this, or the Victorians thought that, while my own difficulty was
to find anything on which they agreed: any assumption which was
not at some time or other fiercely challenged. 'Victorian History',
I had said, 'is before all things a history of opinion. To see ideas
embodying themselves in parties and institutions: institutions and
parties closing in upon ideas: to show old barriers sometimes
sapped, and sometimes stormed, by new opinions: positions once
thought impregnable abandoned overnight, and forces once
thought negligible advancing to unforeseen victories, that is to
4 understand Victorian history.' And the historian must be in
sympathy with them all.

So conceived, my final draft did not dissatisfy me. I thought the
outlines were true, the incidents fairly selected, the omissions justified, though I might with advantage have found space for the
Mutiny and the transfer of India to the Crown. But, when I was
asked to expand my chapter into a survey of the whole reign, I
found myself involved in difficulties which I could not always
master. I see now that I should have carried my book to 1914,
and treated Late Victorian and Edwardian England as the *ancien
régime* of the England in which I was writing. I could then have
shown, more clearly than I have, the ecumenical significance of
the age, revealed not only in the foundation of the great Dominions but in that marvellous network of commerce and finance

which may truly be called a World Economy, and which was created by the genius, and sustained by the strength of Victorian England. That is what I should try to set out if I were beginning afresh. But as the greatest of our masters has said, 'where error is irreparable, repentance is useless'. 5

G. M. Y.

1952

PORTRAIT OF AN AGE

I

A BOY born in 1810, in time to have seen the rejoicings after
Waterloo and the canal boats carrying the wounded to hospital, to remember the crowds cheering for Queen Caroline, and
to have felt that the light had gone out of the world when Byron
died, entered manhood with the ground rocking under his feet as   1
it had rocked in 1789. Paris had risen against the Bourbons;
Bologna against the Pope; Poland against Russia; the Belgians
against the Dutch. Even in well-drilled Germany little dynasts
were shaking on their thrones, and Niebuhr, who had seen one
world revolution, sickened and died from fear of another. At home,   2
forty years of Tory domination were ending in panic and dismay;
Ireland, unappeased by Catholic Emancipation, was smouldering
with rebellion; from Kent to Dorset the skies were alight with
burning ricks. A young man looking for some creed by which to
steer at such a time might, with the Utilitarians, hold by the laws of
political economy and the greatest happiness of the greatest
number; he might simply believe in the Whigs, the Middle Classes,
and the Reform Bill; or he might, with difficulty, still be a Tory.
But atmosphere is more than creed, and, whichever way his
temperament led him, he found himself at every turn controlled,
and animated, by the imponderable pressure of the Evangelical
discipline and the almost universal faith in progress.

Evangelical theology rests on a profound apprehension of the
contrary states: of Nature and of Grace; one meriting eternal
wrath, the other intended for eternal happiness. Naked and
helpless, the soul acknowledges its worthlessness before God and
the justice of God's infinite displeasure, and then, taking hold of
salvation in Christ, passes from darkness into a light which makes
more fearful the destiny of those unhappy beings who remain
without. This is Vital Religion. But the power of Evangelicalism
as a directing force lay less in the hopes and terrors it inspired,
than in its rigorous logic, 'the eternal microscope' with which it

pursued its argument into the recesses of the heart, and the details of daily life, giving to every action its individual value in this
3 life, and its infinite consequence in the next. Nor could it escape the notice of a converted man, whose calling brought him into frequent contact with the world, that the virtues of a Christian after the Evangelical model were easily exchangeable with the virtues of a successful merchant or a rising manufacturer, and that a more than casual analogy could be established between Grace and Corruption and the Respectable and the Low. To be serious, to redeem the time, to abstain from gambling, to remember the Sabbath day to keep it holy, to limit the gratification of the senses to the pleasures of a table lawfully earned and the embraces of a wife lawfully wedded, are virtues for which the reward is not laid up in heaven only. The world is very evil. An unguarded look, a word, a gesture, a picture, or a novel, might plant a seed of corruption in the most innocent heart, and the same word or gesture might betray a lingering affinity with the class below.

The discipline of children was becoming milder, because it was touched with that tenderness for all helpless things which we see increasing throughout the eighteenth century, and with that novel interest in the spectacle of the opening mind which was a characteristic product of the Revolutionary years. But it was, perhaps for the same reason, more vigilant; and moral, or social, anxiety made it for girls at least more oppressive.* Yet if, with Rosalind and Beatrice in our eye, we recall Dryden's saying about 'the
5 old Elizabeth way for maids to be seen and not heard', we shall realize how easy it is to misunderstand our grandmothers. The notable Victorian woman is a blend of the great lady and the intellectual woman, not yet professional, and we can graduate the proportions until, at the opposite ends of the scale, we encounter the limiting instances of the Queen herself and Harriet Martineau. In Mrs. Grote, who would have been a far more effective Member of Parliament than her husband, who sat with her red stockings higher than her head, discomfited a dinner-party by saying 'disembowelled' quite bold and plain, and knew when a hoop was off a pail in the back kitchen, the great lady is formidably

---

* But any one who supposes that there was such a thing as a 'Victorian' family or 'Victorian' father should meditate Norris of Bemerton's *Spiritual*
4 *Counsel*, 1694, or *The Ladies' Calling* (Oxford University Press, 1673).

ascendant; in Mrs. Austin the intellectual woman. In Mrs. 6
Austin's daughter, Lady Duff Gordon, in Lady Eastlake—another 7
product of the high secluded culture of the provinces—and, with 8
the emphasis of genius, in Miss Nightingale, the kind achieves its
balance. 9

But for working use the eighteenth century had conceived a
standard type of womanhood, sensitive and enduring, at once
frailer and finer than the man*—in a word, Amelia—and this
type, repeated and articulated in a thousand novels, had blended
insensibly with the more positive type evolved, in a humanitarian age, by the persuasive working of a religion of duty. Helen
Pendennis in fiction, Mrs. Tennyson in life, might serve as
examples; Miss Nightingale's caustic allusion to 'woman's par- 11
ticular worth and general missionariness' as a corrective. In making 12
up the account of English morals in the nineteenth century it is
necessary to bear in mind that the most influential woman were
reared in an atmosphere which made them instinctively Custodians
of the Standard. The two who had most aptitude and most
capacity for rebellion were fanatics, Charlotte Brontë for the
moral, Harriet Martineau for the economic law. Mary Wollstonecraft left, unhappily, no equal successor, and George Sand
could never have grown in English soil. Thus it came about that 13
the pagan ethic which, when faith in God and Immortality had
gone, carried into the next, the agnostic, age the evangelical faith
in duty and renunciation, was a woman's ethic. George Eliot's
rank in literature has, perhaps, not yet been determined: in the
history of ideas her place is fixed. She is the moralist of the
Victorian revolution. 14

That the ethic could be so transposed from a Christian to a
Stoic key shows how native the discipline was. It had its roots
deep down in the habits of a northern race,† vigorous and self-
controlled, not sensitive but not unkindly, in country rectories
and manor houses, in the congregations of City churches, in the

---

*   God! she is like a milk-white lamb that bleats
           For man's protection.
  God! indeed. But this is Keats (1817), and is Rousseau's Sophie rather than
Fielding's Sophia. One does not easily picture Emma Woodhouse (1816) bleating
for Keats. 10

  † I may refer to Hazlitt's contrast of Northern and Southern manners in
Hot and Cold (Plain Speaker). 15

meeting houses of Yorkshire clothing towns. It rose and spread
with the advance of the class which principally sustained it:
Wesley and his followers carried it into regions which the old
churches had hardly touched; Wilberforce and Hannah More
brought wit and fashion to its support; Cowper brought poetry.
By the beginning of the nineteenth century virtue was advancing
on a broad invincible front. The French wars made England
insular, and conscious of its insularity, as it had not been since the
Conquest. The Evangelicals gave to the island a creed which was
at once the basis of its morality and the justification of its wealth
and power, and, with the creed, that sense of being an Elect
People which, set to a more blatant tune, became a principal
element in Late Victorian Imperialism. By about 1830 their work
was done. They had driven the grosser kinds of cruelty, extravagance, and profligacy underground. They had established a
certain level of behaviour for all who wished to stand well with
their fellows. In moralizing society they had made social disapproval a force which the boldest sinner might fear.

By the beginning of the Victorian age the faith was already
hardening into a code. Evangelicalism at war with habit and
indifference, with vice and brutality, with slavery, duelling, and
bull-baiting, was a very different thing from Evangelicalism
grown complacent, fashionable, superior. Even its charity had
acquired what a Yorkshire manufacturer once grimly styled a
16 'diffusive, itinerant quality'. The impulses it had quickened
showed at their best in the upper ranks of society, where they had
been absorbed into an older tradition of humour, culture, and
public duty; or at the Universities, where they blended with new
currents of intellectual eagerness and delight. The piety of a fine
scholar like Peel or a haughty Border lord like Graham, of Gladstone or Sidney Herbert, had not much in common with the
soul-saving theology of the money-making witness-bearers,
those serious people whose indifference to national affairs Bright
17 was one day to deplore. But, morally, their way of life was the
same. Evangelicalism had imposed on society, even on classes
which were indifferent to its religious basis and unaffected by its
economic appeal, its code of Sabbath observance, responsibility,
and philanthropy; of discipline in the home, regularity in affairs;
it had created a most effective technique of agitation, of private
persuasion and social persecution. On one of its sides, Victorian

history is the story of the English mind employing the energy imparted by Evangelical conviction to rid itself of the restraints which Evangelicalism had laid on the senses* and the intellect; on amusement, enjoyment, art; on curiosity, on criticism, on science.

19

II

THE Evangelical discipline, secularized as respectability, was the strongest binding force in a nation which without it might have broken up, as it had already broken loose. For a generation and more the static conception of society† had been dissolving because society itself was dissolving. 'A nobleman, a gentleman, a yeoman,' Cromwell told one of his Parliaments, 'that is a good interest.' But the good interest was splitting into a hundred aristocracies and a hundred democracies, button-makers and gentlemen button-makers,‡ all heels and elbows, jostling, pushing, snubbing, presuming. On the whole, the articulate classes, whose writings and conversation make opinion, were gainers by the change—it has been estimated, for example, that between 1815 and 1830 the purchasing capacity of the classes above the wage-earning level was all but doubled—and the Victorian belief in progress was bottomed on the complacency which comes of steadily rising incomes and steadily improving security. Mixed with this, no doubt, was the vulgar pride in mere quantity, the thoughtless exultation of a crowd in motion. But no one can read for long in the literature of the thirties and forties without touching a finer and deeper pride, portentously draped in tables of trade and revenue and the publications of the Useful Knowledge Society, but glowing with the authentic sense of war and victory, man against nature, and reason against the traditions of the elders.

2

4

5

* Kingsley (who described Shelley as a lewd vegetarian) correctly diagnosed Byron as an Evangelical gone wrong. Byron's objection to mixed bathing, even when the parties are married, as 'very indelicate', comes from his Venetian period.

18

† As explained, for example, by an Irish judge in 1798. 'Society consists of noblemen, baronets, knights, esquires, gentlemen, yeomen, tradesmen and artificers.' The jury found that, as the subject had ceased to be a breeches maker without becoming a gentleman, he must be a yeoman.

1

‡ For whom there were separate doors in the Birmingham taverns.

3

6   Great things are done when men and mountains meet.

To travellers descending from the moorlands, the smoke and
roar of Lancashire seemed like the smoke and roar of a battle-
field, and the discipline of the factories like the discipline of a great
army. It is hardly an accident that the first history of the Renais-
7 sance came from Liverpool* and that the most conspicuous
9 memorial of the Utilitarians is a History of Greece. Across the
ages, the modern Englishman recognized his peers.

But we must be careful if we are to keep the picture true, not to
view the early Victorian age of production through that distort-
ing medium, the late Victorian age of finance. Science touched
10 the imagination by its tangible results. It was immersed in matter,
and it conformed directly to the Augustan canon of historic progress by its immediate contribution to the 'order, regularity,
11 and refinement of life'. Romance and the Revolution bred ideas
of human purpose which only slowly permeated the English
mind. Even in 1830—far more powerfully in 1840—they were
beginning to work. But the common intelligence was still dominated by the solid humanism of the Augustans, to which the
Eighteenth Proposition of Oxford Liberalism would have seemed
a self-evident truth:

Virtue is the child of Knowledge: Vice of Ignorance: therefore education, periodical literature, railroad travelling, ventilation, and the
arts of life, when fully carried out, serve to make a population moral
and happy.†

'The objects of this Society', so ran the prospectus of the Rochdale
Pioneers, 'are the moral and intellectual advancement of its members. It provides them with groceries, butcher's meat, drapery
13 goods, clothes and clogs.' Gas-lighting of the streets was hardly an
improvement so much as a revolution in public security;‡ cheap

* 'The historian of the Age of Leo (Roscoe) has brought into cultivation the
8 extensive tract of Chatmoss.' (Mrs. Barbauld, 1811.)
† Newman, *Apologia*, Note A. But what does *serve* mean? The almost magical
effect of ventilation on the moral habits (temper and sobriety) of a poor quarter
12 was demonstrated again and again.
‡ 'Without presuming to play on words,' said the Lambeth magistrate, 'I
regard gas as essential to an enlightened police.' It was once proposed to illuminate
thieves' quarters with lamps of a special construction so that law-abiding pedest-
14 rians should pass by on the other side.

cotton goods in personal cleanliness, colza lamps in domestic 15
comfort. Finance, the manipulation of wealth and credit as
things by themselves, three or four degrees removed from the
visible crop or ore, was an adjunct. Production was the thing
itself.

A generation which has come to take invention for granted
and is, perhaps, more sensitive to its mischief than its benefits,
cannot easily recover the glory of an age when knowledge, and
with it power, seemed to have been released for an illimitable
destiny.* The Englishman might reluctantly allow that in social
amenity the French, in care for the well-being of the people the
Prussians, went beyond him. He might at moments be chilled by
the aesthetic failure of his time, so profuse and yet so mean:
alienated by its ethical assurance, at once so pretentious and so
narrow. In a petulant mood, he would talk, with Grote, of the
Age of Steam and Cant, but all the while he knew that in the 17
essential business of humanity, the mastery of brute nature by
intelligence, he had outstripped the world, and the Machine was
the emblem and the instrument of his triumph. The patriotism
of early Victorian England, not yet blooded by the Crimean
War and the Indian Mutiny, irritated by Napoleon III, or exalted
by the vision of empire, was at heart a pride in human capacity,
which time had led to fruition in England; and in the great
humanist, who brought all history to glorify the age of which
he was the most honoured child, it heard its own voice speaking.†

To articulate the creed of progress, to state its evidences and
draw out its implications, was the mission of that remarkable
group of men variously known as the Utilitarians, or the Philosophic Radicals. In discipleship or reaction no young mind of the
thirties could escape their influence. Bentham's alliance with James
Mill, Mill's friendship with Malthus and Ricardo, had created a

---

* The admiration of Bacon, almost amounting to a rediscovery, is very
characteristic of the period. So is the Utilitarian preference for the more scholastic,
less imaginative Hobbes. When his editor, Molesworth, stood for Southwark
the populace paraded the streets shouting NO OBBS.   16

† *Il a son orgueil d'homme*. Taine's fine saying of Macaulay is true of his whole
age. 'That wicked XVIII century' died hard: under his Romantic ornament
Macaulay is through and through Augustan; and contemporary critics (Brougham
and Harriet Martineau are examples) reproduce against him the charges which
the early Romantics had laid against Gibbon—materialism and want of philosophy.   18

party, almost a sect, with formularies as compact as the Evangelical theology, and conclusions not less inexorable. However far the Benthamite disciple went, he would find the old sage had been there before him; every trail was blazed, every pitfall marked, and in every path stood a lion, the Sinister Interest of Privilege. Between rulers and ruled there exists an inherent antagonism* which can only be resolved if rulers and ruled are identified by means of universal suffrage and the ballot-box, and the identity is preserved by publicity and a cheap press.† The sovereignty thus created is to be exercised through a carefully balanced system: of Parliament to legislate, central organs to direct, local organs to execute. On the question of Women's Suffrage, the Utilitarians were somewhat inconsistently divided; Bentham, a flirtatious old bachelor, being more logical than James Mill, who, in spite of Malthus, had begotten more children than he could afford on a female whom he despised. On all other matters, above all on the sovereign authority of Economic Law, they spoke with one voice.

Reduced from an aspiration to a schedule, progress might seem a gloomy business for the mass of mankind. It rests on competition, and always and everywhere competition is reducing the profits of the employer, and the wages of the workman, to the level of bare subsistence. Only the landowner, the common enemy of all, continually profits by the growing demand for sites, and for food, because, always and everywhere, population is pressing on the means to live. Such is the law. But Nature has not left her children without all hope of escaping the fate to which her mathematics seem to have consigned them. By industry, and abstinence, the employer may enlarge the market for his goods; by industry, and continence, the workman may increase the purchasing power, and limit the numbers, of his class: progress, like salvation, is the reward of virtue; of diligence and self-

---

* Translate this into economic terms, substitute for the antagonism of rulers and ruled the antagonism of employers and employed, and some curious conclusions will follow which the Socialists of the next age were ready to draw.

† 'The principle of human nature, upon which the necessity of government is founded, the propensity of one man to possess himself of the objects of desire at the cost of another, leads on, by infallible sequence, not only to that degree of plunder which leaves the members (except the instruments and recipients) the bare means of subsistence, but to that degree of cruelty which is necessary to keep in existence the most intense terrors.'—James Mill on Government.

education; of providence and self-control; and all the evolution-
ary speculation of the next age has for background Malthus's
Stoic vision of that remote, austere, divinity 'whose purpose is
ever to bring a mind out of the clod'.   22

In the early thirties the Philosophic Radicals were a portent,
men whose meetings were watched, the spearhead of a revolution
beginning with the ballot and going on, Heaven knew how far, to
compulsory education and a federated Empire. Then, frigid and
scholastic, as a party they fade from the view. The popular
Radicals, hotter against Church and Lords, and readier champions
of the unprivileged and the oppressed, made more noise; the
people preferred the Tories. Grote lived to decline a peerage;
when the ballot was at last conceded in 1872 John Mill had decided that he did not want it and had moved on to proportional
representation instead; Leader vanished into an aesthetic Italian
exile; Molesworth's features are more familiar at Ottawa than his
name at Westminster. The case for Free Trade was taken out of
their hands by men who had learnt their economics in the
counting-house, their logic on the platform, and their rhetoric in
the pulpit.* But they had done inestimable service. They came
down into a world where medieval prejudice, Tudor Law, Stuart
economics, and Hanoverian patronage still luxuriated in wild
confusion, and by the straight and narrow paths they cut we are
walking still. The Gladstonian Liberals have gone where the   24
Peelites followed the Canningites; the Evangelical creed long ago
foundered on the Impregnable Rock of Holy Scripture, and the   25
great Whig name has not been heard for fifty years. But it would
be hard to find any corner of our public life where the spirit of
Bentham is not working to-day.

It is dangerous to force historic movements into exaggerated
symmetry. But the parallel operation of Evangelicalism and
Utilitarianism cannot be ignored. Their classics, Malthus on
Population and Wilberforce's *Practical View*, appeared almost   26
simultaneously, one in 1797, the other in 1798. Their greatest
victories in public affairs, the Abolition of Slavery and the
Reform of the Poor Law, were won in 1833 and 1834. When a
distracted Government threw the Old Poor Law at a Royal Commission, the Benthamites rose to the height of their opportunity.

* The supersession of Charles Villiers by Cobden, Bright, and W. J. Fox is
typical.   23

The Secretary of the Commission was Edwin Chadwick, whom
the Patriarch had selected to be his apostle to the new age, and
in his hands there was no fear lest the faith should grow
cold. Born in 1800, in a Lancashire farmhouse where the children
were washed all over, every day, the mainspring of Chadwick's
career seems to have been a desire to wash the people of England
all over, every day, by administrative order. In practical capacity
Chadwick was the greatest, in the character of his mind, in the
machine-like simplicity of his ideas and the inexhaustible fertility
of his applications, the most typical of the Benthamites. Napoleon
III once asked him what he thought of his improvements in Paris.
'Sir,' he answered, 'it was said of Augustus that he found Rome
brick and left it marble. May it be said of you that you found Paris
stinking and left it sweet.' It might stand for Chadwick's epitaph.
He found England stinking. If he did not leave it sweet, the fault
was certainly not his. Through the Poor Law Commission, the
Benthamite formula—inquiry, legislation, execution, inspection,
and report—was incorporated in our working constitution. It was
rounded off by the invention of the Public Audit and the Grant-
in-aid to tighten central control and stimulate local activity.
But the corresponding formula for unofficial effort—information,
agitation, the parent society, the local branch, the picture,*
and the handbill—had been discovered by the Evangelicals and
humanitarians in their warfare against slavery, and by them it
was imparted to the Chartists and the Free Trade League.

The Evangelical and Utilitarian movements both rested on a
body of doctrine which to question was impious or irrational;
in both cases the doctrine was the reflection of an exceptional experience, the religious experience of a nation undergoing a moral
revival, its social experience during a revolution in the methods of
production; and in both cases a larger view was certain to show
that neither was a more than provisional synthesis. In the meantime they furnished England with a code and a great company of
interpreters: with their almost Genevan rigour, and almost Latin
clarity, they imposed themselves like foreign task-masters on the
large, ironic English mind, and their great doctrines were all too
readily snipped into texts for the guidance of those who did not
wish to think at all, and the repression of those who wished to

---

* For example, the fine colour prints by Smith after Morland, of the ship-
wrecked crew entertained by natives, whom they return to carry into slavery.

think for themselves, into Cant for Practical Men and Cant for
Serious Men. Finally, they were alike in this, that each imparted
its peculiar virtue: the Evangelicals their zeal for holiness, the
Utilitarians their faith in reason, to the movements, even to the
reactions which sprang out of them, to Tractarians and Agnostics
who denied their introspective ethic, to Tories and Socialists who
challenged their conception of the competitive State.

III

MUCH of accident goes to the making of history, even the history
of thought, which might seem to be most exempt from contingencies. The Victorian record would have been very different if
Canning had lived to the years of Palmerston, if the new writers
had grown up under the shadow of Byron, Keats, and Shelley.
But the old men lived and the young men died. A strange pause
followed their departure, and the great Victorian lights rose into a
sky which, but for the rapid blaze of Bulwer Lytton, was vacant.
Tennyson and Macaulay, Caryle and Newman, Gladstone and
Disraeli, Arnold and Dickens appear above the horizon together.
In Sydney Smith's stately compliments to the Graduate of Oxford,* the eighteenth century bows itself off the stage and intro-
duces its successor. With the appearance of *Vanity Fair* in 1847,   2
the constellation is complete and the stars are named. It was part   3
of the felicity of the fifties to possess a literature which was at
once topical, contemporary, and classic; to meet the Immortals in
the streets, and to read them with added zest for the encounter.   4

Anchored to its twofold faith in goodness and progress, the
early Victorian mind swung wide to the alternating currents of
sentiment and party spite, but the virulence of the Press,† and the
gush of the popular novel were play on the surface of a deep
assurance. There are whimperings, sometimes bellowings, of

---

* 'He said [*Modern Painters*, I] was a work of transcendent talent, presented
the most original views in the most elegant language, and would work a complete revolution in the world of taste.' (*Praeterita*: Chapter ix.)   1
   † It was a Cambridge joke that

> The abysmal deeps of personality

meant *The Times*.   5

self-pity, but defiance was no longer the mode. The greater and better part of English society accepted the social structure and moral objective of the nation, as a community of families, all rising, or to be raised, to a higher respectability. To those postulates their criticism of life was not directed: they were satisfied, not indeed with the world as it was, for they were all, in their way, reformers, but as it would become by the application of those reasoned and tested principles which made up the scheme of progress and salvation.

Poised and convinced, they could indulge, too, in a licence of feeling impossible to a generation bred in doubt, and they could take their ease in an innocent vulgarity which to a later age would have been a hard-worked and calculated Bohemianism. They could swagger and they could be maudlin. In public they could be reserved, for they were a slow and wary race, and reserve is at once the defence of the wise and the refuge of the stupid. But cynicism and superciliousness, the stigmata of a beaten age and a waning class, were alien to the hopeful, if anxious, generation which had taken the future into its hands. In their exuberance and facility, the earlier Victorians, with their flowing and scented hair, gleaming jewellery and resplendent waistcoats, were nearer to the later Elizabethans; they were not ashamed; and, like the Elizabethans, their sense of the worthwhileness of everything—themselves, their age, and their country: what the Evangelicals called seriousness; the Arnoldians, earnestness; Bagehot, most happily, ⁶ eagerness—overflowed in sentiment and invective, loud laughter, and sudden reproof. Once at Bowood, when Tom Moore was singing, one by one the audience slipped away in sobs; finally, the poet himself broke down and bolted, and the old Marquis was ⁷ left alone. We are in an age when, if brides sometimes swooned at the altar, Ministers sometimes wept at the Table; when the sight of an infant school could reduce a civil servant to a passion of tears; and one undergraduate has to prepare another undergraduate for the news that a third undergraduate has doubts about the ⁸ Blessed Trinity—an age of flashing eyes and curling lips, more easily touched, more easily shocked, more ready to spurn, to ⁹ flaunt, to admire, and, above all, to preach.

A young man brought up in a careful home might have heard, whether delivered or read aloud, a thousand sermons; an active clergyman was a social asset to a rising neighbourhood, his popularity a source of spiritual danger to himself. The form of preachers was canvassed like the form of public entertainers, and the circulation of some Victorian sermons is a thing to fill a modern writer with despair. If we consider the effect, beginning in childhood, of all the preachers on all the congregations, of men loud or unctuous, authoritative or persuasive, speaking out of a body of acknowledged truth to the respectful audience below them, we shall see why the homiletic cadence, more briefly Cant, is so persistent in Victorian oratory and literature. It sufficed to persuade the lower middle classes that Tupper was a poet and the upper middle classes that Emerson was a philosopher. Mr. [10] Gladstone formed his style by reading sermons aloud, and his [11] diaries are full of self-delivered homilies.* Old Sir Robert Peel trained his son to repeat every Sunday the discourse he had just heard, a practice to which he owed his astonishing recollection [13] of his opponents' arguments and something, perhaps, of the unction of his own replies. The sermon was the standard vehicle of serious truth, and to the expositions and injunctions of their writers and statesmen the Victorian public brought the same hopeful determination to be instructed, and to be elevated, which held them attentive to the pleadings, denunciations, and commonplaces of their preachers.

The body of acknowledged truth, out of which this early Victorian literature speaks, appears, at first sight, to consist of little more than all those dogmas which a victorious middle class had imposed on the nation. There is not much in it which the Compleat English Tradesman could not understand, and still less [14] that he would not approve; as he could not understand Browning, Browning had to wait outside. But to take the height of the [15] Victorian classics we must view them from the waste land of dreary goodness, useful information, and tired humour, stretching all about them, and no one who has survived the exploration will underrate the genius which could raise such a fabric on such foundations. The world desired to be instructed: it was given Grote and Thirlwall, Milman and Macaulay, Lyell's *Principles of Geology*, Mill's *Logic*, Mill's *Political Economy*; to be elevated: it had *Past and Present*, *Modern Painters*, and *In Memoriam*; it asked [16] for theology and got Newman, for education and got Arnold.

* He once delivered an address on Preaching (City Temple, March 22, [12] 1877).

17 Out of the Minerva Press came Disraeli, out of the horseplay of
18 sentimental Cockneys, Dickens.

It is only necessary to set these names down in order to realize
what potent agencies of dissolution were working in the early
Victorian years. English society was poised on a double paradox
which its critics, within and without, called hypocrisy. Its practical
ideals were at odds with its religious professions, and its religious
belief was at issue with its intelligence. We, for example, should
probably count an employer who kept children of nine working
nine hours a day in a temperature of 98 degrees as, at least, a very
stupid man. If he went farther and insisted that, when they
wished to lift up their hearts in song, it must not be in carnal
ditties like 'A Frog He Would A'Wooing Go', but in hymns—

> By cool Siloam's glassy rill
> How sweet the lily grows,
> How sweet the scent upon the hill
> Of Sharon's dewy rose—

19 we might credit him with a touch of diabolical humour. We
should be wrong in a matter where it is both important and
difficult to go right. He may have been a low hypocrite who slept
with pretty mill girls on the sly. He may have been a kindly and
intelligent man who had convinced himself that only by production, kept down to the lowest cost, could the country be fed, and
that the sufferings of the poor in this present time were not worthy
to be compared with the glory which should be revealed in them
hereafter. Or, like most of us, he may have been something in
between: borne along partly by conviction, partly by example,
and neither disposed nor able to analyse ideas which proved
themselves by their material results. Cheap labour meant high
profits; respectable workpeople meant good work.*

It could not last. It was impossible to maintain for ever the

---

* In the eighteenth century the mill often furnished the millowner's harem:
in our period rarely. I cannot resist the conclusion that the current religion
did sometimes act as a provocative to sadism. A ghastly story came out in the
Courts of a private tutor who prayed with a backward pupil, beat him to a
jelly, kissed him, and left him to die. The connection between religious professions and fraudulent dealing started many criminals on the downward path—
or so they assured the prison chaplains. But, again, this is an old story. In *Areo-*
20 *pagitica* the City Man and his Religion almost twists a smile from Milton.

position that Christian responsibility was a duty everywhere except in economic life, and that strength and vigour, the control of nature by science, of events by prudence, are good things everywhere except in the hands of the State: not less impossible to suppose that the criticism which was unravelling the constitution of the rocks and the legends of antiquity, would always consent to stand in respectful submission before the conventions, or the documents, of contemporary Protestantism. So long as the fear of subversion persisted, criticism could not act with freedom: clerisy* and *bourgeoisie* stood together, and, where they differed, the clerisy, on the whole, preserved a loyal silence. Indeed, in State affairs they did not differ greatly. When, in his tract on Chartism, Caryle essayed to translate the verities into practice, he had nothing to suggest that half the parsons in the land did not know already: that everybody should be sent to school and the odd man to the colonies. In religion they were coming to differ 22 deeply, as the strong surviving vein of Augustan rationalism was reinforced by the conclusions of Victorian science. But the sanctions of orthodoxy were still formidable, and in a world where *Prometheus Unbound* might be judicially held to be a blasphemous libel,† a certain economy in the communication of unbelief was 23 evidently advisable.

The sense of being under a Code accompanies us through the early Victorian decades. To the age of revolt, which runs from Rousseau to Shelley, succeeds the age of acquiescence; the Titans are dead, or they have been tamed. It seems as if speculation had ceased; there is an answer to every question and usually the answer is no. Milman is ostracized for calling Abraham a sheik; Miss 25 Mitford is publicly reproved for calling a pudding a rolypoly; old lords have to guard their words for fear of shocking 26 young lords, and a Member of Parliament wishing to say contracted pelvis must put it in the decent obscurity of a learned language. A Parliamentary Committee, who asked a factory woman 28 if she had ever miscarried, brought on themselves the anger of *The Times* for violating the principles which should preside over such inquiries, 'a dread of ridicule and an anxious avoidance of indecency', and *The Economist*, a paper of exceptional intelligence, 29 declined to go into the details of the Public Health Bill of 1847

---

* Coleridge's useful word for the educated classes acting as a body.   21
† As *Queen Mab* actually was found to be in 1841.   24

30 and fill its columns with a number of unpleasant words. A guilty conscience has never betrayed itself by a more superior sniff. Absurdity and impropriety, like domesticated dragons, guard the stability of society and the peace of the home, and absurdity seems to mean any way of thinking, impropriety any way of behaving, which may impair the comfort, impeach the dignity, and weaken the defence of the middle class. We remember with surprise that we are dealing with a race which had once, and not so long ago, been famous in its island for an independence and even eccentricity which it now only displayed abroad, and we ask what has happened to make it submit its behaviour, its language, and its ideas to this drastic and vigilant censorship.

IV

EVERY period of history may be interpreted in various ways, and the richer it is in event or thought the more numerous will be the interpretations. Early Victorian history might be read as the formation in the thirties of a Marxian *bourgeoisie* which never came into existence, the re-emergence in the forties of a more ancient tradition, a sense of the past and a sense of social coherence, which never fulfilled its promise, and a compromise between the two which possessed no ultimate principle of stability.* But we must all the time remember that the Victorian age is only the island counterpart of a secular movement, as significant as the turn from the Greek middle ages in the time of Socrates or the Latin middle ages at the Renaissance. Twice the European mind had been carried to the verge, and twice it had been baffled. In the nineteenth century it won the top and saw stretching before it that endless new world which Bacon had sighted, or imagined, where nothing need remain unknown, and for everything that is known there is something that can be done; the world of organized thought where even modern scientific man was only the rudiments of what man might be. But European currents have a way of changing their direction when they touch our shores; it was so with the Renaissance, it was so with the Reformation. We borrowed our

* The three phases are conveniently marked by Miss Martineau's *Illustrations*
1 *of Political Economy, Coningsby,* and Bagehot's *English Constitution.*

Party names from France and Spain; only Radical is all our own.* 2
But the Conservative Party is a far more vital element in the
State than a Parti Conservateur, and Continental Liberalism had
little to teach a people who counted their freedom not by revolutions but by dynasties. 'You see,' said Mackintosh, when the latest
French pamphlet on Liberty was exhibited for his admiration,
'in England we take all that for granted.' Of Continental Social- 4
ism we may say we gave as good as we took, and the Nationalism, which was to glorify the heroisms and to poison the conflicts
of a century, made little appeal to a race which had no memories
of foreign oppression to brood over, and is always more disposed
to grudge the cost of its victories than to spend fresh money in
avenging its defeats. On the other hand, the special and domestic
preoccupations which give the European movement its English
colour, being of a kind which our peculiar and isolated history
had engendered, the call of the sea, the constant embarrassment
of English policy by Irish agitation, the persistence of the religious
interest into a secularist age, aristocracy into a commercial age,
and monarchy into a radical age, cannot be expounded in European terms.

To all these themes, the ground-tone was given by the growth
of population, the result of many combining tendencies, humanitarian and scientific, which since the middle of the eighteenth
century had operated with ever-increasing force.† In 1730 it
seems that of every four children born in London three failed to
reach their fifth birthday. A hundred years of improvement had
almost reversed the proportion.‡ Life was safer and longer, and 6
every census was swelled by the numbers of babies who now
grew up, young people who now lived into manhood, old
people who lingered on the earth which a hundred years before
they would have quitted in middle life. But if the process was a
just ground for pride, the results could not be contemplated without deep apprehension, and the gravity of the problem was at once

* Possibly Communism, which is claimed, as a colloquial inspiration, for
Mr. Barmby of Hanwell. He must be distinguished from Mr. Baume, who
planned a Communist University at Colney Hatch. 3

† It was a European phenomenon. The French death-rate seems to have
fallen from 39 to 29 between 1780 and 1820. 5

‡ This in London over all. The infantile mortality about 1840 was—upper
classes 1/10; middle classes 1/6; lower classes 1/4. In Manchester and Leeds the
mortality under 5 was about 57/100. 7

demonstrated and accentuated by the state of Ireland, from which, crossing St. George's Channel at deck cargo rates, the starving Papists swarmed by thousands to gather the harvest in English
8 fields or fill the slums of English towns. Those who traced them home, in books, or by the new tourist route to Killarney, and heard or saw for themselves the worse-than-animal wretchedness of a people withal so intelligent and so chaste, might well ask themselves what relief was in prospect unless Nature intervened and ordained depopulation on a scale from which Cromwell might have shrunk, and whether the misery of Ireland was not a foreshadowing of the doom of England herself.*

The only visible relief was by way of emigration, and already some minds had been fired by the thought of the great spaces waiting to be peopled or, with an even larger sweep of the imagination, by the picture of a vast Eastern Empire ruled from Australia. But the English of 1830, with six generations of the Law of Settlement behind them, were not easily up-rooted, and, publicly, the only restraint that could be recommended was late marriage and the abolition of those provisions of the Poor Law which set a premium on reckless unions. There was much active, if furtive, discussion of birth-control in Radical circles: John Mill was once in trouble for poking pamphlets down area rail-
10 ings; and one writer proposed that instruction in the subject should be included in the rules of all Trade Unions.† But contraception did not seriously affect the birth-rate until, in the seventies, it returned from America, to which it had been carried by the
12 younger Owen. Malthus had raised a spectre which could be neither ignored nor laid.

* Down to the French wars England had been on balance a wheat-exporting country. After Waterloo it was plain that the balance had been reversed and that foreign wheat, though there were still years when the import only amounted to a few days' consumption, was normally required to make good the English harvest. The sliding scale of 1828 was contrived to steady home prices, and therefore rents, while admitting foreign supplies as they were needed: in theory the Radicals preferred Free Trade, in theory the Whigs were for a fixed duty; but in the early thirties the issue was not raised, the schism between the com-
9 mercial and landed interests was latent and speculative.

† Wade in his *History of the Middle Classes* (if indeed I have correctly inter-preted his mysterious hintings). Place gave instruction at Charing Cross; Mrs. Grote, I suspect, more than instruction to her village neighbours. Croker's attack on Miss Martineau was quite unpardonable, but it is fairly clear that Miss Martin-
11 eau did not know what she was talking about.

More immediately significant than the growth of population was its aggregation in great towns. Down to the French Wars the moral habit of society was definitely patrician and rural, and had still much of the ease, the tolerance, and the humour which belongs to a life lived in security and not divorced from nature. What differences existed in the lives and outlook of a gentleman, a yeoman, and a cottager were mitigated by their common subjection to the ebb and flow of the world, the seasons, and the hours. In correspondence with its traditional structure, the traditional culture and morality of England were based on the patriarchal village family of all degrees: the father worked, the mother saw to the house, the food, and the clothes; from the parents the children learnt the crafts and industries necessary for their livelihood, and on Sundays they went together, great and small, to worship in the village church. To this picture English sentiment clung, as Roman sentiment saw in the Sabine farm the home of virtue and national greatness. It inspired our poetry; it controlled our art; for long it obstructed, perhaps it still obstructs, the formation of a true philosophy of urban life.

But all the while Industrialism had been coming over England like a climatic change; the French wars masked the consequences till they became almost unmanageable. It is possible to imagine, with Robert Owen, an orderly evolution of the rural village into the industrial township, given the conditions which he enjoyed at New Lanark, a limited size and a resident, paternal employer. Belper under the Strutts, Bolton under the Ashworths, the cosy houses and flourishing gardens of South Hetton, to which foreign visitors were carried with special pride, the playing fields of Price's Candle Works, the Lancashire village where Coningsby met Edith, all have some affinity with the Owenite Utopia, bold peasants, rosy children, smoking joints, games on the green; [13] Merrie England, in a word, engaged in a flourishing export trade in coal and cotton.* But any possibility of a general development along these lines had already been lost in the change-over from water to steam power, in the consequent growth of the great urban aggregates, and the visible splitting of society, for

* I have read an Owenite fancy of the thirties in which the world is organized as a federation of Garden Cities. One episode is the return of a delegation, clad in chitons, from Bavaria, where, if I remember right, they have been showing their German brethren how to lay a drain. [14]

which the Enclosures had created a rural precedent, into posses-
sors and proletariat. The employers were moving into the
country; their officials followed them into the suburbs; the better
workmen lived in the better streets; the mixed multitude of
labour, native or Irish, was huddled in slums and cellars, sometimes newly run up by speculative builders, sometimes, like the
labyrinth round Soho and Seven Dials, deserted tenements of
the upper classes. In a well-managed village with a responsible
landlord and an active parson, with allotments for the men and a
school for the children, the old institutions and restraints might
still hold good; in a neglected village, and in that increasing
part of the population which now lived in great towns, they
were perishing. Off work, the men could only lounge and
drink; the girls learnt neither to cook nor to sew. Lying
outside the orbit of the old ruling class, neglected by their
natural leaders, the industrial territories were growing up as
best they might, undrained, unpoliced, ungoverned, and un-
schooled.

Yet the physical separation was not so complete that the world
beyond the pale could be ignored, and the Evangelical ascesis was
imposed on a generation to which the spectacle of bodily existence was at once obtrusive and abhorrent. Physically, the national
type was changing; the ruddy, careless Englishman of the
eighteenth century, turbulent but placable, as ready with his
friendship as his fists, seemed to be making way for a pallid, sullen
stock, twisted in mind and body. And if the eye which ranged
with such complacency over the palaces of Regent's Park, the
thronging masts of wide-wayed Liverpool, the roaring looms of
hundred-gated Leeds, descended to a closer view, of Finsbury, say,
or Ancoats, it would have observed that the breeding ground of
the new race was such that in truth it could breed nothing else. The
life within the factory or the mine was doubtless rigorous, and to
children often cruel, but the human frame is immensely resilient,
and with such care as many good employers took, the working
hours of a labourer's life were probably his happiest. But the
imagination can hardly apprehend the horror in which thousands
of families a hundred years ago were born, dragged out their
ghastly lives, and died: the drinking water brown with faecal
particles, the corpses kept unburied for a fortnight in a festering
London August; mortified limbs quivering with maggots;

courts where not a weed would grow, and sleeping-dens afloat with sewage.*

And while the new proletariat was falling below the median line of improving decency on one side, the middle classes were rising above it on the other, becoming progressively more regular, more sober, more clean in body, more delicate in speech. But not only were the middle classes drawing apart from the poor, each stratum, in a steady competition, was drawing away from the stratum next below, accentuating its newly acquired refinements, and enforcing them with censorious vigilance. The capriciousness, the over-emphasis, of Victorian propriety betrays its source. When we have set aside all that England shared with New England, all that nineteenth-century England had in common with nineteenth-century France† and Germany, and all that the England of Victoria had in common with the England of George III‡ and Edward VIII, there remains this peculiar element, what Clough called 'an almost animal sensibility of conscience', 18 this super-morality of the nerves and the senses, of bodily repulsion and social alarm.

Cleanliness is next to godliness. The Victorian insistence, whenever the poor are the topic, on neatness, tidiness, the well-brushed frock and the well-swept room, is significant. 'The English', Treitschke once told a class at Berlin, 'think Soap is

* The following figures tell their own tale:

Expectation of Life at Birth

	Bath	Rutland	Wilts.	Derby	Truro	Leeds	Manchester	Liverpool
Gentlefolk	55	52	50	49	40	45	38	35
Traders & Farmers	37	41	48	38	33	27	20	22
Labourers	25	38	33	21	28	19	17	15

In London the mortality was twice as great in the East End as in the West. In adjacent streets it varied from 38 to 12. 15

† Much nonsense about 'the Victorians' is dissipated by the reflection that it was the French Government that prosecuted *Madame Bovary*. 16

‡ In 1804 Crabb Robinson wrote from Germany: 'To express what we should call Puritanism in language, and excess of delicacy in matters of physical love, the word Engländerei has been coined.' 17

19 Civilization.' Neatness is the outward sign of a conscious Respectability, and Respectability is the name of that common level of
behaviour which all families ought to reach and on which they can
meet without disgust. The Respectable man in every class is one
whose ways bear looking into, who need not slink or hide or
keep his door barred against visitors, the parson, or the dun, who
lives in the eye of his neighbours and can count on the approval
of the great and the obedience of the humble. 'The middle classes
know', Lord Shaftesbury once said, 'that the safety of their lives
and property depends upon their having round them a peaceful,
20 happy, and moral population.' To induce, therefore, some
modicum of cleanliness and foresight, to find some substitute for
savage sport and savage drinking, to attract the children to school
and the parents to church, to awaken some slight interest in books
and the world beyond the end of the street, on such limited,
necessary ends as these was bent that enormous apparatus of early
Victorian philanthropy: of individual effort by squires and parsons
and their wives and daughters,* of organized effort by Hospital
Committees, City Missions, Savings Banks, Mechanics' Institutes,
and Dispensaries, by institutions of every creed and size and
object, from the Coal Club, the Blanket Club, and the Ladies'
22 Child Bed Linen Club up to the great societies for the diffusion
of useful knowledge, religious knowledge, education, and
temperance, and the provision of additional Curates. Respectability was at once a select status and a universal motive. Like
Roman citizenship, it could be indefinitely extended, and every
extension fortified the State.

* As early as the twenties, the young lady in the country was expected to do
her district-visiting seriously, with a register and account book. It is, I think,
true to say that the pruriency which we find so offensive in Victorian morals
(the Blush-to-the-Cheek-of-the-Young-Person business) is mainly an urban,
and therefore middle-class, characteristic. There could not have been much
about the 'facts of life' that a country girl who taught in school and visited
21 in cottages did not know.

V

IN 1830 one aspect, and not the least formidable, of the new civilization, was suddenly forced on every mind. For half a generation, the cholera had been wandering at large across Asia and eastern Europe. It spread, in spite of the most active precautions, into Germany; from Hamburg it crossed to Sunderland; in a few weeks it was in London. Measures were hastily improvised to meet a visitation which might, for all that science could tell, be as destructive as the Great Plague. A Central Board of Health was established in London; local boards in the provinces; a day of fasting and humiliation was proclaimed. Of the local boards the most active was in Manchester, and the report of their secretary— it is only thirty pages long—is one of the cardinal documents of Victorian history. For the first time the actual condition of a great urban population was exposed to view. There was no reason to suppose that Manchester was any worse than other towns, and the inevitable conclusion was that an increasing portion of the population of England was living under conditions which were not only a negation of civilized existence, but a menace to civilized society.

Nor, it seemed, was the country-side in better condition. The Labourers' Rising of 1830 served, like the cholera, to call attention to a problem which without it might have been neglected till it was too late. The land was breaking under the burden of the poor rate, and the administration of the Poor Law was degrading the labourer whom it was designed to support. But the rural problem was simplicity itself compared with the problem of the towns. Let the able-bodied man be given the choice of earning his own living or going into the workhouse, and then, if he still cannot find work on the land, send him to the factory or the colonies. So long as the Poor Law Commissioners were at work in the south, pauperism disappeared as by magic. But, as they moved northwards, unexpected difficulties appeared. 'We grasped the nettle all right,' one of them ruefully acknowledged, 'but it was the wrong nettle.' Machinery had so reduced the value of labour that at any moment the workman might find himself starving in the midst of a plenty which his own hands had helped to create. But the urban problem could not be solved by marching the unemployed in and out of the workhouse as times were bad or good. That rural England was over-populated, the slow increase, in some counties a decline, through the years of prosperity proved. Industrial England was neither over-populated nor under-populated, but periodically over- and under-employed.

Unemployment was beyond the scope of any ideas which Early Victorian reformers had at their command, largely because they had no word for it.* Their language and their minds were dominated by the Malthusian conception of over-population. Sanitation and education were within their reach. But these are remedies which need time do their work, and in the interim the catastrophe might have happened. A fermentation unknown to an earlier England was stirring in the commons. Eighteenth-century society was stable, and felt itself to be stable. From the Revolution to the fall of the Bastille, the thought of subversion, of any social crisis more serious than an election riot or a no-popery riot, never entered the mind of Governments. From Waterloo to 1848 it was hardly ever absent. Looking back from the serene and splendid noon of mid-Victorian prosperity, Kingsley wrote of the years when 'young lads believed (and not so wrongly) that the masses were their natural enemies and that they might have to fight, any year or any day, for the safety of their property and the honour of their sisters'. Young lads will believe anything. But men old enough to remember the French Revolution, or the Committees of Secrecy and the Six Acts of 1819, had their fears too, when they reflected that as the country became more and more dependent on machines, its stability turned more and more on the subordination and goodwill of the savage masses which tended them.

To fortify the State against these and all other perils by admitting the respectable class as a body to the franchise was the purpose of the Reform Bill. For two years, beginning with the Paris Revolution of July 1830, England lived in a sustained intensity of excitement unknown since 1641. But when the dust had settled down Tories might have asked themselves what they had been afraid of, Radicals what they had been fighting for. Never was a revolution effected with more economy in change. The right of the magnate to appoint the representatives of the lesser boroughs had gone: his influence, if he chose to exercise it

---

* It only becomes common in the eighties. Thornton's (very able) *Treatise on Overpopulation* (1845) is really an analysis of unemployment.

with discretion and decorum, was hardly impaired, and it soon appeared that if there was less rioting and less bribery at an election, there was still much bribery, and more intimidation, and election day was still a carnival which usually ended in a fight. Open voting kept the tenant under his landlord's eye; the tradesman under his customer's; and in every county the fifty-pound tenants at will, prudently enfranchised by a Tory amendment, made a solid block of dependable voters. The country was satisfied: even the Radicals accepted the Reform Bill as a fair instalment of their demands without pressing to know when the other instalments—the ballot, one man one vote, one vote one value—would be paid.★

The reforming impulse of the Whigs was exhausted with the passing of the Municipal Reform Act of 1835. The reorganization of the Judicature which Brougham ought to have effected in 1833 was left for Selborne in 1873. Graham, their best administrator, Stanley their best debater, left them. Lord Grey gave up; Lord Melbourne lounged along. The genial Althorp, who kept the Commons in good temper, was taken from them to the Lords. Harried by the Irish, baited by the Radicals, blocked by the Peers, divided among themselves, equally unable to pass their Bills or balance their budgets, the Whigs sank in public esteem and dragged Parliament with them. Their one admitted success did them as much harm as their numerous failures. They kept Ireland quiet, but their pacts with O'Connell seemed to English opinion a disgraceful subservience to a rebel. They accepted Penny Postage, but on a falling revenue it sent their finance to pieces. Palmerston, marching steadily and buoyantly on a line of

★ The figures of the first registration show how oligarchical the new Constitution was:

| Counties, England 345,000 | Scotland 33,000. |
| Boroughs ,, 275,000 | Scotland 31,000. |

The £10 householder in town was in effect a man with £150 a year and upward: without exaggerating it, as the Tories were inclined to do, one must still remember that Reform did disfranchise a large number of working men. Boroughs of 200 and 300 voters were still common: Thetford had 146. In very general terms one might say that from 1832 to 1867 one man in six had a vote, after 1867 one in three. In the same period over fifty returns were set aside for malpractices. *Electorate* is a L[ate] V[ictorian] word: *constituency* which appeared (colloquially) for the first time in 1830/1 originally meant *the whole body of electors*: then, *a particular body*.

his own, brightened their last days with a diplomatic triumph over France and a naval victory over Mehemet Ali, of which, perhaps, in the long run, the most that can be said is that it gave England something to think of beside the misery of 1840. All through the thirties we are aware of a growing disaffection, of which Carlyle and Dickens are mouthpieces, with the delays and irrelevancies* of parliamentary government, which, as the years went on, seemed to be degenerating more and more into an unseemly scuffle between Ins and Outs. The political satire of Dickens is tedious and ignorant. But it registers, what *Past and Present* conveys more passionately, the disillusionment which followed on the hopes of 1830.

Socially, the first reformed Parliaments were hardly distinguishable from their predecessors. The days of extravagant expenditure, when the poll was open for three weeks and a candidate might spend, as the virtuous and religious Acland did in Devon, £80,000 on four contests, were over and done with. But an election might easily cost a candidate £5,000.† The just influence of landed property was preserved, and the old humanity of the South was still politically ascendant over the new industry of the North. The Whigs had introduced a self-adjusting device into the constitution, but it worked slowly. So late as 1845 three notes of exclamation were required to convey Prince Albert's amazement at the thought of Cobden in the Cabinet. The Tories had learnt by experience to adopt capacity from whatever quarter it appeared: they admitted Peel, the son of a cotton-spinner; Canning, whose mother was an actress; and Huskisson, whose origin, if possibly more respectable, was even more obscure. The Whigs in exile had drawn closer together and farther from the main stream of English life; they came from the eighteenth century, where privilege was taken for granted, and they brought the eighteenth century with them; and one result of the Reform was to give

---

* And mysteries. The procedural history of Parliament is a struggle between an old principle (freedom of debate) and a new one (to make a programme and get through it). In the thirties, freedom, exercised through (*a*) a multitude of formal stages, (*b*) irrelevant amendments on going into Committee or adjourning, was in the ascendant. The public, intensely interested in Parliament, was in consequence often baffled to know what Parliament was doing or why.

† Bringing voters to the poll (abolished in 1885) was the main item. The commonest malpractice was impersonation. In one borough election in 1838, out of 310 votes given, 109 were challenged on that ground.

England, growing more and more resentful of privilege, the most aristocratic Government that any one could remember, and to set the Lords almost in equipoise with the Commons. And all the while, with a suspicious, but obedient, party behind him—150 in '32, 250 in '34, 300 in '37—Peel was biding his time. With the return of the Conservatives in 1841 and the impending grapple of Land and Industry, Parliament recovered its standing as the debating-place of public issues, and, what to the new electorate was even more important, as the guardian of the public purse. The country preferred an Income Tax from Peel to one deficit more from Baring. [18]

Until 1834 the traveller approaching London over Westminster Bridge saw on his left a foreshore where watermen lounged among their boats: behind it a walled garden fronting a low range of red-brick Tudor houses. At the far left the Chapel of St. Stephen projected almost to the water's edge, and high above all stretched the grey roof of the Hall. The towers of the Abbey were just visible behind. After the fire of 1834 the Commons found room in the old House of Lords, the Peers sat in the Painted Chamber, while the palace of Barry and Pugin was rising to overshadow both Abbey and Hall: the Lords entered their new house in 1847: the Commons in 1852. Business commonly began at four, mornings being kept for Committees, with questions, few, but often involving voluminous reply, and followed by some desultory conversation, and the presentation of petitions. These opportunities for demagogic eloquence, which at one time threatened to overwhelm the House, were cautiously restricted, and finally abolished in 1843. Two nights were reserved for Government business. Lord John Russell tried to get a third and was refused. Party allegiance was loose, party management dexterous and sharp. Private members had more freedom and opportunity than in a modern Parliament, and much legislation was drafted, introduced, and carried from the back benches.* After the first few speeches the audience scattered to dinner and left the bores in possession. From nine the attendance and the excitement increased. There was no eleven o'clock rule, and often [19]

* The career of Ewart (son of Mr. Gladstone's godfather) is typical. He was in Parliament thirty-four years. He carried three important bills (capital punishment, defence of felons, public libraries) besides being very active on free trade, schools of design, and competitive examinations. But he was never in office. [20]

the sun was up before the Commons, with parched throats and throbbing heads, escaped to enjoy, if they could, the majestic spectacle of London from the bridges, before the smoke had risen to make every street dark and every face dirty. [21]

The manners of Parliament in the thirties seem to have been the worst on record, and they were not improved when, in 1835, the Whigs, in their brief interval of Opposition, chose to put out a strong Speaker, Manners Sutton, and put in a weak one, Abercromby.* Under his amiable governance, with the windows shut —and the stench of the Thames made it impossible to keep them open—the mooings, cat-calls, and cock-crows, what O'Connell once called the 'beastly bellowings', of the faithful Commons, could be heard fifty yards away. The eloquence which could master such an audience was of a new kind. The great rhetorical tradition which begins with Halifax and runs through Pitt to Canning, sent up an expiring flash in Macaulay. The modern manner was less declamatory and more closely reasoned: we might call it more conversational if we remember that conversation still kept some of the amplitude of an earlier day.† Speeches were very long, but the contentions over the currency and the fiscal system had created a new style, of which Huskisson was the first exponent, Peel the most specious master, and which Mr. Gladstone wielded like a Tenth Muse: knowledge of the facts and an apt handling of figures was now the surest proof of capacity, and among the most memorable feats of Victorian oratory are speeches on finance. [22] [24] [26]

In this development Parliament reflected a movement in the national mind. It was the business of the thirties to transfer the treatment of affairs from a polemical to a statistical basis, from Humbug to Humdrum.‡ In 1830 there were hardly any figures to work on. Even the Census was still far from perfect: in that of [27]

* Lord John Russell urged the view, which fortunately did not become canonical, that the Speaker should always be in sympathy with the majority. [23]

† The Brookfields in the fifties claimed to have introduced the new style of conversation, brisk and allusive. Mrs. Carlyle used to torture London parties with the elaboration of her anecdotes. [25]

‡ As a symbol of the age, one might cite the Lords' Report on 'the expediency of Discontinuing the present Mode of Engrossing Acts of Parliament in Black Letter and substituting a Plain Round Hand'. But until Lord Thring took it in hand, the actual drafting of statutes came far short of these good intentions. [28] [29]

1831 the acreage of England is given twice over, with a discrepancy as large as Berkshire. Imports were still reckoned by Official Values based on the prices of 1690. But statistical inquiry, fostered very largely by the development of the Insurance business, was a passion of the times. The Statistical department of the Board of Trade was founded in 1832; the department of the Registrar-General in 1838; the Royal Statistical Society sprang out of the Cambridge meeting of the British Association in 1833. Two private compilations of the thirties, McCulloch's *Statistical Account of the British Empire*★ and Porter's *Progress of the Nation*, are still the best approach to Victorian history. Then come the great 31 inquiries, by Parliamentary Committees or Royal Commissions, following the Poor Law Commission of 1832. To Sydney Smith it seemed that the world had been saved from the flood to be handed over to barristers of six years' standing, and a Prussian 32 visitor apprehended that the object of the Whigs was to Germanize England by means of Royal Commissions. In a few years the 33 public mind had been flooded with facts and figures bearing on every branch of the national life, except agriculture: the collec- 34 tion of agricultural statistics was resisted till the sixties. No community in history had ever been submitted to so searching an examination.† Copied or summarized in the Press, the Blue Books created a new attitude to affairs; they provided fresh topics for novelists and fresh themes for poets. *Sybil* is a Blue Book in fic- tion; *The Cry of the Children* a Blue Book in verse. With the 35 parliamentary inquiries must be ranged the local investigations made by individuals, societies, and municipalities. I have spoken of Kay-Shuttleworth's Report on Manchester. In a few years a score of great towns, Bristol, Westminster, Southwark, Hull, Liverpool, Leeds, had all been put through the same mill and with much the same results.‡ Douglas Jerrold, who had once produced an

★ Which gives more space to Oxford then to Canada. *Empire* in E[arly] V[ictorian] English is stylistic for *realm*, *kingdom*, and imports no overseas reference. 'Dog's Hole Lane has been widened! Main drainage has been installed! Soon X will take her rightful place among the Cities of the Empire!' I quote from memory from the history of some 'glad aspiring little burg'.   30

† The Parliamentary papers were first put on sale in 1835; division lists first published in 1836.

‡ The impulse came from the Statistical Society of Manchester, which, as a control experiment, also investigated Rutland. Leeds was, I believe, the first municipality to investigate itself.   36

unsuccessful play called *The Factory Girl*, complained that in 1833 no one was thinking about the poor and in 1839 no one was thinking about anything else. But in 1839 the depths had not been sounded.

37

VI

THE years following the Reform Act were for the towns a time of quiet prosperity, which culminated in the golden harvest of 1835. Towards the end of 1836 a warning shiver ran through the commercial world: over-production and speculation were producing their natural consequences. There was a parallel depression in America, and the European States were raising their tariffs. Lancashire went on half-time; the harvest of 1838 failed; gold was exported to buy food, and the Bank of England was barely saved from default by credits in Paris and Hamburg. That a bad period was approaching was evident. But few could have guessed through what misery the country would have to pass before the clouds lifted again. In Stockport nearly a fourth of the houses were empty. Thousands of families were living on relief administered at the rate of a shilling a head. Out of 15,000 persons visited, not one in ten was fully employed. Wages had fallen from a pound and more to 7s. 6d.; the average weekly income was less than 1s. 6d. Manchester and Bolton were in like case: the Potteries, the Black Country, the cloth towns of the west, all told the same tale. It was the background of Chartism and the Free Trade League.

The Chartists wished to make a revolution: the Leaguers asserted that the revolution had happened, and drew out the consequences. Lancashire, the home of the movement, was the most typical product of the new civilization, and it needed little argument to prove that Lancashire could not live without imported cotton, could not maintain her increasing population without expanding markets, could not expand her markets unless the foreigner was kept in funds by the sale of food to England. Did the workshop of the world need a hobby farm, with a subsidized gentry to manage it, especially a gentry which was beginning to show an inconvenient interest in factory children, and the

tendency of the fourteen hour day *minuere et contrahere pelvem*?* 4
The League was founded in January 1839. For the first years of its
existence it was fighting on two fronts, against the Protectionists
and against the Chartists. Free Trade lecturers ran the double risk
whenever they stood up in a market-place of being fined by the
magistrate and ducked by the mob. To hungry men the prospect
of relief by Free Trade was more remote than the prospect of
relief by direct action, and it was as easy to represent the League
as a coalition of mill-owners bent on reducing their wages bill,
as a coalition of democrats bent on destroying the landed interest.
'You are a Chartist, Sir; you are a leveller,' the Home Secretary
shouted at the respectable Mr. Ashworth, manufacturer, when he
came on a Free Trade deputation. The self-protective instinct of 6
the aristocracy felt in the League its most dangerous enemy. But
the instinct of society as a whole was more sensitive to the
growing menace of Chartism.

The political creed of the Chartists was an amplification of the
Radical formula, one man one vote, one vote one value. How they
were going to get the vote was not so clear, and what they were
going to do with it remained, even to themselves, unknown.
Judged by what they did, they might be considered a body of
decent, hardly used, and not particularly intelligent men, whose
allegiance, given with equal readiness to high-minded leaders like
Lovett and Hetherington and to pitiful demagogues like Feargus
O'Connor, would probably be at the service of the first Conservative or Liberal who showed that he deserved it. Judged by what
they said, or by what O'Connor, 'false, malignant, and cowardly', said for them, both their objects and their methods seemed 7
to involve a bloody progress from confiscation, through anarchy,
to famine and a dictatorship. The Socialism of Robert Owen, the
doctrine that industrialism was not an impersonal force to be
adored or bewailed, but a way of life to be controlled by co-
operation, had gone underground. The young Queen was gracious to him for her father's sake, who had been his friend in the
days when Napoleon had studied his projects in Elba, and Castlereagh had laid them before Congresses. But his mind was failing,
and to most people Owenism meant a crazy multiplication of

---

* Lord John Manners let the cat out of the bag when he talked, apropos of
a Factory Bill, of 'putting a curb on the manufacturing interest and making it
know its rider'.

Trade Unions with long names, and the combination of economic
8 heresy with irreligion and sexual depravity. 'You tell us', a
Parliamentary Committee once said to a clergyman, 'that the
railway navvies are mostly infidels. Would you say that they are
also socialists?' 'In practice, yes; because though most of them
9 appear to have wives, few of them are really married.' The more
intelligent workmen professed a belated rationalism,* nourished
on the writings of Tom Paine, with which often went, for philosophy, a wondrous addiction to the phrenology of George
Combe.† The older sects meant little to the working classes. The
Wesleyans, whose services in humanizing the masses were hand-
somely recognized by authority, on principle held aloof from
political contests; and Chartism, which disgusted fair-minded
men by the violence of its invective, terrified a still larger class
by its supposed designs, not only on movable property, but on
religion and the family. Yet there was much silent sympathy with
the Chartists as men; if the new rich had been their only enemies,
many young gentlemen would have been glad to strike a blow
for the old poor. Young England was a sincere if boyish gesture
of goodwill, and to play King Richard to somebody else's Wat
12 Tyler has always been a Tory fancy.

How far the mass of the workpeople were at any time seriously
engaged is a question not easy to answer. The Londoners, who
were most closely allied with the Parliamentary Radicals, stood
for caution and constitutional methods. The admixture of cheap
Irish labour and cheap Irish rhetoric alienated the Englishman, and
the party of physical force were unlucky in their choice of military advisers. In no age are Count Chopski and Colonel Macerone
names to conjure with in English working circles. The Conven-

---

* The term Secularism was invented by Holyoake and first appears in his
paper, *The Reasoner*, 1846. The badge of the Secularist was the defiance of
10 Sabbatarian restrictions.

† Which was shared by Cobden. Phrenology was regularly taught in Mechanics'
Institutes, and did, I think, help to keep the idea of personality alive under the
11 steam-roller of respectability. Otherwise, science (for want of apparatus) did not
much affect the workman. The culture of the self-educated man was still literary.
He began with the Bible and its commentators and worked up through Milton
to the economists, philosophers, and historians. This was of some importance
politically. If the speeches of Bright, Gladstone, or Disraeli *ad Quirites* are examined, they will be found to imply a considerable body of literary culture common
to the speaker and at least a great part of his audience.

tion summoned to London withdrew to the less frigid air of Birmingham: it was known that Lancashire was arming; regiments were recalled from Ireland, the army was increased by 7,000 men, a White Guard instituted, and Sir Charles Napier, a wise and sympathetic choice, was sent to take command of the Northern Division. In 1839 the Charter was presented and rejected: the Convention considered a general strike and a march on London. There was no strike; no one marched, and the insurgents had to be content with a wild riot in Birmingham. In a few weeks 400 Chartists were in prison, and the revolution ended in a splutter of musketry and a dozen men killed outside the Queen's Hotel, Newport. Chartism, though there was some brief, fierce rioting in 1842, when the Charter was again presented and rejected, was effectively dead. 13

It is impossible to gauge the danger of a revolution which refused to happen. But in estimating the alarm we must allow for the melodramatic streak in the early Victorian temperament. When Wellington said on the morrow of the riots that no town sacked in war presented such a spectacle as Birmingham, he did not mean that he had gone to see it for himself, any more than when Lord Shaftesbury said that *Ecce Homo* was the foulest book ever vomited from the jaws of hell, he meant that he had read all the others. Events, like books, still came widely spaced, with time 14 between to set the imagination working; and that generation was still overshadowed by the revolutionary years and read itself in their volcanic light. In 1840 there were many men living who could recall the flight of the French nobility. The sacking of Bristol was still fresh in all memories, and England had hardly the ele- 15 ments of a civil force capable of stopping disorder before it reaches the point where factories are burnt and the troops must shoot.

London was provided for by the Peelers and the mounted patrol who kept order within five miles of Charing Cross. The parish had its constable, and the police of the boroughs were reinforced in emergencies by specials: on election days and other occasions of riot the specials might be numbered by hundreds. There were five hundred private associations for the prosecution of felons; but there was no county police;* and the mainstay

* This is not without its bearing on Victorian psychology. With 25,000 vagrants on the pad, and all the village idiots at large, the unprotected female really had something to be afraid of. 16

of the public peace was not the constable but the yeoman, and behind the yeoman, though cautiously and reluctantly employed, the soldier. Lord John Russell, accounting to the Queen for the progress of the Tories at the elections of 1838, added that the Military had in all cases conducted themselves with great temper

17 and judgement. They were employed on even humbler duties: once, at least, troops were called out to enforce the Act of 1823 and save a poor ox from being baited on his way to market. England as a whole, and the country gentlemen in particular, were highly suspicious of anything in the nature of a national police, and the Act of 1839 went no further than to permit the Justices of a County to appoint a Chief Constable and form a police force if they so desired. The boroughs already had the power. But in that alarming year it was discovered that neither Birmingham nor Manchester could maintain a paid force, and an emergency detachment had to be sent from London. So sensitive was the feeling of sound constitutionalists in the matter of police, that Lord John, having sent London constables to Bradford to help with a Poor Law riot, decided on reflection to withdraw

18 them and enjoined the magistrates to use dragoons instead. The Permissive Act of 1839 was generalized by the Compulsory Act of 1856. The interval had been well employed. Essex selected as Chief Constable a retired Naval Officer. He very soon made it appear that a paid constabulary was not only more efficient but actually cheaper than the gratuitous service of Dogberry and Verges. One by one the counties adopted the model he had devised, and all that was necessary in '56 was to bring the laggards into line. There are many famous men to whom England owes less than she owes to Captain M'Hardy, Chief Constable of

19 Essex.

But his career, and his achievement, are typical of a general rule. The English administration was made by administrators throwing out their lines until they met and formed a system. In the fustian phrase which exasperated clear-headed Radicals, it was not made, it grew. In 1830, except for the collection and management of the revenue, for defence, and the transmission of letters, there was hardly anything which a Frenchman or a Prussian would have recognized as an administration. The national expenditure was £50,000,000, of which the debt absorbed £29,000,000, defence £15,000,000 leaving £6,000,000 only for collection, for the

Crown, and the whole civil service. The total and the proportions did not vary greatly till the Crimean War. But by 1860 the cost of defence was £26,000,000, the balance for civil purposes £15,000,000. These figures, which point to the emergence of the armed administrative State, show also with what a slight equipment early Victorian government operated. Local revenue was about a quarter of Imperial, and on an average one-half went in the relief of the poor. The rest was spent on Police, Bridges, and Highways; on Lunatics; on the upkeep of Parish Churches. The Church rate, an inconsiderable sum, but the occasion of much agitation and some painless martyrdom, was persistently evaded, made voluntary in 1853, and abolished in 1868.

The Civil Servants who ran this light machinery were of two sorts: clerks, infallible in accounts, writing a fair hand, the repository of precedent; gentlemen, or the protégés of gentlemen, of the political class, whose position when young might be anything from a copying clerk to a private secretary, and who when old were rather assistants and advisers to an executive chief than executants themselves. There was much routine, so much that by the time the juniors were seniors they were usually unfit for anything else, and the higher posts had to be filled from outside. But almost everything that rose above routine was, except at the Treasury, policy, requiring the personal attention of the Minister: the intermediate sphere of administration did not exist, because there were hardly any laws to administer. Readers of Disraeli's novels must sometimes have been puzzled by the importance of the Under-Secretaries as a class. When the Cabinet was open only to birth, to exceptional genius or exceptional influence, men of excellent gifts had to be content, and were content, with Under-Secretaryships, and the unbroken Tory régime had given some of them a very long innings. Croker was of this class, so was 'gray-headed, financial' Herries; and the Whigs of 1827 could not master their wrath when they were asked to accept as a Cabinet colleague a fellow whom they had always looked upon as a Tory clerk. A Treasury official in Early Victorian English means a Junior Lord.

Well on into the reign the line between politics and administration could be crossed and recrossed as it was by Endymion. Cornewall Lewis was a Civil Servant for fourteen years before he entered Parliament, where he reached Cabinet rank in eight.

Benjamin Hawes from Parliamentary Secretary became Permanent Secretary to the War Office. William Blamire made his mark in Parliament with a speech on tithes, and was given a post which made him, in effect, for twenty years a non-parliamentary Minister of Agriculture. But the dismissal of the Under-Secretaries with their chiefs in 1830, the inexperience of the new Whig Ministers, and the reform of the Poor Law, made a fresh departure. The Benthamite conception of a trained staff dealing with specific problems entered the Civil Service at the very point where the Civil Service impinged most forcibly on the public. The Poor Law filled the whole horizon in 1834. And here, there, and everywhere were Chadwick's young crusaders, the Assistant Commissioners, scouring the country in stage-coaches or post-chaises, or beating up against the storm on ponies in the Weald, returning to London, their wallets stuffed with the Tabular Data so dear to philosophic Radicals, to draft their sovereign's decrees declaring the Union and stating his austere principles of administration, and then back to see that they were carried out. It was an exciting life. Once they had to be protected with cavalry. When they appeared at Todmorden, Fielden rang his factory bells and beat them out of town. In so splendid and imperial a manner did the English Civil Servant first take his place in the national life.*

The Radicals had conceived the possibility of applying disinterested intelligence to social problems. Chadwick realized the idea and created the organ of application. The administrative temper was in being before there was an administration to give it effect. The Poor Law schools at Norwood were taken as a model by the new Education Department. The Poor Law framework was adopted in 1838 for the registration of births, marriages, deaths, and the causes of death. In the same year a London vestry, baffled by an outbreak of fever, turned to the Poor Law Board for help, a step from which descends by regular stages the

---

* The distinction between administrative and clerical duties which lies at the root of the Northcote–Trevelyan reforms in '53 was carried out at the Poor Law Commission from the first. James Mill had already introduced it at the India House. The confusion of functions reached its height at Dublin Castle, where the duties of the Under-Secretary were, *inter alia*, to deputize for the Lord-Lieutenant, to docket incoming letters in red ink, to advise on all criminal business, and to see that the stationery was not wasted.

Health Board of 1848, the Local Government Board of 1870, the
existing Ministry of Health. What was growing up, in fact, in the   26
thirties, under the vigorous impulsion of Chadwick and Kay and   27
the bewildered gaze of Ministers, was a Public Welfare Service,
which was bound sooner or later to demand compulsory powers,
and to receive them as soon as the public mind was sufficiently
moved, enlightened, or alarmed.

But the rapid growth of our administrative services is on the
whole due less to head-quarters than to the Inspectorate. Inspection was in the air: the Factory Inspectors of 1834 were followed
by the Prison Inspectors, and these by the School Inspectors, the
Railway Inspectors, and the Mines Inspectors. The Inspectors,
like the higher officials, were often men of mature experience who
came to their duties with ideas already formed. Leonard Horner,
whose reports underlie so much of our industrial legislation, was
nearing fifty when he entered the Factory department, and was
already a man of note in education and science. Hugh Tremenheere, joining the Education department at thirty-five, had fourteen Acts of Parliament to his credit when he retired. With them   28
must be ranked the specialists in public health; above all, Southwood Smith and John Simon. Smith, a Unitarian minister, whose
devotional writings must have had some singular quality to be
admired both by Wordsworth and Byron, came late to the profession of medicine, but he found his place at once with an Essay
on Fever. Cholera was a visitor: typhus a resident who Southwood
Smith believed could be expelled. Joining forces with Chadwick
he became, in effect, Medical Adviser to the Poor Law Commission. His junior, Simon, a cultivated surgeon of French descent, 29
a connoisseur and the friend of Ruskin, covered in his official life
the development of the Board of Health into the Local Government Board, of which he was the first medical officer. In the   30
careers of men like these, or of Arthur Hassall, who took the
adulteration of food for his province, we see the impact of the   31
educated intelligence on the amorphous, greedy fabric of the new
civilization, and I know nothing which brings the epic quality
of the early Victorian warfare against barbarism into such vivid
relief as the reports, eloquent, impassioned, and precise, which
from 1848 onwards Simon addressed to the Corporation of the
City of London.

VII

THE thirty years from Waterloo have the unity and, at times, the
intensity of a great drama. Castlereagh and Canning adjusted our
insular relations to the Old World and the New. The Reform
Act and the Municipal Reform Act gave the islands a rational
political framework; steam unified their economic structure.
Of all these processes, the Repeal of the Corn Laws in 1846 was
the logical and historical culmination. The operations of the
League, which had gone with a swing all through the bad years,
flagged with the return of prosperity in 1843 and the absorption
of the unemployed by the railway boom; by 1845 manufacturers
did not know where to turn for hands. Peel himself was slowly
moving towards Free Trade in corn, but he was restrained, not by
a political, but by an economic scruple: the belief that cheap food
meant low wages and that the loss of rents to the land-owner
would be followed with no compensating advantage to the working classes. When this doubt was resolved his way grew clear.
The great Budget of 1842, in which he had swept away the
accumulated muddles of the Whigs and raised an income tax to
lower the customs, marks the opening stage of classical Victorian
finance. Incidentally, the sliding scale of 1828, which had refused
to slide, was readjusted. In 1845 he repeated his stroke, and circumstances were gradually imposing a larger policy on his mind.
Of his young men, Gladstone, Lincoln, Canning, Ramsay were
Free Traders already, and Peel, behind the repellent front which
he turned to the world, and which, indeed, cost him his life, was
exceptionally sensitive to the ideas, and the sufferings, of others.
The prosperity of the mid-forties had not spread to the villages;
whatever the cause, the consequences were plain enough: 'I be
protected and I be starving.' One good harvest more, to keep the
League quiet, and he would go to the country as a Free Trader,
with the compensating offer of a credit for the re-conditioning of
the land and the absorption of the next wave of unemployment,
and return with the middle-class Conservatism he had created,
solidly based on the gratitude of the towns and the regeneration of
the farming interest. The disaster which depopulated Ireland shat-

tered the Conservative party on the threshold of a generation of power.*

The Irish difficulty went deeper than the philosophy of the age could reach. The twin cell of English life, the squire administering what everybody recognizes as law and the parson preaching what everybody acknowledges to be religion, had no meaning in a country where the squire was usually an invader and the parson always a heretic. England had staked the good government of Ireland on a double speculation, that the Irish would conform to the Protestant establishment and that they would accept the English use of landlord, farmer, and labourer. The Irishry preferred to misgovern themselves as Catholics and small-holders, and the Englishry, after a few generations, were all too ready to take up the part of tribal chiefs. To analyse the Irish trouble into racial, religious, and agrarian is impossible because in Irish history these three are one, and when England had conceded Catholic emancipation against her own Protestants, and insisted on agrarian reform against the Irish landlords, and both in vain, the logic of history left her no alternative but to concede all the rest, never quite understanding what it was the Irish wanted or why they wanted it.

Thus throughout the nineteenth century Ireland was an uneasy place in the body politic which could be neither forgotten nor assuaged. In the thirties it is tithes and crime. The establishment was a grievance which an English government might alleviate if it could not remove. Disorder was a pestilence which it was bound to stamp out. Hence the history of Lord Grey's Government is taken up very largely with Irish Church bills and Irish coercion bills. On the whole the Whigs were successful, mainly because they sent two honest gentlemen, Drummond and Ebrington, to the Castle and left them alone, and in '41 they handed over to their successors an Ireland neither prosperous nor contented, but at least reasonably quiet. The nationalist agitation 6

* Peel's long-distance programme will be found in a memorandum by Prince Albert, Christmas 1845. His character is not easy to read, because his mastery of Parliamentary methods masked an intense dislike of the party system, while his frigid efficiency covered an almost passionate concern for the welfare of the people. On his last ride an acquaintance, who recognized his horse as a bolter, was afraid to warn him, but in a begging letter-writer's list of people most likely to be touched for a fiver, Peel's name was found with good Queen Adelaide and Dickens.

which sprang up suddenly in the following years, round Gavan Duffy and his friends, was unexpected. Had it fallen a little earlier so as to coincide with the Chartist movement in England, and if O'Connell could have overcome his aversion to physical force, the results might have been memorable. But in 1839 Ireland was so peaceful that soldiers could be spared for England, and in 1843 England was in such good humour that they could be safely sent to Ireland. On October 5 a great demonstration was to assemble at Clontarf; it was proclaimed and O'Connell arrested. Convicted, almost of course, by a Protestant Dublin jury, he was set at liberty by the House of Lords. The incident added a phrase to the language—Lord Denman saying that trial by jury as practised in this case was 'a delusion, a mockery, and a snare', and the Nationalist movement died down.* Peel's Government used their victory not unwisely. They issued a Royal Commission of Enquiry into Irish land tenure and, in the teeth of a frantic Protestant opposition, they carried their proposal to increase the grant for training Irish priests at Maynooth. On the report of the Commission, a classic document for the history of the Irish question, they introduced a Bill to secure compensation for improving tenants. The Lords objected and the Bill was withdrawn for further consideration. The occasion had passed and it did not return.

Early in August 1845, at the end of a successful session, with a thriving country and a full exchequer, Peel received a letter from a potato-dealer, warning him that the crop was diseased and the disease spreading. Half the population of Ireland lived on potatoes, and by the beginning of October it was doubtful whether half the crop would be saved. England had been accustomed to take on an average 2,000,000 quarters of wheat from Ireland. It looked as if she would have to send 2,000,000 quarters to keep the Irish alive, and the English harvest was short. It was out of the question to ask the English to pay duty both on the corn they ate themselves, and on the corn they bought for the Irish: equally impossible to suppose that the Corn Laws, once suspended, could ever be reimposed, or that the Conservative party, as it stood, would ever consent to repeal them. Peel, with the support of the Whigs and with a fragment of his own party, undertook to admit foreign

---

* And split up, the split being signalized by the foundation of the *United Irishman* in opposition to *The Nation*.

corn at a nominal fixed duty.* Supported by imminent famine, the arguments of the League could not be answered: they could only be opposed. It seemed as if nature, which was solving the Irish problem in the sense of the economists by killing off the surplus population, would solve an English problem in the sense of the Radicals by killing off the superfluous landlords. In fact, it did no harm to the English gentry, and it made the Irish problem insoluble. The Encumbered Estates thrown on the market were bought up by investors who proceeded to reorganize them economically by wholesale evictions, and for years hardly a ship sailed to the west without its freight of exiles carrying to America an unappeasable passion for vengeance on the dispossessor.

Yet there was never an Irish tragedy without its satyric afterpiece. In 1848, Smith O'Brien, a respectable and humourless Member of Parliament who seems to have been drawn to Repeal by simple despair of the Union, was caught levying war on the Queen's Majesty in the widow McCormack's cabbage garden. The campaign was brief, as O'Brien had forgotten to provide his army with anything to eat. He was sentenced to the usual penalty, 12 which was at once commuted to transportation. With the maddening logic which Irishmen have at command he argued that as he had not been convicted of anything deserving transportation, he must be pardoned or he must be hanged. The Law Officers admitted his contention, and a short Act had to be passed providing that, in spite of the earnest expectation of the creatures, O'Brien and others in like case might lawfully be required to remain alive. 13

VIII

LATER Victorians, to whom Free Trade had become a habit of mind, tended almost instinctively to divide the century into the years before and after 1846. But in the sixties one social observer laid his finger not on the Repeal of the Corn Laws in '46, but on the Factory Act of '47, as the turning-point of the age and, with our 1

* It is characteristic of Early Victorian manners that in the Cabinet paper announcing his conversion, Peel can hardly bring himself to call That Root by its proper name. It was observed that in all prayers offered up for our Irish brethren, potatoes were never mentioned.   11

longer perspective, we can hardly doubt that he was right. Of facts which, in Gibbon's phrase, are dominant in the general system, by far the most significant in this period is the emergence of a new State philosophy, of which the overt tokens are the Factory Act, the Public Health Acts,* and the Education Minute of 1846. The great inquiries of the thirties and forties were the Nemesis of the middle-class victory of 1830; an unreformed Parliament would never have persisted in them, and they led, silently and inevitably, to a conception of the State and its relations to its subjects which the electors of the first Reformed Parliaments would almost unanimously have repudiated. The cataclysm of 1830 proved to have been the beginning of a slow evolution, by which, while an aristocratic fabric was quietly permeated with Radical ideas, an individualistic society was unobtrusively schooled in the ways of State control. Engels's *Condition of the Working Class*, which projected the image of the exploiting capitalist on the mind of the European proletariat, appeared in 1845; it was based on the English Blue Books. So was the legislation of 1847. History, which sometimes condescends to be ironic, had chosen her dates with meaning.

From 1832 to 1847 the student of Victorian history finds himself the bewildered spectator of a warfare between Radicals who upheld Factories and Workhouses, Tories and Chartists who abhorred them both, infidel Benthamites leagued with Conservative Anglicans against dissenting manufacturers, landowners denouncing the oppressions of Lancashire, and cotton masters yearning over the sorrows of Dorset. The movement for Factory Reform and against the New Poor Law, against Protection and for the Charter, are mixed in an inextricable confusion of agitation, of which, nevertheless, the main pattern is clear. The Factory Act of 1833 introduced, in all textile factories, the ten-hour day for young persons under eighteen and a forty-eight-hour week for children under thirteen, with the obligation to attend for two hours every day at a school which often did not exist. In this last provision, and in the four inspectors appointed to observe the operation of the law, we see the Radical hand. Otherwise the Act is a watering down of the demands made by the Evangelical Tories, Oastler, Sadler, and Lord Ashley, on the

---

* The principal are: Baths and Washhouses Act '46 and '47; Town Improvements Clauses '47; Public Health '48; Lodging Houses '51; Burials '52.

basis of the Ten Hour movement in the West Riding. To the work-people it was a disappointment, and their resentment went to animate the growing body of Popular Radicalism. Thrown on themselves, they turned towards Direct Action, Trade Unions, and the Charter. To the employers it was a warning, since the reduction of children's hours of necessity brought with it a rearrangement of all working hours, which ultimately the State might generalize. Outside the factories, indeed, the seventy-two-hour week was becoming common in many trades.

But for the next few years the focus of agitation was not Factory reform, but the New Poor Law. The resources of the Poor Law Commissioners were limited; the Benthamite watchword—aggregate to segregate—remained a watchword only; and their comprehensive scheme for dealing separately with the young, the sick, the aged, the vagrant, and the destitute was never put into effect. In its place nothing was visible but the New Bastilles, and the proposal which the workhouse system seemed to involve of applying factory discipline—if not prison discipline—to the pauper, lashed the working classes to fury. It was at this time that The House acquired its sinister meaning, and the Poor Law first inspired that repulsion which has hobbled our administration ever since. The Forty-third of Elizabeth, which declared the Right to Work, had degenerated into the Right to Relief without working. But it was the Charter of the Poor. The New Poor Law was the charter of the ratepayer, and it was failing of its purpose. The formula which had worked in the rural south failed when it was applied to the industrial midlands and the north. Reluctantly the Commissioners surrendered their principles and set the people to task work, or road-making, as if they had been Tudor magistrates faced with a short harvest. And the poor rate rose again.

The failure of the New Poor Law to fulfil its promise, the inevitable harshness of a new administration suddenly applied to a people with no idea of administration at all, the brutality that went on in some workhouses and the gorging in others,* the petty tyranny of officials and the petty corruption of Guardians,

* Against the oft-repeated tale of the Andover gristle set the dietary discovered in one workhouse: bread 72 oz., gruel 7½ pints, meat 15 oz., potatoes 1½ lb., soup 4½ pints, pudding 14 oz., cheese 8 oz., broth 4½ pints, and compare it with the tables, in Chapter II of *Early Victorian England*, of ordinary working-class food.

discredited the scientific Radicals and brought the sentimental Radicals to the front. *The Pickwick Papers* is not a Victorian document: it belongs to a sunnier time, which perhaps had never existed. The group of novels that follow, *Oliver Twist, Nicholas Nickleby, The Old Curisosity Shop*, is charged with the atmosphere of the thirties. They have the Radical faith in progress, the Radical dislike of obstruction and privilege, the Radical indifference to the historic appeal. But they part from the Radicalism of the Benthamites in their equal indifference to the scientific appeal. Dickens's ideal England was not very far from Robert Owen's. But it was to be built by some magic of goodwill overriding the egoism of progress; not by law, and most emphatically not by logic.

The economists and the reformers had drawn the bow too tight: it almost snapped in their hands. But so, too, had the Evangelicals, and even goodwill was suspected if it came arrayed in religious guise. At the sight of Wilberforce, Cobbett put his
8 head down and charged. Young Anglicans were prepared to defend black slavery only because the Evangelicals were against
9 it. Sir Andrew Agnew's Sunday Observance Bill, the most rigorous piece of moral—and, indeed, class—legislation since the Long Parliament, supported by 128 members of the Commons, with Lord Ashley at their head, brought the two humorists of the age into the field together. Dickens riddled it in words; Cruik-
10 shank in pictures. But in all Dickens's work there is a confusion of mind which reflects the perplexity of his time; equally ready to denounce on the grounds of humanity all who left things alone,
11 and on the grounds of liberty all who tried to make them better. England was shifting uneasily and convulsively from an old to a new discipline, and the early stages were painful.★ To be numbered, to be visited, to be inspected, to be preached at, whether the visitors were furnished with a Poor Law Order or a religious mission, whether they came to feed the children or to save their souls, frayed tempers already on edge with mechanical toil, and hurt—often unreasonably, but still it hurt—that very sense of personal dignity on which the scientific reformers, as strongly as the sentimentalists, relied for the humanization of the poor.

The one field in which they might have co-operated without

★ It has been suggested to me that the Railway Time-table did much to discipline the people at large. I think this is true.

reserve was the care of children. The Factory Act of 1833 was incidentally an Education Act as well, though a very imperfect one, since for the purposes of the Act any cellar might be returned as a school and any decayed pedlar as a schoolmaster. The year [12] 1840 saw the chimney-sweeping children brought under public protection. The next advance was inspired by the revelations of [13] the Employment of Children Enquiry of 1840 and registered in the Mines Act of 1842. In the following year Peel's Govern- [14] ment tried to carry the Act of 1833 one step farther. They were beaten by a union of manufacturers and dissenters: 'worthy and conscientious men', Brougham wrote, 'who hate the Established Church more than they love education.' In 1844 Graham re- [15] introduced his Bill, omitting the educational clauses which had given so much offence, but reducing the hours of children's labour to six and a half, of men's to twelve. Lord Ashley stood out for ten: the Government resisted. Peel pointed out that the Bill dealt only with textile factories and that notoriously the conditions in other workshops were worse. 'Will you legislate for all?' he asked. It was a rhetorical question. But it was answered with a solid shout of 'Yes'. Without meaning it, the House of Commons had undertaken to regulate the factory system throughout the land, and a few nights later they recalled their decision. [16] But the tide was running fast and the conversion of Macaulay is symptomatic. As a young man he had dealt his blows impartially between paternal Toryism and deductive Radicalism, between Southey, Owen, and James Mill. His economics, like those of [17] most Englishmen, were in descent not from Ricardo, but from Adam Smith and Burke.

'It is one of the finest problems in legislation, and what has often engaged my thoughts whilst I followed that profession, "what the State ought to take upon itself to direct by the public wisdom, and what it ought to leave, with as little interference as possible, to individual discretion". Nothing, certainly, can be laid down on the subject that will not admit of exceptions, many permanent, some occasional. But the clearest line of distinction which I could draw, while I had any chalk to draw it, was this: that the State ought to confine itself to what regards the State, or the creatures of the State, namely, the exterior establishment of its religion; its magistracy; its revenue; its military force by sea and land; the corporations that owe their existence to its fiat; in a word, to everything that is *truly and properly* public, to the public peace, to the public safety, to the public order, to the public prosperity. In its preventive police it ought to be sparing of its efforts, and to employ means, rather few, unfrequent, and strong, than many, and frequent, and, of course, as they multiply their puny politic race, and dwindle, small and feeble. Statesmen who know themselves will, with the dignity which belongs to wisdom, proceed only in this the superior orb, and first mover of their duty steadily, vigilantly, severely, courageously: whatever remains will, in a manner provide for itself. But as they descend from the State to a province, from a province to a parish, and from a parish to a private house, they go on accelerated in their fall. They *cannot* do the lower duty; and, in proportion as they try it, they will certainly fail in the higher. They ought to know the different department of things; what belongs to laws, and what manners alone can regulate. To these, great politicians may give a leaning, but they cannot give a law.'*

A great body of principle, self-interest, and sentiment had to be shifted, before the public mind could pass this point. Of principle, because State intervention was still commonly pictured as that system of State regulation of industry which Adam Smith had confuted. Of self-interest, because it does undoubtedly mean a restriction of a man's right to do what he will with his own. Of sentiment, because the intense dislike of interference and domiciliary visits which history had bred in us, took into its field the workpeople and the factory; and the religious, the economic, and the social codes all combined to emphasize the vital importance of individual effort, whether the prize was domestic comfort or heavenly joy. But experience tells, and by 1845 it was becoming evident that the line between what the State may do and what it must leave alone had been drawn in the wrong place, and that there was a whole world of things where the individual simply could not help himself at all. He could not build his own house, or even choose his own street. He could not dispose of his own sewage or educate his own children. In Macaulay's mind the sphere of State interest now includes not only public order and defence, but public health, education, and the hours of labour. It includes, what is most remarkable of all, that triumph of private enterprise—the railways.

[18]   * Burke, *Thoughts on Scarcity*, 1795.

'Trade considered merely as a trade, considered merely with regard to the pecuniary interest of the contracting parties, can hardly be too free. But there is a great deal of trade which cannot be considered merely as trade, and which affects higher than pecuniary interests. Fifteen years ago it became evident that railroads would soon, in every part of the kingdom, supersede to a great extent the old highways. The tracing of the new routes which were to join all the chief cities, ports and naval arsenals of the island was a matter of the highest national importance. But unfortunately those who should have acted refused to interfere. That the whole society was interested in having a good system of internal communications seemed to be forgotten. The speculator who wanted a large dividend on his shares, the landowner who wanted a large price for his acres, obtained a full hearing. But nobody applied to be heard on behalf of the community.'*

Was Hudson listening that night? For Hudson, 'Mammon and Belial in one', was nearing his apogee and his fall. The Midland 21 and North-Eastern systems were under his control: he had carried the Sunderland election against Bright and Cobden in 1845, when *The Times* chartered a special train to bring the news of his return; his financial triumphs, his country houses, his parties in Albert Gate, his friendship with Prince Albert, gave him an almost legendary prestige.† But Hudson was one of those not uncommon characters who persuade themselves that an aptitude for business carries with it a genius for fraud. He kept one block of shares in demand by paying the dividends out of capital: with even greater simplicity he helped himself to others which did not appear in the books and sold them at a profit. Naturally he was the strenuous, and, no doubt, the sincere, opponent of Government supervision; and naturally when the bubble burst, with a loss to the investor, it was reckoned, of nearly £80,000,000, the public attitude to Government supervision underwent some change. 22

In this atmosphere Fielden's Bill was finally carried. Those who have read the debates may perhaps think that the opponents had the best of the argument. The 58-hour week (which, in effect, was

* Speech on Fielden's Factory Bill, May 22, 1846. In the Government, the 19 same view was strongly urged by Dalhousie, who was able to give effect to it in India. 20

† Mrs. Hudson hardly kept pace with her husband's elevation; once, on a visit to Grosvenor House, she was shown a bust of Marcus Aurelius: 'It ain't the present Markis, is it?' she inquired.

what the Bill established) was a plunge, and an opposition supported by Peel, Graham, and Herbert for the Conservatives, by Brougham, Roebuck, and old Jo Hume for the economists, and backed by the warnings of the most experienced officials, is not to be ignored. But the debates mark at once the waning of the economics of pure calculation and the growth of that preoccupation with the quality of life which is dominant in the next decade. There is a remarkable passage in Peel's speech, in which he refers to the criticism of the Italian economists that their English colleagues concentrated on wealth and overlooked welfare.* But he need not have gone to Italy for it. He could have heard it from Sadler and Southey and Young England; he could have read it as far
23 back as 1832 in the *Quarterly Review*. This alternative economic was not thought out; it remained instinctive, sentimental, feudal; and the natural alliance of the scientific Benthamite administrator and the authoritative Tory gentleman was never fully achieved, or
24 achieved only in India. But it was creeping in and on. 'Of course, all legislative interference is an evil—but' runs like an apologetic refrain through the speeches of those who supported the Bill. And the 'but' grew larger as the conviction of evil grew less assured.†

* Peel was probably thinking of Sismondi's *Nouveaux Principes*.

† I may here refer to Mrs. Tonna's *Perils of the Nation*, hurriedly compiled for the Christian Influence Society in the alarm following the Chartist Riots of 1842. It undoubtedly represents a great body of educated opinion of, broadly speaking, a Tory Evangelical cast, and furnishes a link between the Sadler–Ashley thought of the thirties and *Unto this Last* of 1860. Her analysis of the social trouble is (a) defective conceptions of national wealth; (b) exorbitant power of the employing class; (c) unwillingness to legislate between employer and workman; (d) competition, which had (i) destroyed the notion of fair wage, fair price, and fair profit, (ii) lowered the quality of goods. It will be seen how near all this comes to the Ruskin of twenty years later. Mrs. Tonna's remedies are naturally somewhat vague: specifically, education, housing, and direct industrial legislation; generally, the organization of a better opinion among the upper and professional classes. Incidentally she believes the beautiful doctrine that when God sends mouths he sends meat, and regards contraception (and Harriet Martineau) as the 'most horrifying abomination of Socialism'. The book had a wide circulation, but I refer to it, not as an agent, but as a symptom, in the struggle to get away from the impersonality of Capital and Labour to the idea of a fair deal and a decent population. Directly, Carlyle contributed little: but the atmospheric effect of his
25 insistence on personality, immaterial values, and leadership was immense.

IX

'RAILWAY companies may smash their passengers into mummy and the State may not interfere!* Pestilence may sweep our streets and the state may not compel the municipalities to put their own powers in operation to check it! We have heard of the Curiosities of Literature and some day this book will be numbered among them.' So did *Eliza Cook's Journal* dispose of the already antiquated individualism of Herbert Spencer's *Social Statics* in 1851. Eliza Cook knew what the lower middle classes were thinking about. 'There have been at work among us', a Nonconformist preacher told his people, 'three great social agencies: the London City Mission; the novels of Mr. Dickens: the cholera.' It had never been forgotten: it was always due to return. It came in '48/'49 and again in '54.   2

The Health Legislation of the Victorian age is a blended product of Poor Law and Municipal Reform. By 1830 the old boroughs were falling into imbecility; they had for the most part ceased to perform any useful service; improvements in lighting, draining, gas, water, markets, streets, even in police, were carried out under special Acts by special commissioners, and the corporations were little more than corrupt electoral colleges. When the franchise was bestowed on the ten-pound householders at large, the corporations had lost their reason for existing unless some one could find something for them to do, and make them fit to do it. One article in the Benthamite code prescribed representative local bodies for all purposes—miniatures of Parliament and Cabinet, with trained officials selected by open competition. The Municipal Reform Act did not go so far as this: it 3 created 178 elected corporations, but with limited powers and little supervision from above. London was reserved for separate treatment: even a Benthamite quailed before the magnitude of the metropolis, which was misgoverned by four counties, innumerable vestries and commissions, the Bailiff of Westminster, and the Corporation of the City of London. The field of the new municipalities was the police and good government of the towns. They were allowed, though not compelled, to take over

* Railway travelling was much more dangerous in England than on the Continent. Fatal accidents were more than fifteen times as frequent as in Germany.   1

the duties of the Special Commissioners, and it was by the gradual assumption of these activities that the great municipalities mastered the problems of town life.

That of all these problems health, in the widest sense, was the most important, had been realized at the time of the cholera visitation, and the lesson was constantly hammered home by Chadwick from the Poor Law Commission. All that the science of the day could discover or suggest—and the discoveries were as awful as the suggestions were drastic*—was embodied in his
5 Report of 1842. In 1848 the results were brought together. In the early Poor Law administration, the Commissioners had no representative in Parliament, so that the Tyrants of Somerset House were without a Minister either to control or to defend their masterful proceedings: they really were bureaucrats, as Palmerston explained the new word to Queen Victoria, from *bureau* an office and *kratos* power. The defect was made good in 1847, and the Commission was provided with a Parliamentary President. The Act of 1848 created a parallel Board of Health in Whitehall with power to create Local Boards and compel them to discharge a great variety of duties, from the regulation of slaughter-houses, to the supply of water and the management
6 of cemeteries. It was a patchy and cumbrous piece of legislation: one municipality might adopt the Act and its neighbour not, and cholera might bear down on a district, while the average mortality of the last seven years had been too low to give the Board a ground for intervention. And when they were allowed to intervene, they must first inquire and then report, and then make a provisional order and then get the order confirmed, and then, most difficult of all, see that it was not evaded by local jobbers, backed by the Private Enterprise Society.† There was not enough staff to go round: the local doctors could not be got to report their wealthy patients for maintaining nuisances: it is not supposed that municipal affairs as a rule engage either the most intelligent or the most

---

* The principal were: municipal water supply, scientific drainage (land and town), an independent health service (with large summary powers for dealing with nuisances), and a national interment service. Why this last was regarded as important will be understood by any one who looks at Walker's *Gatherings*
4 *from Graveyards.*

† Founded in 1849 to resist the operation of the Act. There is a good account of the working of the Act in *Two Years Ago*, which is drawn from the Mevagissey
7 outbreak of '54.

disinterested of mankind, and the impact of the irresistible Chadwick on the immovable incuriousness of the small municipal
mind could only end in explosions.* The virtue of the Act of
1848 lay less in its immediate results than in the large opportunities
it gave for local initiative and scientific intelligence to work together. Gradually, over the country as a whole, rapidly in some
aspiring boroughs, the filth and horror which had crawled over
the early Victorian towns was penned back in its proper lairs,
and perhaps the first step towards dealing effectively with slums
was to recognize them as slums and not as normal phenomena of
urban existence. In the mid-fifties returning exiles were greeted
by a novel sight. The black wreath over London was thinning;
the Thames was fringed with smokeless chimneys. The Home
Office had begun to harry offenders under the Smoke Nuisance
(Metropolis) Act of 1853.   9

But the great development of municipal administration belongs to the next generation. The advance of education was much
more rapid. In fact, by 1846 it had already passed out of its first
phase of mass production by monitors and private initiative into
the phase of trained teachers and public control. Under the
monitorial system, the more forward children imparted the elements to the juniors in groups. As a device for getting simple ideas
into simple heads as fast as possible it was successful.† Up to a
certain point the Bell and Lancaster children made astonishing
progress; most children like playing at school; and the system
was not intended to carry them further than the Three R's. The
British and Foreign School Society backed Lancaster and simple
Bible reading; the National Society for Promoting the Education
of the Poor in the Principles of the Established Church stood for
Bell and the Catechism. A fine class-distinction tended to keep   11
them apart through the Victorian age; the British Day scholar
was not, as a rule, of the poorest class. The success of the two
societies in diffusing elementary instruction was admitted, and the
first intervention of the State in the education of the people took
the shape of a grant in aid, in 1833, for school-building; of £11,000
to the National Society and £9,000 to the British and Foreign.

* He was retired in '54. One of his last feats was a circular enjoining Local
Authorities to consider 'insolvency, bankruptcy, and failure in previous pursuits
as presumptive evidence of unfitness' for official employment.   8
† It was adopted for a time at Charterhouse.   10

Six years later the distribution was entrusted to a Committee of Council, nominally: effectively, to their Secretary, Kay-Shuttleworth of the Manchester Report.

A survey of elementary education in the thirties revealed to thoughtful contemporaries a profoundly disquieting picture. School-buildings were rarely good, often indifferent, sometimes thoroughly bad. The same might be said of the teachers. The average school-life was perhaps two years, perhaps eighteen months. The Society Schools, which represented the best practice of the time, were helped out by Sunday Schools which also gave a little instruction in reading and writing, sometimes in arithmetic, and by a mob of private ventures, of which the one kept by Mr. Wopsle's great aunt and attended by Pip was, if anything, a favourable specimen. At Salford it was found that of 1,800 children nominally at school, less than half were taught to read or write. In Liverpool less than half the child population under fifteen went to school at all, and the other half did not miss much. The fees were 6*d.* for readers, 9*d.* for writers, 1*s* for counters. Masters made 17*s.* a week, Dames 6*s.* A curious difficulty occurred in the collection of these statistics. 'Catch me counting the brats,' one Dame replied. 'I mind what happened to David.' At Newcastle half the children escaped from schools which are briefly described as horrible. Bristol was rather better; more than half the children were at school, paying a penny or twopence a week. Leeds was worse, for there 15,000 went untaught altogether; Sunday schools provided for 11,000, and less than 7,000 were in such rudimentary secular establishments as existed. In Hull a close investigation revealed that of 5,000 children who had been to school, 800 could not read, 1,800 could not write, and just half could not do a sum. It was much if the victims could write their names. From the marriage registers it would appear that in the thirties about one-third of the men and two-thirds of the women could not. Nor was there much evidence of improvement in the past thirty years. In Manchester, about 1810, the Signers were 52, the Markers 48; by 1838 the proportion had only moved to 55 and 45.

Clearly no society could be left to rest on a substratum of ignorance so dense as these figures show, especially after the Reform Bill had divulged the arcanum of party government, that the franchise might be extended. Of what use were cheap papers to a population which could not read them? The passion for an educated people, which united all reformers and gives a lasting nobility to the tortuous career of Brougham,* was frustrated by the absence of any foundation on which to build, and the Mechanics' Institutes from which so much was hoped sank into play-centres for serious clerks. The Philosophical Radicals had | 15 their solution. As usual, it was entirely right, and, as usual, it was entirely impracticable. In dealing with the difficulties of Victorian administration it is necessary to remember that hardly any one had yet thought of the county as an administrative unit, except for its ancient functions of justice and highways. Twice in the thirties a Radical Bill for the creation of elected County Boards fluttered for an evening in the unfriendly air and died. There was the Imperial 16 Government: there were the boroughs. But between Whitehall and the people at large there were, except for the Poor Law Unions, no administrative links or gradations. Chadwick, who thought of everything, had meditated a system of local authorities for all purposes based on the Poor Law Unions, but he was darkly suspected of a design for abolishing the counties to begin with and cutting up the immemorial map of England into Benthamite rectangles. The Radicals proposed to divide the country into 17 School Districts, levying an education rate, maintaining infant schools, elementary schools with a vocational bias, continuation classes, and training colleges. In process of time the schools would be wholly staffed by trained teachers; education should be compulsory from six to twelve, and it should include instruction, by means of Government text-books, in political economy. The 18 Radicals had substituted the inspiration of Ricardo for the inspiration of Scripture. Otherwise, this project has a very modern air. Radical projects always have, after their origin has been forgotten.

It was far too modern for 1843. Parliamentary Government can only operate with the equipment and feelings of the current age. The Voluntary Schools were there. And any attempt at educational reform had to reckon with the most intense of Victorian emotions, sectarian animosity. It must be allowed for everywhere, and a few years later it flamed up with a vehemence which consumed the most promising experiment yet projected. Immediately

---

* The appointment of Panizzi to the British Museum was one of Brougham's best jobs.

on his appointment Kay-Shuttleworth produced, and the Committee of Council accepted, a plan for a Training College, complete with model school and practising school. It broke down on the question of religious instruction. The Dissenters would not stand the parson in a State school. The Establishment would not stand any one else. Even the Church of Scotland, which might have minded its own business, took a hand in the game. The plan was withdrawn. With an energy typical of himself and his age its author opened the College himself and for some years lived a double existence, as an official at Whitehall and the Principal of a Training College at Battersea. The example was decisive. Voluntary training colleges sprang up in quick succession, and the
19 foundations of a teaching profession were laid. The system was consolidated by the Minute of 1846—apprenticeship to a master, a course in a Training College, the Certificate, additional pay for the Trained Teacher, and the unkept promise of a pension at the
20 end. Charley Hexam—surely the most detestable boy on record—
21 was apprenticed to Bradley Headstone. Sue Bridehead was a Queen's scholar at Salisbury Training College when she made her
22 disastrous expedition to Wardour with Jude. They are products, perhaps unusual products, of the Minute of 1846.

But the new grant system which the Minute established—£1 from the Treasury, in augmentation of salaries, for every £2 raised locally—brought up the whole issue of State intervention or State abstention. The Dissenters, who had wrecked Graham's Bill of 1843 for educating factory children in Church schools with a conscience clause, took the field against the Committee of Council. As of all the churches the Church of England was the richest and, in fairness it must be added, the most generous, it was foreseeable that the two pounds would be more readily forthcoming for Church schools than for any other. In effect, therefore, and in the circumstances inevitably, the Government grant would be a subsidy in aid of the education of little Churchmen, or the conversion of little Dissenters. That the bulk of the child population might better have been described as little heathen seems to have escaped the notice of the reverend opponents to the measure. But the onslaught of the Voluntarists was encountered with a conviction equal and an eloquence superior to their own, and probably the only speech on Education which has ever been read with pleasure by any one except the author is Macaulay's defence of the

new grants against Mr. Duncombe, Mr. Baines, the Congregational Union, and John Bright. Henceforth the education of the
people was admitted to be a primary function of the State. From
this admission it is not far to the Radical position—education universal, compulsory, and secular—and the only question remaining
was how slowly and by what devious routes and compromises it
would be reached, and how much energy would be squandered
by the way on the interminable rancours of Church and Dissent.

X

THE Tory ascendancy under George III had modified the political
colour of the Anglican body. In the earlier Hanoverian decades,
the hierarchy, nominated by the Government, was, on the whole,
Whig; the clergy, appointed by lay patrons, Tory. Then,
gradually, the Sees came to be filled with men in closer sympathy
with the mass of the clergy, men, too, for the most part, of a type
superior in piety and learning to the bishops of the first two
Georges, while, with the improvement of the land, Holy Orders
became a more and more attractive profession for the sons of
gentlemen. Thus the Church of England after its long lethargy
was reconsolidated, with a distinctly aristocratic colouring, about
the time when the Evangelical example was raising the moral level
of its ministers. The result was that phase which Froude declared
to be the golden age of the Church, when her princes were still
princes,* and her pastors enforced the simple morality and
administered the simple consolations, of village life, with the
authority due rather to personal character, birth, and learning
than to any pretensions as priests.

There was another side to the picture. The ministers of the
Church were at once too rich and too poor. The Archbishopric of
Canterbury and the Bishopric of Durham were each worth
£19,000 a year; Rochester, £14,000; Llandaff less than £1,000.
Of 10,000 benefices, the average value was £285. Less than 200
were worth £1,000 and upward, but among them were livings of

---

* The last, I suppose, was Charles Sumner, Bishop of Winchester till 1869,
whose hospitality was the most conspicuous of his many virtues. Froude was
thinking of his own father, the Archdeacon of Totnes.

I

£2,000, £5,000, and one of over £7,000 a year. The poor parson was therefore very poor, the curate poorer still, best off in Rochester on £109 a year, worst off in St. David's on £55. The mischief was aggravated by pluralism, non-residence, and nepotism. A great Church family, taking sons, nephews, and sons-in-law together, might easily collect £10,000 a year among them and leave the greater part of their duties to be discharged by curates at £80. The best of parsons could not help being a little too much of a magistrate and landowner, and not enough of a pastor.* Into the gaps left in his spiritual ministrations crept dissent, with its opportunities for personal distinction,† close converse, and mutual inspection. At the beginning of our period it was estimated that the Church, the Dissenters, and the Romans were in the ratio of 120, 80, and 4. The figures of Church attendance taken in 1851 show the Establishment decidedly preponderating in the south and south-west, except in Cornwall; and holding its own, with varying majorities, everywhere, except in the old Puritan strongholds of Bedford, Huntingdon, and the West Riding, and in Northumberland. An absolute figure of effective membership it is impossible to give. Out of a population of 2,000,000 in the diocese of London it was reckoned that there were 70,000 communicants.‡ But a distinction must be drawn between the country and the old towns on one side and the new agglomerations on the other. In the one, everybody, except the free-thinking cobbler, would at least have called himself one thing or the other, and there were few families which were not sometimes represented at the Sunday service. In the other, great multitudes were as indifferent to the distinction as the inhabitants of Borrio-

* Whately of Cookham is the best example. 'A Whately in every parish' was a catchword of Poor Law reformers.

† In 1860 H. F. Tozer wrote of Norway, 'The priest's residence is usually the nicest house in the neighbourhood, and the priest's daughters are the most eligible young ladies. It is surprising in these circumstances that dissent does not spring up.' The implication is as illuminating as P. G. Hamerton's remark that few educated people had ever seen a dissenter eat.

‡ Lord Robert Montagu's statistics in 1860 are at least amusing. He reckoned: Baptists, Congregationalists, Jews, Mormons, &c., 16½ per cent.; Wesleyans (seven sorts) and Roman Catholics, 16½ per cent.; Church of England, 42 per cent.; Irreligious Poor, 25 per cent. I fancy they are pretty near the mark. Of the great underworld, Lord Shaftesbury said that only 2 per cent. went anywhere. The figures of 1851 are not very trustworthy, but it would appear that of 100 possibles 58 went somewhere.

boola-Gha. It was to these masses that the Churches, often in unfriendly rivalry, had next to address themselves.

In dogma there was little to choose between a worthy clergyman of an evangelical cast and a worthy dissenting minister. Socially, by their University education, and their relations with the gentry, the clergy as a body stood in a class apart and, with the preachers who collected little congregations about them in hamlets and the back streets of towns, who ministered in Zoar and Bethel and Mizpah and Shebaniah, they had little in common. But the ministers of the older bodies were often as learned as the clergy, and their congregations more exclusive than the mixed multitudes who, from habit as much as conviction, were gathered in the parish church. The Unitarians were, on the whole, the most intellectual of the dissenting bodies: they went to the theatre. The Independents represented traditional middle-class Puritanism: the more fervent, and more rhetorical, Baptists struck lower in society, among the tradesmen in small streets. With them and with the dissident Wesleyans we approach that brand of unattached Nonconformity with which Dickens was so familiar, and which is represented for us by Mr. Stiggins and Mr. Chadband.* The 4,000 Quaker families were a body, almost a race, apart.

But between them all there was, at the beginning of the nineteenth century, a state of stable equilibrium which the political advance of the middle classes, the Oxford Movement, and the growth of the Wesleyans destroyed. As it left the hands of its founder, the Wesleyan body was a society, autonomous in government and independent in action, but essentially supplementary to the Established Church. Under his successors, especially Jabez Bunting, it developed into a church itself. Active, zealous, and resourceful, it gave a personality to the somewhat formless individualism of earlier Dissent, and it satisfied, and steadied, thousands of men and women who, but for the Wesleyan church, would, in the break-up of the old society, have drifted without direction or restraint, into vice, or crime, or revolution. By providing a far larger sphere of action for the laity than the Church or the older denominations furnished, it brought romance and ambition into a

* See also Theodore Watts (Dunton's) account of Ebenezer Jones's childhood in Canonbury, and the 'tea-and-toast' ministers who terrified the children who waited on them (*Athenaeum*, 1878).

class which, under the pressure of the new civilization, was losing both purpose and aspiration; and the Wesleyan organization—the class meeting, the circuit, the conference, the Legal Hundred—has powerfully affected the constitution of political parties and Trade Unions. The activity of the Wesleyans radiated through the older denominations and was not without effect on the Church itself. By 1840 it was supposed that they numbered half a million members in England and Wales, and their attitude on any political question was anxiously calculated by the managers of both politi-

12 cal parties. They were as a body not unfriendly to the Church: they were zealous upholders of the Constitution. 'Wesleyanism',

13 Bunting said, 'is as much opposed to Democracy as it is to Sin'; and among the causes which led to the defeat of Chartism and the great pacification of the fifties must be numbered the resolute opposition which the Wesleyans offered to subversion in society or the State.*

In the eighteenth century the ancient opposition of Rome and Oxford had died down; courteous gestures were exchanged across the frontiers; in the French wars the Pope became an almost attractive figure. Yet the growth of a new anti-Roman feeling was inevitable. Evangelicalism emphasized the points of difference and gave them alarming value for the individual soul; travellers reported the shocking condition of the Papal States. And there was always Ireland. To be misgoverned in this world and damned in the next seemed to many thousands of sober English families the necessary consequence of submission to Rome. Nor could it be comfortably pretended that the claims or activity of Rome were abating, and no Englishman could read the contemporary history

---

* The writings of Mark Rutherford show E[arly] V[ictorian] Nonconformity at its selfrighteous worst. Of its other side, as a civilizing agency, credulous, conceited, but of heroic tenacity, one of the most sympathetic records I know is *Warminster Common* by W. Daniell. Daniell (who had gifts of healing, the nature of which he did not recognize) must have been very like an early Christian bishop up country. Incidentally, this little work enables me to determine one important question of social history—the origin of the chapel tea-fight. It was invented by Daniell, and the first was held on December 13, 1815. Tea was an expensive and select drink, and the tea-drinkings at Warminster were, as the following extract shows, almost Eleusinian in their rapture:

'Christmas 1829. Drank tea at Chapel with the Christian friends (a purely religious meeting). A holy unction attended and great was the joy. We could

14 all say (we trust experimentally) "Unto us a child is born".'

of France without a running commentary in which Louis XVIII played the part of Charles II and Charles X stood for the fanatical James. If the Bishops had seen their way to vote for Reform in 1831, they would have made themselves as popular as the Blessed Seven in the Tower. It was the misfortune of the Church that her politics should be officially branded as illiberal just when her theology was about to come under suspicion of Romanism. The combination, coinciding with the Radical drive against privilege, produced that Political Protestantism which waxed with the growth of the middle-class electorate and waned in our time with the spread of religious indifference and with the dilution of the middle-class vote by universal suffrage.

The immediate occasion of the Oxford Movement was the suppression of ten Irish bishoprics by the Whig Government. The danger to the Church was exaggerated, but in 1833 much seemed possible that time proved imaginary. It was believed that Government emissaries had directed the attack on the Bishop of Bristol's palace in 1831. It was known that James Mill, an official man in the confidence of the ruling powers, had prepared a plan for the conversion of the Church into a Benthamite institution of public utility. Sunday services, without, of course, any form of prayer or worship, were to be preserved: the parish would attend, in its best clothes, to hear a lecture on botany or economics and receive prizes for virtuous behaviour. The day of rest and gladness would end with dances expressive of the social and fraternal emotions, but avoiding any approach to lasciviousness, and an agape at which, naturally, only soft drinks would be served. In principle there is no difference between amalgamating the see of Ossory with the see of Ferns, and applying the revenues of the Church to magic lanterns and muffins. In their alarm, certain divines, their imagination outstripping the practical difficulties in the way (and, in fact, the Whig Government having rearranged the revenues of the Irish Church split on the question what to do with the surplus) decided to act before it was too late. Seven thousand clergy assured the Archbishop of their attachment to the Church: a lay address, signed by 230,000 heads of families, followed. Eminent Nonconformists allowed it to be known that they could countenance no aggression against the Establishment, which was still the national bulwark against infidelity; and the storm blew over. In the peace that followed, the rulers of the Church showed that they

15

16

17

had taken their lesson.* The vexatious question of tithes was equitably settled by the Commutation Act of 1836. Pluralities were regulated, the grosser inequalities of church livings levelled out. There the movement, having demonstrated, and stimulated, the vitality of the Church, might have been re-absorbed into the main stream of invigorated Churchmanship. But feelings had been too deeply stirred. In any case, it was inevitable that in a generation which had been enchanted by Scott and bemused by Coleridge,† the corporate and sacramental aspect of the Church should re-emerge, and that religion would have to find a place for feelings of beauty, antiquity, and mystery, which the ruling theology had dismissed or ignored as worldly or unprofitable or profane. Now, too, the question had been raised, on what foundation could the Church of England, disendowed and disestablished, take her stand, and it had to be answered even though the danger had passed. Hitherto, Churchmen had taken their Church for granted as the

20 mode of Protestantism established by law. The Oxford Movement created an Anglican self-consciousness, parallel to the self-consciousness of the Protestant denominations, based on the assurance of apostolic descent, and inevitably, therefore, tending to sympathy, at least, with the one Church whose apostolic origin could not be denied.

Apart from these two processes, the crystallization of Anglicanism round the Tractarians and of Nonconformity round the Wesleyans, a larger and more fluid conception of the Church was gathering strength. The Oxford divines took little note of Nonconformity. Their object was to brace and fortify the Church against the coming onslaught of Liberalism and infidelity, and in the thirties, after the Oxford leaders, Newman and Pusey themselves, perhaps the most conspicuous, certainly the most influential, figure in the English Church was one who by his own profession was a Liberal and in the eye of his critics was not much better than an infidel.‡ But neither Anglicans nor Protestants had

* The guiding hand was Blomfield of London, who also edited Aeschylus, and was a principal originator of the Sanitary Enquiry of 1839. But he would
18 not allow ladies to attend Geological lectures at King's College, London.

† One critic divided the rising generation into fluent Benthamites and muddled Coleridgians. S.T.C. once said to Miss Martineau: 'You seem to regard society as an aggregate of individuals.' 'Of course I do,' she replied. There is much
19 history implicit in that encounter, and by 1850 Coleridge had won.

21   ‡ 'But is Dr. Arnold a Christian?' Newman once asked.

any real conception of the forces which were gathering against that stronghold of their common faith, the inerrancy of Holy Scripture; they were only beginning to learn, when they went out of the University or the seminary, how little religion meant to the half-barbarized population of the great towns. The diffusion of scientific knowledge among the educated, the spread of old-fashioned rationalism downwards through the masses, had created a new problem for the religious teacher. Milman, walking through the City early one morning, was held up by a group of porters and made to deliver his opinion: did God really command the Israelites to massacre the people of Canaan? It was the test [22] question. Macaulay, putting himself on Butler, wrote that in the Old Testament we read of actions performed by Divine command which without such authority would be atrocious crimes. Lyell— who could sometimes be led on, in a small company after dinner, to admit that the world was probably 50,000 years old—called [23] on him and asked him to speak out. He refused. At the height of such a reputation as no other English man of letters has enjoyed, he could not face the storm that would have broken on the head of the infidel who questioned the humanity of Joshua or the veracity of Moses.★ [24]

Here, not in schism or disendowment, in the rabbling of bishops for their votes, or the burning of their palaces in a riot, lay the danger which only Arnold clearly apprehended. The union of the Churches was an incidental stage in his programme. The foundation was a new conception, in which, no doubt, we can detect something of Lessing, something of Coleridge, something of Carlyle, but which in purpose and direction was Arnold's own, of the significance of history as the revelation of God. The world, as he conceived it, needed new rulers, and the rulers needed a new faith, which was to be found in the historic record, in the Bible, doubtless, most of all, but in the Bible—and here he broke definitely with Oxford and current Protestantism alike—interpreted not by tradition, but by science, scholarship, and, above all, political insight. 'He made us think', a pupil wrote, 'of the [26] politics of Israel, Greece and Rome.' In this sentence we come as [27] near as we can hope to get to the secret of Arnold's power. He

★ When Lyell, then aged 62, came forward in support of *The Origin of Species*, Darwin wrote: 'Considering his age, his former views, *and his position in society*, I think his conduct has been heroic.' [25]

took the self-consciousness of the English gentry, benevolently authoritative, but uneasily aware that its authority was waning, and gave it religious and historic justification.*

XI

OF these three schools, united in their emphasis on personal conduct, the Protestant, on the whole, accepted the social philosophy of the age, the Anglican ignored it, the Arnoldian challenged it. The Nonconformist business man, like Bright, severe with himself and others, within reason generous and within reason honest, is one of the central Victorian types. So, and of the same ancestry, is the preaching politician, like the Corn Law
1 rhetorician, Fox. Another, of which Mr. Gladstone may serve as the representative, is the new High Churchman, instructed in his faith but submissive to his teachers, touched by the art and poetry of old religion, inclining to regard the Church as the one immovable thing in a changing and shifting world, and therefore less concerned with its future than with its past, less with the application of his faith to the circumstances of the world than with its integrity as transmitted from the fathers. As individuals, the High Churchmen worked as manfully as any: Walter Hook in Leeds created a new standard of duty for every parish priest who has come after him. But as a school, they shook off with well-bred impatience the humanitarian professions which had become associated with the Evangelical creed, and few Tractarian names will be found connected with the reforms which are the glory of the
2 Early Victorian Age. This rather was to be the sphere of action of the third school. In the forties we are aware of a new type issuing from the Universities and public schools, somewhat arrogant and somewhat shy, very conscious of their standing as gentlemen but very conscious of their duties, too, men in tweeds who smoke in the streets, disciples of Maurice, willing hearers of Carlyle, passionate for drains and co-operative societies, disposed to bring everything in the state of England to the test of Isaiah and Thucydides, and to find the source of all its defects in what, with youth-

---

* On the whole, William Arnold's *Oakfield* seems to me to convey most com-
28 pletely the effect that Arnold made on those who came under his influence.

ful violence, they would call the disgusting vice of shopkeeping.
These are the Arnoldians. 3

In the meantime the Oxford Movement had gone into liquidation. Through the thirties it advanced, in the face of authority,
with irresistible force. But the farther it went, the more certain
appeared its ultimate objective, and with the publication of
Tract XC it seemed to have unmasked itself. The purpose of the
Tract was to clear away the popular interpretations which had
grown up round the formularies of the Church, to prove that the
Articles rigidly construed were more susceptible of a Catholic
than a Protestant meaning, or, as Macaulay put it, that a man
might hold the worst doctrines of the Church of Rome and the
best benefice in the Church of England. In this sense, at least, the 4
Tract was received and condemned by the Heads of Houses, and
the Tractarians stigmatized as Romanists without the courage of
their convictions. And by 1843, when Newman left St. Mary's,
Protestantism was beginning to work almost hysterically even on
sober English opinion, which, having accepted Catholic emancipation as the completion of the Union, was now challenged by
O'Connell to regard it as the basis of disruption to be achieved, if
need be, at the price of civil war. Deviations of doctrine, like
novelties of observance, were watched by ten thousand critical
eyes; the Hampden controversy and the Gorham controversy 5
were followed as attentively as any debate in Parliament, and, far
away in Borneo, Rajah Brooke wrote home to his mother that he
had not had much time for theology, but he had composed an
answer to Tract XC. The decision of Pope Pius IX to revive the 6
Roman Hierarchy in England was answered with an outburst of
frenzy of which the Tractarian clergy were almost as much the
objects as the Papists themselves.

But to the new Englishman of the late forties and fifties, a
travelled man bred up on Carlyle and Tennyson and the romantic
classics, the world was a far more interesting place than it had been
to those late Augustans, imprisoned in their island, among whom
Evangelicalism struck root, and his religion conformed to the
awakening of his senses. The theology of Oxford he still viewed
with distrust: at sisterhoods and processions he frowned with
dark suspicion. Insensibly, however, the Tractarian influence was
affecting his notions of public worship. The Hanoverian vulgarity
of a Royal christening, with a sham altar loaded with the family

7 plate and an opera singer warbling in the next room, shocked a
taste which was insensibly forming for simplicity and reverence
and the beauty of the sanctuary. Churches were swept; church-
yards tidied; church windows cleaned. High pews behind which
generations of the comfortable had dozed the sermon out, red
velvet cushions on which the preacher had pounded the divisions
of his text, the village band in the gallery, the clerk under the
pulpit, gradually disappeared: very cautiously, crosses were introduced, and flowers and lights. Liturgical science became a passion
with the younger clergy, and the wave of restoration and church
building brought with it a keen, sometimes a ludicrous, preoccupation with symbolism. Dickens was not far out when he
observed that the High Churchman of 1850 was the dandy of 1820
in another form.*

   The great ritualist controversy belongs to later years: its origin-
ating issue was the fashion of the preacher's garment.† The custom
at the end of the morning prayers had been for the minister to
retire and reissue from the vestry in the black gown of a learned
man. As the practice spread of reading the Ante-Communion
service after the sermon, the double change from white to black
and back into white again was felt to be unseemly. But preaching
in his whites—his vestments as a minister—the parson might be
thought to claim for his utterances an authority more than his
own, the authority of a priest, and so surplice riots became a
10 popular diversion of the forties. In 1850 the ritual of St. Barnabas,
Pimlico, was holding up the Sunday traffic, and we have a glimpse
of Thackeray testifying in the crowd: 'O my friends of the
11 nineteenth century, has it come to this?' Ten years later blas-
pheming mobs stormed St. George's in the East in defence of the
12 Reformation Settlement. But gradually new standards of dignity, reverence, and solemnity assimilated the worship in the
ancient meeting-place of the village, the portentous assembly
room of a London parish, and the Gothic churches which were
rising by hundreds in the populous suburbs and industrial towns.
Protestant vigilance was easily alarmed, but even an Ulsterman

   * Newman, in *Loss and Gain*, has put the same point with more dexterous
8 satire.
   † And the material, wood or stone, of the Holy Table. In the ruling case
(Holy Sepulchre, Cambridge) a document was tendered under the title *Restora-*
9 *tion of Churches the Restoration of Popery*. Which, after all, was what Pugin wanted.

could hardly suspect that the hand of the Pope was at work when the Communion Table ceased to be a depository for hats, the font a receptacle for umbrellas.

Like the Philosophic Radicals, the Tractarians vanish as a party to work in widening circles out of sight, and when, years afterwards, their memory was recalled by Kingsley's tempestuous challenge and the genius wasted on Rome was at last recognized by England, it was in an age less concerned to know whether Newman's faith or some other faith was the right one, than whether in the modern world there was any room for faith at all. For all this vehemence of surface agitation, it had been growing 13 every year plainer, on a deeper view, that neither Pauline nor Patristic Christianity, neither the justification theology nor the infallibility of the Church, could be maintained as a barrier against the 'wild, living intellect of man'. Religion had, somewhat 14 hastily perhaps, made terms with the astronomers. The heavens declare the glory of God, and the better the telescope the greater the glory. The geologists, attacking one of the prime documents of the faith, the Mosaic cosmogony, were more difficult to assimilate or evade. One of the earliest of them had taken the precaution of inviting his theological colleague to sit through his lectures, as 15 censor and chaperone in one; and, on the whole, the religious world seems, in the forties, to have been divided into those who did not know what the geologists were saying and those who did not mind. A far more serious onslaught was preparing from two quarters, abroad and at home. English divinity was not equipped to meet—for its comfort, it was hardly capable of understanding— the new critical methods of the Germans: it is a singular fact that England could not, before Lightfoot, show one scholar in the field of Biblical learning able and willing to match the scholars of Germany. Thirlwall, whom good judges declared to be the ablest 16 living Englishman, was silent, and what was passing in that marmoreal intellect remained a secret. The flock was left undefended against the ravages of David Strauss. On the other side, the English mind was particularly well equipped to grasp the arguments of the biologists. The natural sciences in all their branches—rocks, fossils, birds, beasts, fish, and flowers—were a national hobby; the *Vestiges of Creation*, issued with elaborate secrecy and attributed by a wild surmise to Prince Albert, was a national excitement; translated into golden verse by Tennyson, 17 evolution almost became a national creed. *In Memoriam,* which is nine years older than the *Origin of Species,*★ gathered up all the doubts of Christianity, of providence, of immortality, which the advance of science had implanted in anxious minds, and answered them, or seemed to answer them, with the assurance of a pantheistic and yet personal faith in progress.

In Memoriam is one of the cardinal documents of the mid-Victorian mind, its ardent curiosity, its exquisite sensitiveness to nature, and, not less, perhaps, its unwillingness to quit, and its incapacity to follow, any chain of reasoning which seems likely to result in an unpleasant conclusion. In his highest mood, Tennyson sometimes speaks like an archangel assuring the universe that it will muddle through. The age was learning, but it had not mastered, the lesson that truth lies not in the statement but in the process: it had a childlike craving for certitude, as if the natural end of every refuted dogma was to be replaced by another
20   dogma. Raised in the dark and narrow framework of Evangelical and economic truth, it wilted in the sunlight and waved for support to something vaguely hopeful like the Platonism of Maurice, or loudly reassuring like the hero worship of Carlyle. New freedom is a painful thing, most painful to the finest minds, who are most sensitive to the breaking-up of faiths and traditions and most apprehensive of the outcome. The stress of the age is incarnate in Arthur Clough. Deeply influenced by Arnold in his boyhood, he had stayed long enough in Oxford to feel all the exhaustion and disillusionment which succeeded the excitement of the Tractarian movement. In the Church was no satisfaction. He had lost, as most educated men were losing, his hold on what had been the middle strand of all Christian creeds, faith in the divine person of
21   Christ. The natural way of escape was into the open mockery to which Clough's temperament inclined him,† or into such a pagan equanimity in face of the unknown as the agnostics of the next age

18   ★ Some of the evolutionist parts of *In Memoriam* are actually older than *Vestiges.* Tennyson really understood the workings of the new scientific mind, as of the upper class political mind. He was the natural laureate of an age morally conservative and intellectually progressive. Party zeal has claimed Newman's *Essay on Development* as a forerunner. But have the partisans read Milman's rejoinder?
19   Or the *Essay on Development* perhaps?

       † His conjecture that the First Cause would turn out to be a 'smudgy person with a sub-intelligent look about the eyes' is very much in the manner of Butler,
22   and therefore of Mr. Shaw.

practised and proclaimed. But to his generation, so powerful still was the appeal of lost faith, so intricate the associations of right belief and right conduct, that that way was closed. Ruskin's final assurance, that it does not matter much to the universe what sort of person you are, was impossible to a generation impressed by its 23 teachers with the infinite importance—and therefore self-importance—of the individual soul. The Tractarians by pointing to the Church, the Arnoldian school by their vivid realization of history, had relieved the intense introversion of Evangelicalism.* But lacking faith, the individual was released from his own prison only to find himself alone in an indifferent universe.† Kingsley was relieving many souls of their burden by communicating his own delight in the body, in the ardours of exploration, sport, and sex. Unluckily the world is not entirely peopled by young country gentlemen, newly married to chastely passionate brides, and it is perhaps, rash to identify the self-contentment which comes of a vigorous body and an assured income, with the glorious liberty of the children of God. Nevertheless, the name of Kingsley, naturalist, health reformer, poet and preacher, on the one hand silenced as an advocate of socialism, on the other denounced as a propagator of impurity, may stand for the meeting-place of all the forces 27 at work on the younger imagination of the years when, as it seemed to those who recalled the sordid and sullen past, England was renewing her youth, at Lucknow and Inkerman, with Livingstone in the African desert, with Burton on the road to Mecca, and speaking to the oppressors of Europe in the accents of Cromwell and Pitt. Of all decades in our history, a wise man would choose the eighteen-fifties to be young in.

* For Newman, see the profound diagnosis of Evangelicalism at the end of the Lectures on Justification, which, translated out of the technical terms of theology, is applicable to the whole age. Introspection within a closed circle of experience was the trouble. I cannot doubt that if Arnold had not been a school- 24 master he would have been a fine historian. *Introverted* is, somewhat surprisingly, a word of the forties: Wilberforce used it of Peel. 25

† This mode of pessimism can be followed through *Dipsychus* and *Obermann* down to bedrock in the *City of Dreadful Night*. 26

XII

MR. GLADSTONE, dwelling on the responsiveness of the people to good government, once said that every call from Parliament had been answered by a corresponding self-improvement of the masses. The years through which we have been passing afford some confirmation of this sanguine philosophy. The labouring Englishman in the fifties was much better governed than the labouring Englishman of 1830, and he was, taken in the mass, a much more respectable man. He was better governed, inasmuch as the State had definitely resolved to concern itself with the condition of his life and labour and the the education of his children. He was more respectable because, with rising wages and cheaper food, with some leisure at home and the grosser kinds of insanitation put down, he was recovering his self-respect. More strictly, it might be said that the proletariat, which in the thirties seemed to be sinking into a dull uniformity of wretchedness, had been stratified. In this light, the contradictions which we encounter whenever we turn our eye to the condition of the people in mid-Victorian England are resolved. There was a vast, untouchable underworld. But the great industries were manned with families, often much better off than the neighbouring curate or school-master, and not burdened by the middle class necessity of keeping up a position. This right wing, hopeful, comfortable, within sight of the franchise, the Respectable Poor, the Conservative working man, drew away. Crime, poverty, and drunkenness, which had reached their peak about 1842, were dropping year by year. The maypole had gone: the village feast and the club-walk were going; but the zoo, the panorama, the free-library, the fête, and the excursion ticket were bringing hundreds of thousands within the reach of orderly and good-humoured pleasure. It is a curious observation of the early fifties that the workmen were wearing the same clothes as the gentlemen. Still more oddly, the French artist, Delacroix, noticed that the gentlemen were wearing the same clothes as the workmen.

One grey patch remained, growing drearier as the life ebbed out of the villages; but the brooding apprehension of thirty years had lifted. The testing time had come in 1848. The last Chartist demonstration was a demonstration only; for the artillery men who lined the Thames from Waterloo Bridge to Millbank, the shopkeepers who patrolled the streets, the Government clerks who laid in muskets and barricaded the windows with official files,* and the coal whippers who marched from Wapping with a general idea of standing by the Duke and a particular intention of breaking every Irishman's head, it was a demonstration and a 5 festival. The storm which swept away half the Governments of Europe passed harmlessly over the islands, and the words which Macaulay wrote at the beginning of his history, that his checkered narrative would excite thankfulness in all religious minds and hope in the breast of all patriots, had a deep significance for his first readers, watching the nations of Europe sink one by one from convulsive anarchy back into despotism, and seeing, in the recovered unity, as much as in the prosperity of England, a triumphant vindication of the historic English way. The Great 6 Exhibition was the pageant of domestic peace. Not for sixty years had the throne appeared so solidly based on the national goodwill as in that summer of hope and pride and reconciliation. After all the alarms and agitations of thirty years the State had swung back to its natural centre.†

Victoria was not in her girlhood a popular Sovereign.‡ She was tactless: she was partisan: the tragic story of Lady Flora Hastings showed her heartless as well. The figure that made its way into the 9 hearts of the middle classes was not the gay, self-willed little Whig of 1837, but the young matron, tireless, submissive, dutiful. Her Court was dull, but the Royal nursery was irresistible. Prince Albert had seized the key positions—morality and industry§— behind which the Monarchy was safe. A revolt of the special

* The Foreign Office consented to receive reinforcements from the Colonial Office 'if we lose any men'. 4

† In 1848 Thackeray declared himself 'a Republican but not a Chartist'. In 1851 he was writing odes to the Crystal Palace. But *Punch* was still Radical enough to resent the sight of Goldsticks walking backwards. 7

‡ But in Ireland, the young queen who was to rebuild the Church on the Rock of Cashel, was for a time an object of intense affection—partly, no doubt, because she was not her uncle, Ernest the Orangeman (and other things). Her failure to draw on this fund of loyalty was the gravest error of her life. 8

§ Again, like most things in Victorian England, this was a European episode. The English Court struck a mean between the pietism of Berlin and the bourgeois decorum of Louis-Philippe. The King of Prussia and Elizabeth Fry once knelt together in prayer in the Women's Ward at Newgate. 10

constables would have been formidable: a virtuous and domestic Sovereign, interested in docks and railways, hospitals and tenements, self-help and mutual improvement, was impregnable. Such a Sovereign, and much more beside, Prince Albert would have been, and in this mild, beneficent light he displayed his Consort's crown to the world. As its power pursued its inevitable downward curve, its influence rose in equipoise.

In 1834 King William had strained prerogative to the breaking-point by putting the Tories into office before the country was quite ready for them. In 1839 the Queen had kept the Whigs in office when the country was heartily tired of them. But ten years later the Crown was called upon to exercise that power of helping the country to find the Government it wants, which makes monarchy so precious an adjunct to the party system. After repealing the Corn Laws, Sir Robert was defeated by a combination between his late allies, the Whigs, and his own rebels, the Protectionists. Lord John Russell came in, with Palmerston at the Foreign Office, Disraeli leading the Opposition. In 1850 Peel died, the only English statesman for whose death the poor have cried in the streets, and it soon appeared whose hand had kept the Whigs in power. In 1851 they were defeated; Stanley tried to form a Tory Government, failed, and the Whigs came back. Palmerston was dismissed for impertinence to his Queen, and Lord John groped about for a coalition. He was unsuccessful, and in 1852 Palmerston had the gratification of turning him out. Stanley (now Lord Derby) and Disraeli formed a Government, struggled through a few months against united Whigs, Peelites, and Radicals, and resigned. Old Lord Lansdowne was sent for, and dear Lord Aberdeen was commissioned, to form one coalition more. He succeeded, and went to war with Russia. Went is hardly the word. But the mismanagement of the opening campaign in '54 broke up the Cabinet, and with universal applause, superb assurance, and the recovered confidence of his Sovereign, Palmerston bounded into the vacant place. A brief eclipse in '58 hardly impaired his ascendancy, and till his death at eighty-one, with a half-finished dispatch on his table, in the eyes of the world and his country Palmerston was England and England was Palmerston. The political comedy has never been more brilliantly staged, and at every turn the Crown was in its proper place, selecting, reconciling, and listening, its dignity unimpaired by party conflicts and its impartiality surmounting individual distastes. 'I object to Lord Palmerston on personal grounds,' the Queen said. 'The Queen means,' Prince Albert explained, 'that she does not object to Lord Palmerston on account of his person.' In place of a definite but brittle prerogative it had acquired an indefinable but potent influence. The events of 1846 to 1854 affirmed for some generations to come the character of the new monarchy, just at the time when events abroad—Australian gold discoveries, India, and the Crimea—were giving the nation an aggressive, imperial self-consciousness. [13]

From 1815 to the Revolution of '48 foreign affairs had engaged but a small share of the public attention. First came the depression after Waterloo and the slow recovery, with a terrible set-back in 1825. Then Ireland and Catholic emancipation took the stage, then Reform and the Poor Law, and Ireland again with O'Connell; then come the Oxford, the Chartist, and the Free Trade movements, the depression of the first years of Victoria, Ireland once more, and the Repeal of the Corn Laws. But from 1850 onwards the focus of interest is overseas; the soldier, the emigrant, and the explorer, the plots of Napoleon III and the red shirt of Garibaldi, take and fill the imagination. Domestic politics are languid. Once, if not twice, in twenty years, the franchise had brought England in sight of civil war: in the fifties a Franchise Bill was four times introduced

> Quater ipso in limine portae
> substitit, atque utero sonitum quater arma dedere,*

and was forgotten; the annual motion on the ballot became an annual joke. Ireland was prostrate, Old Chartists were lecturing on Christian evidences, or, more usefully, working quietly in the new trade unions; old republicans were shouting for war; old pacifists declaiming to empty halls. Nothing is so bloody-minded as a [15] Radical turned patriot. Roebuck was all for bombarding Naples.

* Bob Lowe, Disraeli's 'inspired schoolboy'. I put this second among Virgilian quotations, the best being Gladstone's, when the Spanish Government unexpectedly met some bills and so stopped a hole in the budget.

> 'via prima salutis
> Quod minime reris, Graia pandetur ab urbe.'

Pitt's 'Nos ubi primus equis', when the dawn came through the windows of St. Stephen's, is not quotation, but inspiration. [14]

Bentham's former secretary, Bowring, crowned his astonish-
16 ingly various career by actually bombarding Canton. Only those
whose memories went back fifteen years could understand the
change of sentiment which made the arming of the volunteers in
'59 possible, or how completely the confidence which inspired
that gesture was vindicated by the patience of Lancashire in the
cotton famine.

Adventurous and secure, the ruling class in the years of Palmerston was excellently qualified to found a commonwealth or re-
conquer an empire abroad, and, within the range of its ideas, to
legislate wisely at home. Ireland, unhappily, lay outside that
range. But University reform, divorce reform, the management
of the metropolis, the resettlement of India, colonial self-government, the creation of the Public Accounts Committee, the Post
Office Savings Bank, the Atlantic cable, that generation took in
its stride, and the conversion of the vast and shapeless city which
Dickens knew—fog-bound and fever-haunted, brooding over its
dark, mysterious river—into the imperial capital, of Whitehall,
the Thames Embankment and South Kensington, is the still
visible symbol of the mid-Victorian transition.*

Parties were changing; the strong and steady currents of Whig
and Tory opinion were splitting into eddies. The friends of the
late Sir Robert Peel, as they move to and fro across the stage,
make Conservatism a little less Tory, and Liberalism a little less
Whig. A new and popular Liberalism is forming of definite
grievance and redress, Church rates and University tests, Army
Purchase and Irish Disestablishment, and a humane and frugal
distrust of Empire, aristocracy, adventure, and war. The re-
education of the Conservatives, paralysed by the Free Trade
schism, has begun, and the field is setting for the encounter of
Gladstone and Disraeli when once Palmerston has departed. But
the virulence of party conflicts is abating in a humorous, sporting
tussle, where Palmerston keeps the ring against all comers, while
Gladstone's budgets swing majestically down the tideway of an
unexampled prosperity. In twelve years our trade was doubled,
and the returns, indeed, of those years are a part of English litera-
18 ture because they furnished footnotes to Macaulay's third chapter.

* Modern hotel life begins with the Langham. The Prince of Wales, who
attended the opening in 1865, remarked that it reminded him of the Astoria,
17 New York.

In four years from 1853 the profits of agriculture increased by a fifth. The whole debt left by the Russian war was less than one-half of a year's revenue and the revenue no more than a third, perhaps not more than a fifth, of the annual savings of the nation. But age and crabbed youth cannot live together; age is full of pleasure, youth is full of care; and the unfriendly and mistrustful 19 union of Palmerston and Gladstone, a union almost breaking into open hostility over the French panic and the fortification of Portsmouth, and again over the Paper Duties, is typical of the poise of the age, looking back to the proud, exciting days of Canning and Pitt and another Bonaparte, and forward to a peaceful prosperity of which no end was in sight; an ignorant pride which forgot that Prussia had an army, a thoughtless prosperity which did not reckon with American wheat.

Parliament was changing, too. Till 1832 it was in effect and almost in form a single-chamber assembly, since a large part of the Commons were appointed by the Lords, and a man might easily have one vote—or one proxy—in the Upper House and half a dozen in the Lower. Separation implies the possibility at least of conflict. That it was avoided, that, for all the hostility of the Radicals to the Peers, neither reform nor abolition of the Lords was seriously mooted, followed from the fact that socially the landed interest ascendant in the Commons had no hostility towards its chiefs in the Lords, and that politically the Duke could always induce the Tory Lords, in a crisis, to give way to the Whig Commons. They yielded in 1832; they yielded in 1846; and by neither surrender did the Lords as a House, or the aristocracy as a class, lose any particle of real power. 20

After the first shock of dismay they had rallied to the land, and the upward tilt of prices gave them the confidence they needed. Rents did not fall; they even began to rise; between '53 and '57, helped by the war, they rose by more than a tenth. The basis of mid-Victorian prosperity—and, indeed, of society—was a balance of land and industry, an ever enlarging market for English manufactures, and a still restricted market for foreign produce. The home harvest was dominant: a short crop meant high prices, low prices meant an abundant crop. If all other grounds were absent, the obstinate survival of aristocracy in Victorian England is capable of economic explanation. They were the capitalists and directors of the chief English industry: 3,500,000 acres under wheat, crops from 30 bushels upwards to the acre:* encircled by a prosperous and respectful tenantry, as proud in their own way as themselves, and a landless peasantry at the feet of both.

But their ascendancy rested hardly less on immaterials. If they had the one thing the plutocracy most respected in themselves, they had all the other things which the people missed in the plutocracy. In morals and intellect they were not disturbingly above or below the average of their countrymen, who regarded them, with some truth, as being in all bodily gifts the finest stock in Europe. By exercise, temperance, and plebeian alliance, the spindle-shanked lord of Fielding had become the ancestor of an invigorated race. They had shed their brutality and extravagance; their eccentricities were of a harmless sporting kind; they were forward in good works; they habitually had family prayers.† Of two rich men, or two clever men, England was not ashamed to prefer the gentleman, and the preference operated for the benefit of many gentlemen who were both poor and stupid. Mr. Podsnap is not a bad man: in the one crisis he has to face he acts with right decision. But Dickens's heart is with little Mr. Twemlow, who never made a decision in his life and would probably have got it wrong if he had. If they had stood against each other for a borough constituency in the South it is not improbable that the ten-pound householders would have chosen Mr. Twemlow. England is large, there is room, and a future, for Sir Leicester and the Iron-
23 master, but Mr. Podsnap is a belated and sterile type.

Mr. Gladstone had two names for this peculiar habit of mind. Once he called it 'a sneaking kindness for a lord'; at another time, more characteristically, 'the shadow which the love of freedom
24 casts or the echo of its voice in the halls of the constitution'. The philosophic historian may take his choice, and it is easier to frame a defence or an indictment of the Victorian attitude to aristocracy than to understand why, in a money-making age, opinion was, on the whole, more deferential to birth than to money, and why, in a mobile and progressive society, most regard was had to the element which represented immobility, tradition, and the past.

* All these statistics contain an element of guess-work. But the best opinion seems to be that, in the mid-fifties, England had rather more than $3\frac{1}{2}$ million
21 acres, with crops running to 40 bushels. The yield over all was $26\frac{1}{4}$ bushels.

† Lord Hatherton used to say that in 1810 only two gentlemen in Stafford-
22 shire had family prayers: in 1850 only two did not.

Perhaps the statement will be found to include the solution. The English *bourgeoisie* had never been isolated long enough to frame, except in the spheres of comfort and carnal morality, ideals and standards of its own. It was imitative. A nation, hammered into unity by a strong crown, had ended by putting the power of the Crown into commission, and the great houses, in succeeding to the real authority, had acquired, and imparted to the lesser houses, something of the mysterious ascendancy of the royal symbol. For a hundred years they ruled, and almost reigned, over an England of villages and little towns. The new urban civilization was rapidly creating a tradition of civic benevolence and government, but it had no tradition of civic magnificence. To be anything, to be recognized as anything, to feel himself as anything in the State at large, the rich English townsman, unless he was a man of remarkable gifts and character, had still to escape from the seat and source of his wealth; to learn a new dialect and new interests; and he was more likely to magnify than to belittle the virtues of the life into which he and his wife yearned to be admitted, the life, beyond wealth, of power and consideration on the land. From time immemorial a place in the country had been the crown of a merchant's career, and from the first circle the impulse was communicated through all the spheres down to the solid centre of the ten-pound franchise and the suburban villa.

Within the limits thus marked out by instinctive deference, the electorate was free, and not, on the whole, ill qualified to make a general choice between parties and policies. Through its educated stratum, which was proportionately large as the electorate was still small, through the still costly newspapers written for that stratum, through the opportunities which the orders of the House still gave to private members,* it could maintain a fairly

* This is of great importance for the character of Victorian Parliaments. After the disappearance of Speeches on Petitions in 1843, questions to Ministers steadily increased. The Government had only Mondays and Fridays, and on the motion for adjournment to Monday any member could raise any question, the result being, as Disraeli said, a conversazione. (The present system of numbered questions goes back to a proposal for regulating the conversazione made in 1860.) Moreover, every Monday and Friday before Easter, on the motion for going into Committee of Supply, the same liberty existed. As a result, I find in one fortnight, besides several useful little Bills introduced or advanced, the following subjects reviewed by the Commons, often in great detail, on the initiative of private members (sometimes, of course, by arrangement with the Government):

even pressure on Parliament, and the work of Parliament was correspondingly increased. Parliaments in the eighteenth century and in the French wars were not in the first instance legislative bodies: they met to ventilate grievances, vote taxes, and control the executive. From about 1820 the age of continual legislation begins, and, as it proceeds, the ascendancy of the business end of Parliament over the debating end, of the Cabinet over the back benches, is more and more strongly affirmed. But between the two Reform Acts the executive and deliberative elements in Parliament were still in reasonable equipoise: Mr. Gladstone's punctilious phrase, that the Government would seek the advice of the House, was not quite a formality in an age when the Government commanded less than half the time of the House; and the fact that a large minority, sometimes a majority, of the Cabinet were Peers relieved the congestion of debate by spreading it over two Houses. As a branch of the legislature, the House of Lords is of limited utility, and it could neither compel nor avert a change of Ministry or a Dissolution; but it was an admirable theatre for the exposition or criticism of policy, and Peel, a House of Commons man through and through, came late in life to the opinion that public business might be advantaged if the Prime Minister were relieved of the management of the Commons and set to
26 direct operations from the security of the Upper House.

XIII

In the great peace of the fifties the lines of force released in the earlier decades, lines best remembered by the names of Arnold, Newman, and Carlyle, come round into pattern. It is about this time that the word 'Victorian'* was coined to register a new self-consciousness. 'Liverpool below, Oxford on top,' was said of Mr.

---

25 Corruption at Elections, Criminal Appeal, Civil Service Economy, Defective Anchors, the Shrubs in Hyde Park, Publication of Divorce Reports, Church Rates, Indian Finance, the Ballot, Naval Operations in China (by the Admiral Commanding, at great length), Flogging, Manning the Navy, Competitive Examination, and the Export of Coal.

1 * The first example I have noted is in E. P. Hood, *The Age and its Architects*, 1851.

Gladstone, and it might be said more generally of the English 2
intelligence of the fifties. Work shapes the mind, leisure colours it;
the grim discipline of the years of peril was relaxed: life was richer,
easier, and friendlier. To turn from the stark, forbidding dogmas
of James Mill on Government to the humorous wisdom of
Bagehot's *English Constitution*, with its large allowances for the
idleness, stupidity, and good nature of mankind, is to enter
another world of thought, at once less logical and more real, and
the contrast not unfairly represents the change that had come
over England in thirty years.

In the general movement of the English mind few episodes are
so instructive as the revulsion which in the fifties reduced the
Economic Evangelicalism of 1830 from dominant philosophy to
middle-class point of view, and so prepared the way for the teaching of Pater and Arnold, the practice of Morris and Toynbee, the
recognition, after years of derision or neglect, of Ruskin and
Browning. 'Nothing', Bagehot once wrote, 'is more unpleasant 3
than a virtuous person with a mean mind. A highly developed
moral nature joined to an undeveloped intellectual nature, an
undeveloped artistic nature, is of necessity repulsive,' and in the 4
fifties England was becoming keenly aware of the narrowness and
meagreness of her middle-class tradition. A process very like that
which was stratifying the proletariate into the Respectable and the
Low, was creating out of the upper levels of the middle class a new
patriciate, mixed of birth, wealth, and education, which might be
Liberal or Conservative in politics, Christian or nothing in religion, but was gradually shedding the old middle-class restraints on
enjoyment and speculation. And of this readjustment of classes and
values, if the basis was security and prosperity, the principal agents
were the Universities and the public schools.

In 1831 Brougham had defined The People as 'the middle
classes, the wealth and intelligence of the country, the glory of the 5
British name'. In 1848 a pamphlet appeared under the title *A Plea
for the Middle Classes*. It was concerned with their education. The 6
Barbarians and the Populace were provided for. Strenuous work, 7
and what seemed to economists a formidable expenditure, were
giving popular education in England a dead lift to a level not much
below Prussia, on paper, and, on paper, well above France and
Holland, the three countries from which much of the inspiration
had come. It was the education vote, indeed, which opened the 8

eyes of the public to the cost of the social services, and there was a
growing doubt, which the Newcastle Commission of '58–'60
9 confirmed, of the value received for the money spent. The leaving
age had been forced up to eleven and the school life lengthened to
four years. But the cellar and the pedlar still flourished, a substantial proportion of the children were still not taught to write and
only a tiny fraction got very much beyond. Robert Lowe, introducing payment by results, with the catchword 'if dear efficient,
10 if inefficient cheap', succeeded for the first and last time in interesting the English public in an education debate without the sectarian spice. Nor can it be doubted that his policy was right. If he
levelled down the best schools, he levelled up the worst, and so
made sure that, when compulsion came in the seventies, those who
were compelled to go to school would learn something when
they got there, to write a letter, to make out a bill and hem a shirt.
It was not much, but in the thirties it would have seemed a vision-
ary ideal. That the ideal had been so imperfectly realized, that the
late Victorian democracy was not altogether unfit for its responsibilities, was in the main the work of one man, and, if history
judged men less by the noise than by the difference they make, it is
hard to think of any name in the Victorian age which deserves to
11 stand above or even beside Kay-Shuttleworth's.

In the early nineteenth century England had possessed in seven
or eight hundred old grammar schools an apparatus for giving the
middle classes an education as good as public opinion required for
the class above and below, and by a disastrous miscalculation she
let it run down. Not that it was wholly wasted. A good country
grammar school, neither over-taught nor over-gamed, with a
University connection and a strong local backing, gave probably
as sound an education as was to be had in England: such was
Wordsworth's Hawkshead, and the King's School at Canterbury
where Charles Dickens looked wistfully through the gates at the
12 boyhood he had never known, and Tiverton and Ipswich and
many more. They made good provision for the sons of the lower
gentry, superior tradesmen, and farmers; a sound stock and fertile
in capacity. When they were not available, the deficiency had to
be made good by the private school of all grades, or the proprietary school. But beneath the level of schools which were in touch
with the Universities all was chaos, where those which aimed
lowest seem to have done best. The rest, the rank and file of the

secondary schools, under-staffed by untaught ushers, were turning out, at fifteen or so, the boys who were to be the executive of the late Victorian industries and professions, and could be fairly described as the worst educated middle class in Europe.

The Taunton Commission, which in 1861 reviewed the whole system of secondary education, found that the girls were even 13 worse off than the boys. In the better classes their education was still a domestic industry staffed in the first place by the mother, who might delegate the routine to a governess, and by visiting masters. Those families who could afford an annual stay in London added some intensive teaching by specialists in music, drawing, and the languages. The domestic system involved the employment of untrained gentlewomen as teachers, and the figure of the governess, snubbed, bullied, loving, and usually quite incompetent, is a standby of Victorian pathos. Lady Blessington first introduced it into literature, it reached its apotheosis in *East Lynne*. The silliness and shallowness of the boarding school is an 14 equally constant topic of Victorian satire, but, like the boys' schools, they were of all degrees. Browning's aunts had an admirable establishment at Blackheath, and George Eliot was excellently taught at her Coventry boarding school. London was 15 ringed with such institutions, through which the drawing-master and the music-master wearily circulated on foot from Battersea over the river to Chiswick and up by Acton to Hampstead and Highgate. Below the boarding-school class was that unfortunate stratum just too high to make use of the charity school, the National school or the British Day. For them there was rarely anything better than a superior dame's school in a parlour or a very inferior visiting governess.

That the education of girls, as codified by eighteenth-century manners and moralized by nineteenth-century respectability, tended to a certain repression of personality in the interests of a favourite sexual type, can hardly be denied. But in the Victorian age this type was moulded by the pressure of an uncompromising religion: if the convention was that eighteenth-century man preferred his women fragile, and nineteenth-century man liked them ignorant, there is no doubt at all that he expected them to be good; and goodness, in that age of universal charity, imported the service of others, and if service then training for service. Children and the sick had always been within the lawful scope of women's activi-

ties, and, in a generation not less scientific than benevolent, the
evolution of the ministering angel into the professional teacher,
16 nurse, or doctor was inevitable. Often obscured by agitation for
subordinate ends—the right to vote, to graduate, to dispose of her
own property after marriage—the fundamental issue of feminism
was growing clearer all through the century, as women, no longer
isolated heroines but individuals bent on a career, drew out into
the sexless sphere of disinterested intelligence, and the conception
of autonomous personality took body; a process which may be
truly named Victorian if only for the horror with which Victoria
17 regarded it. 'I want', said Bella Rokesmith to her husband, 'to be
something so much worthier than the doll in the doll's house.' In
the profusion of Dickens, the phrase might pass unnoticed. But
18 Ibsen remembered it.

The demand for a better sort of woman was not a new one:
Swift had urged it vehemently in eighteenth-century England,
Montesquieu in France. But the curriculum was still dominated
by the economic uniformity of women's existence and the doc-
19 trine of the Two Spheres. Every girl was prospectively the wife of
a gentleman, a workman, or something in between. For the few
unmarried there was a small annuity, or dependence as companion, governess, or servant, in house or shop. Education, therefore,
meant a grounding of morals and behaviour to last all through
life, and a top dressing of accomplishments intended partly to
occupy the girl's mind, partly to attract the men, and, in the last
resort, to earn a living by if all else failed. For the intelligent girl in
a sympathetic home there was a most stimulating provision of
books, travel, and conversation. But this was no part of the
curriculum at Chiswick or Cloisterham, and it would have been
20 thrown away on Dora Spenlow. Economically the two spheres
had hardly begun to intersect. Intellectually, the overlap was
steadily increasing, and it was for this common province of taste,
criticism, intelligence, and sympathy that wise mothers trained
their daughters, sensible girls trained themselves, and the more
fortunate husbands trained their brides.

Tennyson, always the most punctual exponent of contemporary
feeling, published *The Princess* in 1847, a year in which many
minds were converging on the problem. With the express approval of Queen Victoria, a Maid of Honour planned a College for
Women, King's College undertook to train and examine govern-

esses, and Bedford College started with classes in a private house. [21]
From these three movements all the higher education of women
in England has proceeded, but by the sixties it had not proceeded
very far. At Cheltenham and North London College, where those
distinguished but unfortunately named ladies, Miss Beale and Miss
Buss, held sway, the country had models capable of a rich
development, and the age of development begins when, in 1865,
Cambridge, with qualms, had just allowed girls to sit for Local
examinations. London was still refusing to let them sit for matri-
culation. The collision of the Two Spheres is a Late-Victorian [22]
theme, almost a Late-Victorian revolution: in Mid-Victorian
England only the first mutterings of the revolution can be heard.

XIV

COMPARED with the uncertain aims and methods of middle-class
and female education, the growth of the Universities and public
schools has all the appearance of a concerted evolution aiming at
the production of a definite type.

The institution of serious examinations, at Cambridge in 1780,
at Oxford in 1802, had created at the two Universities fields of
keen intellectual emulation. The distinction of pass and honours
not only set up an objective for the ambitious, but united them in
an intellectual aristocracy where form was studied as eagerly as, in
later days, athletic gifts.* By tradition Cambridge was mathematical and Oxford was classical, but Oxford had an honours
school in mathematics before Cambridge established the classical
tripos, and the awe-inspiring double first, whatever it may signify
in feminine fiction, properly meant a first in the two final schools:
it was correctly used of Peel and Gladstone. For men who took [2]
their reading seriously, the standard was high and the classical
impression lasting. Except Brougham, who was educated at
Edinburgh, it is not easy to recall any public man of eminence
who could have talked science with Prince Albert; but many of [3]
them were competent scholars, several were excellent scholars,

* Peel's translation of *suave mari magno*: *suave*, it is a source of melancholy
satisfaction, was remembered all his life. Hogg and Shelley (in Hogg's *Life*) [1]
seem to me the first undergraduates, recognizable as such, on record.

and the imprint of a thorough, if narrow, classical education is visible in Hansard whenever the speaker is Peel or Lord John Russell, Gladstone or Derby. It was equally diffused over Whigs and Tories, who could point back to the great examples of Fox and Windham; and the Radicals, who on principle might have been expected to be averse to a purely literary discipline, numbered by accident in their ranks the most illustrious classical scholar and the most exacting classical tutor of the age—George
4 Grote and the elder Mill.

The Universities were definitely Anglican. At Cambridge a man could not graduate, at Oxford he could not matriculate, without signing the Thirty-Nine Articles.* The Commons in 1834 passed a Bill enabling dissenters to graduate. The Lords threw it out. Practically, it was not a matter of much consequence, as dissenters were not, as a rule, of the class whom Oxford and Cambridge served, and a new private venture called the London University was already at their disposal. It was strongly Radical in origin and affinity, it was entirely secular, and its curriculum was very much wider than that of the old Universities. The foundation of the University of London marks the entry of a new idea; the conception of a University as training for a specific profession, for medicine, law, engineering, or teaching, was in England a novelty to which the examples of Germany and Scotland both contributed. But as a seat of instruction University College rose at once to the first rank, and there are few pictures of the young Victorian mind so attractive as the pages in which Hutton set down his memories of Long and de Morgan, and their brother sophists, and of his walks with Bagehot up and down Regent Street in search of
5 Oxford Street and truth. Liberal, accessible, and utilitarian, it might have been expected that the example of the Londoners would have been widely and speedily followed. That it was not, that the northern colleges emerged late and slowly from their original obscurity, shows how alien to the middle classes was the idea of higher education not connected with practical utility or social distinction, and how much was lost with the disappearance of the Nonconformist academies of the eighteenth century.† A

* To which, incidentally, Wesleyans took no exception.

† Owens College, founded in 1851, begins to count from about 1860. Readers of *Endymion* will remember how the younger Thornbury was diverted from Mill Hill and Owens to Radley and Oxford. Of another Manchester father, Disraeli

feeble effort to provide the north with inexpensive culture was made by the Dean and Chapter of the richest of English cathedrals, but the historian of Victorian England will not often have occasion to mention the University of Durham.

Both at Oxford and at Cambridge the career of the pass-man was little more than the prolongation of his school days without the discipline. In fact, as Freeman put it, prospective parsons and prospective lawyers, young men of rank and fortune, were provided for; if they had any intellectual ambitions they were admirably provided for; if they had not, the Universities had little to give them, and outside the circle of the Church, the Bar, and the landed gentry, they had nothing to give at all. In their internal discipline they were overgrown with a picturesque tangle of privileges, distinctions, and exemptions; founders' kin and local fellowships, servitors and sizars, gentlemen commoners and fellow commoners: New College and King's took their degrees without examination,* and the tuft, the golden tassel on the cap, survived until 1870 at Oxford as a mark of noble birth. The governing oligarchy of heads of houses stood aloof from the general body of residents; and the fellows, except where personal influence drew together groups of disciples, stood aloof from the under-graduate. Compared with the eighteenth century, the intellectual life was intenser, manners and morals were more refined. Compared with the later nineteenth century, studies and sports were far less standardized, manners and morals were still barbaric. There was much unscientific cricket and rowing, a fair amount of riding and hunting, occasional street fighting, some wenching, and much drinking. But there is universal agreement that the state of the Universities was steadily improving as the juniors became less childish and the seniors less remote.

On the world outside their walls the ancient Universities exercised an exasperating fascination: they were clerical; they were idle; they were dissipated; they reflected those odious class distinctions by which merit is suppressed and insolence fostered; their studies were narrow, their teaching ineffective. And on every count of the indictment the reformers found themselves supported

7

---

told the Queen that he sent his sons to Oxford to be made into gentlemen, 'but unfortunately they only became Roman Catholics'.   6

*   πάντων πλὴν ἵππων ἀδαήμονές ἐστε κυνῶν τε
        καίτοι γ' οὔθ' ἵππων εἰδότες οὔτε κυνῶν.   8

by eminent friends within the gates, by Thirlwall at Cambridge and by Tait and Jowett at Oxford. The Commission of 1850–2 and the Acts of 1854 and 1856 only accelerated, and consolidated, a process of internal reform which had proceeded somewhat faster at Cambridge than at Oxford, partly because for ten years the activities of Oxford had been diverted to religious agitation, while Cambridge had had the good sense to profit by

9   her Chancellor's experience as an undergraduate of Bonn.

The object of the Commission was to clear away the constitutional obstructions to internal development and to make the Universities more accessible to the middle classes, more useful to the pass-man, and more serviceable to pure learning. But in principle the Universities affirmed their essence, against Germany and Scotland, as places not of professional but of liberal education in a world which still acknowledged that public life, in the Church, in Parliament, or on the County Bench, was not only a more distinguished, but a better life than the pursuit of wealth by industrious competition. If we imagine Victorian England without Oxford and Cambridge, what barrier can we see against an all-encroaching materialism and professionalism? Even in their alliance, their too close alliance, with the aristocracy there were elements of advantage. The Clergyman was rarely an instructed theologian, but he was not a seminarist. The scholar growing up among men destined for a public career took some tincture of public interests; the Schoolmaster, the Barrister, the Politician, the Civil Servant, and the gentleman unclassified acquired the same double impress of culture and manners; and the Universities broke the fall of the aristocracy by civilizing the plutocracy.

The old Universities were fed by the public schools, and by the private tutor, commonly a clergyman; the preparatory schools for young boys were in existence, and one of them, Temple Grove at East Sheen, was famous. Some details have been preserved of the life lived by the boys: hands, face, 'and perhaps the neck', were washed daily; feet once a fortnight, heads as required; a vernal dose of brimstone and treacle purified their blood, a half-yearly dentist drew their teeth, it was the custom under flogging to bite

10   the Latin Grammar. Not a bad preparation, one may think, for Long Chamber, where boys of all ages were locked up from eight

11   to eight 'and cries of joy and pain were alike unheard'. But the system was not yet stereotyped, and much education was still

received at home or in the study of the neighbouring rector. Apart from the ceremonial of Eton and Christ Church for the aristocracy, a public-school education was no necessary part of the social curriculum. Of Victorians born in good circumstances, neither Macaulay nor Tennyson, Newman, Disraeli, or Harcourt got their schooling that way, and at the University or in after-life it made no difference. The Old Giggleswickian was not yet a named variety.* Indeed, if the grammar schools had been equipped for their task, it is very probable that our higher education would, to our great advantage, have developed on a less expensive, less exclusive, basis. Practical parents disliked a purely classical curriculum; sensitive parents were dismayed by the tales of squalor, cruelty, and disorder which were told of almost every public school; and religious parents, warned by Cowper's *Tirocinium*, hesitated to entrust young boys to institutions which gave   12 only a formal security for piety and morals.

Arnold reconciled the serious classes to the public school. He shared their faith in progress, goodness, and their own vocation; incidentally, he was convinced that, with some modest enlargement on the side of history, the classical curriculum was best fitted to produce the type of mind both he and they desired to see in authority. But for Arnold's influence, it is not at all improbable that out of the many experiments then being made in proprietary schools some more modern alternative might have struck root and become ascendant.† Arnold led us back with firm hand to the unchangeable routine of the Renaissance; indeed, he could not have helped it if he had wished. To all complaints of the classical curriculum there was one convincing answer: there were hundreds of people who could teach it, there was hardly any one who could teach anything else. 'If you want science,' Faraday told a Royal Commission, 'you must begin by creating science teachers.'   14

In the eye of the law the public schools were nine in number,   15

* The first Old —an I have noticed is, as might be expected, an old Rugboean in 1840. A man born in the fifties told me that until he was twelve he was intended for the local grammar school, as the family could only support one son at Eton. A discovery of coal on the estate altered the position. He had to begin by learning English in place of the N. Riding dialect which was his native speech.

† For example, in the schools run by that remarkable family, the Hills, from which Rowland Hill issued to reform the Post Office, or George Edmondson's Queenwood.   13

but in effect, in the sense of regularly preparing boys for the University, the list was continually enlarging. By 1860 they were not dominant, but they were ascendant in the Universities, and, as they grew, the private tutor fell away, leaving his ample rectory as a burden to his impoverished successor; the career and type of the public-school boy became standardized, and the preparatory schools rose in corresponding importance. The outlook of the newer schools was to some degree modernized by the demands of

16 Woolwich and the Civil Service Commissioners for science and modern languages; but the Renaissance tradition was not seriously impaired, and when Lord Clarendon summed up all the charges against the public schools in a question to the Headmaster of Eton, 'We find modern languages, geography, chronology, history and everything else which a well-educated Englishman ought to know, given up in order that the whole time should be devoted to the classics, and at the same time we are told that the boys go up to Oxford not only not proficient, but in a lamentable deficiency in respect to the classics', the Headmaster could only

17 answer, 'I am sorry for it'.* But public opinion did not want knowledge. It wanted the sort of man of whom Wellington had said that he could go straight from school with two N.C.Os. and fifteen privates and get a shipload of convicts to Australia without

19 trouble. With the reconquest of India and the reform of the Army after the Crimea, it needed them in increasing numbers; and it was satisfied that the best way to get them was to begin by producing public-school boys and overlooking their deficiencies in 'everything which a well-educated Englishman ought to know'. For the civil branches, indeed, something more was required which Oxford and Cambridge would supply. Macaulay annexed the Indian Civil Service to the Universities: Jowett and Trevelyan, beaten in '53, had their victory in 1870, when Gladstone annexed the administrative grades of the English Civil Service.

Isolated by history as much as by the sea, the English ruling

---

* The Headmaster of Westminster claimed that of his sixth form two-thirds could read Caesar and half could read Xenophon at sight. Perhaps the Queen was thinking of this when she told Mr. Gladstone that education was ruining the health of the Upper Classes. But contrast the account we have of Sedbergh in the fifties. 'It was part of the tradition that every one should have read Homer, Thucydides and Sophocles before he went up.' Everything depended on the

18 *genius loci*, which might vary from one decade to another.

class had bred true to the barbaric type from which absolutism and revolution had deflected the foreign aristocracies; round this type, with its canons of leadership—respect for the past, energy in the present, and no great thought for the future—Victorian England formed a new ideal, in which the insolent humanism of the eighteenth century was refined by religion, and the industrious puritanism of the early nineteenth century was mellowed by public spirit; and to disengage, to affirm, and to propagate the type, no better instrument could have been devised than the Universities and public schools, with their routine of authority and old books and their home background of country life and sport. That the ideal was in many ways defective is too obvious to be asserted or denied: it was the flower of a brief moment of equipoise, Protestant, northern, respectable. It omitted much that a Greek or Italian would have thought necessary to completeness: artistic sensibility, dialectic readiness, science, and the open mind— Aristophanes would have thought Sidney Herbert exceedingly superstitious:* Ariosto, one fears, would have set him down as a prig—and to its defects must be in large measure ascribed the imprecision of late Victorian thought and policy which contrasts so ominously with the rigorous deductions of the early Victorians. Yet in the far distance I can well conceive the world turning wistfully in imagination, as to the culminating achievement of European culture, to the life of the University-bred classes in England of the mid-nineteenth century, set against the English landscape as it was, as it can be no more, but of which, neverthe- less, some memorials remain with us to-day, in the garden at Kelmscott, in the hidden valleys of the Cotswolds, in that walled 21 close where all the pride and piety, the peace and beauty of a vanished world seem to have made their last home under the spire of St. Mary of Salisbury.

* But Aristophanes has given the best definition of the type that I know, 'an insider who enjoys his privileges and is regular in his duties to the outsiders'.

μόνοις γὰρ ἡμῖν ἥλιος
καὶ φέγγος ἱλαρόν ἐστιν,
ὅσοι μεμνύημεθ' εὐ-
σεβῆ τε διήγομεν
τρόπον περὶ τοὺς ξένους
καὶ τοὺς ἰδιώτας.

XV

In surveying a period of history it is sometimes useful to step outside and see what happened next. Of late Victorian England the most obvious characteristics are the Imperialism of Beaconsfield and Chamberlain and the counterthrust of Gladstonian Liberalism; the emergence of a Socialist and, in a lesser degree, of a Feminist movement as calculable forces; the decay of the religious interest and the supersession of the aristocracy by the plutocracy, a process masked by the severe and homely court of Victoria, but growing precipitate, after the agricultural depression, with the influx of South African money and American brides. Early Victorian had become a term of reproach when Victoria had still ten years to reign.

It was the good fortune of England in the years we have been surveying to confront a sudden access of power, prosperity, and knowledge, with a solidly grounded code of duty and self-restraint. In the fifties and sixties, the code still held good, but the philosophy on which it was based was visibly breaking up. It had rested on two assumptions which experience was showing to be untenable: that the production of wealth by the few, meant, somehow, and in the long run, welfare for the many; and that conventional behaviour grounded on a traditional creed was enough to satisfy all right demands of humanity. At our distance in time we can see the agnostic and feminist turn impending: we can understand the connection, peculiar to England, between the socialist and aesthetic movements of the next age. But life was too leisurely and secure for agitation. The reforms of the forties satisfied the aspirations of the poor and the consciences of the rich, until a new tide set in and carried us forward again with the Education Act of 1870, and the legislation of Disraeli's Government, with which Young England, now grown grey, redeemed the promise of its far-off fantastic youth. In the fifties the main current of Utilitarianism was running in the channels which the great administrators had dug for it: the springs of religious feeling opened by the Evangelicals had been led over the new fields which Newman, Arnold, and Carlyle—miraculous confederacy— had won or recovered for English thought; and Economic Evangelicalism was no more than a barren stock. The first Victorian generation had built with the sword in one hand and the trowel in the other: in the fifties the sword was laid aside and the trowel was wielded, quietly, unobtrusively, anonymously, by civil servants and journalists, engineers and doctors, the secretaries of Trade Unions and the aldermen of manufacturing towns. Early in the thirties, Nassau Senior had boldly declared, against the current Malthusianism, that if the influx of Irish labour could be checked and the outflow of English labour assisted the population question could be left to settle itself. Now his words seemed to be coming true. A race so tenacious of its immemorial village life that in 1830 a Sussex family could hardly be persuaded to seek its fortune in Staffordshire, or a Dorset family that Lancashire existed, was flocking by the hundred thousand in quest of the Golden Fleece, or the land where the gates of night and morning stand so close together that a good man can earn two days' wages in one. By 1860 the whole world was the Englishman's home and England was at peace.

Released from fear, the English mind was recovering its power to speculate, to wonder, and to enjoy. The dissolvent elements in Early Victorian thought, romance and humour and curiosity, the Catholicism of Oxford, the satire of Dickens, the passion of Carlyle, the large historic vision of Grote and Lyell and Arnold, were beginning to work. One of the last survivors of the mid-Victorian time spoke of those years as having the sustained excitement of a religious revival. Excitement was Lord Morley's word also, and all through the fifties we are aware of the increasing tension of thought. The Christian Socialists rose in ill-directed but fruitful revolt: the Pre-Raphaelites struck out for a freedom which they had not strength to reach. Tennyson, in *Maud*, Dickens in *Hard Times* turned savagely on the age that had bred them. We miss the precise objectives, the concentrated purpose of the earlier time. Science and poetry, business and adventure, religion and politics are not yet divided into separate, professional avocations; but they are thrown together in an irregular, massive synthesis, of which the keynotes still are competence and responsibility, a general competence not always distinguishable from a general amateurishness, a universal responsibility sometimes declining into a universal self-importance. Not for a long time had the English character seemed so upright, or English thought so formless, as in that happy half generation when the demand for organic change was quiescent, the religious foundations were perishing, and the balance of land and industry was slowly toppling.

We are nearing the years of division. In 1859 the last of the Augustans was laid by Johnson and Addison, and the Red House was begun at Bexley: in 1860 Ruskin issued as much of *Unto this Last* as Thackeray dared to print, and how great a part of late Victorian thought is implicit in five books of those same years, in the *Origin of Species*, Mill on *Liberty* and *Essays and Reviews*: in FitzGerald's *Omar* and Meredith's *Richard Feverel* we can appreciate now better than their own age could have foreseen. We are approaching a frontier, and the voices that come to us from the other side, *Modern Love* and *Ecce Homo*, Swinburne's first poems and Pater's first essays, are the voices of a new world, of which the satirist is not Cruikshank but du Maurier, the laureate not Tennyson but Browning, the schoolmaster not Arnold but his son. The late Victorian age is opening.

7

XVI

BUT the Englishman, growing towards maturity in those years, felt himself no longer isolated, but involved in a world of accumulating and accelerating change. Swiftly, under the impulsion of Bismarck, the European pieces were setting to a new pattern. The North German lands ranged themselves with Prussia. To the south, Austria and Hungary had come together again over the body of their depressed and resentful Slavs. Italy, enriched by the cession of Venetia, had established her capital at Florence and her hands were closing on Papal Rome. The only barrier remaining between the old Europe—Congress Europe, the Europe of Canning and Palmerston—and the new, was the incalculable and untested stability of the French Empire.

Official incidents are rarely of much account in history, and the greater part of what passes for diplomatic history is little more than the record of what one clerk said to another clerk. But it is allowable to speculate on what might have happened if the Queen had had her way, and Robert Morier, who knew Germany as Palmerston knew Europe, had been kept in Berlin from 1866 to 1870. But Bismarck was an astute man: our Ambassador, a stupid man:

Hammond, the Permanent Under-secretary, a jealous man. So
Bismarck worked, unobserved, unsuspected; and in the June of   1
1870 Hammond could confidently assure Lord Granville that
never had Europe been so profoundly at peace. War was declared   2
on July 15. On August 6 the armies of France and Germany met at
Saarbruck. Napoleon III surrendered at Sedan on September 2.
On September 20 the Italian army entered Rome by the gate of
Michelangelo. On December 18, in the Hall of Mirrors at Ver-
sailles, the King of Prussia was acknowledged German Emperor.
Europe had lost a mistress and found a master.* After the Siege,
the Commune. 'Let us go to Montmartre,' an English visitor was
overheard to say: 'It is the best place to watch Paris burning.'   4

The Prussian campaign against Austria in 1866 had imposed on
the world a new standard, almost a new conception, of efficiency.
But no one had ever taken Austria very seriously as a military
power, and the swoop of the German armies on Paris came, to
England at least, as a revelation. At the opening of the war, sym-
pathies were on the whole with Germany: Englishmen had no
great cause to trust Napoleon, they knew something of the corruption of government in France, and had seen more of the corruption of society in Paris. Feeling veered when the Empire had
fallen, and France at bay began to show her natural bravery, the
victorious Prussian his native brutality. Our public attitude, un-
ruffled by the abuse discharged on us by both the combatants,
remained entirely correct. But the Prussians had reached the
Channel. There was no reason, yet, to suppose they would wish
to cross it, but six months before there had been no reason to
suppose they would fall on France. If the Almighty, with whose
designs the new Emperor showed so intimate a familiarity, chose
to direct a crusade on London, it was reasonably certain that the
Army could not oppose him and not quite clear whether the Navy
could stop him.† The prudence of Bismarck gave better assurance
of the peace of Europe and the security of England.

Fortunately, at a time when the country might easily have run
into panic, the War Office was in the hands of one of Peel's best
pupils, Edward Cardwell. He had already to his record one of the

---

* The phrase is Henry Bulwer's.   3
† The loss of the *Captain* in 1870 had raised grave doubts as to the efficiency
of our naval administration. See the scathing inscription on the memorial in
St. Paul's, and Chesney's *Battle of Dorking*.   5

useful codifications of the age, the Merchant Shipping Act of
1854* and the draft, at least, of one of its most memorable Statutes, the British North America Act of 1867. Behind the convenient clamour over the abolition of Purchase, he worked steadily at
the unification of the Line, Militia, and Volunteers, at the equipment and training of the Army for the new scientific warfare, the
improvement of material, the formation of a Reserve. So steadily
and so well, indeed, that England, which, when the Germans were
before Paris was inclined to wonder whether she had an army at
all, was, a few months later, when the Germans were back in
Germany, ruefully considering the cost of an efficient one. To
abolish Purchase the debt was increased by £7,000,000: to add
20,000 men to the Army and modernize its equipment the taxpayer had to find £3,000,000 in a year: a price well worth paying
for the removal of those uneasy, fitful alarms which had been
before, and were to be again, the parents of bad counsel and
improvident administration.† The Army, as Cardwell left it, was
a good machine: and it was not his fault if his successors, and the
Duke of Cambridge, and public opinion always more and more
concerned with naval defence, let the machine run down.

An island power needs an army as a defence against casual
raiders, and as an expeditionary force. But its main strategy must
be oceanic and its diplomacy will naturally aim at friendship with
the chief military power of the Continent. Only when that power
grows strong at sea must the island look for another friend. So in
the sixteenth century we had swung from Burgundy to Valois: in
the seventeenth from Bourbon to Hapsburg, and the time had
come for a new variety of an old combination: England at sea,
Germany by land, watching the Channel and the Rhine, the Polish
frontier and the Indian passes, an equipoise which would hold until
Germany looked seaward too. Russia, urged by that strange power
of growth which had spread the Orthodox People from the Black
Sea to the Arctic, and from the Baltic to the Pacific, was still
moving forward. How near in truth she was to India was a question few could answer. But the completion of the Suez Canal in

* When 516 clauses went through Committee at one sitting. Is this a record?
† Field manœuvres were introduced by General Hope Grant in 1870. With
the Volunteers' annual Field-day at Brighton, they did much to create that
interest in the army and its doings which is characteristic of the later decades of
the reign.

1869 had opened a new route from India to England, and on its flank lay Constantinople, and behind Constantinople the Black Sea Fleet. The board was set, and the pieces in their place.

XVII

AT home, the forces so long restrained by the genial ascendancy of Palmerston were seeking their traditional outlets, the abatement of privilege and the extension of the franchise. Mill was in for Westminster, and Gladstone out for Oxford. In 1866, Russell and Gladstone, unmuzzled at last and member for South Lancashire, introduced their Reform Bill. They were defeated, and for one bright summer evening London enjoyed the forgotten thrill of a battle between Reformers and Policemen. Derby and Disraeli succeeded and fell.* The Tenpound Householder imparted his privilege to the Householder at large, and the Lodger: the Forty Shilling Freeholder to the Twelvepound Householder. For another eighteen years the distinction of Borough and County persisted: and though, after 1867, the social composition of Parliament began to alter rapidly to the advantage of the business man, the ascendancy of the rural gentry was not yet fatally impaired. Fortune was still on the side of her old favourites, and the Civil War in America postponed for half a generation the menace to the land. But the return of the Liberals in 1868 dealt a threefold blow to the Gentlemanly Interest. Purchase of Commissions was abolished, the Universities were thrown open to dissenters, the Civil Service to competition. Radicalism was making itself felt again, and two cycles of Benthamite reform were rounded off by the Ballot Act in 1872 and the fusion of Law and Equity in 1873. Never, it was said, had new members talked so much as they talked in 1868. Never had they had so much to talk about: never since 1832 had there been so many of them: the quiet time was over.

In its six years of office, this great but unfortunate administration contrived to offend, to disquiet, or to disappoint, almost every

---

* Having, incidentally, purchased the telegraph system for the Post Office. Proxies in the House of Lords, Church Rates, and public executions, came to an end in the same year, 1868.

interest in the country. Of its three chief measures, Irish Disestablishment failed to placate the Irish and left English Churchmen uneasy. Forster's Education Act satisfied neither the Church nor the Dissenters. The Irish Land Act did not go to the root of the Irish land trouble and it planted a lasting anxiety in the mind of the English landowners. Lowe's fancy budget of 1871 ended in a squalid riot in Palace Yard, twopence on the income tax, and a lesson to the new electorate that they might be extravagant at
6 other people's expense. The neutrality of the Black Sea, the prize of 1856, had to be surrendered: the *Alabama* indemnity had to be
7 paid. After 1871 nothing went right. There were political jobs
8 almost amounting to public scandals: there was a departmental
9 scandal almost amounting to malversation of public money:
10 Epping Forest was all but sold for building lots. Finally, Mr. Gladstone, overrating both his ascendancy and his ingenuity, failed to reconcile the Catholic hierarchy and the Nonconformist Conscience to an Irish University which should teach neither
11 modern history nor philosophy. England turned to the Tories, and in 1874 the Ballot sent Disraeli back with a majority that recalled the triumph of 1841.* Of the next thirty years, the Conservatives were in power for twenty-two.

But to any observant mind it was manifest that a revolution of far deeper and wider import than any shift of the balance of power in Europe, or the centre of electoral or social gravity in England, was impending. Such a change as had come over the human mind in the sixteenth century, when the earth expanded from Europe to a globe, was coming over it again. Now space was shrinking, time expanding. The earth had given up her most mysterious secret when in 1856 Speke stood on the shores of Victoria Nyanza and
12 saw the Nile pouring northward. The Atlantic cable was laid at last in 1866. Even in domestic life the contraction was making itself felt: the Metropolis was becoming compact: its satellite villages, from Blackheath round to Chiswick, suburban. But as the home of mankind grew smaller to the imagination, so the history of the race was perceived to stretch in longer and longer perspective. Before the first ferment over the *Origin of Species* had subsided, a new window had been opened on to the past. In 1860 John Henslow, famous throughout Europe as a botanist, and to

* I remarked to an old Gladstonian how quiet the Election of 1935 had been. 'Yes,' he said, 'like 1874. Very different from 1868. But then he had *driven* us so.'

his neighbours better known as an exemplary parish priest, crossed the Channel to examine for himself the prehistoric discoveries claimed by Boucher de Perthes in the valley of the Somme. Convinced, his authority carried with it the consent of English science: a new age, not to be reckoned by the centuries of Europe or even the millennia of Egypt and Babylon, was thrown open to explorers, and close on the discovery of primitive man followed the discovery how much of man, not least his religion and his morality, was still primitive. 13

We are passing from the statistical to the historical age, where the ground and explanation of ideas, as of institutions, is looked for in their origins: their future calculated by observation of the historic curve. As Early Victorian thought is regulated by the conception of progress, so the late Victorian mind is overshadowed by the doctrine of evolution. But the idea of progress—achieved by experiment, consolidated by law or custom, registered by statistics—had, without much straining of logic or conscience, been made to engage with the dominant Protestant faith, and this, equally, in both its modes: in the individualism of the soul working out its own salvation, in the charity which sought above all things the welfare of others. Now, of the main articles of the common Protestant faith, the Inerrant Book was gone, and it had carried with it the chief assurance of an intervening Providence. To propose an infallible Church, in compensation for a Bible proved fallible, was a pretension which the Church of England had expressly, and in advance, disclaimed,* and which no Protestant sect could maintain. The only valid alternative was agnosticism, or a religion of experience. But in those very years when the historic impact was loosening the whole fabric of tradition, we can see, and it is one of the strangest paradoxes on record, historic speculation engaged in building an inerrant system of economics, and demonstrating, with inexorable scholastic rigour, the future evolution of society through class war into its final state of Communism. Disraeli about this time spoke of a 'craving credulity' as the note of the age. The human mind is still something of a troglo- 15 dyte. Expelled from one falling cavern, its first thought is to find another.

Religion, conceived as a concerted system of ideas, aspirations, and practices to be imposed on society, was losing its place in the

* Articles XX and XXI. 14

English world, and the Oxford scholars about Sanday who were to settle the documents of the faith with an exactness and integrity which Germany could not have outmatched, delivered their results to a generation which had ceased for the most part to be interested in the faith or the documents. The ethical trenchancy of the Evangelicals was passing over to the agnostics, who in their denunciation of the Sin of Faith, their exaltation of scientific integrity, could be as vehement, as dogmatic, and at times as narrow, as any of the creeds which they believed themselves to have supplanted. Agnosticism had the temper of the age on its side, and the believers were hampered by the ancient ravelins and counter-scarps which they could not defend, and would not abandon. There are times when the reader of Victorian apologetic, whether the theme be miracles or inspiration or the authorship of the Gospels, whether the book before him be the *Speaker's Commentary*, or Drummond's *Natural Law in the Spiritual World*, or Pusey on Daniel or Gladstone on the Gadarene Swine, is nauseated by the taint of sophistry and false scholarship, and feels, as the better intelligence of the time did feel, that if men could force their intellects to think like that, it cannot matter much what they thought.★ This was not the way, and nothing could come of it but a certain disdainful indifference to all such speculations, or a flight of perplexed unstable minds into the Confessional, into Spiritualism, into strange Eastern Cults.

A saner instinct counselled those who were not satisfied with the purely immanent order, physical or moral, propounded by science, to hold fast to the historic forms of devotion, and compel them to yield what they still promised and once had yielded: the certitude of experience as the reward of faith, insight into the nature of the transcendent, and the renewal, by the sacraments, of the saving impulse which Christ had through his Church imparted to the race. There, in the balanced emphasis on individual conduct and social coherence, on the personal origin and historic transmission of the faith, was the new Via Media. In this fusion of the Evangelical, the Arnoldine and the Tractarian teaching, this return to a faith more primitive than the creeds or the Bible, and shot with strands of Plato and Hegel, we can feel rather than dis-

---

★ Or as an Edinburgh Reviewer (Bishop Wilberforce, I think) once said: 'Such intellects must be left to the merciful apologies of Him that created them.' But to whom is He to apologize?

cern the religious philosophy of Later Victorian England moving towards its next objective, while from *In Memoriam* to *The Woods of Westermain*, from *The Woods of Westermain* to the Choruses of *The Dynasts*, we can follow the secular intellect seeking its way to such an apprehension of Being as Process as might hereafter reconcile the spiritual demands of humanity with the rapt and cosmic indifference of Evolution. 19

XVIII

IN the life of a nation, to dispose of one problem is to start another. To an observer of a benevolently Utilitarian disposition in 1865, it might well have appeared that the problem of progress had been solved. Few able-bodied men lacked employment, and indeed it seemed quite possible that at no distant date England would have to import foreign labour to adjust the balance of native emigration. That a great part of the population was under-nourished did, it is true, go to show that the distribution of wealth was less efficient than its production. But, even here, remedies were available within the accepted scheme of things: Trade Unions to keep wages in some correspondence with the earnings of industry: co-operation and profit sharing for the mechanic: free sale of land for the farmer, and small holdings for the labourer. Fawcett★ was not following a flight of fancy, but a sober speculation, when he looked forward to a society of well-fed, well-educated citizens, with skilled artisans and peasant proprietors at the base, scavenged for and waited on by negroes and Chinese. It is the Early Victorian ideal of the Respectable Family, set upon the economic basis of free, but not uncontrolled, competition, and steady, but not unaided, self-help.

To the question: progress whither? the answer is agreed. But poetry and philosophy, the new history and the new science, had together posed a more fundamental question, evolving what? And the dominant minds of the seventies were those who had faced the question most boldly: who had, like Darwin himself, grown slowly to fame, and spoke with the equal authority of unquestioned genius and long meditation, who embodied in

★ *Economic Position of the British Labourer*, 1865. 1

themselves the revolution in English thought, who were masters of the tradition and had found the tradition wanting. These are, beyond all others, Ruskin, Browning, and George Eliot. They had all been reared in the same atmosphere of middle-class industry and piety; they shared the same gifts of observation and analysis; and they were, one audaciously, the other dramatically, and George Eliot gravely and philosophically, in revolt.

Round them, growing up under their shadow, we see a younger group, marked with the same imprint, and bearers of the same ideas—the agnostics, Morley and Leslie Stephen: the romantics, Morris and Burne-Jones, Philip Webb and Swinburne: aesthetic Pater and disconcerting Meredith. They form no school, their derivation is various, and their allegiance divided. But there is a spiritual bond between them in the sense of personal value. A Socratic search for the good had begun again, to replace ideals which were toppling as their religious foundations cracked: we can count the schools that will come out of it, and name their manifestoes: *An Agnostic's Apology*, the *Renaissance*, the *Essay on Comedy*, *News from Nowhere*. And crowding into the picture are the pessimists and the pagans, the strenuous and the decadent, strong, silent men, and not so silent feminists, Celts and aesthetes, spiritualists and theosophists, Whistlers and Wildes and Beardsleys, all the fads and all the fancies into which the compact and domestic philosophy of Victorian England dissolved.

2

But if, again, we seek a clue to this phantasmagoria of a late afternoon, we shall find it best, I think, in Meredith. He had, in virtue of his birth-year, 1828, the strong decency, the vigour, gusto, and ebullience of the Early Victorians; but he charged them with a new spirit, the searching criticism of his maturer time. Browning and Ruskin had taken the same path. But Browning was preoccupied, as George Eliot was, with problems which could be stated, if not solved, in the terms of old theology and old ethics, God, Duty, and Immortality: righteousness and temperance and judgement to come; and the mind of Ruskin, endowed with every gift except the gift to organize the others, was more tumultuous than the tumult in which it was involved. The deceptive lucidity of his intoxicating style displayed, or concealed, an intellect as profound, penetrating, and subtle as any that England has seen; and as fanciful, as glancing, and as wayward as the mind of a child. But if Ruskin is all dogma and no system, Meredith's

3

grotesque is the vehicle of a philosophy which is all system and no dogma.

What, we may ask—and it is the fundamental problem at once in Meredith's work and in all Late Victorian Ethic—what are the duties which the conception of Being as Process imposes on those to whom it has been revealed and who acknowledge no other revelation? It was not a new problem, and answers could be read in the ethereal verse of *Prometheus*, in the gritty prose of Harriet Martineau; more lucidly, and with an almost mystical clarity, in the closing stanzas of *In Memoriam*. Perfectibility was returning from the exile to which the reign of the economists had consigned her, enriched by the experience of two absorbing generations, and heartened by their victories, with a new objective and method, the gradual improvement of the race, by the transmission of a life more and more at harmony within itself, and more and more sovereign over circumstance. But whether the end was to be reached by the segregation of finer types, or the general elevation of the community at large; whether evolution had established competition as Nature's first law, or had indicated the emergence of a moral law above itself: heredity against environment, nature against nurture: the weakening of fibre by too much help, the degeneration of tissue by not help enough: the lessons to be drawn from the progress of fifty years, and to be drawn also from their failures; it is in such roving, ranging debates as these, that the thought of England is now involved; debates which, being grounded on no acknowledged premises, could issue in no accepted conclusion; explorations, rather; definings of problems, not solutions; the ideas of the future shaping themselves in the language of the past; and still set out with something of the romantic urgency of a more pious, a more confident, time. Some closeness of the northern fibre, the slow rising of the northern sap, keeps the years and the decades tight to each other. But the sap is rising: silently, inevitably the tissue is transformed.

It may well be thought that if England had been visited by such a calamity as befell Europe in 1848, America in 1861, or France in 1870, the urgency of reconstruction would have drawn the new conceptions into a new and revolutionary configuration which would have shaped new institutions to match. The Church of England would have followed the Church of Ireland, and the Throne the Church; and a rapid extension of the suffrage would have involved the fall of the aristocracy and the redistribution of their still rich lands. All the necessary ideas were in the air: whisperings against the Crown, more than whisperings against the Church and the Lords; against primogeniture and the aggregation of estates: and the ground-tone, always growing louder, is the discord of progress and poverty. But England, watching Paris burn, was in no mood to go too far or too fast, and a greater destiny was beginning to absorb her thought. Mistress of India and the seas, mother of nations, she might well see in her worldwide sovereignty the crown and demonstration of evolution in history.* The very contraction of the world was making the thought of Greater Britain † more intimate and familiar, and giving to Imperial hopes and aspirations an ascendancy over domestic doubts and fears.

XIX

Doubts and fears there were. The roaring slapdash prosperity of a decade had worked itself out to its appointed end: overtrading, speculation, fraud and collapse; and the misery of East London in 1866 was a grim but timely comment on the complacency of ¹ Fawcett in 1865. In spite of a buoyant revenue and a record expansion of the export trade, there was already a chill in the air. The company promoter was beginning to take his toll of the surplus wealth accumulating for a decade past. After a century of immunity, the Cattle Plague returned. The advance guard of militant Fenianism reached Ireland from America, and that simmering cauldron began to bubble once more. In the spring of 1866

---

* Ille populus qui cunctis athletizantibus pro Imperio mundi praevaluit, de Divino iudicio praevaluit. Dante, *de Monarchia*, ii. 9.

It has always seemed to me (and I am speaking of what I remember) that, in its exaltation and in its almost Darwinian reasoning, this part of Dante's tract is a perfect rendering of the philosophic Imperialism of the end of the century; the distinction between the races, *apti nati ad principari*, and those *apti ad subiici*; the final cause of Empire, *subiiciendo sibi orbem, bonum publicum intendit*; natural disposition, *natura locum et gentem disposuit ad universaliter principandum*; and the survival of the fittest in *certamina* and *duella*. One might even deduce the Statute ⁵ of Westminster from the principles laid down in i. 14.

† The phrase was Dilke's, then a Republican, and first used as the title of ⁶ his travel book in 1868.

a catastrophe far beyond the mercantile panics of 1847 and 1857 fell on the City. The failure of Overend and Gurney, in its magnitude, and in its social consequences recalled rather the disasters of 1825. The new system of Limited Liability had brought into the area of speculative finance thousands of quiet-living families who had hitherto been satisfied with the Funds or a few well-established Railways or Foreign Loans. They were now the chief sufferers, and the contraction of their expenditure, and the loss of their confidence weighed on the country for years. It seemed as if the resiliency of old days had gone, as if we were moving from our apogee, yielding, as Cobden had foreseen, to the larger resources of America,* yielding, too, to the higher efficiency of the Germans.

'On the speedy provision of elementary education,' Forster warned the Commons in 1870, 'depends our industrial prosperity, the safe working of our constitutional system, and our national power. Civilized communities throughout the world are massing themselves together, each mass being measured by its force: and if we are to hold our position among men of our own race or among the nations of the world, we must make up for the smallness of our numbers by increasing the intellectual force of the individual.' A movement long maturing was taking shape in action, and with it a controversy which of all Victorian controversies is perhaps the hardest to recall with patience.

It may be admitted, and by this time it was almost universally agreed, that simple instruction should be brought within the reach of all who needed it. Not universal, but still dominant, was the opinion that the instruction should include the Bible and the elements of religion. No party would have dared to turn the Bible out of the schools, and no two parties could agree as to the terms upon which it should be admitted. Had the ground been unoccupied, or had it been completely occupied by the Church schools, the solution was obvious. In the one case, voluntary arrangements by all denominations:† in the other, a conscience clause for all dissenters, would have satisfied most reasonable

---

* It is not always remembered that Cobden regarded Free Trade, not as a law of nature, but as a device for postponing the inevitable consequences of American competition. In his heart Cobden preferred the pre-industrial civilization in which he was born, and there is as much bitterness as belief in his economic creed.

† This was the solution actually proposed by Walter Hook as early as 1838.

men. But sectarians are not reasonable men: and it was plain that the vast deficiencies in elementary education could now only be made good by public effort; by schools tax-aided and rate-provided; and that the effort was bound either to enlarge or diminish the influence of the Church: enlarge it enormously if the parson was admitted into the new schools; diminish it, more slowly but as certainly, if he were excluded, and his own schools gradually sapped by the superior resources of the School Boards, and the superior efficiency of the Board Schools. So a debate was started which the compromise of 1870—plain Bible teaching in one school and the Catechism in another; increased assistance to Church schools where they were efficient, and Board Schools to supplement them where they were not—did not end. Thirty years later the controversy flamed into life again over the Act of 1902, and even to-day a statesman who tampered with the settlement might find that the ashes were not quite cold.

But William Forster, a Dorset quaker, a Bradford manufacturer, and a Volunteer of 1859, had a sound eye for essentials. It is not without its significance that, while Mr. Gladstone found him 6 'an impracticable man', he was among the Queen's most trusted friends, for the Queen loved plainness as much as she hated Mr. Gladstone: and in 1870 the essential was to get the children, somehow, into some sort of school. The incidental consequences of his great measure were of hardly less importance than its direct effects. The Education Act of 1870 was, for most English people, the first sensible impact of the administrative State on their private 7 lives; the Beadle, vanishing figure of fun, underwent a strange rejuvenation into the School Board Man, the Attendance Officer; and how forcible and disturbing his appearance was we may divine from the consideration that in Birmingham, before the Act, forty children out of a hundred, in Manchester fifty, were running loose in the streets. Spiced with sect, moreover, the School Board Elections were, particularly in London, as hot as a parliamentary contest. To great numbers they gave a novel interest in local government: to a smaller circle, women as well as men, their first experience of administration. Nor, in any history of the Victorian age, should the school-builders be forgotten. Those solid, large-windowed blocks, which still rise everywhere above the slate roofs of mean suburbs, meant for hundreds of thousands 8 their first glimpse of a life of cleanliness and order, light and air.

XX

THE Educational controversy points the sagacity of Disraeli's observation in 1868 that religion would give the new electorate something to take sides on. At no time since the seventeenth century had English society been so much preoccupied with problems of doctrine and Church order: at no time had the Establishment been so keenly assailed, or so angrily divided within itself. A misjudged appointment to a bishopric or deanery might influence a by-election, or provoke a Cabinet crisis. Church policy could shake a Government.

In the circumstances of nineteenth-century England, the argument for an Establishment must in fairness be pronounced to be convincing. The parochial system, worked by a married clergy, was unquestionably a civilizing influence which nothing else could have replaced. Whether it was in equal measure a religious influence may be doubted: the English Churchman was rarely so well informed in his faith as the Irish Catholic or the Scotch Presbyterian, and he was not called upon to be so active in his membership as the English Dissenter. The Church was on the defensive: Nonconformity had the strategic initiative. The Church was aristocratic: the Church was the greatest landed proprietor in the kingdom: and in the sixties even well-disposed men might wonder anxiously whether the Church was still the bulwark it had once been against Popery and Infidelity.

Viewed in perspective, the Anglo-Catholic movement is the emergence, in a prepared season, of the Caroline tradition, transmitted not only through the non-jurors but through many of the parochial clergy, unnamed, unknown, who had been bred in the writings of the Caroline divines. As both Newman and Pusey proved, it is possible to construct from those writings such a body of permitted belief as makes the barriers between England and Rome transcendible at all save two or three insuperable points. Perhaps at two only, because, if it be admitted with Hooker that transubstantiation is no matter for churches to part communion on, then all that remains is papal supremacy, and the veneration of the Virgin and saints. In other words, and to unspeculative English minds, the Anglo-Catholics had only to take one step more into idolatry, and the last step of all into Popery. Meanwhile, the

movement which might by turns be labelled Latitudinarian or
Rationalist,* or more simply and vaguely Broad Church, had
been gaining steadily in force and authority. In the widest terms,
it could be defined as the response to the challenge of science, as
the effort to reformulate the Christian faith in language adapted to
the outlook of the age, an age profoundly impressed with the
uniformity of nature, and increasingly critical in its acceptance of
evidence. The question which the Zulu convert put to Bishop
3 Colenso: Do you believe all that? could not be evaded for ever,
and it would be difficult indeed to say with what inner acceptance
the Gospels were read and the Creed recited by Thirlwall or
Jowett or Stanley. The laity, not restrained even by the vague and
liberal terms of subscription which the Act of 1865 imposed on the
clergy, might speak more openly, and for a while, and to a certain
number of serious souls, Seeley and Matthew Arnold seemed to
4 offer a possible standing ground in a rising flood of doubt. But
even the clergy, recruited, as they still for the most part were,
from the families of clergymen and gentlemen, could not in the
long run be bound to beliefs inconsistent with the views of the
educated laity: and the intimate association of the professions,
sacred and profane, from the Universities onwards; the social
activity of the clergy from the bishops downwards; had together
brought about the paradox which Mr. Gladstone once set before
the Queen—the tenacious vitality of a Church whose ministers,
5 many of them, rejected both her authority and her creeds.

But proceedings for heresy being of a penal character, the law
required an exact and circumstantial statement of the offence
alleged, and the wise ambiguity with which the Church had
formulated the mysteries of her faith, made it almost impossible to
frame a charge which could, or a defence which could not, be
sustained. In 1850 the Gorham judgement which allowed a clergy-
6 man to disbelieve in Baptismal Regeneration,† had produced a
formidable secession to Rome. In 1860 a group of scholars put

---

* Add Arnoldine, Germanist, and Neologist, all terms of abuse rather than
terms of art.

† It was not uncommon for Low Church parents to have their children
christened by Nonconformist ministers, so as to avoid the awful words 'seeing now that this child is by baptism regenerate'. In 1864 Spurgeon preached
a sermon calling on the Evangelicals to quit an establishment which admitted
7 the doctrine. Over 200,000 copies were sold.

forth a volume of *Essays and Reviews*, not very remarkable in themselves, which was taken as a challenge to orthodoxy. After much agitation, not altogether creditable to the good sense or good faith of the orthodox, it was brought before the Judicial Committee of the Privy Council. An adverse judgement now would have forced many conscientious men to lay down their orders and would have checked the inflow of educated candidates, already shrinking as the Universities grew more secular. The Privy Council held, however, that though Scripture contains the Word of God, it is not in itself the Word of God, leaving it to the individual judgement and conscience, it must be supposed, to determine which part is and which part is not. To any Christian   8 minister convinced that the Word of God to mankind is conveyed in the person, the example, and the teaching of Christ, the liberty of interpretation thus accorded would seem to be enough.* By this decision the Philosophic party, the party of Free Speculation, were kept within the Church. The Sacramental school won their liberty in 1872 when the Privy Council acquitted Bennett, Rector of Frome Selwood, and authorized a view of the Real Presence as exalted as Pusey or his teachers had ever entertained. The Privy Council had rendered it so difficult for a Churchman to be a heretic that prosecutions for heresy almost ceased,† and the public mind turned with the greater avidity to the persecution of ritualism.

'I do profess *ex animo*,' Newman wrote in 1862, 'that the thought of the Anglican service makes me shiver,' and, indeed,   11 abstracted from the gregarious joy of hymn-singing, the Anglican rite as he had known it did little to evoke the imagination, to gratify the senses or to stir any but the soberest emotions. But since then a combined movement, romantic, antiquarian, doc-

---

* It is worth quoting one passage to show what passed for heresy in 1861: 'When the fierce ritual of Syria, with the awe of a Divine voice, bade Abraham slay his son, he . . . trusted that the Father, whose voice from heaven he heard at heart, was better pleased with mercy than with sacrifice, and his trust was his salvation.' Of all the anfractuosities of the Victorian mind, none perplexes me more than Thirlwall's concurrence in the prosecution of the Essayists.   9

† The only one of consequence, the Voysey case in 1871, elicited from the Privy Council the opinion that a clergyman may follow 'any interpretations of the Articles, which, by any reasonable allowance for the variety of human opinion, can be reconciled with their language'. But in the matter of ritual, the Court is bound itself to determine the meaning of rubric and enforce it.   10

trinal, had transformed the worship which he found so dreary. In religion, as in poetry and art, the appeal of the Middle Ages was irresistible: and the whole tendency of the Tractarian movement was to exalt the priestly character, and to isolate the Eucharist as the chief act of worship. The law was obscure: the opinion and practice of the clergy were divided. But on the whole the laity were suspicious even of such modest and venerable symbols as altar lights and the mixed chalice: the attitude of the minister at the Communion Table might import doctrinal views of the deepest significance: and the younger clergy, going far beyond the practice or intention of the old Tractarians, were now bringing into the Anglican service vestments and gestures, which, as they had no ground in any living tradition, could only be interpreted as an accommodation to a foreign, and still suspect church. Indeed, set forth in the downright English of aggrieved Protestants, some of the new rites, such as rubbing black powder on the faces of people, sprinkling the candles with water, and giving the acolyte a decanter to hold, do not commend themselves as either seemly or sensible. To prepare the way for legislation a Royal Commission was issued in 1867. There were twenty-four minority reports. The Public Worship Regulation Act was passed in 1874. There were scenes: there were scandals: a few obstinate ministers retired to jail from which they were quickly, and with some embarrassment, released. In quiet times, their misdoings or their sufferings might have excited some popular commotion. But the times were not quiet and by 1880 the electorate had other things to take sides on.

12

It can hardly be maintained that these controversies engaged the better or deeper part of the public mind or that they were governed by any ardent desire for truth or the spiritual welfare of the people. When we have abstracted the condescension of middle-class Anglicanism and the social envy of middle-class dissent; the deep-bitten suspicion of Rome, recently enflamed by the Vatican decrees; timidity in face of new ideas, and pertness in face of old prejudices; we shall probably conclude that what remained might have been adjusted by a very moderate exercise of forbearance and common sense: by recognizing that the Church of England without ceasing to be Protestant had outgrown the formularies of the Protestant Reformation. But it was simpler then to say Mass in Masquerade and have done with it. And it is better now to

13

14

remember that this distracted Establishment was still the home of men not inferior in life or learning to the greatest names in its history, of Westcott, and Lightfoot, and Dean Church.

XXI

THERE are moments when an English student of nineteenth-century history must wish that birth had given him for his central topic something less vast and incoherent than the growth of England from the compact, self-centred organism of 1830 to the loose and world embracing fabric of 1900. Not that the growth of the Empire is itself inexplicable or even intricate, because the orderly process of expansion and devolution was a natural function of geographical position and inherited self-government. But from about 1870 onwards we feel that the inner development of the race and its institutions is constantly interrupted, confused, and deflected, by urgent and exciting messages from its sensitive periphery, from the outposts and the seaways: messages which we must postpone for a while. Soon enough they will become insistently loud.

In 1867 a statutory commission sitting at Sheffield, long notorious as a disturbed area, elicited the fact that the Secretary of the Saw-grinders Union was responsible for one murder and twelve other serious assaults on unpopular employers and their work-people. These outrages were isolated and irresponsible. But they called attention sharply to the growing discord between the law and the economic system which it reflected on the one side, and on the other the necessary conditions of labour. Less reluctantly than ignorantly, Parliament had in 1825 conceded a modified recognition to the Trade Unions, but behind the Act of 1825 lay the whole body of law, going back to the days of villeinage, relating to Master and Servant. The status of the Unions was obscure: they could not protect their funds against embezzlement by their own officers: the rights and wrongs of persuasion and incitement, the definition of molesting and intimidating, were vexed topics to which, on the whole, magistrates were not disposed to apply the more lenient construction. The law was still dominated by the old apprehension of combinations in restraint of trade, and, in more

personal relations, by the frank acceptance of the Master as a privi-
leged person. On a breach of contract, the servant could only sue:
the master could prosecute. The master could only be cast in
damages, the servant could be imprisoned. For a time, after the
Chartist collapse, the relations of capital and labour called for little
public notice. But close on the commercial disorders, which followed the financial crisis of 1857, had come a long succession of
strikes, to make it clear that whether Trade Unions were good or
evil they had become a power in industry which must either be
put under the ban, or brought within the scope, of ascertained law.

In 1875, Parliament recognized in its entirety the freedom of
contract and the right of collective bargaining. The author of this
wise and timely measure of pacification, which in our social
history may rank with Fielden's Act of 1847, was a typical product
of Early Victorian training. Of comfortable Lancashire stock: a
Rugbeian of Arnold's time and a Trinity man; churchman,
magistrate, and banker; Cross represents that combination of old
sagacity and new intelligence which marks the blending of the
traditional and authoritative element in public life with the
exploratory and scientific. In history he does not rank as a great
man: on the crowded canvas of Victorian politics he is barely an
eminent man. Yet it might fairly be questioned whether any
measures ever placed on the Statute book have done more for the
real contentment of the people than the Employers and Workmen
Act, and the Protection of Property Act, both of 1875, and the
consolidation of the Factory Acts in 1878. It was a singular chance,
or an act of rare judgement, that gave Disraeli, rapt in the dreams
of *Endymion*, a colleague to realize the aspirations of *Sybil*: 'Mr.
Secretary Cross, whom I always forget to call Sir Richard.'*

We are moving rapidly away from Cobdenism and the Joint
Stock State. Both in Whitehall and in the municipalities, the
wheels of administration, no longer a spasmodic intervention but
part of the ordinary habit of life, are turning faster, and nowhere
are they producing more remarkable results than in Birmingham.
In many ways the change from Early to Late Victorian England is
symbolized in the names of two great cities: Manchester, solid,
uniform, pacific, the native home of the economic creed on which
aristocratic England had always looked, and educated England at

---

* And who, one fears, is now only remembered as the man who once heard a
² smile.

large was coming to look, with some aversion and some contempt: Birmingham, experimental, adventurous, diverse, where
old Radicalism might in one decade flower into a lavish Socialism,
in another into a pugnacious Imperialism.

> If the Devil has a son,
> It is surely Palmerston. 3

Hardly a generation had passed from Palmerston's death, before
Europe had seen cause to suspect that the infernal dynasty had
been continued in Chamberlain.

But in the seventies, Birmingham was best known as the seat,
Chamberlain as the director, of an exceptionally vigorous experiment in political organization, and, more beneficially, in municipal order. Between 1831 and 1861 the population of the borough
had almost doubled, and within the same years it had become,
from one of the healthiest, one of the sickliest of English towns. In
1851 the physical welfare of nearly a quarter of a million people
(less than 8,000 had the parliamentary vote) was supervised by one
inspector of nuisances and one medical man, whose office, though
unpaid, was on the grounds of economy allowed to lapse. In the
diseases which come from dirt and pollution the Borough as late
as 1873 held the record against all England, a condition of affairs
which is partly explained by the opinion strongly held in the
Council that sanitary inspectors were unconstitutional, un-
English, and a violation of the sanctity of the home: in short, cost
more than the ratepayers of Birmingham were willing to spend.
Indeed, any one who wishes to understand why the legislation of
the forties and fifties was so ineffective, and what the invincible
resistance was that frustrated the energy of reformers, will find the
answer as clearly written in the proceedings of the Borough
Council of Birmingham as in those of any corrupt and languid
corporation left over from the reform of 1834. But it was in
Birmingham that John Bright made his appeal to the boroughs to
be 'more expensive'* and his younger colleague's municipal

---

* 'I only hope that the Corporations generally will become very much more
expensive than they have been—not expensive in the sense of wasting money,
but that there will be such nobleness and liberality amongst the people of our
towns and cities as will lead them to give their Corporations power to expend
more money on those things which, as public opinion advances, are found to be
essential to the health and comfort and improvement of our people.' Jan. 29, 1864.
Note the Ruskinian touch in 'nobleness'. 4

career was the answer. The purchase of a Gas Company in 1873, the adoption of the Public Health Act in 1874, the summoning of a Municipal Conference in 1875 are not things that show large in history. Yet if we put to ourselves the question—of all the doings of the mid-seventies, which in the long run mattered most?—we might find that our difficulty lay in deciding between the municipal administration of Chamberlain and the industrial legislation of Cross.

XXII

THE events of 1874 and 1880 lend some colour to the view that the electors never vote for a party but only against one. Disraeli came in because the country was tired of the Liberals, and the Liberals came back because the country distrusted Disraeli. The brief recovery of the early seventies had been followed by a long depression and a series of calamitous harvests; and the whole world was labouring under the disturbance of the French indemnity, and the wild speculation which had followed it in Germany. For four years, too, the country had lived under the costly excitement of Imperial politics, war, annexation, debt, and a contingent liability for fresh debts, fresh annexations, and fresh wars. It was time to call a halt.

The contraction of the world, which was bringing the army of every great power closer to its neighbours' frontiers, was bound, in the Near East, either to consolidate or to disrupt the Turkish Empire. It existed on sufferance, based on mutual jealousies and the well-grounded belief that the Turk was no despicable fighter. France was for the time being out of action: Germany was recovering from her victory in 1871, and its consequences, and was so far disinterested. Austria was easily satisfied. There remained the two half Asiatic powers: England, watching the Mediterranean, the Canal, and the Persian Gulf; and Russia, heir of Byzantium and protectress of the Orthodox people as far as the Adriatic. It was unfortunate that this natural antagonism cast England also for the part of protectress of the Turk, while leaving her without any power to make her protectorate effective. The Turk remained a foreign body in the European system, and the bad humours that generated about him necessarily infected our domestic politics as well.

All through 1875 the Conservatives were busy carrying their social and industrial legislation through the House, no difficult task with a leaderless opposition: and they crowned a successful year with the purchase of the Suez Canal Shares.* Meanwhile, a tithe revolt, not very unlike the agrarian agitation in Ireland, had broken out in Bosnia. The powers addressed a homily to the Porte: the homily was followed by a memorandum: the Sultan was deposed by his Prime Minister, the memorandum withdrawn, and the homily ignored. By the summer of 1876, Serbia, Montenegro, and the province of Bulgaria were all involved, and rumours began to circulate that in Bulgaria the conduct of the Turk had been such as even his old protectress could hardly condone. At this moment, the Prime Minister, now past seventy, decided to seek the ease of the Upper Chamber, and Gladstone, issuing from his lettered retirement,† leapt into life as the leader of the Liberals, against the Turk and Disraeli. The clash of armies on Rhodope was echoed in a personal contest as hot as the encounter of Pitt and Fox.

> Like fabled gods, their mighty war
> Shook realms and nations in its jar:

and never perhaps have Englishmen contrived to find themselves so greatly excited over issues with which so few of them were concerned.

---

* Besides the two Trade Union Bills already mentioned, other measures of this fruitful session were the Food and Drugs Act, the Merchant Shipping Act (Plimsoll's line), a Public Health Act, and the Artisans' Dwellings Act. Disraeli suggested that the Queen should become Patroness of the Artisans' Dwellings Company. She declined on the ground that she knew nothing about its finances. Two years later, the chairman, who bore 'the inauspicious name of' Swindlehurst, after a life of good works, went to prison for embezzling its funds. Victoria was no fool.

Might one add the Public Entertainments Act, which legalized matinée concerts? The day-return ticket for the outer suburbs, the tea-shop, and the visit to the Grosvenor Gallery, count for something in the greater liveliness of Late Victorian England.

† He published *Homeric Synchronisms* in 1876 and was engaged on *Retribution* (the theme of the Bampton Lectures for 1875). It is pleasant to find Professor Shewan, in his last volume of Homeric Essays, adhering to views first put forward by Mr. Gladstone, long before Minos was revealed.

On the broadest view, it might be acknowledged that in maintaining the integrity of Turkey and negativing the Russian protectorate in 1855, England had assumed a certain responsibility towards those races whom it pleased Palmerston to describe as the Nonconformists of Turkey. In quiet times their position was probably not worse than that of the Irish Catholics in the eighteenth century, and Palmerston himself had drafted a plan of reform which would have given them such rights as Irish Catholics enjoyed after the Emancipation, or as had been promised to the people of India by the Queen's proclamation in 1857: toleration, equality before the law, access to all military and civil office. But twenty years had made it clear that the Turk would never of his own accord accept or execute any plan or reform whatever. Always a ruler, he meant always to rule: to the sentiments and civilization of Europe he was indifferent: in its jealousies and divisions he was deeply versed. He is also credited with a sense of humour, and it must have found exercise in contemplating the proposals put forward by his enemies in England: that the Ottoman should be bodily transferred from Europe elsewhere; that England should garrison the Balkans with 100,000 men; that the Balkans should be delivered to Austria and German Austria ceded to Prussia in compensation; or their sudden discovery that Russia was a liberating and civilizing power.

Those who kept their heads in this tornado of irresponsible altruism were right in thinking, first, that the English Government might have joined more heartily in the homily; second, that it should have taken the Bulgarian atrocities more seriously. Between the Turk and his Christian victims no Christian power could be neutral. Between the Turk and the Russian no English Government could be disinterested. When, therefore, in November 1876 the Tsar made a private gesture of friendship at Livadia and the overture was publicly declined at the Guildhall, the practical conclusion to be drawn was that the Government had subordinated its interest in the Christians to its suspicion of Russia: in a word, considerations of morality to considerations of Empire. This was the theme of the oratorical carnival held at St. James's Hall on December 8, 1876, an occasion which would have been even more edifying if some of the historians, novelists, and divines, who met to settle the business of the world, had explained how England was to get 100,000 men into Turkey, how much it would cost,

and how many of them would come home again. Instead, Lord
Salisbury went to Constantinople.   6

By this step the Government recovered its control of the situation. The Conference of the Powers did, indeed, fail of its immediate object, to enforce a settlement in Bosnia and Bulgaria. But it
made clear to the Turk that he could expect no assistance against
Russia, and to the public at home that no armed intervention on
behalf of the Nonconformists was contemplated or was possible:
in other words, that a policy of British Interests was to be pursued,
that within the limits thus indicated Russia might do as she liked,
and that the issue of peace or war turned, therefore, on Russia's
willingness to recognize them. Fortunately they were plain to all
men: Constantinople and the Straits, the Gulf and the Canal: and
the history of the years 1877 and 1878 comes in brief to this, that
Russia accepted the invitation and respected, or was forced to
respect, its restrictions. In European Turkey 11,000,000 souls were
transferred from Mohammedan to Christian rule, and the map of
the Near East was settled for another generation. England
emerged with a trifling addition to the National Debt, the Island
of Cyprus, and an undefined protectorate over Asiatic Turkey and
all its Christian inhabitants. That results so gratifying to the
imagination and the moral sentiments should have had so little
effect on the General Election of 1880 is one of the most instructive facts in the history of Victorian England. Instructive and
intelligible: because the Conservative rout can be interpreted as
the last effort of liberal, detached England, the England of Peace,
Retrenchment, and Reform, which still brought to its politics
something of the shrewdness of a Lancashire board meeting, and
something of the fervour of Exeter Hall, to save itself from the
complications and costs of world empire, to cut the glory and get
on with the business. It was time to call a halt: it was time to look
at Ireland.

But there is an epilogue to be disposed of first. We stayed in
Cyprus. In 1882 the Navy was called upon to perform what Mr.
Gladstone called 'the great and solemn act' of bombarding Alex-
andria, and the egg of a new Empire had been laid. In 1885   7
Canadians were sailing to the war in the Sudan and fleets and
armies were gathering for war with Russia. A party which takes
office with no programme except to reverse the course of history
invites such ironies.

XXIII

But Ireland will be kept waiting no longer, and if we endeavour to contemplate the Irish question as a problem of pure politics, we shall probably judge that it was capable of two solutions only. Either Ireland was an integral part of a really United Kingdom, under a sovereignty as much Irish as English, or it was a subject province. But in either case, a territory in which the Sovereign cannot protect loyal subjects from gross and continual outrage cannot be regarded as effectively part of his dominions, and it must either be recovered or abandoned. Between these two ideas, Reconquest and Separation, modified into Resolute Government and Home Rule, Late Victorian policy wavered. As early as 1865, John Bright had suggested that the Conservative and Liberal leaders should bring forward a joint scheme for the government of Ireland.* It is not easy to conceive the formula on which they could have come together, unless it was that, as the Irish would be content with nothing short of Home Rule, they had better have it at once, with the reservation that, as they would not long be content with Home Rule, they had better not have it at all.

But the formula would have had to provide for the facts that a certain part, whether large or small, of the Irish people was definitely hostile to the English connexion, that socially and economically the structure of England and Ireland was fundamentally different, and that what England and the Scottish Lowlands, which had shared and in part directed her development, regarded as normal, was in fact a peculiarity of their own. Nowhere else in the world had the factory system of capitalist, manager, and labourer been so thoroughly applied to the land: nowhere else was the cultivator a precarious tenant of the soil he cultivated.† It was no doubt conceivable, and it was often argued, that a secure administration would attract capital to Ireland, that capital alone was required to create that balance of land and industry which in England provided a market for the farmer's produce, a demand for the

---

* It is a curious fact that the land system of the Free State rests on the Bright clauses (land purchase) of the Act of 1870, developed by three Conservative and one Liberal Act, of 1885, 1898, 1903, and 1909.

† The only man who thoroughly grasped this historic dissidence was John Mill.

labourer's work, and a steady revenue for the landlord, the merchant, and the investor: in short, that the missionary efforts of the
Anglican Church having failed to make the Irish good Protestants,
Ricardian economics might be applied to making them good
tenants. But the precedent was not encouraging.

The Devon Commission, on the eve of the great famine, had
diagnosed the malady; and the Land Act of 1870 was an attempt   4
to apply the remedy they had indicated. The object of all agrarian
legislation must be to keep the land and the people on it in a good
heart, and, in the last analysis, the prosperity of Ireland depended
on the contentment and energy, and therefore on the security, of
the tenant cultivator. Here was no powerful class of resident,
improving landlords, or rich and masterful farmers; and what
history had not created, no law could provide. Instead, circumstance had produced, generally in Ulster and sporadically in the
other provinces, a custom which made the tenant effectively
part owner of the land. So definite was the custom that the Ulster
tenant could sell his leasehold, his successor stepping into his
rights without any new contract with the owner. In effect, where
the Custom of Ulster held full sway, the landlord had a rentcharge on the land, the tenant had the rest. This was the formula
now to be applied by Parliament to the whole soil of Ireland.
Palmerston had characterized it in advance in the last, and not the
least effective, of his popular phrases: Tenant's right is landlord's
wrong. The Act of 1870 was an act of confiscation to redress a   5
process of confiscation which had lasted for centuries, and it failed
because it did not confiscate enough. The landlord was left with
the right of eviction,* in a country where there is not enough land
to go round. From the evictions after the Famine came the Migration, which gave the Irish a place of arms in America, and out of
the evictions of the late seventies came the Land League, Home
Rule, and in the far distance Civil War.

The phases of a controversy which hung over public, and infected private, life for so many years, a controversy in which the two
fixed elements are the steely resolution of Parnell and the serpentine persistence of Gladstone, can be briefly enumerated. The Land
Act of 1881 recognized the Three Fs: Fair Rents, Fixity of Tenure,
Free Sale. Parnell set out to test its efficacy, and was sent to

---

* Either by raising rents in good times, or not lowering them in bad, and
1879 was as bad a year in Ireland as it was in England.

Kilmainham Gaol. Six months later Parnell was released and Lord Frederick Cavendish murdered. Spencer, with a new Coercion Act, went to Dublin to save what seemed to be a society on the eve of dissolution. The fearful disorders of the preceding years somewhat abated, and, in the Cabinet, opinion so far matured that in May 1885 the Prime Minister was able to enumerate in a letter to the Queen almost as many Irish policies as he had
6 colleagues. Except on one point they were not irreconcilable. But the creation of a Central Irish Board, 'a vestry striving to become
7 a Parliament', was a reef in the fairway. At this point the Government was defeated on its Budget and the Conservative policy was announced. It began with the cessation of all special or coercive legislation, and it went on . . . how far? Parnell believed, or pretended to believe, as far as Home Rule, and in this faith the Irish voters throughout Great Britain were ordered to vote for Lord Salisbury.

But what little the Conservatives got from the Irish alliance in the boroughs they more than lost by the labourer's vote in the counties, where their old Protectionism was still remembered against them. Ulster went Conservative and the rest of Ireland followed Parnell. Together, Conservatives and Nationalists almost exactly matched the Liberals. But, once in office, the Conservatives gave no ground for supposing that any Irish hopes would be realized, and they were dispatched. The Liberals returned. Hartington and the Whigs held aloof: John Bright had called the
8 Nationalists rebels, and when he said rebels he meant rebels, like those whom his idolized North had crushed to preserve another Union. The first Home Rule Bill was laid before the Cabinet and Chamberlain resigned. It was introduced into Parliament, together with a Land Purchase Act, and it was defeated. Ninety Liberals followed Bright, or Chamberlain, or Hartington, and at the General Election of 1886 the Unionist parties were in a majority of 110: Mr. Gladstone's attempt to reverse the decision in 1893 brought them back with a majority of 152 and a policy of Land Purchase and Resolute Government. Ireland receded from the foreground of politics. The Irish party broke up, but the issue of reconquest or separation remained.

'It will lumber along,' Melbourne used to assure his agitated
9 young mistress. But how much longer Parliament could lumber along if it was not relieved of some part of its burden, had by

1880, if not earlier, become a matter of serious consideration. Its efficiency depended very largely on mutual forbearance and the recognition of certain unwritten rules; and when, in 1877, Parnell kept the Commons sitting for twenty-six hours on a Bill in which he was not in the least interested, the House as a body was quick to scent danger. But how to guard against it was a puzzle to which no obvious answer was forthcoming. Four years later, on the introduction of Forster's Coercion Bill—the fifty-eighth, someone calculated, since the Union—a forty-hours sitting was brought to an end by the intervention of the Speaker, acting on his own responsibility and from a sense of duty to the House. Parnell had paralysed the law in Ireland, and the legislature at Westminster. The legislature could protect itself by new rules for the conduct of debate. But the framing of those rules with due regard to freedom of speech and the rights of minorities was not easy, and it was not of good omen that the oldest and most august of Parliaments should have to borrow from the youngest and most uproarious, the device of *clôture*, to preserve its dignity and efficiency. And, that nothing might be wanting to impair the repute of the House, night after night, and session after session, it found itself employed in extruding Bradlaugh, whose only difference with many of those who voted against him was that they did not believe in God and he said he did not.   10

Devolution was one remedy for congestion, and one of the most tempting arguments for Home Rule was that it would get rid of the Irish, and Irish legislation, together. Shorter and less frequent speeches were recommended rather than tried. More relief was promised by the creation of two Standing Committees, on Law and Trade. But the physical fact remained that there were not hours enough in the day for the House to get through its work, if half the hours were spent in the repetition of exhausted arguments and motions to adjourn. The New Rules of 1882 were designed to strengthen the hands of the Speaker or Chairman in controlling the course of debate: to reduce the opportunities of talking at large: to deliver the House from the habitual offender, while leaving it still at the mercy of the habitual bore. On the whole they produced their intended results: an occasional Irish night wasted less time than a constant blockade: they are the basis of modern Parliamentary procedure. But by the older hands they were accepted as a humiliating necessity; another melancholy proof that the days of government by gentlemen were over. Those who knew their precedents were not slow to remark that the Irish had learnt their tactics from the phalanx of Tory Colonels in 1870, bent on opposing the abolition of Army Purchase.

11

It was one of Lord Salisbury's paradoxes that only uncontentious legislation should be brought before Parliament: if it were contentious, then public opinion was not ripe for it. The notion that a party should enter office with a ready-made list of things it meant to do, begins to take hold in the years just after Palmerston's death, when the press rang with policies and predictions of what the returning spring of Liberalism would bring forth. This legislative ardour was somewhat checked by the experiences of 1868 to 1874, and not legislation, but relief from legislation, was the promise held out by Disraeli. Gladstone was in closer touch with the spirit of his time when, in 1880, he included neglect of legislation among the sins of his predecessor's Government. The charge was no truer than most of his statements about Disraeli, but it told. The age of programmes is on us, and of programmes Chamberlain was a master-maker.

12

13

To raise, by agitation, a powerful head of opinion; through the Caucus, to embody it in a solid well-drilled party; to cast it into legislative form, and then by means of the closure to force it swiftly through the Commons; these, to certain masterful and aggressive spirits, were the tactics proper to modern politics. Two difficulties indeed there were. One was the House of Lords and its incurable Conservatism, which sooner or later, and sometimes very soon indeed, assimilated even the Liberals who entered it. The other was the absence of any clear and definite object on which opinion could be excited. Between the Repeal of the Corn Laws and Home Rule, no domestic issue came before the public on which a powerful agitation could be founded and sustained: and the aspiring agitator was baffled not by any apathy of the public so much as by the distraction of its interests. Orators might thunder, processions might stream along the Embankment to testify against the insolence of the Lords in holding up the Franchise Bill in 1884, knowing all the while that the minds of the people were set not on the Lords or the Franchise, but on a lonely and heroic figure far away in Khartoum. Between Ireland and the Empire there was not room enough to plant an agitation or time enough for it to grow. The great Free Trade leaders were neither in office nor candidates for office, and could devote themselves for years wholly to one cause. The new Radicals had half a dozen causes on their hands, and the responsibilities, actual or future, of office as well. The Unauthorized Programme of 1885 was, to some serious minds, a portent of revolution. But a great deal of it was carried out by Conservatives who hardly remembered that it had ever been a programme at all.

14

If Lord Salisbury was right, or serious, it would follow that public discussion is of greater consequence than Parliamentary discussion. In this respect, the England of his prime was better served than it had ever been before. In argument, information, and style the higher journalism of the seventies and eighties had reached a remarkable level. First, in order of dignity, were the Liberal *Edinburgh* and the Conservative *Quarterly*, and the three new monthlies, the *Fortnightly*, the *Contemporary*, and the *Nineteenth Century*: the squibs and arrows of the *Saturday*; for Sunday reading the mellow gravity of the *Spectator*. In London there were eight dailies of the first political importance, in the provinces perhaps as many more. Salisbury himself, Gladstone, Harcourt, Dilke, Morley, Chamberlain, were constant contributors to the press. If the public was not well informed, it was not for want of instructors; and if the political leaders could not always commend their views, they could at least count on having them known and understood. Disraeli found that, in office, he could not write; and, out of office, he preferred to express himself in works of imagination. This reticence may have been designed, as it certainly assisted, to sustain the note of mystery which was so grateful to his inward ear. But it also kept him at a distance from the public, and it is probably true to say that the most famous scenes in his career were acted before an audience, of which the majority was hostile and the minority puzzled. He took no pains to stand well with educated opinion: the others did, and the Reviews were their forum.

15

To the people they spoke from another stage. Earlier Victorian history is punctuated with famous platform feats. From the later seventies the noise is continuous, the reverberations in the press incessant. The newspapers had begun to notice that the public was less interested in parliamentary debates than of old, but its appetite for oratory was insatiable. Whether it was an inherited craving for the spoken word, or the pleasure of making the great ones feel the

approval or the censure of the people, whether speeches satisfied
an intellectual or a dramatic taste, to hundreds of thousands
speech-going was a delight as keen as a Puritan's joy in sermons.
But on whichever side the orator takes his stand, what an ancient
would have called the Common Places are the same: justice and
freedom, welfare and security, the greatness of the Empire, its
dangers, its moral obligations; from which might be deduced, as
occasion served, the duty of giving votes to all men over twenty-
one, and of not giving votes to women at all; of staying in Egypt
and abandoning the Sudan; the capitulation to the Boers in 1881
and the defiance of Russia in 1885; Establishment in England and
Disestablishment in Wales. In issuing from the Curia to the
Forum, eloquence did not at once put off her senatorial robes, and
the speakers of the eighties, though none could recapture the
enchantment of Midlothian, could always rise, were expected by
their tense and patient audiences to rise above the sentiment and
invective* which is the staple of party speaking, to the reasoned
articulation of great principles, which is the essence of political
oratory. A sound body of political philosophy might still be
extracted from the rich information of Dilke and the fine reasoning of Courtney, the robust indiscretions of Salisbury, the close
argument of Goschen, and Hartington's grand good sense. We are
far from Limehouse still. But Lord Randolph had pointed the
16   way.

By 1886 every argument on either side of the Irish case had
been stated, confuted, reiterated, and shredded to the last syllable.
But still Mr. Gladstone was there, always ready to fan the tiring
ardour of his followers with a moral emotion which may seem to
17   us to be strangely in excess of the occasion. Surely it is possible to
be a religious man and an intelligent man, and yet not deem it
necessary to enter into the chamber of the soul, the recesses of the
heart, yea, the presence of Almighty God, when the question at
issue is whether in the last Irish tussle, the policeman or the
Ribbonman hit the other first; be it in politics or in poetry, few
English optics are fine enough to determine whether a pale light
in the western sky is the birth of a star or the dust above a Dublin
street fight. Released from power, the old man employed the most
wonderful resources of voice, presence, experience, fame, of

---

* In 1905 an old woman in Warwickshire warned a young candidate: 'We
don't like to hear the gentlemen becalling one another.'

scholarly and religious accomplishment, ever given to an English statesman, to keep Ireland before the eyes of a people already stirring away from Liberalism towards an Imperialism or a collectivism of which he understood nothing. But in those same years, the West Britons were gathering material for a new statement of Irish nationality, a new assault on the impermeable arrogance of the conqueror, and imparting to English thought not a little of their own resentment, impatience, and disaffection. To a foreigner, the age through which we ourselves have been living is the age of Galsworthy, Wells, and Shaw; before them of Wilde. Something, doubtless, beside literary enjoyment guides his taste, and in his malicious preference for what is most critical and most subversive, we catch an echo of that passionate jealousy of England which for a generation was the most widely diffused emotion in Europe, a generation when it seemed at times not wholly out of reckoning that a second League of Cambrai might be formed for the spoliation of a greater Venice. But two Irishmen in a list of four. It is to be thought of. 18

XXIV

THE Reform Movement of 1830 resulted in ten years of Whig government, and a sharp Conservative reaction. The Reform of 1867 gave the Liberals six years of office, and the Tories another six. The last extension of the suffrage in 1885 eclipsed them for six months and then put them in power for seventeen years. Disraeli's forecast that the enlarged electorate would be preponderantly Conservative was justified, but by accident perhaps as much as by any inner necessity. 1

The election of 1868 was fought, partly on a general, abstract Liberalism, and partly on the personality of Gladstone: and 1874 was far more a defeat for the Liberals than a victory for Conservatism. The country wanted not a programme but peace. The results of 1880 were equally astonishing to both parties, neither of whom had expected or feared much more than a slight majority either way. What the country hoped for, beyond the cessation of Imperialist adventure, it is not so easy to determine. Few of the myriads who waited in the snow for hours to hear Mr. Gladstone speak, held up their babies to see him pass, and decorated their tables with Sweet Williams, could have guessed that in five years they would be called upon to make their choice between the abandonment of a lifelong loyalty, and surrender to the Irish party.

Practical men, without underrating the other elements in the catastrophe of 1880, were disposed to assign no small part of the results to the working of the Caucus, or as it was often called, the Birmingham System, the organization on a democratic basis of the whole party in the borough. But in 1880 the borough for electoral purposes was still the borough for municipal purposes: burgesses and voters could be organized on parallel lines, and rewarded for their political constancy by municipal honours, appointments, and contracts. The Act of 1885 which broke up the boroughs into single-member constituencies, made it less easy to drill or corrupt the constituents. The Caucus had not time to take root, and the course of events was against it. In 1886 the Birmingham Caucus stayed Liberal. Chamberlain went Unionist and carried Birmingham with him.

The Liberal split had other consequences. Hitherto, the historical parties had not been unevenly represented at all levels of society, and of the two, the Whig houses were more conspicuous than the Tory. But as they crossed the floor, the balance altered. There was a concentration of wealth, titled and untitled, on the Unionist side, and there ought to have been a corresponding concentration of Radicalism—or Socialism—on the Liberal side. But the chief Radical crossed the floor too. History seemed to have decided once more, as in the thirties, that while there was room for Whigs and Tories, or Liberals and Conservatives, there was no room for any one else. The debates of two centuries had channelled the political landscape down to bedrock, and into one of the two great streams all the minor affluents must find their way, or be wasted in the desert.

But meanwhile, partly from the natural operation of time, and partly, no doubt, from the delicate impulsions which Disraeli gave to that operation, the relations of the Crown with Ministers and people had been subtly transformed. Between them, the Queen and the Prince Consort had created a position which the Queen alone could not fill. For a while the Albertine practice had kept its sway; vigilant, impartial, imperturbable. Then a character, long suppressed, gradually lifted its head: vigilant indeed, laborious, fearlessly truthful: but excitable, impassioned and self-willed: Melbourne's Victoria, grown middle-aged; respected for her virtues and pitied for her sorrows, rather than loved, as she was hereafter to be loved by a people to whom her Consort had become a dim figure of their fathers' time: who had long forgiven, if ever they remembered, the acerbity of her warfare with one Minister, the too compliant ear she turned to the Imperial wiles of another. In 1870 perhaps the most general, though secret, opinion among thoughtful observers was that the virtues of its wearer would preserve the Crown for one successor, hardly for more than one. Professed or active republicans were few, and the spectacle of Paris had diminished their numbers: but the scandalized horror with which the Commons howled down Auberon Herbert's avowal of his principles in 1872 may have masked a certain misgiving. Republican simplicity is appropriate to a Republic: but a Court which does not allure the intelligent, attract the smart, or dazzle the many, makes the worst of both worlds if it is not frugal as well: and Victoria's demands for dowries and allowances were unconscionable. Fifty-three members voted to reduce the grant to Prince Arthur, Duke of Connaught, and the invective with which Gladstone met Dilke's request for light upon the Civil List was heard in a glum silence on the Liberal benches. It is worth reflecting—it is a pity Victoria did not reflect—what a turn our history might have taken if the greatest Liberal of all time had not been to his innermost fibre penetrated with a veneration for all ancient, all established things: for the Church, the Universities, the Aristocracy, the Crown. 3

The lengthening experience of the Queen, laid up in a most retentive and faithful memory, was making her an excellent person to talk things over with; if she had mastered the nervous horror of London which drove her to Balmoral and Osborne, and had kept her Ministers under the charm at Buckingham Palace, her influence would have grown with her experience; if she had been a woman on the intellectual level of her Consort, her influence might have become very great. On three occasions after the Prince's death she intervened with decisive effect: in checking the hysterical fussiness with which Palmerston and Russell were behaving over Schleswig-Holstein under the grim contemptuous eyes of Bismarck; in promoting the passage of the Reform Bill of

1867; in releasing the deadlock of the Houses over Reform and Redistribution in 1884. But Disraeli made her a partisan: the hoarded experience which might have been freely at the disposal of all her Ministers was reserved for such favourites as Salisbury and Rosebery, and the influence was dissipated in reprimands and injunctions, often shrewd, always vigorous, but sometimes petulant and sometimes petty.

But on the people the figure of the Queen was growing in power and fascination. Her Conservatism did her no harm with a nation which was beginning to think, and dream, and shout Imperially, and which, politically, was outgrowing certain of the limitations of its fathers. Early Victorian England, with some of the defects, had the one great merit at least of oligarchic government: a clear and rational political philosophy. Certain men, whose rank and wealth gives them influence and standing, are appointed by the respectable classes to consult for the people, to the end that they may be well ordered. Of these, the most influential and capable are in turn selected to administer the finances and the chief offices of State. They are Ministers of the Crown, but like Pitt in Johnson's famous distinction, they are ministers given to the Crown by the people; that is by the limited and stable body of householders and freeholders, by whom in turn they are judged, upheld or removed. The mere existence of a Crown in such a system imparts an element of mystery and make-believe not very easy to reconcile with its philosophy. Rationally considered, the Monarchy was only an accident, a legal fiction or an historical survival; and if Victoria and her young husband had chosen to devote themselves entirely to the other avocations and accomplishments of their class, to travel, society, and good works, the machinery of Government could with very little difficulty have been adjusted to gratify their wishes; the wheels would have revolved without any loss of power from their abstention.

Walter Bagehot's restatement of the philosophy of the Constitution in 1867, turns on two points for which the stricter theory, Whig or Radical, had not provided. One is, the presence in every community of an irrational appetite, call it emotional or imaginative, which Monarchy satisfies, and also stimulates; a desire for dignity, serenity, and grandeur. The other is the advantage, even the necessity, of having somewhere in the state a person beyond the competition for office, who is entitled to be heard in any

matter on which he may think it his duty to speak; who has the
right to warn, to encourage, and, therefore, to be consulted by,
the agents of authority.

Of Victoria it must be said that she did associate herself in too
lively a manner with the competition for office, she did speak too
often on matters which were not within her competence; her
distribution of warning and encouragement was far from impartial; and her facility in reproof exposed her to snubs which her
wiser consort would never have allowed her to incur. Now that
her relations with her ministers are known with some degree of
intimacy, it is permissible to say that if she never overstepped the
limits of her admitted powers, she did not always behave well
within them: she did her duty, but often with a reluctance and
temper which in a more critical age might have been even
dangerously resented. In so doing, she undoubtedly weakened the
political authority of the Crown. But, more and more fully with
advancing years, she was able to satisfy the imagination of her
people: such resentment as the followers of Mr. Gladstone not
unjustly felt—and feel still—could do nothing against a Queen so
august, so homely, so doubly armed with the reverence and affection of her people: and rational criticism of the Monarchy was as
powerless, because as irrelevant, as it always is when applied to
any creation of affection, reverence, and imagination.

To go below the respectable class for voters, and to oust the
gentlemen from government, is Democracy: and, as the Queen
once said 'a democratic monarchy is what she never will belong
to'. The elections of 1868 showed a voting strength, in England,   6
of a little over 2,000,000; in Scotland, about 150,000; in Ireland,
less than 100,000. The redistribution of seats had left England,
south of the Thames, and apart from London, with 119 members,
against 101 for the six Northern counties. Eighty peers had sons in
the Lower House. Democracy, it was plain, was advancing at no
formidable pace: and the elections of 1874 showed an equally well
marked fondness for old ways and old families. Even 1880,
though it planted two advanced Radicals, if not Republicans,
Fawcett and Dilke, in office, and Chamberlain in the Cabinet, did
not make any violent alteration in the general composition of
Governments and Parliaments. In Beaconsfield's Cabinet of
thirteen, there were six peers: in Gladstone's of fourteen there
were five.

For the measure which was to change completely the old political landscape of England, the two parties made themselves jointly
responsible. The Franchise Bill of 1884, by extending the household and lodger franchise to the counties, added some 2,000,000
voters to an electorate of 3,000,000. The Conservatives insisted
that a Redistribution Bill should be produced as well, and by their
majority in the Lords they were able to suspend the Franchise Bill
until their demand was satisfied. To the other alarms of an anxious
year was added the prospect of a conflict between the Houses, and
a concerted attack on the Lords by Chamberlain and the Radicals.
But, privately asked to say what they wanted, the Conservative
leaders produced a plan even more drastic than the Cabinet had
contemplated. No less than 107 boroughs, with a Parliamentary
history often going back to the origins of the Constitution, were
to be swept away, and 166 seats released for redistribution, Yorkshire getting 18, Lancashire 24, London and its suburbs 37. It is
impossible not to share some at least of the regrets with which
contemporaries regarded the disappearance of the little boroughs,
and the variegated representation of interests which their existence
had ensured. The independent member may have been correctly
defined as the member whom no one could depend on, but his
presence saved Parliament from becoming merely the register of
party opinions. The success of the Birmingham Caucus had given
party managers a new idea of their importance and power; and
there were plenty of candidates ready to pay for their admission to
a political career by bargains which the traditions of the political
class had hitherto discountenanced. 'The old type of judicial
member,' Salisbury told the Queen, 'who sat loose to party, and
7 could be trusted to be fair, has disappeared. They are all partisans:'
delegates, bound by the contract that if the electors vote as the
candidate asks them, the member shall think as the organization
bids him: 'greedy place-seekers', the Queen sobbed, 'who do not
8 care a straw for what their old sovereign suffers,' bearers of such
unhistoric names as Asquith and Morley and Bryce.

XXV

But if we survey this landscape in another light, we are aware of a certain fading of one familiar tint. An observer from a distant planet, able to watch the seasonal changes on the earth's surface, would have noticed that everywhere the golden area was growing, except in England, where the green was winning against the gold. He would rightly have concluded that a change of cultivation was in progress. He would not have known that he was witnessing the end of a social order.

That English farming was the best in the world, all the world acknowledged. It had to be, because, as the saying went, with wheat at fifty shillings it only began to pay after a crop of twenty-eight bushels to the acre had been got. One might, perhaps, say further, that a wealthy landowner, understanding the economics of agriculture, a farmer master of its practice, a village not over populated, with pure water, decent houses, allotments, and a school, made up the most successful experiment in social organization that England had so far seen. There were, it is true, many points at which the experiment might go wrong. The landlord might be encumbered: the rain unseasonable. 'Is there anything about the weather in your rules?' a farmer once asked his Union men. But so long as prices kept up, a new landlord or a good harvest might put all right again. In the war year, 1855, wheat was at 74s. After 1877 it never touched 50s. again;* in 1884 it dipped below 40s.; in 1894 it was at 22s., and the harvest of that year of panic sold at 19s. The grazing counties stood the storm best. But, the corn counties were stricken, it seemed, beyond recovery. Great wars have been less destructive of wealth than the calamity which stretched from 1879 the wettest,† to 1894 the driest, year in memory.

Never again was the landed proprietor to dominate the social fabric. Indeed, if the broad acres of the gentry had been acres of wheat and grassland only, there would soon have been a cry for a Land Purchase Act in England as well as in Ireland. But they were

* I am referring to the yearly average.
† This is the year of Tennyson's lines:

> The cuckoo of a joyless June
> Is calling through the dark.

acres of coal and acres of dock: they included the most fashionable
streets in London, the most popular watering places, miles of
suburban villa and wastes of urban slum. For two generations,
moreover, the surplus profits of the land had passed into industry
or commerce or foreign bonds. The agricultural depression completed the evolution from a rural to an industrial state which the
application of steam to machinery had begun, and it accelerated
the further evolution from an industrial to a financial state.

Great figures, Derby, Shaftesbury, Salisbury, Hartington,
Spencer, still kept the aristocratic idea alive and forcible. But
gradually the deference which had been directed to birth, when
birth meant commonly land and wealth, moved, as the land grew
poorer, towards wealth itself. And not only the landed man, but
the merchant and manufacturer also were coming to be overshadowed by the financier, the swiftness of his winnings, the riot
of his display.* When in 1890 it was revealed that the old and
sober house of Baring had lost its foothold in the torrent of
4 foreign speculation, it was revealed also that hardly one English
name figured any longer among the leaders of high finance. As the
historic associations of wealth grew fainter, the imaginative or
sentimental defence of inequality grew less assured: the world
which had taken it as a natural thing that a Duke of Devonshire
should grow the Victoria Regia in a glass-house like an Arabian
palace, grew restive when Whittaker Wright began to display his
ill-gotten glory in a subaqueous billiard room on the Surrey
5 Heaths. It would have been hard to find even a Conservative who
felt for a rich man, or a titled man, as such, the respect which Early
Victorians had, not wrongly, paid to the founders of great industries or the heads of historic houses, on whose capacity they depended for good government and progress. There is a taint in the
air recalling the corruption of the Second Empire, and the leanings
of the Prince of Wales gave the new plutocracy a standing which
cast some shadow over the whole world of rank and splendour.

---

* There had been bursts of company promoting before, in the twenties,
forties, and sixties. But the first man to appreciate the unlimited possibilities
of limited liability was Albert Gottheim, otherwise Baron Grant, towards
whose great house on the outskirts of Kensington Palace, a trustful public had
contributed, it was reckoned, some twenty million pounds.

3
Honours a King can give, honour he can't:
And Grant without honour is a Baron Grant.

Men spoke still of the land, but more and more the land was coming to mean house property or industrial sites. If it be true that in the long run every country gets the land law that its soil and circumstances require, history seemed to have determined that England was made for landlord and tenant, and Ireland for the Peasant Proprietor. But no owner of rural property expected to make a trading profit, and an old rule laid it down that no gentleman should try to get more from his land than he would have got from its value in Government Stock. Urban property, on the other hand, might at any moment owe a sudden and enormous increment of value to some shift of population; to a new industry, a new railway station, a new municipal tramline; and the public was equitably entitled to a share in the wealth which it had created.* In this way, the nebulous project of land nationalization came to be condensed about one topic, the principle of betterment and the taxation of site values. In 1889 the new London County Council projected a Bill to secure for the ratepayer the whole of the increment due to public improvement. So far and so fast are we moving. So necessary is it for us to recall from time to time that we are in an age of transition: to remember, for example, that a boy who had heard Arnold say that railways had given the death blow to feudalism, might have lived to hear Bernard Shaw say that dynamite had given the death blow to capitalism, or Bramwell at the British Association in 1881 prophesy that within the lifetime of his audience steam would have made way for internal combustion. In that audience, doubtless, there were gentlemen whose lands were still ploughed with oxen.

But along with this dipping of the balance from country to town, we can discern another process at work, which, if the word had not been taken for other purposes, might most compactly have been described as the socialization of wealth. Economists may talk of the manufacturer or the labourer. But on a closer view, one is rather the symbol of a ramifying organization, the ownership of which rests in innumerable shareholding hands;† the other, a unit

6

7

8

---

* Which follows strictly from Ricardian doctrine. Because, if rent is the price of all differential advantages, any advantage bestowed by the community properly belongs to it.

† Of the scale on which trade was now thinking, Sir Henry Eliot's project for amalgamating the whole coal industry into a single trust is the most grandiose example.

in a disciplined force, which, if it supports him when he cannot work, may compel him to remain idle when he could. One becomes aware, too, when projects of expenditure are under discussion, of a subtle shift of speech. The older generation tends to speak of the taxpayer, the younger of the State. With reason, because the electorate of 1832 to 1867 had to pay its own way. After 1867, much more after 1885, there is a feeling abroad that the electors have only to give their orders; some one else will meet the bill.* The control of industry is more searching and regular; the volume of departmental legislation grows yearly. Free Trade is no longer an unquestioned dogma; even compulsory military service can be debated. In Forster's phrase, the nations are massing themselves; the temperature is rising under the inter-pressure of competition; and the rocky core of old individualism is being metamorphosed into something new. We may think of English history in the years, let us say between the Jubilees, the years of the great London strikes and the first Colonial Conference, as the epilogue to one age, or the prehistory of another. One picture is dissolving fast. Into what pattern the emergent lines and colours will fall, we cannot tell. But the proud and sober confidence which irradiates the mid-Victorian landscape, that will not be seen again.

XXVI

WHEN I think of old people I remember, people whose first memories were rich with stories of how Nelson stood and how Nelson fell; who saw the prentices marching with marrow-bones and cleavers through the streets of the City in 1821,† and heard

* In the common discourse of the seventies and eighties, this is the meaning of Socialism; so that a Radical capitalist who was in favour of Disendowment and expropriation of the landowner might call himself a Socialist, as Chamberlain sometimes did.

† As I have never seen their song in print, I may as well set it down, as it was told me by one who had heard it:

> May Scotland's thistle never grow,
> May Ireland's shamrock never blow,
> May the Rose of England still decay,
> Till the Queen of England's gained the day.

the great bell of St. Paul's tolling in 1901; of the next generation, whose span covered the last stage-coach and the first aeroplane, who had sat waiting for news from Lucknow and Sebastopol, and lived to listen for the guns defending London; when I consider their assured morality, their confident acceptance of the social order, their ready undertaking of its obligations; I have a sense of solidity, tenacity, and uniformity, which all the time I know to be in large part an illusion of distance, and I shall have failed of my purpose if I have not made it clear that the very word 'Victorian' may be used to mask a fallacy and a misconception.

I was born when the Queen had still nearly nineteen years to reign; I saw her twice, Gladstone once; I well remember the death of Newman and Tennyson, and my earliest recollection of the Abbey brings back the flowers fresh on Browning's grave. But if I place myself in 1900, and then look forward for thirty-six years, and backward for as many, I feel doubtful whether the changes made in the earlier time were not greater than anything I have seen since. I am speaking of changes in men's minds, and I cannot in my own time observe anything of greater consequence than the dethronement of ancient faith by natural science and historical criticism, and the transition from oligarchic to democratic representation. Yet the generation whose memories went back another thirty-six years had seen and felt changes surely as great: the political revolution of 1830, the economic and social revolution produced by the railway and the steamship, the founding of the great Dominions. I read constantly that the Victorians did this and the Victorians believed that; as if they had all lived within the sound of the town-crier's bell, and at all times behaved, and thought, and worshipped with the disciplined unanimity of a city state on a holy day. I ask myself, Who are these Victorians? By what mark are we to know them? What creed, what doctrine, what institution was there among them which was not at some time or other debated or assailed?

I can think of two only: Representative Institutions and the Family.* I am speaking of sincere debate and earnest assault, of doubts widely felt, and grounded on the belief that there is a better way: and for the ordering of public and private life that age could imagine none better. I know that at times its fancy, flushed perhaps by Carlyle, would stray towards some simpler, more

* If anyone chooses to substitute 'monogamic idealism about sex', he may. 2

heroic mode of government; and that it was not very willing, could readily find reasons for not being willing, to extend the best mode of government to lesser breeds without the law. But, within the pale of civilized humanity, it had no doubts that Representative Institutions, if they were safeguarded from corruption, and if they were dominated by men with a high sense of the common good, afforded the only sure guarantee of public improvement or even stability. They were preservative, they were educative; they reconciled rulers and ruled, the cohesion of society with the rights and aspirations of its members; and the natural shortcomings of all representative bodies, vacillation, short views, slowness in action, were a price worth paying for their inestimable advantages. If, indeed, upon these there were induced faction and deliberate obstruction, then the future took a greyer colour. An age of great cities, Bagehot once said, requires strong Government. An age of great armaments and swift decisive movements by land and sea, required a corresponding rapidity and certainty of authority. Eyes turned anxiously and admiringly towards Germany, her precision and thoroughness, the intelligence with which she was mapping out her future, the energy with which her government provided for the health and good order of her towns.

Really, the elements of strong government were here all the time, if we knew how to use them. The Benthamites had seen, long ago, where the secret lay; and if, as we are told, the ghost of Bentham sometimes walks in Gower Street, it must have danced on the night when Ritchie's Local Government Bill was carried in 1888. That measure might be quoted in proof of Lord Salisbury's paradox. No one had agitated for it; few were greatly interested in it; it was brought out of the departmental pigeonhole where Dilke had left it, was accepted with almost universal approval, and may, without much exaggeration, be said to have transformed the tissue of English existence. Ritchie left the School Boards and the Guardians to be absorbed later. When the transfer of power was complete, the entire range of ordinary life, from birth, or even before birth, to burial, had been brought within the ambit of public interest and observation. In the middle, like a Tudor gateway worked into a modern building, remains the joint control of the Justices and the County Council over the constabulary. Otherwise, the whole system, now so comprehensive and searching, is nothing but the logical evolution of the Benthamite formula—local representation controlled by central experience, public zeal guided by professional knowledge.   4

The other vital article of the common Victorian faith is less easy to analyse. The Family may be regarded as of Divine institution, as a Divine appointment for the comfort and education of mankind. Or it may be thought of as a mode of social organization, based on certain primary facts, the natural attraction of the sexes and the long infancy of the human creature, and affording on the whole, with all its defects, the most satisfactory provision for that education and comfort. A very cursory observation of human affairs is, indeed, enough to show that the attraction may be as transient as it is powerful; that relations within the family family may be both painful and oppressive; and that, while the cessation of affection between the spouses is likely to make itself quickly felt, disaffection between parents and children may smoulder unseen to the mischief of both. To the religious man or woman, boy or girl, the trouble will appear as a cross to be borne, an infirmity or even a sin to be overcome: to others, as a misfortune to be endured as long as possible and then, if possible, thrown off.

The increasing secularism of English thought might have been expected to compel a more critical attitude to the family than in fact we find. Sexual ethic had attracted to itself so great a body of romantic sentiment: it was so closely associated, and even identified, with virtue in general, with the elevated, the praiseworthy, the respectable life, that the faintest note of dissidence might attract a disproportionate volume of suspicion and censure. Examples crowd on one's memory. I will mention only one. In 1873, on the death of Mill, a public memorial was proposed. The story of his youthful Malthusian activities was revived, and Mr. Gladstone ostentatiously withdrew his support.   5

I do not believe that we are at a sufficient distance from the Victorian age to judge with perfect fairness its prevalent philosophy in a matter where only the utmost vigilance can prevent our thought from being at once clouded and coloured with, often unconscious, emotion. I have already indicated what I believe to to be two vital elements in the analysis; physical recoil, exaggerating the ordinary asceticism of religion, and the necessary dependence of the women as a body in society, on the men. To these

must be added the tighter domestic discipline that came from the
management of large families: a discipline not yet enlightened—
or distracted—by the psychological explorations which may perhaps, in the long run, prove to be the decisive achievements of our
age. To go further would, in an Essay of this brevity, be to go too
far. I will only record my belief—and I think I remember enough,
and have read and thought enough to give my belief some weight
—that the preoccupation, social or personal, with one emotion
and its manifestations was mischievous; that it produced much
falsehood and much injustice, much suffering and much cruelty;
but that, on the other hand, in the circumstances of the age, the
instinct of the age was sound in regarding romantic love as the
right starting-point for the family, and family life, administered
with sympathy and intelligence, as the right training ground for
the generations in their succession:

sic fortis Etruria crevit,

scilicet et facta est rerum pulcherrima Roma.

6

The incidents and circumstances, too, of this life: its durable
furniture and stated hours; its evening reading and weekly church-
going; its long-prepared and long-remembered holidays; its
appointed visits from and to the hierarchy of grandparents, uncles,
aunts, and cousins; a life which did not differ in essentials whether
the holiday was spent at Balmoral or Broadstairs; gave to those
who were within it a certain standing with themselves, and a cheerful confidence in the face of novelty, which is perhaps the clue to
the Victorian paradox—the rushing swiftness of its intellectual
advance, and the tranquil evolution of its social and moral ideals.
The advance was in all directions outwards, from a stable and
fortified centre. Of certain reformers of his own day, Morris
tartly remarked that their aim was to turn the working classes
into middle classes. Of Victorian reform as a whole the aim was
the steady diffusion of culture and comfort downwards and outwards in widening circles. This was the ideal which Mill be-
queathed to his disciples, and the better mind of the later nineteenth century was still guided, if no longer dominated, by the
thought of Mill; and it could best be pictured to the imagination
as such a way of life as the middle classes had fashioned for themselves in their families.*

7

8

* The books which, taken together, seem to me to give the truest idea of

XXVII

IN an age of swift transition we constantly need some mark by which to register the rate of change. Especially is this true in a time, and in a country, where change proceeded, as perhaps it always will proceed, rather by massive internal transformation than by any outward or forcible readjustments. The seventies grow out of the sixties, with a slight acceleration after the death of Palmerston, the eighties grow out of the seventies, as the fifties out of the forties. But then; take any test that comes to hand; take, for example, the new, unpietistic handling of childhood by Lewis Carroll, Mrs. Ewing, Mrs. Molesworth; or in the drawings of Du Maurier. A whole world of pious, homiletic convention has passed away, and who can say for certain how and when and why?* The stirring and good-humoured fifties had left a grace and lightness behind them, which we can feel in the dress and decoration of the time; in the layout of dinner tables, no longer burdened with gargantuan tureens and processional silver camels: in the freer fancy and franker manners of fiction. We can hear it in the urbane ironic prose which came natural to a generation whose wisest head was Walter Bagehot; and which, when wielded by Matthew Arnold, kept old Nonconformity in a state of hissing, bubbling wrath. The truculent, the pompous, the gushing, in literature or manners, are still there, but they are not the mode. It is a time of relaxation, and yet with the old undertone of gravity and responsibility. It is the time of George Eliot. Looked at from the Early Victorian years it is a time of licence, of an unrestrained and dangerous scepticism, a perilous trifling with the essential decencies of society and sex. Looking back, we may see it as a time of excessive caution and reserve. Both pictures would be true. Let any one think, for example, of *Middlemarch*, exactly poised between *Esmond* and *Tess of the D'Urbervilles*: and compare the earnest and searching psychology

---

family life, its standards and morals, in the Victorian age, are the first volume of *Praeterita*, *David Copperfield*, Mrs. Ewing's *Six to Sixteen*, the (anonymous) *Book with Seven Seals*, and Mrs. Hughes's *London Child of the Seventies*.

   * It is amusing to find the *British Quarterly* (a Nonconformist organ) standing up in 1868 for *Tom Brown* and *Alice* against *Eric* and goody books in general.

with which the conscience of Bulstrode is explored, and the
4 strange reticence which veils the life of Dorothea with Casaubon.

Or, consider more generally the position of women in 1850
and a generation later; their attitude to themselves and society;
of society to them. At the base, no doubt, we shall find unchanged
a solid block of what some may call convention, some instinct,
and some prejudice; a dislike of disturbance, a real care for the
finer qualities of women, and a genuine fear of the consequences
if they are led out of their proper sphere into a world where, if
they are unsuited to it, they will be wasted; if suited, they may
undersell the men. But at a higher level we encounter the philosophic man, like Mill and Fawcett, who will admit no inequality
of status unless some utilitarian cause can be shown: an attitude
shared by many plain men who cannot see why Miss Nightingale
should not have a vote, and secretly hold that even in the House
of Commons a Women's party could not possibly be a greater
nuisance than an Irish party. There are the professional men, like
5 Henry Sidgwick,* scholars and physicians, for whom sex is
irrelevant to the work in hand. And there are, most effective
perhaps of all, the social observers, of whom Meredith is the type,
to whom a society with women on the secondary plane, without,
therefore, the collisions from which the purifying spark of comedy
7 flies, is a society half finished.

Women's suffrage is not at any time in the nineteenth century
an obtrusive or even a prominent issue in public affairs. It could
not be until there was a sufficient number of women able to conduct a political movement. But those who were able had already
tested their strength and shown that it could be formidable.
Between 1864 and 1868 Parliament, alarmed for the health of
soldiers and sailors, had sanctioned a system for controlling
prostitution, which might be, and in some instances, undoubtedly
was, most gravely misused. Encouraged by Mill and guided by
Fawcett, a group of educated women set out to repeal the ob-

---

* Asked to name his favourite heroine, he wrote Rose Jocelyn. This was
when *Evan Harrington* (1861) was new. No one in the company had ever heard of
her. Swinburne's favourite was Violet North—and who has ever heard of her?
But, put the two together and you get a fair idea of what intelligent men were
attracted by in 1860–80. Back to Sophia Western, and to Beatrice! Saintsbury's
selection, Diana Vernon, Argemone Lavington, and Elizabeth Bennet, shows
6 the same leaning towards the 'frank, young merchant'.

noxious Act. By their exertions, a government candidate was defeated at one by-election, and a Cabinet Minister nearly defeated at another.* From this success it might safely have been deduced that the enfranchisement of women was in the long run inevitable, if only for the reason that no party could afford to lose such efficient allies. But it was never a party question. Strong advocates could be found in both camps; John Bright changed sides,† and the most virile and persistent opponent of women's rights was a Liberal whose experience of life, though he remained unmarried, was generally known to be in all other respects of an exceptional breadth. As early as 1884, ninety-eight Conservatives voted for an enfranchising amendment. In spite of James, as many Liberals would no doubt have voted with them, had not their leader intimated that the question of Women's Franchise was too sacred to be discussed on a Franchise Bill.‡

It is not here that we must look for the ground of the social transformation that our own time has seen, but in the rapid improvement and extension of women's education, and their increasing activity in the professions and Universities, in local administration, in philanthropic work, in the Inspectorates. 'Women', wrote one of the wisest of them, 'are certainly great fools', and if she could have heard some of the cruder feminist utterances of the later Victorian time, she might have doubted whether a hundred years had made much difference. But she would have seen, too, over the whole range of criticism and intelligence, women becoming an effective element in the articulation of the social mind. She would have seen the weight of accomplishments and attractiveness lifting, and the number of things a woman can do or think, without discredit or censure, increasing yearly. She would have seen another burden lifting too.§ About 1875 the birth-rate in the provident and educated classes begins to fall. The Respectable Family is shrinking: and it

8

9

10

11

* Childers at Pontefract, the first election by ballot.

† His reasons are interesting. One was that women had not much to complain of. The other, that they were unduly susceptible to clerical influence.

‡ The cross-voting in 1897 is curious:

> Aye: Balfour, Dilke, Haldane.
> No: Asquith, Chamberlain, Bryce.

§ The earliest public discussion of this topic I have noted is in the *Fortnightly Review*, 1872.

is, though very faintly yet, beginning to lose its old patriarchal cohesion. It is a strange world we look out on when we stand on the slope of the Victorian age and watch the great lights setting: a world which would have startled and dismayed many of those who had helped to make it. But two of them could have faced it with a high confidence. One is Bentham. The other is Mary Wollstonecraft.

<h2 style="text-align:center">XXVIII</h2>

THE great lights are sinking fast. Darwin has gone, Carlyle and George Eliot. Browning, Newman and Tennyson are nearing their term. So long and steadily had they shone that it was not easy to think of the world under other constellations. We are in such a twilight, such a pause again, as we observed sixty years before. But what meteor is this proceeding with as much noise as light across the sky? Once it was Bulwer: now it is Kipling. In their sudden and world-wide popularity they stand together, and the contrast between the sentimental exuberance of the one, and the aggressive ebullience of the other, does not go very deep. The introversion of the early time, its mournful and Byronic self-contemplation, had been relaxed, and turned outward on the world until it was ready to explode into a muscular and masterful

1   self-expression.

When Er the Pamphylian in Plato's *Republic* watched the souls choosing their destiny, he saw one who chose power, having lived its last life in a well-ordered state, practising virtue without

2   philosophy. It is no bad account of the ideal which the mid-Victorian patriciate, the Arnoldians, the Christian Socialists, the believers in God's earth and the healthy mind, transmitted to their successors of the age of iron and empire. More faithfully than any of the sister nations, England had cherished the Renaissance figure of the Courtier, the man of bodily and social accomplishment and learning subdued to an accomplishment, a man of authority but a ready servant of the State. The success of the old public schools for their own purposes, the downward and outward extension of their notions and observances, had given this ideal a wide diffusion throughout English society. But the public schools were designed rather for a governing than an administrative class, for

an aristocracy than for a clerisy, and while an aristocracy can live   3
a long while on its conventions, it is the business of a clerisy to
keep all conventions under review, to maintain an informed and
critical resistance against the propagandist, the advertiser and all
other agents of the mass-mind. The charge against the higher
education of the Late Victorian age is that it surrendered the freedom it was meant to guard. In a world of exact progressive knowledge, where the foundations not of belief only but of daily habit
were perishing, the public schools overstressed and standardized
ideals which were becoming inadequate to the conduct of modern
life, and they did not adjust the balance by breadth of observation
or fineness of reasoning. They preserved, indeed, some of the
most precious things of the past: not untruly can the spirit of
Sidney say, over some who were born in the last Victorian years,
Agnosco discipulos scholae meae. But the larger and freer upbringing   4
of the earlier Victorians made them a more receptive and independent audience for literature and science, for philosophic or
political controversy; and for this closing of the general intelligence, this replacement of the fresh and vigorous curiosity of the
former generation by a vaguely social, vaguely moral, vaguely
intellectual convention, the public schools must take their share of
blame.

Their share only, in a process of greater sweep. It would not be
difficult to draw a parallel between the political, economic, and
intellectual development of England from the middle to the end
of the nineteenth century, a parallel which would be in some
ways, no doubt, fanciful, but in many ways instructive. The
rounded and solid culture of the mid-Victorians corresponds to
the golden age of the staple industries. In a limited electorate, the
educated classes, like the manufacturing and mercantile classes,
still counted as a body; and science, fast as it was growing, was not
yet either so extensive or minute that its achievements could not
be followed and borne in mind. The public which bought 100,000
copies of the *Cornhill* when Thackeray was editor, supported the
stout quarterlies, and paid toll to the proprietor of the *Athenaeum*
at the rate of £7,000 a year clear profit, was, if not a well-informed   5
public, at least a public that desired to take care of its mind, a
public trained in the keen debates of the Oxford and Free Trade
movements, and ready to act as jury if not judge in any controversy that might arise in future. But by successive stages, in 1867

and 1885, the educated class was disfranchised, while the advance of the arts and sciences was withdrawing them from the observation and practice of the individual educated man. Simultaneously the lead of the great industries was shortening: and, in compensation, capital, labour, and intelligence were flowing away to light industry, distribution, salesmanship.* After the age of the great producers: Armstrong, Whitworth, Brassey, comes the age of great shops and great advertisers. Famous names still kept our station in a world which had no naturalist to equal Darwin, and no physicist to surpass Clerk Maxwell, but the springs of invention are failing, and, for the successors of the Arkwrights and Stephensons we must look to America, to France, even to Italy. And where shall we look for the successors of the Mills and Ruskins and Tennysons? Or of the public for which they wrote? The common residual intelligence is becoming impoverished for the benefit of the specialist, the technician, and the aesthete: we leave behind us the world of historical ironmasters and banker historians, geological divines and scholar tobacconists, with its genial watchword: to know something of everything and everything of something: and through the gateway of the Competitive Examination we go out into the Waste Land of Experts, each knowing so much about so little that he can neither be contradicted nor is worth contradicting.

The shrinkage of native genius, or the cooling of native ardour, or the dying down, perhaps, of the old austerer impulses: Protestantism, Self-improvement, Respectability: had left the English mind open to fresh stimulation from without, from France in one way, Germany in another, from Russia, even from Norway. The first Romantic generation had fed, with equal zest, on German fantasy and German philosophy. The next was less susceptible to foreign influences; and the poetry and fiction, the history, art, and economics of mid-Victorian England have all a racy home-made flavour. Some lines of contact were, of course,

---

* It was this readjustment that produced the *malaise* of the eighties. There is an admirable study of the process by Giffen (British Association, 1887) though I do not think he allows enough for the destruction of agricultural values. On this, the best work known to me is *Lage der Englischen Landwirthschaft*, 1896, by König, a thoroughly competent and sympathetic observer. The troubles of London in the eighties might be read as a local Malthusian tension—the result of an influx of disbanded labour from the country, and the stoppage of expenditure following on falling rents.

6

kept open: through the Austins, for example, with Germany; through Mill and the Grotes with France; and the influence of Mazzini might repay some study. But, later, we become aware of [8] a more general, deflecting, pressure from the Continent, and even a certain dominance of continental ideas.

There had always been those who urged a closer acquaintance with French ways, to whom the clarity of the French mind and the social ease of French life were as attractive as the loose, provincial heaviness of English thought, style, and manners was repellent. From Matthew Arnold's early time in the fifties, this French influence steadily increases, repaying the inspiration which had regenerated French poetry and painting in the days of Constable and Scott. It reawakened our art, which to foreign eyes had been asleep for two generations; to our literature it gave fresh standards of accomplishment. A living critic has described the shock of embarrassment and pain with which a generation, toiling after Flaubert in pursuit of the Right Word, read how Trollope did his daily stint of writing before setting out to hunt, or organize the country mails. The quest which led to *Treasure* [9] *Island* was not on a false trail. [10]

But, as the Elizabethans knew, an addiction to foreign ways is a powerful dissolvent of English propriety, and the impact of French Naturalism, in particular, was certain, sooner or later, to call for the intervention of the police. To bards and painters a certain limited eccentricity had always been permitted, but the notion of art as an enclosed world, obedient to its own laws only, did not come easily to a race which took its pictures much as it took its tunes, less for the excellence of the work than the pleasure of the response; and thought of the painter as an upper-class decorator, a recorder of domestic incident, winning landscapes, and right sentiments. On this level the Victorian enjoyment of art [11] was sincere, and curiously uniform. On the whole, what Lord Landsowne liked, the people liked, much as Penny Readings preferred the authors whom Queen Victoria read. How often one has seen this old community of tastes on the bookshelf of a cottage parlour or a country inn: the Works of Tennyson, the Works of Longfellow; some Bulwer, some Macaulay, some Victor Hugo; Dickens, and Motley's *Dutch Republic*; surmounted by a print of the *Shepherd's Mourner* or the *Meeting of Wellington and Blucher*. [12] But who ever saw the *Poems* of Rossetti or a Whistler *Nocturne*?

Lord Morley, wishing to make clear some social stratification,
once divided the public into those who had a Tennyson at home
13 and those who had not. With *Enoch Arden* in 1863 the Laureate
had captured the widest popularity that any great English poet
has ever enjoyed. Only an Historical Index to his works could
make clear at how many points he touched the passing interests
of the day. It might be Evolution or Personal Immortality or the
Nebular Hypothesis. It might be Chancery Procedure, or Company Promoting, or Industrial Insurance, or the Provision of
Coaling Stations.* On all he had spoken with the oracular and
mannered perfection to which his contemporaries submitted and
which drove the next generation to ribaldry and revolt. In his own
lifetime men spoke of him with Virgil as the authentic voice of his
14 race, an Imperial race in its golden prime. The new writers and
artists might fancy that they formed an Estate: it was not an
Estate of the Realm. Down to Lord Morley's line and perhaps
somewhat lower, poetry meant Tennyson, fiction meant Dickens
and George Eliot, art meant Landseer, Millais, Leighton, and
Watts.

To this native uniformity of taste and enjoyment, there succeeds in the later decades a deliberate self-conscious culture, of
which some elements, and those the most elaborately displayed,
are exotic. The Pre-Raphaelites had forced their world to look at
pictures, and their originals, with a new eye: Swinburne had set
the English muse dancing to a new, and in the end an intolerably
wearisome, tune: Pater had furnished the necessary philosophy
with his doctrine of the aesthetic moment and the gem-like
15 flame. Greece, Rome, the Middle Ages; the Renaissance, recovering somewhat from its moral condemnation by Ruskin; the
Catholic Church; Iceland, Paris, Japan; all were made to contribute something to the new ritualism or the new dandyism, of
villanelles and peacock's feathers, Utamaro and Cellini, strange
odours, strange sorrows, strange sins. What rapture to repeat, in a
French accent more strange than all, some sonnet of José-Maria

* It seems I broke a close with force and arms:
  There came a mystic token from the King . . .
  And the flying gold of the ruined woodlands drove thro' the air . . .
  A Mammonite mother kills her babe for a burial fee . . . ,
  Her dauntless army scattered and so small:
  Her teeming millions fed from alien hands.

de Heredia: what ecstasy in the very syllables—Narcisse Virgilio Diaz. 16

Under its iridescent froth, the aesthetic movement, like the Fourth Party in Parliament, was an earnest challenge to that grey respectability which was thinning indeed but had not quite lifted: with all their exotic postures, the aesthetes were the lawful successors or exponents of Ruskin, Arnold, and Browning,* much as Balfour and Lord Randolph were the true inheritors of Disraeli and Young England. They brought, or brought back, into English life much that we should be poorer without: they recovered for us something of a European standing, and something of a European outlook: refining form and opening new sources of delight. The mischief lay in the addiction to what was less excellent so long as it was less known, to mere paradox and mere perversity. But the movement furnished its own corrective in the comedy which it created or provoked. We may easily forget how deeply our picture of the Victorian age is coloured by its satire, and how much that we call Victorian is known to us only because the Victorians laughed at it; how persistently, in the classes accessible to comedy, defective types and false postures were ridiculed into a sulky self-suppression; worn-out fashions blown away, and new attitudes approved. And, whether for censure or encouragement, few of the Victorian satirists were so timely or so effective as Wilde, Du Maurier, and the Gilbert of *Patience*.

But while in art, and now in literature, we were becoming a suburb of Paris, in other ways we were falling into an unexpected dependence on Germany, a dependence resulting in part from the sincere respect of the educated classes, in part from the equally sincere alarm of the business classes. The establishment of the German Empire in 1870 had stripped off a film of insular self-

* One might go further back to Pugin and the Ecclesiologists. And who wrote 'The report of their deeds and sufferings comes to us musical and low over the broad sea'? Wilde? No. Pater? No. John Henry himself (*Lives of the English Saints*). The grandfather of aestheticism is James Garbett of B.N.C., Professor of Poetry, 1842–52, of whom I should like to know more than I have been able to discover. His remark at a viva: 'Not read Dante? Cruel Man! Take him, Williams', sounds like the parent of more than one Pater anecdote. I have been assured by those who were in a position to know that the ripostes with which Wilde took the town were the current backchat of clever undergraduates, 1870–80. One of the most famous has an even homelier origin: it will be found in *Guy Livingstone*, 1853, as 'an old Irish story'. 17

confidence which was very imperfectly replaced by the glittering panoply of Imperialism. It is not only in the light of later events that we are constantly impelled to measure England against Germany: the compact, authoritative structure of the one, with the indolent fabric of custom and make-believe here called a Constitution and an Empire. There, across the North Sea, not in the armies only, but in the factories, schools, and universities of Germany, Late Victorian England instinctively apprehended its rival or its successor. Germany was abreast of the time, England was falling behind.

Thus, before Rosebery had put the word into circulation, the conception of efficiency as the Germans understood and practised it; of technical, professional competence in every sphere of life; was gaining ground, to overshadow and, in the end, dislodge, the old faith in experience, in practical, instinctive capacity. The Later Victorian was not so sure as his father that a stout heart and a cool head would do more to make a soldier than all the diagrams of Jomini. Indeed, the South African war was to prove that, even without diagrams, hearts were not always so stout or heads so cool as a public school education might have been expected to ensure. It was becoming doubtful how long the personal energy of the manufacturer, even the high quality of his wares, would make up for an ignorance of chemistry and the metric system, and a lordly indifference to the tastes and requirements of his customers. The age of the pioneers was over, and for an age of close cultivation we were imperfectly equipped. It was once the boast of Manchester that if a railway were opened to Jupiter, Lancashire could provide all the Jovians with shirts in a year. Fifty years later it seemed more probable that the first traveller would find a German already established and doing good business.

But the German secret was an open secret. There was no reason to suppose that they were individually or in the mass more intelligent or determined than their neighbours. They were simply, and for the particular need of the time, better educated. Thus in the widest sense the Later Victorian age became an age of technical instruction. The men who understood their time best, now put their benevolence less into charity than into education, and especially scientific education, or research. City companies and borough councils catch the movement and pass it on through

schools and colleges. In 1887 we are by our own confession out-
classed.* By 1897 the handicap is shortening. But no real or solid
progress could be made until the great Victorian omission had
been made good, and the executive class educated up to the level
of the demands now making on it in a trained and scientific
world. Over all those late Victorian years hovers the airy and
graceful spirit of the School Inspector, ingeminating *Porro unum
est necessarium*: organize your secondary education; and in the   21
background, at the end of every avenue, stands the lonely and
uncomprehended figure of the Prince Consort, surrounded by the
Commissioners of the Great Exhibition of 1851.

XXIX

A SENSE of vagueness, of incoherence and indirection, grows on us
as we watch the eighties struggling for a foothold in the swirl
and wreckage of new ideas and old beliefs. We must allow, it is
true, for the distraction of interest by external affairs. But if we
could, in imagination, first neutralize the Irish deflexion, and then
remove the preoccupation with questions of Empire and defence,
thus studying the England of 1890 as a direct outgrowth of the
England of 1860, we should notice as the chief symptoms of
internal change, first a greater care for the amenities of life,
natural and domestic; and, behind this, a far more critical attitude
towards the structure of society which few could any longer think
of as divinely ordered, or logically irrefutable. The mind of 1890
would have startled the mind of 1860 by its frank secularism, not
less than by its aesthetic and Socialistic tone.

More particularly and concretely, especially if our eye falls on
the winters of 1889 and 1890, we should observe a new, and
grave, attention to the problem of poverty as exemplified by
London. The Union Chargeability Act of 1865 had finally detached the labourer from his place of settlement, which in the

* 'As a result of this stirring of the national pulse we see schools, colleges,
and universities, now rising in our midst, which promise by-and-by to rival
those of Germany'.—Tyndall's farewell speech in Jubilee week. When Abney
became Inspector of Science Schools in 1873, they had six laboratories between
them. In 1903 there were more than a thousand.   20

country was usually his place of birth, and created that mobility of labour which the economist had desired or sometimes assumed.* Those who stayed on the land profited: of the three partners in agriculture, it seems certain that the labourer, relatively to his condition, lost less than the landlord and the farmer in the years of depression. From the time of Joseph Arch and the Labourers' Union in 1870 the standard of rural welfare ceases to
2 fall: after the Reform of 1885 it begins to rise. But those who could not stay on the land, and could not emigrate, joined the reserve of labour in the towns; in that town above all which had always provided the largest market for casual and unskilled labour; and thus London in the eighties was for the first time confronted with troubles of a kind which hitherto had been associ-
3 ated mainly with the distant midlands or the north.
4   Of all the great capitals, London was the most orderly, and the good tradition was hardly interrupted by the comedy of 1848, or the Sunday Trading riots of 1857 and the Hyde Park riots of 1866, neither of which in truth was much more than a procession which got out of hand. In the eighties Trafalgar Square became the scene, and, in a way, the symbol, of Metropolitan disaffection, and in 1886 the police and the nerves of the capital were put to the test and found wanting. A demonstration, or two demonstrations,† met in the Square on a Sunday in February, and before the police recovered control of the situation the attendant roughs had helped themselves, it was rumoured, to some £50,000 of shop-keepers' goods. A second performance in 1887 was more vigor-
5 ously encountered; for the rest of the reign London maintained its habitual good-humoured tranquillity; and the Dock Strike of 1889 showed the world that patience and self-discipline under suffering were not the virtues of Lancashire alone.

The alarm had been intensified by the magnitude of the London underworld, and the unknown efficacy of dynamite. Assassination was the rarest of crimes in England, and the indiscriminating violence of the time fuse and the bomb had always been associated with foreigners. Now, in quick succession, there were attempts on Westminster Hall, on the House of Commons, three great railway stations, the Tower, London Bridge, and the Nelson

---

   * Hardy and Rider Haggard, observers of unquestioned competence, agreed
1 that village tradition came to an end about 1865.
   † One to discuss, of all depressing topics, the Sugar Bounties.

column. But whether Fenians or foreigners were behind them, the absurdity of some of the objectives, and the futility of most of the enterprises, suggests less a concerted attack on order than the exasperated exhibitionism which afterwards characterized the militant Suffragists. With the insane attack on the Royal Observatory in 1895, this spasmodic terror came to an end. Like the 6 Fenian movement, of which it was an outlier, it had hardened rather than terrified the public; and, like all unsuccessful insurgents, the Trafalgar Square Socialists had alienated more than they had converted, and in the end perhaps amused more than they shocked. This was not the way. But the disturbance of London in the eighties had effected a concentration of interest upon poverty, its grounds, and incidents and consequences, which could not again be relaxed. That there was something wrong, whether it was remediable or not, every one had always known. But now they had seen it, and the sight left many of them asking whether it was remediable without organic change, not in the political but in the economic system. They asked: and we have not yet heard the answer.

That they could ask, and at least project an answer, shows how profoundly the attitude of the thoughtful classes to the State and its problems had changed. And yet the change was natural, and explicable. To use a word which does not very well go with English conditions, the bourgeois ascendancy which the thirties seemed to promise was never fully achieved. The resistance of the gentry, entrenched in Parliament, the Church, the Universities, and the land, was too strong: their wealth too great, their way of life too attractive. In the course of a generation or little more, the productive *bourgeoisie* had evolved, was tending at least to evolve, into a financial plutocracy, with a subordinate executive class: and the natural line of development for the gentry was to become the administrators of a State and Empire which they could no longer claim to govern as of right, advisers and leaders of a people whom they could no longer hope to rule. The impulse was much the same, whether it sent young men, in the footsteps of Edward Denison, to Whitechapel, or to Egypt and South Africa on Milner's staff. 7

A second age of inquiry, recalling the investigations of the thirties, is setting in, and, as of old, literature begins to consult the Blue Books. A forgotten but remarkable novel, Gilbert's *De*

Profundis, is the link between *Sybil* and *Alton Locke*, and the literature of the Social Deposits so much in vogue in the Late Victorian
years, of which in its day *All Sorts and Conditions of Men* was the
8 most influential, *Esther Waters* is the classic, example. The bleak
logic of the Philosophic Radicals, that indeed we shall not find.
Instead, we have a very much wider psychology, of the individual
and of the community, than they had possessed; a greater range
of observation; a saving doubt of the imposing generality. The air
is charged with a subtle potency, the product of the same ferment,
which bred by turn the Christian Socialists and the Pre-Raphaelites, and took body in the republicanism of Swinburne, the economics of Ruskin, the workshops and romances of Morris. But
this potency is controlled now by the exacter methods, the more
rigorous scrutiny of evidence, which science was imposing upon
all inquiry, and the ferment is charged with foreign elements; a
strong infusion of Henry George, a dash of Mazzini, a dash of
Tolstoi, not much Anarchism, rather more Internationalism, and
a gradually solidifying contribution from Engels and Marx.
9 In that hospitable, lightly-policed London, among whose most
respectable citizens were Russian Nihilists and Paris Commun-
ards, all theories might be propounded, and all would have to
run into the English mould or else evaporate in air.

Politically old Radicalism was not far from its goal of universal
suffrage, and the final identification of rulers and ruled. So near
was it indeed that the rest might be taken for granted, and the
younger Radical mind was thinking of another course and another objective. In politics there is no Utilitarian stopping place
short of pure democracy. In economic life is the identification of
rulers and ruled conceivable at any point short of pure collectivism? Are not the organs, in outline, there, in Whitehall, in the
Counties and County Boroughs? Of the two lions in the way, one
was dead, the other stricken. The determinism of the classical
economists got its death-blow when Thornton exploded, and
10 Mill recanted, the doctrine of the Wage Fund. The administrative Nihilism of the Manchester school had been confuted by
experience, the example of the School Boards, the example of
Birmingham. The old Radical passion for logic and improvement,
the old Tory confidence in leadership and authority, were again
moving towards their natural alliance. But whether the inscription
on the Union flag should be read Tory Democracy or Socialism

depended mainly on the point of view of the beholder, who might perhaps in some lights read it as Birmingham, in others Fabianism.

Any one who set himself to collect all occurrences of the word Socialism in the Victorian age would probably conclude that it might be taken, or made to mean everything which a respectable man saw reason to disapprove of or to fear: Macaulay detected Socialism in Wordsworth's *Prelude*. From France it had brought 11 with it associations, alarming and unsavoury, with subversion, plunder, and sex, which were strengthened by the spectacle of 1848, the National Workshops and the swift revulsion to despotism; and, though the Commune of 1871 had no more necessary affinity with Communism than it had with the Book of Common Prayer, the desolation of Paris, the massacres and the reprisals, gave both names a terrifying significance, which was not unfelt by the electors who returned the Conservatives in 1874. The industrial legislation of 1875, the extension of the franchise in 1885, and the Local Government Act of 1888, made it certain that, 12 whatever the driving force might be, the channels within which English Socialism would run would be insular and traditional: the Trade Union, the Municipality, the Parliamentary Committee.

It was certain also that in the circumstances of that time the driving force would be in large degree religious: not only because the officials of the Trade Unions were often religious men, chapel leaders, and preachers, trained in the administrative habits of Methodism, equally accustomed to declamation and conference, but because the higher intelligence of the movement was impregnated with all those ideas, which descending from Coleridge, Arnold, and the Tractarians, had enriched the humanitarianism of the eighteenth century and the Evangelicals with a reverence for historical and social relations in themselves. Even an anxious mind in the eighties might, on a fair review of persons and possibilities, have consoled itself that a revolution led by Morris and Cunninghame Graham, would certainly be picturesque: looking 13 towards Gore and Dolling and the Christian Social Union, that it would very likely be High Church. 14

That it would be Utilitarian, both in scope and method might also safely be assumed, because the Philosophic Radicals had created a way of thought to which every administrator instinctively conformed; a body of practice so extensive and solid that it left little room for any invasion of Utopian concepts. True,

the central idea of their administrative philosophy, the Local Authority for all purposes, had been blurred by special legislation, the creation of sleepy rural School Boards and obstructive urban Health Boards. But time was enforcing its wisdom. Alexander Macdonald said in 1880 that the Conservatives had done more for
15 the working classes in five years, than the Liberals in fifty. A modern Tory might add that his party did more for Socialism in 1888 than the Socialists themselves did in another fifty. The permeation of local government by Fabian ideas is the Late Victorian counterpart of the assault and capture of the Poor Law administra-
16 tion by Philosophic Radicalism in the fighting person of Chadwick.

But we should be out in our analysis if we failed to give its due place also to the tidal surge of a movement which had been gathering momentum from the fifties onward. Right from the beginning, from Robert Owen and the Christian Socialists, the notions of industry and the good life had been kept together: from Pugin onwards, the Gothic Revival had presented the strangest blend of ethics and aesthetics, where it was of equal importance that the mason and the carver should present eternal truth in sym-
17 bols and that they should not drink or swear. We must think, too, that never perhaps had the natural world appeared so beautiful as it did to a generation whose senses had been trained to the last fineness by the art and literature of a century, by Constable and the water-colourists, by Tennyson, Ruskin, Kingsley, and all the school of word painters. But against this world, so intimately seen and cherished, what way of life for modern man to live by could be devised by minds enchanted with the vision of some lightly populated, machineless time of guilds and craftsmen, villages and their Common Halls, and white towns, if towns there must be, mirrored in the streams, and walled and gated towards the
18 forests of old romance? Along that line there was no future. The machine, the tenement, the multiple shops were there. Yet it was something that over the heads of philosophic administrators and humanitarian reformers there should have hovered the belief,* or even the fancy, that for the satisfaction of human needs,

---

* It was not absent from Chartism. In 1849 Gerald Massey's poem on the *Chivalry of Labour* has the refrain: Come, let us worship Beauty. Massey made his name by reciting, at Chartist meetings, George Smythe's Ode to the Jacobins. Smythe is Coningsby, and Massey ended with Imperialist Odes of his own, which
19 are a forecast of Kipling's *Seven Seas*. So the web is woven.

one thing more was wanted than the equitable and scientific distribution of material resources among the community of Respectable Families.

But we must observe, as we saw before about 1870, that there is no overt or general failure on which disaffection can seize to confute the ruling order. Judged by the standards of 1840, the state of England in 1890, when the dark shadow of the eighties was lifting, was most enviable: and that, whether the eye rested on the imposing stability of the whole, or the steadily growing comfort and freedom of its component parts. In that year two veterans spoke their last word. In the Reichstag, Moltke rose to warn his countrymen against seeking by violence what could only be won by patience. In Parliament, Bradlaugh, round whom so fierce a storm had once raged, denounced the revolutionaries as men who would apply caustic to a cancer, and were impeding, not advancing, the progress to which he himself could bear testimony, and of which the land might be proud. But the standards 20 had themselves changed, and the conceptions both of freedom and comfort were at once more exalted, more spacious, and less precise than those which had satisfied an earlier, more tight-lipped time. To attend a place of worship, to abstain from spirits, to read a serious newspaper and put money in the savings bank, was in 1840 as good an ideal as could be set before a man. To pursue it gave him rank as a citizen, the promise of a vote, and a share in a solid civilization. If thereto the State added a safe and healthy workshop, a decent house, and a good school, what more was there left to think of? By Early Victorian conceptions, little or nothing. By Late Victorian, much. Security remained; and leisure; the defence of the standard against the inrush of underpaid labour, casual or unskilled: protection against contingencies, support in old age. These are the ideas of the new age; and they embody themselves in a series of measures which pick up the thread of social legislation, dropped in the political convulsions of the Russian years and the Irish years, and culminate in what, though out of time, are in spirit the last of the great Victorian statutes, the Education Act of 1902 and the Insurance Act of 1911.*

* An expert was explaining its provisions to a journalist. 'I think I understand', he said: 'we have got to find a lot of money to set a crowd of Early Victorian benefit clubs on their legs.'   21

XXX

IF we range the forces operating on society at any moment into the Conformist and the Dissident, or the Stabilizing and the Exploratory, and apply this canon to the development of Victorian England, we shall remark how singularly detached they are from the traditional alignment of parties. There is one pattern of ideas, and another of parties, and of ideas neither party seems to be more or less receptive than the other. The most we can say is that on the whole for a generation after 1830, Liberalism suited England best, for a generation before 1900, Conservatism; while the dominant tendency is checked and deflected by a strong reaction towards Conservatism in 1840, and towards Liberalism in 1880, a reaction demanding in the one case greater efficiency in government, in the other greater moderation in policy. But of all those who shared on whichever side the impassioned expectations of 1868, how many would have ventured to prophesy that within twenty years the old Whig name would be heard no more?

Broken by the disaster of 1885, the Liberal party was nearing exhaustion. Traditionally reluctant to face the responsibilities or to yield to the excitements of Empire, it was reduced to peddling reforms for which there was no general or hearty demand: Welsh Disestablishment, Scotch Disestablishment, registration, drink, one man one vote:* or else evading argument on the eight-hour day, and anxiously reckoning the gain of the workman's vote against
1 the loss of the employer's subscription. Yet there was a Liberal, a man equally conversant with problems of labour and defence: an Imperialist, a Radical, a Home Ruler: a man to whom in 1886 opinion would almost unanimously have pointed as the leader of future Liberalism. The long Conservative ascendancy was something of a mystery to Conservatives themselves. How long would it have lasted if, besides the fame of Gladstone, the Liberals could have opposed to the weight and fire of Salisbury, Hartington, and Chamberlain, the capacity of Dilke? Lord Acton used to say that the course of history in the nineteenth century had been
2 altered twenty-five times by assassination. In ten years Victorian history was twice deflected by a divorce. The fall of Parnell left

* Thus making up the Newcastle Programme of 1891, ambiguously described by an adherent as a Blooming Plant.

Ireland with a dead god instead of a leader, and the fall of Dilke left Liberalism without a brain. 3

But the history of great nations is not written in the minuscule of personal incident, and if we could set against each other, in a Melian★ debate, the spirit of Conservative and Liberal England, we should hear an argument proceeding thus. 'We still demand, as we always have demanded, that wherever privilege exists, it shall be abated, in such degree and measure as the welfare of the State requires. It was we who delivered industry and the Middle Classes from the domination of the landed interest, the Dissenter from the ascendancy of one Church; who opened the Army, the public service, the Universities, to merit; who gave the people their schools and the labourer his vote; who forced you to emancipate the Catholic and to repeal the Corn Laws.' And on the other: 'But who is to decide what the welfare of the State allows? And when you have admitted every man to vote, delivered the Welsh tithe-payer from his parson, unsettled your own settlement of 1870, and destroyed whatever faint preponderance our constitution gives to education and property at the polls, what is there left for you to do? Will you deliver the poor man from the rich man, or will you be satisfied with watering his beer? And are you so sure that we are not nearer the heart of the matter than you? If you gave the labouring man his vote, who first stood up on behalf of the labouring children? Who made their schooling free? If you took the people at large into partnership in government—and we could say something about your disfranchisement in 1832 and our re-enfranchisement in 1867—who gave them the administrative organs by which their welfare is assured? If you emancipated the Jews, who emancipated the Trade Unions?'

'We own that we were behind you in some matters, as you were behind us in others. But we are ready to learn the lesson of our times. We have ceased to be Whigs. We no longer hold by the pre-eminent sanctity of property. And we think that your own forwardness in well doing is neither so philosophic nor so disinterested as you would have people believe. We seem to see that it

★ Not used at random. Many young men felt that the South African War was our Syracusan expedition. A friend of mine told me that nothing ever affected him so painfully as the change of Orange Free State into Orange River Colony. The evolution of Euripides from a pro-Boer into a League of Nations lecturer began about the same time. 4

has been sensibly quickened since you took Birmingham into your councils, and the rural labourer got his vote. But are there not dangers ahead for both of us? When there is no more political privilege to impart—and the women are waiting their turn—do you mean to outbid us with offers of public money, called Social Reform? Is it Protection you mean, or only Old Age Pensions? Do not forget you brought the Income Tax into existence. Can you set limits to the leverage of that instrument for the subversion of property? And are not our Estate Duties a more potent engine still?'

'We agree with you that the public corruption of great masses is the worst mischief that can befall a people. But we think that your practice in the abatement of privilege has given you a taste for innovation in itself, and a habit of setting class against class which we both fear and deplore. Both of us doubtless hold that a contented people will be a united people, and that unity is the only sure pledge whether of progress in peace or victory in war. But when we look abroad we see ourselves in a more dangerous world than you conceive. Our lead is shortening: our markets closing: and still our numbers are increasing. How many of the nations acknowledge your Free Trade? How far does your call for Peace and Retrenchment carry? Blame Nature, if we are Imperialists; or blame Fate, which set these islands at the meeting of the great sea-ways on the verge of an armed Continent. Hereafter, in a less perilous age than this, there will be room for you again. But unless you are Imperialists also, you will not be there to fill it.'

To an Englishman of 1870, Imperialism meant, in the first instance, the mode of government associated with Napoleon III, or more vaguely with Austria or the Tsar, and the association made the title of Empress* distasteful to many devoted subjects of the Queen. Its application under other conditions was defined by Lord Carnarvon, who, as a young Under-Secretary, had presided over the federation of Canada; who afterwards tried to federate South Africa, and nursed the fancy, at least, of federating Great Britain and Ireland; and who, in 1878, had broken with the imperialism of Disraeli.† The age of indifference, he told an

* Martin Tupper claimed to have thought of it first.

† This Disraelian Imperialism of ascendancy in Europe was an episode of no lasting importance. For the popular view of Disraeli as 'founder of modern

audience in Edinburgh, was over; we were at the parting of the ways. One led to a mere material aggrandizement of territory and armaments, of restless intrigue and reckless expenditure. The true Imperialism was a flexible and considerate policy of guidance, of justice between natives and settlers, of reconciliation, emancipation, and training for self-government. 8

Just twenty years later the *Oxford Dictionary* wrote:

'In recent British politics Imperialism means the principle or policy (1) of seeking, or at least not refusing, an extension of the British Empire in directions where trading interests and investments require the protection of the flag; and (2) of so uniting the different parts of the Empire having separate Governments, as to secure that for certain purposes, such as warlike defence, internal commerce, copyright, and postal communication, they shall be practically a single state.'

Between these three there is room for many half tones, and for 9 all the emotions, from an almost religious fervour to an almost religious horror, with which the name and idea of Imperialism affected Late Victorian minds, according as it was regarded as the Mission of an Elect People, or Exploitation by Superior Power.

The notion of Mission, adapted from the religious conception of the duty laid by the Lord upon his prophets, was popularized by Carlyle. Poet, novelist, statesman, journalist, every one who 10 wished to give his doings the importance which in his own secret judgement, perhaps, they did not possess, put them down to the credit of his Mission. Nations have their Mission too, and by 1870 the conception had taken body in the Indian Civil Service. The purification of that service from the time of Clive onwards; its arrogant detachment from native life; its self-devotion and efficiency; its close association with the English Universities and Public Schools: all these things had combined to create, and to diffuse, such an ideal of a distinterested ruling class as could be accepted by the national pride and not disowned by the national conscience.

But the mention of India is enough to remind us that not for many generations to come can the contribution of Victorian England to history be assessed, because no one can yet say which

---

Imperialism' I can see little evidence. In any case, these things are not 'founded': they come about. But the first man to state the new ideas clearly was Dilke. 7

of the ideas or which of the institutions generated in an age so
fertile and constructive will in the end be found to have taken root
and to be bearing. In the India of to-day, who will undertake to
determine what elements come from the East India Company,
what from Macaulay's Education Minute, what from the Queen's
Proclamation of 1857? The Company, in a dispatch which shows
the hand of the elder Mill, had laid it down that in compensation
for the authority they had ceded to their conquerors, young
Indians of rank should be trained for the administration of India:
a policy of which an education in the arts and sciences of the
West was the necessary outcome and agency, and which the
Proclamation might be thought to have converted into a promise.
Was the Queen's promise kept? The Queen did not always think
so. The Mutiny could not be forgotten; and the colour bar, of
which the earlier invaders were hardly conscious, grew firmer as
easier communications brought women in increasing numbers to
India. The material framework of the Peninsula, its language, its
communications, its administrative order, are the creation of the
Indian Civil Service. But whence will come the ideas with which
they will be charged? Go through the list of great names in the
Indian service and then consider: to an Indian a hundred years
hence will any of them be so familiar as the name of Herbert
11 Spencer, or will he be forgotten too?

But in India there was no body of white settlers: in Australia
the aboriginal element was unimportant: in Canada, the West
Indies, and New Zealand, relations had been stabilized by experience and time. The new Empire, in the Pacific, and above all in
Africa, was being built by such enterprises and encounters, raids,
martyrdoms, murders, and reprisals, as are inevitable when frontiers are shifting momentarily, a stronger race is bearing down upon
a weaker, and trader, hunter, pioneer, and missionary are all upon
the trail at once, and they are not all of one race: Arab slave
dealers, French priests, Portuguese majors; remittance men,
beachcombers, and determined colonists; seekers after rubber,
seekers after ivory, seekers after souls; all the world in search of
gold or diamonds, and fifty thousand Dutchmen in possession
of the land where the gold and the diamonds were to be had.

Of this Imperialism, where much was exalted and much corrupt, much, and perhaps the greatest part, was no more than adventurous. We must consider the influence of the telegraph and

the war-correspondent, in vivifying messages which had once trailed through, months after the event, in official dispatches borne by sail; of the newer, livelier press, rapidly surrendering the make-believe that newspapers were the instructors of the people or that the Board-school population desired to be instructed;* of the ever-growing literature of travel and adventure, always pushing farther into the unknown and always leaving something for the next pioneer. Still armies might march into the mountains and be lost for weeks, as Roberts marched on Kandahar: into the desert and be lost for ever, as Hicks was lost at El Obeid. Still false prophets might arise in the wastes beyond Wady Halfa, still Lhassa was unvisited, and a man might make himself as famous by riding to Khiva in fact, as by discovering King Solomon's Mines in fiction. The ways of adventure stood wide open, and in Stanley [13] the world had seen the last of the great adventurers. Those who measured him against Livingstone might qualify their admiration with no little distaste. [14]

Thus to the slowly gathering, powerfully discharging emotions of an earlier day, when the grounds and preliminaries of war might be debated for a year, there succeeds a quick and clamorous sensibility: easily started, easily diverted, from Khartoum to Afghanistan, from Fashoda to the Transvaal; always there to be inflamed, one day by messages, pert or menacing, from the Kaiser or President Cleveland: another by truculent exchanges between Chamberlain and Caprivi. All the world is alike, whether it be [15] Pan-Slavs trumpeting their designs on Trieste, Pan-Germans on Denmark, or Mr. Olney informing the Queen's Majesty that her sovereignty in Canada is unnatural and transitory. We can [16] observe the areas of special tension: there is the Far East, there is the North-West Frontier; there are always the Balkans; and in any one the discharging spark may suddenly flash. The service vote for 1890 was £31,000,000 showing an increase of no more than £6,000,000 since the death of Palmerston twenty-five years before. But by 1895 it was close on £37,000,000 and in 1899, the last year of Victorian peace, it had reached £47,000,000. These figures are evidence of the same preoccupation which discloses itself in the immense contemporary literature devoted to prob-

---

* One old Chartist of '48 lived long enough to rebuke, in the reign of Edward VII, a professor turned journalist for the American vulgarity of his headlines. I fear the object of this censure was the philosophic L. T. Hobhouse. [12]

lems of Empire and defence,★ a nervous and ranging preoccupation which seems at times to be reflected in a nervous and bewildered diplomacy, conforming to circumstances which no man
could control.

But we may easily censure the diplomacy of the Imperialist
age too harshly if we forget in what Titanic chaos it was involved.
A still increasing population supported increasingly on foreign
food; an industrial and commercial lead that was steadily
lessening; the longest of frontiers guarded by the smallest of
armies; communications encircling the world, but threaded on
coaling stations that a venturesome squadron might annihilate in
an afternoon; Australians snarling at the German flag in the
Pacific; Newfoundland threatening to join the United States;
English and Dutch eyeing one another for the mastery of South
Africa; West Africa undelimited; China collapsing; Russia in
search of an open sea; markets closing or opening as new tariffs
are set up or spheres of influence staked out: what policy, one
may ask, was possible in such a world, except the seeming no-
policy of maintaining the frail Concert of Europe, of easing all
contacts, with Germany in Africa, with France on the Mekong;
and making the Fleet invincible at all costs? Isolation, splendid or
not, was forced on the England of Rosebery and Salisbury as it
had been chosen by the England of Canning and Palmerston, and
isolation in that tense encroaching time bred a temper by turns
self-critical and arrogant, reckless and earnest, and a diplomacy
which the foreigner might read as a stony and unscrupulous
egoism, or a flurried search for friends in a universally hostile
world.

Yet all through this turmoil we hear the insistent note of a growing Imperial unity under the Crown. What formal bonds still
linked England to the Colonies were rapidly parting, and there
were none to link them to each other. Whether elements so dis-
parate would fall apart by mutual consent, or reunite in a new
order; of what shape or nature that order would be—a Customs
Union or Union for Defence, with representation at West-

★ Add a prodigious growth of popular, feuilleton stuff, about the Next War,
with which is mixed up the Apocalypse, Daniel, the Second Coming, the Restoration of the Jews, and the Great Pyramid. Only one sentence remains in my
memory: 'Then the Lord arose: the British Government decided to send troops
17 to Egypt.'

minster or without—such topics might be debated in peace, but who would say what answer the strain of war might give? The Empire stood in such a precarious equipoise of parts that only some inner cohesion of feeling or purpose could create a habit of unity, and the one thing common to all subjects of the Queen was that they always had been subjects of the Queen. Her reign stretched out of memory, giving to the youngest of democracies its share in a majestic and immemorial tradition.

When we think of all the forces, all the causes, at work in the sixty-three years of her reign; with how few of them she was in sympathy, how few she understood; we must find it originally strange that Victoria should, by the accident of a youthful accession and a long reign, have been chosen to give her name to an age, to impose an illusory show of continuity and uniformity on a tract of time where men and manners, science and philosophy, the fabric of social life and its directing ideas, changed more swiftly perhaps, and more profoundly, than they have ever changed in an age not sundered by a political or a religious upheaval. If the Queen, and not Prince Albert, had died in 1861, we might have set against each other the Victorian and Edwardian ages, and seen in the contrast the most striking example in our history of pacific, creative, unsubversive revolution. But upon the English race Fate had imposed the further, ecumenical function of Empire: and for all time that we can foresee, great nations in all Continents will look back, for the origins of their polity, and their institutions, to the years when they were first united in freedom, or the hope of freedom, under the sceptre of Victoria.

There are in our nineteenth-century history certain moments of concentrated emotion which seem to gather up the purposes of a whole generation. One is the determination which, fifteen years after Waterloo, drove England past all barriers into a resolute Liberalism. Another is the passion of goodwill and confidence which swept the country in 1851. A third is the second Jubilee. The homely and somewhat slipshod festivities of 1887* were for domestic enjoyment and were indeed overshadowed by the

---

* The Office of Works put the decoration of the Abbey into the hands of an undertaker, Banting. Thinking that the Coronation Chair looked shabby, he gave it a lick of brown paint and a coat of varnish, supplying missing crockets out of stock. The Bantings are the only undertakers who have found a place in O.E.D., D.N.B., and Hansard.

ensuing misfortunes of Miss Cass.* The magnificence of 1897 was an Imperial defiance. After Cyprus, Egypt, Burma, Nigeria, Uganda, Baluchistan, Rhodesia: what with chartered companies and protectorates, an area fifty times as large as Britain had in ten years been added to the Queen's Dominions. Some Nemesis was due, and Nemesis had already shown its hand. The Committee of Inquiry into the Jameson Raid had closed its proceedings abruptly. No one knew why, and every one thought the more.

The rash annexation of the Transvaal in 1877 and its precipitate abandonment in 1881 had left on either side a sentiment of apprehension and humiliation, which might have subsided into such a friendly indifference as commonly prevailed between the Empire and the other Republic on the Orange River. But in 1886 gold was discovered on the Witwatersrand; in 1888 Rhodes amalgamated the Kimberley Diamond Companies, and in 1889 the South African Company was incorporated. In the person of Rhodes, all the Imperialisms of the age seem to exist in a confused, inextricable embodiment. Of the stock and origin which has bred so many conquerors, he went out from his father's rectory in Hertfordshire to grow cotton in Natal, to hunt for diamonds and keep up his classics, and to nourish two ambitions. One was to become a graduate of the University of Oxford: the other to federate the Empire, an Empire so vastly enlarged that it could impose its Peace on all the nations of the world. He was barely thirty-six when, thrusting past the raids and outflankings with which Germany, Portugal, and the Transvaal were seeking to enclose the Cape Colony, he had carried the frontier from the Orange River to the Zambesi.

But in England, where Empire meant either the self-government of kindred communities, or the just rule of a superior caste, this new African venture had awakened many misgivings. Names of a kind not greatly honoured, Beit, Joel, Barney Barnato, were too conspicuous on its foundation stones. Serious men were apt at times to wonder whether more was not at stake than the suzerainty of the Queen; whether, if the safety of the Empire required the extinction of the Republics, the integrity of the Eng-

---

* A sempstress of irreproachable character who went out on Jubilee night to post a letter and was arrested for soliciting. Chamberlain took up her cause: the adjournment of the House was carried against the Government: the policeman prosecuted for perjury.

lish character was not bound up with the resistance they might offer to the tactics of the company promoter and the morals of the mining camp. A stain was left on the year of Jubilee; a discord 22 had made itself heard, growing louder through the disasters and ineptitudes of the South African War, till it merged into the triumph song★ of Liberalism reunited and victorious, but with a small, vigorous, and disconcerting auxiliary operating on its left flank. The Imperialism of the nineties had burnt itself out in the Mafeking bonfires, and the Conservative overthrow of 1905 recalled, in its grounds and its magnitude, the defeat of 1880. But 24 in twenty-five years much had happened that could not be undone. The Empire was a thing in being. Germany had thrown down her challenge at sea.

The Victorian age was over. The old queen was dead. She had lived long enough. The idol of her people, she had come to press on the springs of government with something of the weight of an idol, and in the innermost circle of public life the prevailing sentiment was relief.†

XXXI

IN January 1874 a number of Liberals met in London to congratulate the Emperor William I and Bismarck on the strong action they were taking against the Catholic Church in Germany. Lord Russell signified his support and was honoured with a letter of thanks from the Emperor, saluting him as the Nestor of European Statesmen. In the following winter, the *Deutschland* sailed from 1 Bremen, having on board certain Franciscan nuns, exiles under the laws which the Liberals of London, with the Vatican Decrees still fresh in their memory, so heartily approved.

> She drove in the dark to leeward,
> She struck—not a reef or a rock
> But the combs of a smother of sand: night drew her
> Dead to the Kentish Knock. 2

★ *The Churchman and the Brewer, we will drive them from the land,*
For the Nonconformist children are marching hand in hand. 23

† Sir Charles Dilke wrote: 'The Accession Council (of Edward VII), attended almost solely by those who had reached power under her reign, was a meeting of men with a load off them.'
25

As life is short and knowledge boundless, is there any canon by which we can determine whether, in the history of Victorian England, Lord Russell's letter or Gerard Hopkins's poem better deserves to be recorded?

Philosophies of History are many, and all of them are wrecked on the truth that in the career of mankind the illuminated passages are so brief, so infrequent, and still for the most part so imperfectly known, that we have not the materials for a valid induction. Of historic method, indeed, nothing wiser has ever been said than a word which will be found in Gibbon's youthful *Essay on the Study of Literature*. Facts, the young sage instructs us, are of three kinds: those which prove nothing beyond themselves, those which serve to illustrate a character or explain a motive, 3 and those which dominate the system and move its springs. But if we ask what this system is, which provides our canon of valuation, I do not believe we can yet go further than to say, it is the picture as the individual observer sees it.

If we trespass across this boundary, we may find ourselves insensibly succumbing to one of the most insidious vices of the human mind: what the Germans in their terse and sparkling way call the hypostatization of methodological categories, or the habit of treating a mental convenience as if it were an objective thing. 'Painting', Constable once said, 'is a science of which pictures are 4 the experiments.' That there is a painter's eye, an attitude or disposition recognizable as such in Giotto and Gauguin, no one will question. Yet Giotto and Gauguin confronted with the same object will make very different pictures, of which no one can say that one is truer than the other: and to impose an Interpretation of History on history is, to my mind, to fall into the error, or to commit the presumption, of saying that all Virgins must look like Piero's, or that, if we were sufficiently enlightened, we should see all chairs as Van Gogh saw them.

History is the way that Herodotus and Fra Paolo and Tocqueville and Maitland, and all those people, saw things happening. And I dwell on the name of Maitland partly because, outside his own profession, England has never done justice to that royal intellect, at once as penetrating and comprehensive as any historian has ever possessed: but more because no other English writer has so perfectly apprehended the final and dominant object of historical study: which is, the origin, content, and articulation of

that objective mind which controls the thinking and doing of an
age or race, as our mother-tongue controls our speaking; or poss-   5
essed, in so full a measure, the power of entering into that mind,
thinking with its equipment, judging by its canons, and observing
with its perceptions.

Capacity like that is no more imitable than the capacity which
hung the dome of St. Paul's in the sky. But one need not travel
far in England to discover that, not Wren's genius, but Wren's
way of thinking about brick and stone, the uses they can be put
to, the spaces they can be made to enclose, was once the possession of craftsmen innumerable. Some day we may recover the
builder's eye which we lost a hundred years ago. Some day we may
acquire, what as a race we have never possessed, the historian's
eye. Is it worth acquiring? I think it is. Any serious and liberal
habit of mind is worth acquiring, not least in an age which the
increase of routine and specialism on one side, the extension of
leisure and amusement on the other, is likely to make less liberal
and less serious. But if I needed another argument, I should say:
Look at Ireland. There we have the great failure of our history.
When I think of the deflexion and absorption of English intelligence and purpose by Ireland, I am inclined to regard it as the
one irreparable disaster of our history; and the ground and cause
of it was a failure of historical perception: the refusal to see that
time and circumstance had created an Irish mind; to learn the
idiom in which that mind of necessity expressed itself; to understand that what we could never remember, Ireland could never
forget. And we live in an age which can afford to forgo no study
by which disaster can be averted or eluded.

This may seem an unduly grave conclusion to a slight work.
But one must be in earnest sometimes, especially when one's
theme is the waning of a great civilization. As I see it, the function
of the nineteenth century was to disengage the disinterested intelligence, to release it from the entanglements of party and sect—
one might almost add, of sex—and to set it operating over the
whole range of human life and circumstance. In England we see
this spirit issuing from, and often at war with, a society most
stoutly tenacious of old ways and forms, and yet most deeply
immersed in its new business of acquisition. In such a warfare
there is no victory, only victories, as something is won and held
against ignorance or convention or prejudice or greed; and in

such victories our earlier and mid-Victorian time is rich. Not so the later. Much may be set to the account of accident, the burden and excitement of Empire, the pressure and menace of foreign armaments, the failure of individual genius, the distraction of common attention. But, fundamentally, what failed in the late Victorian age, and its flash Edwardian epilogue, was the Victorian public, once so alert, so masculine, and so responsible. Compared with their fathers, the men of that time were ceasing to be a ruling or a reasoning stock; the English mind sank towards that easily excited, easily satisfied, state of barbarism and childhood which press and politics for their own ends fostered, and on which in turn they fed: 'and we think, with harms at the heart, of a land where, after Titanic births of the mind, naught remains but an
6 illiberal remissness', of intelligence, character, and purpose.

   That time has left its scars and poison with us, and in the daily clamour for leadership, for faith, for a new heart or a new cause, I hear the ghost of late Victorian England whimpering on the
7 grave thereof. To a mature and civilized man no faith is possible except faith in the argument itself, and what leadership therefore can he acknowledge except the argument whithersoever it goes? But the great age is not so far behind us that we must needs have lost all its savour and its vigour. It takes some effort to think of England, in this autumn of 1936, as in any special sense the home of the disinterested mind, as very noticeably illuminated by the lights of argument and reason. But

> Carisbrooke keep goes under in gloom;
8 > Now it overvaults Appledurcombe:

and if they go out here, what ages must pass before they shine again?

                                                              1936

NOTES

NOTES

LIST OF CONTRIBUTORS

BA	Betty Askwith (Hon. Mrs. Miller Jones)
DEDB	D. E. D. Beales
PAB	P. A. Bezodis
RB	Lord Blake
JWB	J. W. Burrow
JPTB	J. P. T. Bury
OC	The Rev. Professor Owen Chadwick
AMHC	Mrs. A. M. H. Chitty
GKC	G. Kitson Clark
JMC	J. M. Collinge
PAWC	Professor P. A. W. Collins
GJC	G. J. Crossick
HJD	Professor H. J. Dyos
DRF	D. R. Fisher
MRDF	Professor M. R. D. Foot
NG	Professor Norman Gash
JPWG	J. P. W. Gaskell
JG	John Gross
GJ	Gordon Johnson
EJK	Professor E. J. Kenney
WAL	Professor W. A. Lloyd
EL	Elizabeth, Countess of Longford
OM	Professor Oliver MacDonagh
FCM	F. C. Mather
HCGM	H. C. G. Matthew
BRM	B. R. Mitchell
KBN	Professor Kevin B. Nowlan
LR	Professor Sir Leon Radzinowicz
RR	Robert Robson
ER	Edward Royle
MJSR	Professor M. J. S. Rudwick
LGS	L. G. Salingar

FHS   Professor F. H. Sandbach
AWS   Anthony W. Shipps
FBS   Professor F. B. Smith
ERT   E. R. Taylor
JTW   Professor J. T. Ward
JAW   J. A. Weir

The following abbreviations have been used:

Finer, *Chadwick*: S. E. Finer, *The Life and Times of Sir Edwin Chadwick* (1952).

Hodder, *Shaftesbury*: Edwin Hodder, *The Life and Work of the Seventh Earl of Shaftesbury* (3 vols., 1886).

Monypenny and Buckle, *Disraeli*: W. F. Monypenny and G. E. Buckle, *The Life of Benjamin Disraeli, Earl of Beaconsfield* (6 vols., 1910–20).

Morley, *Gladstone*: John Morley, *The Life of William Ewart Gladstone* (3 vols., 1903).

Trevelyan, *Bright*: George Macaulay Trevelyan, *The Life of John Bright* (1913).

Trevelyan, *Macaulay*: George Otto Trevelyan, *The Life and Letters of Lord Macaulay*, 2nd edn. (2 vols., 1877).

Letters of Queen Victoria, 1st Ser.: *The Letters of Queen Victoria. A Selection from Her Majesty's Correspondence between the years 1837 and 1861*, ed. Arthur Christopher Benson and Viscount Esher (3 vols., 1907).

Letters of Queen Victoria, 2nd Ser.: *The Letters of Queen Victoria, Second Series. A Selection from Her Majesty's Correspondence and Journal between the years 1862 and 1885*, ed. G. E. Buckle (3 vols., 1926–8).

Letters of Queen Victoria, 3rd Ser.: *The Letters of Queen Victoria, Third Series. A Selection from Her Majesty's Correspondence and Journal between the years 1886 and 1901*, ed. G. E. Buckle (3 vols., 1930–2).

Young and Handcock, *English Historical Documents*: *English Historical Documents*, ed. David C. Douglas, vol. xii (1), *1833–1874*, ed. G. M. Young and W. D. Handcock (1956).

The place of publication of works cited in the notes is London unless otherwise stated.

INTRODUCTION

1. See Sidney's letter to his brother, Robert, 18 Oct. 1580, in which he observed that the historian sometimes became a poet 'in painting forth the effects, the motions, the whisperings of the people' (*The Complete Works of Sir Philip Sidney*, ed. Albert Feuillerat (4 vols., Cambridge, 1912–26), iii. 131). *DRF*.

2. See Frederic William Maitland on the results which he expected from further research into 'ancient English history': 'Above all, by slow degrees the thoughts of our forefathers, their common thoughts about common things, will have become thinkable once more.' (*Domesday Book and Beyond* (Cambridge, 1897), p. 520.) *RR*.

3. Young's use of these specific words has not been traced, but the idea which they embody is expressed in a number of his essays. *GKC*.

4. G. M. Young, 'Victorian History', in *Selected Modern English Essays*, 2nd Ser., ed. Humphrey Milford (1932), p. 272. *DRF*.

5. Marginal comment by Edward Gibbon in his own hand on the first paragraph of Volume I, Chapter 1 of a copy of the new edition (1782) of his *History of the Decline and Fall of the Roman Empire*, now in the British Library. The original reads: 'Where error is irretrievable, repentance is useless.' See *The English Essays of Edward Gibbon*, ed. Patricia B. Craddock (Oxford, 1972), p. 338. The word 'irreparable' appears to have been introduced by J. B. Bury in his edition of *Decline and Fall* (7 vols., 1896–1900), i. p. xxxv. *GKC*.

SECTION I

1. cf. Sir Walter Scott's tribute, dictated to the editor of the *Edinburgh Weekly Journal* the day after he heard of Byron's death: 'we feel as if the great Luminary of heaven had suddenly disappeared from the sky'. See Edgar Johnson, *Sir Walter Scott* (2 vols., 1970), ii. 870. DRF.

2. B. G. Niebuhr (1776–1831), the eminent ancient historian and philologist, who was deeply shaken by the French Revolution of 1830, from which he anticipated the outbreak of another general war, the destruction of his home in the Rhineland, and the relapse of Europe into barbarism. These fears seem to have hastened his death on 2 Jan. 1831, although the immediate cause was inflammation of the chest. GKC.

3. 'Vital Religion' was a phrase commonly used by Evangelicals to describe their own faith, as contrasted with the practice and beliefs of more conventional Christians. Young may have had specifically in mind observations made by Daniel Wilson, Vicar of Islington, and later Bishop of Calcutta, in his Introductory Essay, dated October 1826, to William Wilberforce, *A Practical View of the Prevailing Religious System of Professed Christians, in the Higher and Middle Classes in this Country contrasted with Real Christianity* (Glasgow, 1826 edn.), p. xlvi. Commenting on the progress of the revival of religion since the first appearance of the work in 1797, he wrote: 'The general standard of religious doctrine and practice in our country has been rising ... A spirit of inquiry into the great principles of Christianity has been more and more excited. The importance of religion, of vital religion, has been more generally felt.' That Young was familiar with this passage is clear from *Daylight and Champaign* (1948 edn.), p. 229.

It has not proved possible to trace the phrase 'the eternal microscope', but examples of the repeated and searching self-examination to which an earnest Evangelical subjected himself can be found in the journal of William Wilberforce, of whom Wilson said that 'He had a delicate yet penetrating and microscopic insight into character.' (Robert

Isaac Wilberforce and Samuel Wilberforce, *The Life of William Wilberforce* (5 vols., 1838), i. 181, 207, 241, 329; iii. 123, 135, 425; v. 295.) *DRF, GKC.*

4. John Norris (1657–1711), Rector of Bemerton, near Salisbury, published *Spiritual Counsel, or the Father's Advice to his Children* in 1694. He was the author of a large number of works of divinity, in many of which he dealt with problems of morality. See the *D.N.B.* for further details. The full title of the second work is *The Ladies' Calling; in two parts. By the Author of The Whole Duty of Man* (Oxford, 1673). *The Whole Duty of Man*, first published anonymously in 1658, remained popular throughout the eighteenth century. The author was probably Richard Allestree, D.D., but there are other candidates. See Samuel Halkett and John Laing, *Dictionary of Anonymous and Pseudonymous English Literature*, new edn., ed. James Kennedy, W. A. Smith and A. F. Johnson (7 vols., 1926–34), iii. 228; vi. 231. The content of these works, and the uninterrupted acceptance of *The Whole Duty of Man*, seem to be evidence of a continuous moral tradition from the seventeenth to the nineteenth century, which provided the substance of much that is called 'Victorian'. *GKC.*

5. See John Dryden, *Of Dramatick Poesie*, ed. James T. Boulton (1964), pp. 54–5. *GKC.*

6. Harriet Lewin (1792–1878) married in 1820 George Grote (1794–1871), M.P. for London, 1832–41 (on whom see Section II, note 24). She was a major influence and inspiration in all facets of her husband's career, and his *Personal Life* (1873) was her own most important publication. The stories about her come from the following sources:

Frances Anne Kemble, *Records of Later Life* (3 vols., 1882), ii. 65:
     One evening she came to my sister's house dressed entirely in black, but with scarlet shoes on, with which I suppose she was particularly pleased, for she lay on a sofa with her feet higher than her head, American fashion, the better to display or contemplate them.

ibid. ii. 64–5:

     I remember, at a dinner party at her own table, her speaking of Audubon's work on ornithology, and saying that some of the incidents of his personal adventures ... had pleased her particularly;

instancing . . . an occasion on which, as she said, 'he was almost starving in the woods . . . and found some kind of wild creature, which he immediately disembowelled and devoured.' This, at dinner, at her own table, before a large party, was rather forcible.

Lady Eastlake, *Mrs. Grote. A Sketch* (1880), p. 8, tells of her knowing 'when a hoop was off a pail in the back kitchen'.

Young's suggestion that her abrupt manners were those of a 'great lady', which is reproduced in Mona Wilson, *Jane Austen and Some Contemporaries* (1938), p. 257, is questionable. Mrs. Grote was rather a great eccentric than a typical specimen of the great ladies of high social position, whose characteristics are better illustrated in the lives of Lady Stanley of Alderley (1807–95) and the 2nd Lady Ashburton (1805–57), and in *Miss Eden's Letters*, ed. Violet Dickinson (1919). GKC.

7. Sarah Taylor (1793–1867) married in 1820 John Austin (1790–1859), the eminent jurist and friend of the Mills. Their house in Queen Square, adjacent to that of Jeremy Bentham, became a meeting place for politicians, lawyers, and literary men. A prolific authoress and translator, her most notable work was *Germany from 1760 to 1814* (1854). Between 1827 and 1848 she and her husband spent most of their time on the Continent. Their daughter, Lucie (1821–69), married Sir Alexander Duff-Gordon (1811–72), and their home, also in Queen Square, in turn became an important intellectual centre, and was frequented by Dickens, Thackeray, and Tennyson. Her own published works consisted chiefly in translations. In 1860 she went to the Cape for the sake of her health, and from 1862 until her death, apart from two brief intervals, she lived in Egypt. See Janet Ann Ross, *Three Generations of Englishwomen* (2 vols., 1888); Lady Duff-Gordon, *Last Letters from Egypt* (1875). GKC.

8. Elizabeth Rigby (1809–93), who wrote for the *Quarterly Review* on German and Russian topics, married in 1849 the artist, Sir Charles Lock Eastlake. She continued to publish extensively, and for almost fifty years was at the centre of contemporary literary, artistic, and political society. Her *Journals and Correspondence*, ed. Charles Eastlake Smith (2 vols., 1895), are an important historical record.

In the cases of Mrs. Austin and Lady Eastlake 'the high secluded culture of the provinces' refers to Norwich, of which Harriet Martineau, who spent her youth there, later wrote: 'Norwich, which has now no claims to social superiority at all, was in my childhood a rival of Lichfield itself, in the time of the Sewards, for literary pretension and the vulgarity of pedantry.' (*Harriet Martineau's Autobiography*, ed. Maria Weston Chapman (3 vols., 1877), i. 297–8.) At the same time, Norwich did produce a notable school of artists. *GKC.*

9. It is doubtful whether Florence Nightingale can be regarded as representative of the typical woman of any period. She was an individual genius, who broke out of the conventional life of the society into which she had been born, and won for herself a professional training. By sheer force of character, great organizational ability, and the use of the opportunity presented by the Crimean War (although her most important services were performed later) she secured a unique place in British history., *GKC.*

10. Lines from the last stanza of the poem in the 1817 collection which begins:

> Woman! When I behold thee flippant, vain,
> Inconstant, childish, proud, and full of fancies . . .

The sentiment was applied not to women in general but to the types of women to which Keats was attracted at a particular time, and bore little relationship to his more mature views. The poem seems to have been written in 1815, when Keats was barely 20, very inexperienced, and under the influence of a minor Romantic poet, George Felton Mathew. With Mathew's approbation, he burst into tears at the lines quoted here by Young, 'overpowered by the tenderness of his own imagination'. See Robert Gittings, *John Keats* (1968), p. 46. Sophie is the idealized mate in Rousseau's *Émile*, who had been educated solely to fit her to perform her functions as wife and mother. Sophia Western is the heroine of Fielding's *Tom Jones*, and Emma Woodhouse of Jane Austen's *Emma. GKC.*

11. 'Amelia' may refer either to the heroine of Fielding's novel of that name or to Amelia Sedley (later Mrs. George Osborne) in Thackeray's *Vanity Fair*. On the one hand, since *Amelia* was published in 1751, identification with Fielding's heroine would place her in the eighteenth century, and in many ways she corresponds with the type specified. On the other hand, Thackeray's Amelia, sweet, enduring, and rather stupid, also approximates to the type, and is better known. It is perhaps

significant of a change in values that Thackeray's correspondence reveals that he did not believe his Amelia to be particularly admirable. He did, however, portray as admirable Helen, the devoted mother of Arthur Pendennis, in his novel *Pendennis*. The same practical devotion was shown in real life by Mrs., later Lady, Tennyson in looking after the affairs of her husband, Alfred Tennyson, the poet. GKC.

12. Miss Nightingale's dislike of talk about 'woman's mission' sprang from her contempt for the sentimental Victorian idea that there were services which women were peculiarly fitted by their innate qualities to perform without training: 'It seems a commonly received idea among men, and even among women themselves, that it requires nothing but a loving heart, the want of an object, a general disgust or incapacity for other things, to turn a woman into a good nurse.' She also observed that it was 'alarming, peculiarly at this time, when there is so much talk about "woman's mission", to see that the dress of women is daily more and more unfitting them for any "mission", any usefulness at all.' (*Notes on Nursing for the Labouring Classes*, new edn. (1868), pp. 41, 111.) For her general attitude see Cecil Woodham-Smith, *Florence Nightingale* (1950), pp. 341, 384, 477. See also below, Section XIII, note 19. GKC.

13. In her novel *Jane Eyre* and elsewhere Charlotte Brontë (1816–55) evinced sufficient force and independence to be considered a rebel, and it may be significant that she showed great sympathy for her contemporary, the French novelist George Sand (1804–76), who was herself very much in revolt. See Mrs. Gaskell, *The Life of Charlotte Brontë* (2 vols., 1857), ii. 54, 55, 185–6. While it is true that she was a severe moralist, this does not mean that she was satisfied with existing conditions, and it is worthwhile to consider *her* views on 'Woman's mission' (ibid. ii. 177). Perhaps had she lived longer her views would have developed.

It is difficult to conceive that Harriet Martineau (1802–76), the very successful popularizer of political economy (see below, Section IV, note 1), could have gone further than she did. She lived her own life, propagated her own views, and was perfectly prepared to give publicity to her disbelief in orthodox religion (see below, Section XVIII, note 4).

Mary Wollstonecraft (1759–97) was of an earlier generation. After a stormy and unhappy career she married William Godwin, the philosopher. Her publications included *Thoughts on the Education of Daughters* (1787), *A Vindication of the Rights of Men* (1790) in reply to Burke's *Reflections on the Revolution in France*, and *A Vindication of the Rights of Woman* (1792). Among her posthumous works was a fragment of a novel entitled *The Wrongs of Woman, or Maria*. See above, pp. 157-8. GKC.

14. This no doubt refers to George Eliot's remark that when the existence of God had become unbelievable, and the concept of immortality inconceivable, the demands of duty remained absolute and peremptory (see Section XVIII, note 3). However, it seems extravagant to attribute the very strong moral feelings of late Victorian agnostics at all generally to the example and values of mid-Victorian women. GKC.

15. Hazlitt's essay, which is number XVI in his *Plain Speaker*, published anonymously in 1826, is a comparison of the characteristics of northern and southern races, principally the Swiss and the Italians, based on observations made during his Italian tour and a three-month stay at Vevey in 1825. See *The Complete Works of William Hazlitt*, ed. P. P. Howe (21 vols., 1930-4), xii. 169-78. GKC.

16. The Yorkshire manufacturer has not been identified. GKC.

17. The observation by Bright to which Young alludes has not been traced. GKC.

18. See Kingsley's article in *Fraser's Magazine*, November 1853:

> The age is an effeminate one; and it can well afford to pardon the lewdness of the gentle and sensitive vegetarian, while it has no mercy for that of the sturdy peer. . . . Byron has the most intense and awful sense of moral law—of law external to himself. Shelley has little or none; less, perhaps, than any known writer who has ever meddled with moral questions. . . . His whole life through was a denial of external law, and a substitution in its place of internal sentiment.

Charles Kingsley, *Miscellanies* (2 vols., 1859), i. 311-13.

Byron's disapproval of mixed bathing expressed during his Venetian period has not been traced, but in an earlier letter to Hobhouse, 23 Aug. 1810, he gave some views on the question of decency in bathing: 'it is a curious thing that the Turks when they bathe wear their lower garments as your humble servant always doth, but the Greeks not, however, questo Giovane e vergogno [this young man is bashful].' (*Byron's Letters and Journals*, ed. Leslie A. Marchand, vol. ii (1973), p. 14.) *GKC, RR*.

19. Young overrates the influence of the Evangelicals before 1830, underestimates their significance later in the century, and exaggerates the social and moral changes which occurred 'about 1830'. While it is true that at about that time the grosser forms of cruelty to animals were made illegal, even if the tendency to inflict them did not cease, this was by no means solely the work of Evangelicals. The pioneer was Richard 'Humanity' Martin (1754–1834), M.P. for County Galway, 1801–26, whose efforts were supplemented by successive governments between 1828 and 1835. For details see Sir Spencer Walpole, *A History of England from the Conclusion of the Great War in 1815* (5 vols., 1878–86), iii. 57–62; Brian Harrison, 'Religion and Recreation in Nineteenth-Century England', *Past and Present*, xxxviii (Dec. 1967), 98–125 and 'Animals and the State in Nineteenth-Century England', *English Historical Review*, lxxxviii (1973), 786–820.

Duelling remained fairly common after 1830, but opinion was hardening against it in the forties. The last recorded duel on English soil seems to have been between George Smythe, later Viscount Strangford, and Colonel Frederick Romilly at Weybridge in 1852, although there are credible stories of Englishmen fighting duels on the Continent at a much later date.

There was still much profligacy and brutality in all ranks of society, but it was checked among the aristocracy in some degree by the strict standards of the Court after the arrival of Prince Albert. While Gladstone was at one time an Evangelical, the piety of such men as Peel, Graham, and Herbert probably reflects a general improvement in morals, humanity, and piety from the late eighteenth century, which affected all classes and was not necessarily associated with the theology of the Evangelical revival.

At the same time, it would be wrong to underestimate the importance of Evangelicalism after 1830, when it was by no means always 'complacent, fashionable, superior'. With the rival attractions of the Ritualist movement and the Catholic revival there were probably fewer fashionable Evangelicals after the death of Charles Simeon in 1836 than in the days of Wilberforce. While Evangelicals after 1830 were at times intrusive, intolerant, and oppressive, as indeed they had always tended to be, the careers of the 7th Earl of Shaftesbury and Sir Thomas Fowell Buxton demonstrate the important role which their creed still had to perform in relation to the protection of factory children and of native races, and the abolition of slavery. Less prominent Evangelicals continued to undertake extensive social work. No doubt much of it was of uncertain value and vitiated by narrowness of spirit, but it included many individual services for the degraded and the outcast who would otherwise have been totally neglected. See Kathleen Heasman, *Evangelicals in Action. An Appraisal of their Social Work in the Victorian Era* (1962). *GKC*.

SECTION II

1. The source of this anecdote has not been traced. *GKC*.

2. Cromwell's speech of 4 Sept. 1654: 'A nobleman, a gentleman, a yeoman; "the distinction of these:" that is a good interest of the nation, and a great one! The "natural" magistracy of the nation, was it not almost trampled under foot, under despite and contempt, by men of Levelling principles?' (*The Letters and Speeches of Oliver Cromwell, with elucidations by Thomas Carlyle*, ed. S. C. Lomas (3 vols., 1904), ii. 342.) *GKC*.

3. The source of this statement has not been traced. *GKC*.

4. The source of this estimate is uncertain, and as stated it seems to be too loose in definition and too general in application to be satisfactory. There were certainly groups, such as the farmers and many landowners, who believed that they had become poorer during these years, and there are too few reliable statistics available to pronounce with any certainty on their lot or that of others. Even where there had been an increase in prosperity it might not have been continuous or lasting. A year such as 1825 brought ruin, sometimes final, to a number of people. There was, however, a contemporary belief in a continuous increase in well-being. The successive editions of Porter's *Progress of the Nation* describe an increase in the earning power of all classes, including the upper classes, and the increasing sale of commodities which can only have been of interest to the latter. See G. R. Porter, *The Progress of the Nation* (1847 edn.), pp. 530–46. *GKC*.

5. The Society for the Diffusion of Useful Knowledge was founded under the inspiration of Henry Brougham in 1825, and its introductory volume, written by Brougham, appeared in March 1827. Charles Knight, a publisher, became 'reader' for the Committee in 1828 and subsequently wrote and edited for them. His *Passages of a Working Life during Half a Century* (3 vols., 1864–5) is probably the best account of the organization. *GKC.*

6. The line is William Blake's, and is to be found among the epigrams, verses, and fragments written *c.* 1808–11. See *The Complete Writings of William Blake*, ed. Geoffrey Keynes (1966), p. 550. *RR.*

7. William Roscoe, *The Life and Pontificate of Leo the Tenth* (4 vols., Liverpool, 1805). *RR.*

8. This quotation is taken from an explanatory note to the following lines of Mrs. Barbauld's poem, *Eighteen Hundred and Eleven*:

> Where Roscoe, to whose patriot breast belong
> The Roman virtue and the Tuscan Song,
> Led Ceres to the bleak and barren moor
> Where Ceres never gained a wreath before

The Works of Anna Laetitia Barbauld (2 vols., 1825), i. 240. *DRF.*

9. George Grote, *A History of Greece* (12 vols., 1846–56). *RR.*

10. 'Immersed in matter' was a Baconian phrase, meaning concerned with what is material, practical, and particular, as opposed to what is purely general, theoretical, and abstract. In his *Advancement of Learning*, Book II, Bacon wrote: 'Civil knowledge is conversant about a subject which of all others is most immersed in matter, and hardliest reduced to axiom.' (*The Works of Francis Bacon*, ed. James Spedding, R. L. Ellis, and D. D. Heath (14 vols., 1857–74), iii. 445.) The *O.E.D.* and Johnson's *Dictionary*, under the word 'immerse', give two other examples of his use of this phrase. *GKC.*

11. See William Robertson's *History of the Reign of the Emperor Charles V* (1769):

> From that aera [the close of the eleventh century] we may date the return of government and manners in a contrary direction, and can

trace a succession of causes and events which contributed, some with a nearer and more conspicuous, others with a more remote and less perceptible influence, to abolish confusion and barbarism, and to introduce order, regularity, and refinement.

The Works of William Robertson, new edn. (12 vols., 1817), iv. 25. Young, who appears himself to have added the words 'of life', discussed Robertson's use of this criterion in his *Gibbon* (1932), pp. 79–83.

In this passage he is characterizing what he believed to have been the ideal of the early Victorian period of production, in contrast to later Victorian ways of thought, when Romanticism and the concept of an ideological revolution had penetrated the English consciousness. He saw this ideal as one which combined a belief in moral development and practical achievement, felt that it was congruous with the balanced ideals of the eighteenth century, and found it expressed in the eighteenth proposition of Oxford Liberalism, which Newman condemned in Note A to his *Apologia*, and the 'prospectus' of the Rochdale Pioneers. GKC.

12. See John Henry Cardinal Newman, *Apologia Pro Vita Sua*, ed. Martin J. Svaglic (Oxford, 1967), p. 262. 'Serve' obviously means 'suffice'. See the *O.E.D.* GKC.

13. The Rochdale Pioneers were working men who combined to open a co-operative store in Toad Lane, Rochdale in 1844. The first section of their manifesto read:

> The objects and plans of this Society are to form arrangements for the pecuniary benefit, and the improvement of the social and domestic condition of its members, by raising a sufficient amount of capital in shares of one pound each, to bring into operation the following plans and arrangements.

The objects specified were the establishment of a store for the sale of provisions and clothing; the purchase or erection of houses in which 'those members desiring to assist each other in improving their domestic and social condition may reside'; the manufacture of such articles as might provide employment for members who were out of work, or who were suffering repeated reductions in their wages; the purchase or renting of land to be cultivated by members who were out of employment or badly remunerated. The manifesto is printed in Arnold

Bonner, *British Co-operation*, revised edn. (Manchester, 1970), pp. 522–4. GKC, DRF.

14. Evidence given by M. Wyatt, resident magistrate at the Lambeth Street police office, to a Select Committee of the House of Commons in 1822: 'I consider gas, without presuming to play upon the word, essential to an *enlightened* police.' (H.C. (1822) iv. 153.) See Leon Radzinowicz, *A History of English Criminal Law and its Administration from 1750*, vol. ii (1956), p. 175 n. 18. But cf. ibid. vol. iii (1956), p. 457 n. 4. The source of Young's statement about the proposal to illuminate thieves' quarters has not been traced. *LR, GKC*.

15. The first scientifically constructed oil burner which could be satisfactorily applied to domestic use in place of candles was invented by Aimé Argand (1755–1803), of Geneva, in 1784. Colza oil, obtained from the seeds of the plant *Brassica campestris*, was commonly used for burning in domestic lamps. *GKC*.

16. William Whewell, *History of the Inductive Sciences* (3 vols., 1837), i. pp. vii–xvi provides some evidence of the significance attributed to Francis Bacon in the 1830s and 1840s, when it seemed clear that exact knowledge and the discoveries of natural science were to be of the greatest importance. This view is reflected in Macaulay's famous essay on Bacon in the *Edinburgh Review*, vol. lxv, no. cxxxii (July 1837), pp. 1–104. However, while he conceded Bacon's general importance, he not only condemned his character but also, rather perversely, professed to find nothing out of the ordinary in his philosophy. For Macaulay, the significance of Bacon lay in his belief that the proper object of philosophy was to serve the practical needs of mankind, rather than to discuss those abstractions which had occupied the minds of the ancient philosophers. Macaulay was answered in a series of dialogues by James Spedding (1808–81), privately published as *Evenings with a Reviewer* (2 vols., 1848). Spedding's absorption in Bacon is significant. He was in many ways the acknowledged leader, the 'Pope' of the group which included Tennyson and Hallam, devoted most of his life to Baconian studies, and refused important preferment to pursue them.

Between 1839 and 1845 Sir William Molesworth (see Section II, note 24) published a sixteen-volume edition of the works of Hobbes, which he dedicated to George Grote, a fellow Philosophical Radical.

In September 1845 he stood for Southwark at a by-election, and wherever he went in the constituency he was met with the cry of 'No 'Obbes', directed against Hobbes's reputed atheism. The issue had apparently been introduced into the contest by Edward Miall (1809–81), the prominent Nonconformist, who said on the hustings: 'I tell the hon. baronet that it was not until he, in miserable taste, taunted me with the title of "Reverend", that I referred to him as the Editor of Hobbes.' Molesworth defended Hobbes at some length against the charge, and Miall answered that it was the general opinion that he had been an atheist. It would be hard to say what the issue meant to the electors: 1,943 of them voted for Molesworth and 352 for Miall. See Mrs. Fawcett, *Life of Sir William Molesworth* (1901), pp. 249–56; *Illustrated London News*, 13 Sept. 1845 (vol. vii, p. 175). GKC.

17. Grote to G. C. Lewis, September 1840: 'In this age of *steam and cant*, I find so very few people whose minds take the same track as my own, that the small number who exist become to me as precious as the Sibylline Books, and I treasure them up with equal care.' (Mrs. Grote, *The Personal Life of George Grote* (1873), p. 133.) GKC.

18. It seems possible that the quotation from Hippolyte Taine reflects a passage in his *Histoire de la littérature anglaise*, 2nd edn. (5 vols., Paris, 1866–71), v. 159 where, discussing Macaulay's passion for public freedom, he wrote: 'il l'aime par orgueil, parce qu'elle est l'honneur de l'homme.' For Brougham's criticism of Macaulay see his letter to Macvey Napier, 28 July 1837 (*Selections from the Correspondence of the late Macvey Napier*, ed. Macvey Napier (1879), pp. 196–7). Brougham's criticism in this instance of Macaulay's article on Bacon is justified, but in general his jealousy of Macaulay was so great that his views should be discounted. Harriet Martineau bitterly attacked Macaulay, not so much on the grounds that he was materialistic, or lacked philosophy, as that he was superficial, inaccurate, heartless, and incapable of presenting a case with complete honesty (*Harriet Martineau's Autobiography*, ed. Maria Weston Chapman (3 vols., 1877), i. 348–50). GKC.

19. See above, p. 168.

20. James Mill, *An Essay on Government*, ed. Ernest Barker (Cambridge, 1937), p. 23. GKC.

21. Bentham included women's suffrage in his *Plan of Parliamentary Reform* in 1817 (*The Works of Jeremy Bentham*, ed. John Bowring (11 vols., Edinburgh, 1843), iii. 463). James Mill, however, excluded women from the franchise on the ground that the interest of almost all of them 'is involved either in that of their fathers or in that of their husbands' (*Essay on Government*, p. 45). His son wrote of him:

> in his position, with no resource but the precarious one of writing in periodicals, he married and had a large family; conduct than which nothing could be more opposed, both as a matter of good sense and of duty, to the opinions which, at least at a later period of life, he strenuously upheld.

J. S. Mill, *Autobiography* (1873), p. 3. GKC.

22. See T. R. Malthus, *First Essay on Population, 1798*, ed. James Bonar (1926), p. 353:

> I should be inclined ... to consider the world, and this life, as the mighty process of God, not for the trial, but for the creation and formation of mind; a process necessary, to awaken inert, chaotic matter, into spirit; to sublimate the dust of the earth into soul; to elicit an aetherial spark from the clod of clay.

GKC.

23. Charles Pelham Villiers (1802–98), brother of the 4th Earl of Clarendon, was M.P. for Wolverhampton from 1835 until his death. An associate of Bentham and the Utilitarians, from 1838 he proposed an annual motion for the repeal of the Corn Laws. Sir Herbert Maxwell, *The Life and Letters of George William Frederick, Fourth Earl of Clarendon* (2 vols., 1913), ii. 372 describes his last years: 'he perambulated, feebly and ever more feebly, that House wherein he had won his renown before five-sixths of the members around him had left school, registering dumb and docile votes, and creeping home to a solitary fireside to chew the cud of far-off memories.' Villiers played quite an important part in the campaign of the Anti-Corn Law League, but was undoubtedly overshadowed by Cobden, partly on account of the latter's connection with Manchester and the manufacturing interest, but also probably because of Cobden's superior ability. Cobden and Bright were of course manufacturers. William Johnson Fox (1786–1864), a former Unitarian minister, was M.P. for Oldham, 1847–62,

and a notable anti-Corn Law orator and journalist. See Richard Garnett, *The Life of W. J. Fox* (1910). GKC.

24. In the *Spectator*, 24 June 1871, Bagehot wrote of Grote:

> he belonged to a remarkable class of most vigorous Liberals. They were called the 'Philosophic Radicals' forty years ago, and had a curious, hard, compact, consistent creed. They were in the most anomalous position possible as politicians. They were unpopular Democrats; they liked the people but the people did not like them or their ideas.

Walter Bagehot, *Literary Studies*, ed. Richard Holt Hutton (3 vols., 1905–7), iii. 389.

The decline of the Philosophic Radicals became marked in the general election of 1837, and with that of 1841 the careers of several of them came to an end. Grote retired from public life in 1841, and, apart from his banking, devoted the rest of his life to writing his *History of Greece* and to his work as Vice-Chancellor of London University and President of University College. He declined Gladstone's offer of a peerage in 1869 and in 1870 decided against the ballot, of which he had once been a leading advocate (Mrs. Grote, *The Personal Life of George Grote* (1873), pp. 306–8, 312–13). Mill had in fact done so in 1859: 'It appears to me that secret suffrage, a very right and justifiable demand when originally made, would at present, and still more in time to come, produce far greater evil than good.' (*Thoughts on Parliamentary Reform* (1859), pp. 36–7.)

John Temple Leader (1810–1903), the son of a wealthy London merchant, was returned for Bridgwater in 1835, made his mark as an active Radical, and was elected for Westminster in 1837 and 1841. He abandoned politics in 1844 and went to live on the Continent, first at Cannes with his friend Lord Brougham, and later near Florence, where he bought and restored ancient buildings. His greatest undertaking was the restoration of the medieval castle of Vincigliata. Henry Warburton (1784–1858), another of the group, was M.P. for Bridport, 1826–41. He reappeared in the Commons in 1843 as Member for Kendal, but retired in 1847, maintaining that the reforms which he had most desired had been effected.

There is therefore a case for Young's contention that the Philosophic Radicals disappeared between 1837 and 1847, and the rise to prominence of Cobden and Bright is significant of the increased importance of men 'who had learnt their economics in the counting-house, their logic on the platform, their rhetoric in the pulpit'. Nevertheless, men who had been closely associated with the Philosophic Radicals continued to be of importance in politics. Sir William Molesworth (1810–55), the colonial reformer and founder of the *London Review*, was M.P. for East Cornwall, 1832–7, for Leeds, 1837–41, and for South-wark, 1845–55. He became First Commissioner of the Board of Works in 1853 and Colonial Secretary in July 1855, but died only three months later. His fellow colonial reformer, Charles Buller, M.P. for West Looe, 1830–1, and Liskeard, 1832–48, would no doubt have continued to play an important part but for his untimely death in 1848 at the age of 42. The veteran Joseph Hume, born in 1777, entered Parliament in 1812 as Member for Weymouth and died, after representing a number of constituencies, as Member for the Montrose Burghs in 1855. The careers of other Radicals who owed their origins neither to the manu-facturing districts nor to Dissent continued beyond this period: Thomas Slingsby Duncombe (1797–1861), M.P. for Hertford, 1826–1832, Finsbury, 1834–61; William Ewart (see below, Section V, note 20); and Thomas Wakley (1795–1862), M.P. for Finsbury, 1835–52.

In fact there was more continuity in Radical politics in the mid-nineteenth century than Young suggests. Politics were loosely or-ganized, and an independent Radical could if lucky retain his hold on a constituency, or if rejected, find another, whatever his background. He could still play an important part in the House of Commons by promoting his own particular reforms, as did both Wakley and Ewart. It must, however, be remembered that many of the objects at which the Philosophic Radicals had aimed in the thirties remained part of the common stock of Radicalism till after 1868. See Joseph Hamburger, *Intellectuals in Politics: John Stuart Mill and the Philosophical Radicals* (New Haven and London, 1965); John Vincent, *The Formation of the Liberal Party, 1857–1868* (1966), pp. 28–35. GKC, DRF.

25. *The Impregnable Rock of Holy Scripture*, by W. E. Gladstone, ap-peared in *Good Words* in April 1890. W. Isbister published a revised and enlarged edition later in the year. GKC.

26. For the full title of Wilberforce's *Practical View*, which may be regarded as the manifesto of late eighteenth- and early nineteenth-century Evangelicalism, see above, Section I, note 3. Within six months of its publication on 1 Apr. 1797 7,500 copies had been sold. Fifteen

editions were produced in England by 1824, and twenty-five in America, and the work was translated into French, Italian, Spanish, Dutch, and German. *DRF.*

27. The standard biography is Finer, *Chadwick*, but further personal details can be obtained from the memoir in Benjamin Ward Richardson, *The Health of Nations* (2 vols., 1887), i. pp. xv–lxxiv. Early in his career Chadwick was drawn into very close association with Jeremy Bentham, who offered him an annuity if he would become the official exponent of his philosophy after his death. Chadwick declined the proposal, but accepted a legacy. In 1832 he became an Assistant Commissioner and in 1833 a Commissioner of the Poor Law Commission, whose report he wrote with Nassau Senior. He was responsible for those parts which formed the basis of the Poor Law Amendment Act of 1834 and became Secretary of the Poor Law Commission, which was given ample scope to enforce the Act and to impose its principles on the unions. Chadwick also framed the Factory Act of 1833 which was to be put into effect by inspectors. It has been considered that these inspectors and the Poor Law Commissioners represented the beginning of the modern civil service. *GKC.*

28. See Richardson, *Health of Nations*, i. p. xxiv: 'The mother of Edwin Chadwick died . . . while he was quite a child; but he remembers that she was, by nature, a sanitarian *pur et simple*. Morning and evening ablution of unquestionable quality, was the rule with her for her children.' *DRF.*

29. See ibid. i. p. lxvii:

During this visit [to the Paris Exhibition of 1865–6] he had an interview, more than once, with the Emperor Napoleon III., in one of which interviews the often-repeated story is told, in which Mr. Chadwick, on being asked by the Emperor what he thought of Paris, is said to have answered, 'Fair above, Sire, foul below.' The answer was not quite in that form. The answer really was as follows: 'Sire, they say that Augustus found Rome a city of brick, and left it a city of marble. If your Majesty, finding Paris fair above, will leave it sweet below, you will more than rival the first Emperor of Rome.' Napoleon, mightily pleased with the suggestion, entered into the subject very fully, and, on my friend's instance, directed an inquiry into the subject referred to, and into the application of the sewage of Paris to agricultural purposes.

GKC.

30. Public audit started with the audit of the Poor Law authorities imposed by the Poor Law Amendment Act of 1834. The grant-in-aid of rates effectively began in 1833 with grants to local authorities to subsidize the expense of prosecutions, and was extended in 1846, largely as compensation to the counties for the repeal of the Corn Laws. See Joseph Redlich, *Local Government in England*, ed. Francis W. Hirst (2 vols., 1903), i. 155–62; ii. 268–72. *GKC.*

31. This presumably refers to 'The Slave Trade' and 'African Hospitality', painted by George Morland (1763–1804), apparently in 1791, and engraved by John Raphael Smith (1752–1812). They were probably painted not so much as propaganda, but rather as the illustrations of a moral story, such as those of Hogarth, or Morland's own series depicting the recapture of a deserter from the army. *GKC.*

32. For 'Free Trade League' read 'Anti-Corn Law League'. *GKC.*

SECTION III

1. John Ruskin, who was only 24 at the time, published the first volume of his *Modern Painters* in April 1843, under the name of 'A Graduate of Oxford'. The first edition to bear his own name was that of 1851. For Sydney Smith's compliments see Ruskin's *Praeterita*, Volume II, Chapter 9:

In the literary world, attention was first directed to the book by Sydney Smith, in the hearing of my severest and chiefly antagonist master, the Rev. Thomas Dale, who with candid kindness sent the following note of the matter to my father:—

'You will not be uninterested to hear that Mr. Sydney Smith . . . spoke in the highest terms of your son's work, on a public occasion, and in presence of several distinguished literary characters. He said it was a work of transcendent talent, presented the most original views, and the most elegant and powerful language, and would work a complete revolution in the world of taste. He did not know, when he said this, how much I was interested in the author.'

The Works of John Ruskin, ed. E. T. Cook and Alexander Wedderburn (39 vols., 1903–12), xxxv. 395. *DRF.*

2. The first number of *Vanity Fair*, which was not initially a popular success, appeared in January 1847, and the last in July 1848. Thackeray was 35, had been writing for the press for some ten years, and had enjoyed some success with his work for *Punch*, which included 'Jeames's Diary' in 1845, 'The Snobs of England' in 1846, and 'The Prize Novelists' in 1847. *GKC.*

3. In 1844 R. H. Horne published *A New Spirit of the Age*, in conscious imitation of Hazlitt's *Spirit of the Age*, which had appeared in 1825. His selection of representative literary figures provides an interesting re-flection on Young's description of the way in which at about this time the great Victorian writers replaced those of the early nineteenth century. Of those mentioned by Young, Bulwer Lytton, Tennyson, Macaulay, Carlyle, and Dickens feature in Horne's selection. He did not list Disraeli, but included a number of fashionable novelists, such as Mrs. Gore and Mrs. Trollope, and omitted Newman, while includ-ing Pusey. Although he made no mention of Thackeray, he included his friends, Browning and Elizabeth Barrett. Lord Ashley and South-wood Smith appear as philanthropists, but politicians are explicitly excluded, which accounts for the omission of Gladstone. As Matthew Arnold only graduated at Oxford in 1844, and did not publish until 1849, he was naturally not among Horne's selection, and was, in any case, a man of a later generation. The significance of Horne's work lies both in its demonstration that most of the figures mentioned by Young were already seen to be important in 1844, and in the fact that of Haz-litt's representative writers, only Wordsworth and Leigh Hunt appear in it. *GKC, LGS.*

4. cf. Young's elaboration of this point in *Daylight and Champaign* (1948 edn.), p. 158:

Young men in 1850, reading with the proper avidity of youth, could have found most of their tastes, and most of their curiosities, satisfied by masterpieces published, since their birth, by men who had been pointed out to them in the streets. To watch Mr. Macaulay threading his way through the Piccadilly traffic, book in hand: to see Mr. Dickens running up the steps of the Athenaeum: to recognise the Laureate by his cloak and Mr. Carlyle by his shawl, were the peculiar joys of that time.

DRF.

5. See Charles Merivale to W. H. Thompson, 11 June 1832:

a daily Divan continued to sit throughout the term . . . The *Palace of Art* was read successively to each man as he came up from the vacation . . . the institution did on the whole drag a very slow length along . . . like some of the lines in the *Lotus-eaters*. Though the least eminent of the Tennysonian rhapsodists, I have converted by my readings both my brother and your friend (or enemy?) Richardson, to faith in the latter poem. They rather scoff at the former, and ask whether the 'abysmal depths of personality' means the *Times* newspaper.

Autobiography of Dean Merivale, ed. Judith Anne Merivale (1899), pp. 130–1. The relevant lines of *The Palace of Art* are:

> Lest she should fail and perish utterly,
> God, before whom ever lie bare
> The abysmal deeps of Personality,
> Plagued her with sore despair.

RR.

6. See Fitzjames Stephen's comment on Dr. Arnold in his review of *Tom Brown's Schooldays* in the *Edinburgh Review*, vol. cvii (Jan. and Apr. 1858), p. 183: 'The special peculiarity of his character would seem to have been an intense and somewhat impatient fervour. To him and his admirers we owe the substitution of the word "earnest" for its predecessor "serious".' Bagehot's use of the word 'eagerness' has not been traced. *JMC.*

7. I have not been able to discover any record of the incident as described in the text; but in Moore's diary, 9 Jan. 1838, there is an account of an episode, also at Bowood, which so closely resembles it that it

seems possible that Young's story is an inaccurate recollection of what Moore recorded:

> In the evening, the Duchess [of Sutherland] having expressed a strong wish that I should sing, I sat down, and began, unluckily, with 'There's a song of the olden time,' which I had not sung for a long time; and the state of my spirits not being very good, the melancholy both of the song and of my own voice affected me so much, that before I had sung the first two lines I broke out into one of those hysterical fits of sobbing, which must be as painful to others as they are to myself, and was obliged to hurry away into the next room. . . . The exceeding effort I made to suppress the sobbing only made it break out more audibly; and altogether, nothing could be more disagreeable. . . . Having drunk off a tumbler of sal-volatile and water . . . I returned to the drawing room; and after laughing a little at my own exhibition, sat down again to the pianoforte, and sung through all the gayest of my songs that I could call to remembrance.

Memoirs, Journal, and Correspondence of Thomas Moore, ed. Lord John Russell (8 vols., 1853–6), vii. 215. If this is the incident to which Young alludes, it must be observed that it was not a case of excessive sensibility given unlimited scope, but one of hysteria. It seems likely that the words of the song were associated in Moore's mind with the death of his father in 1825, shortly after which an attempt to sing the same song had also resulted in his breakdown (ibid. v. 28). It does, at the same time, raise the wider question of the relationship of the uninhibited sensibility with which Young is dealing to hysteria, a problem reflected also in the physical phenomena sometimes manifested at eighteenth- and nineteenth-century revivalist meetings, and the 'unknown tongues' at Irving's meetings between 1830 and 1834. For evidence that Moore's singing could have a powerful effect on his audience see N. P. Willis, *Pencillings by the Way* (3 vols., 1835), i. 108–9:

> He makes no attempt at music. It is a kind of admirable recitative, in which every shade of thought is syllabled and dwelt upon, and the sentiment of the song goes through your blood, warming you to the very eyelids, and starting your tears, if you have soul or sense in you. I have heard of women's fainting at a song of M——'s; and if the burden of it answered by chance to a secret in the bosom of

the listener, I should think, from its comparative effect upon so old a stager as myself, that the heart would break with it.

GKC, JMC.

8. cf. John Keble, then a Fellow of Oriel, to J. T. Coleridge, a Fellow of Exeter, 14 Feb. 1819:

> I have not talked with Arnold lately on the distressing thoughts which he wrote to you about, but I am fearful, from his manner at times, that he has by no means got rid of them, though I feel quite confident that all will be well in the end. The subject of them is that most awful one, on which all *very* inquisitive reasoning minds are, I believe, most liable to such temptations—I mean the doctrine of the blessed Trinity. Do not start, my dear Coleridge; I do not believe that Arnold has any scruples of the *understanding* about it, but it is a defect of his mind that he cannot get rid of a certain feeling of objections—and particularly when, as he fancies, the bias is so strong upon him to decide one way from interest . . .

Arthur Penrhyn Stanley, *The Life and Correspondence of Thomas Arnold* (2 vols., 1844), i. 21–2. It should be noted that at this time Arnold was also a Fellow of Oriel. However, that undergraduates could take themselves and these problems seriously is confirmed by the diary of Archdeacon Allen, written during his undergraduate days at Trinity, Cambridge:

> *Feb.* 3, 1830.—Began looking over an essay, but Thackeray came in. We had some conversation, when I affected him to tears. He went away with a determination to live a new life. Fitzgerald and myself afterwards in tears.
> *Feb.* 7, 1830.—After Chapel Thackeray came up. He expressed some doubts of Christ being God; we read over St. Matthew together, and he was convinced. Went to bed very late, but I hope the day was not spent in vain.

Anna Otter Allen, *John Allen and his Friends* (1922), pp. 2–3. GKC.

9. I do not know which civil servant burst into tears at the sight of an infant school, or which Ministers wept at the Table, although I am sure there were not a few of them. Young is making an important point in stressing the great readiness to weep in public, as a feature of the excessive sensibility which was characteristic of the first half of the

nineteenth century. According to Tom Moore, Sir Walter Scott told him that the Duke of Wellington wept when he spoke of the horrors of Waterloo (*Memoirs of Thomas Moore*, iv. 337); and Dr. Arnold burst into tears when, in his own family circle, he heard a comparison which seemed to put St. Paul above St. John (Stanley, *Life of Arnold*, i. 197). Macaulay was liable to be reduced to tears by literature, the theatre, and individual human tragedy throughout his life (Trevelyan, *Macaulay*, ii. 211–12). At the same time, a willingness to show appreciation of 'affecting' literature by uninhibited crying was in many ways a convention of the time, and the ability of particular passages to provoke such a reaction was regarded as a criterion of their success. Macaulay felt well satisfied with a section of his *History* in 1849 after reading it to his sister and brother-in-law, when 'Hannah cried, and Trevelyan kept awake.' (ibid. ii. 231.) Swooning also had strong literary authority, particularly in the sillier forms of novel, as well as being quite common in reality. A public reading by Dickens at Clifton in January 1869 of the murder of Nancy caused 'a contagion of fainting. And yet the place was not hot. I should think we had from a dozen to twenty ladies borne out, stiff and rigid, at various times. It became quite ridiculous.' (Edgar Johnson, *Charles Dickens: His Tragedy and Triumph* (2 vols., 1953), ii. 1106.)

However, proneness to public weeping continued for much longer than Young implies, and even in the present century eminent men, of whom Sir Winston Churchill was one, have not been ashamed to be seen in tears. The convention whereby a lachrymose response to 'affecting' literature was almost obligatory also survived. On 10 June 1879 Tennyson called Mary Gladstone 'a hard little thing' for not crying when his son, Hallam, read the death of Socrates in Plato. Hallam himself broke down suitably and completely (*Mary Gladstone: Her Diaries and Letters*, ed. Lucy Masterman (1930), p. 161). The problem is further complicated by the fact that people who were themselves liable to indulge in what seems to the modern mind uncritical emotion were ready to satirize it in others. Before 1830 Macaulay mockingly kept count of the number of times the characters in Mrs. Kitty Cuthbertson's *Santo Sebastiano* fainted (Trevelyan, *Macaulay*, i. 134), but was himself prone to tears all his life. Thackeray was totally subdued by the death of Paul Dombey in *Dombey and Son*, but in Chapters 22 and 23 of *Pendennis* he drew a sharp picture of Blanche Amory with her poetry, 'bound in blue velvet, with a gilt lock', and called *Mes Larmes*. GKC.

10. Martin Farquhar Tupper (1810–89) was the author of several volumes of *Proverbial Philosophy*, published between 1839 and 1871, which achieved great popular success in Britain, the United States, and elsewhere. Evidently, for twenty-five years seldom less than 5,000 copies were sold in any year in Britain, and the earlier volumes went through more than fifty editions and were translated into German, Danish, and French verse. They are, in fact, merely collections of crass commonplaces, expressed in rather contorted language in rhythmical prose form; and in the second half of the century Tupper became a target of derision and parody. See his autobiography, *My Life as an Author* (1886); Derek Hudson, *Martin Tupper: his rise and fall* (1949); Ralf Buchmann, *Martin F. Tupper and the Victorian Middle Class Mind* (Bern, 1941); and the *D.N.B.*

The works of Ralph Waldo Emerson (1803–82), the American poet, essayist, and transcendental philosopher, also appealed to a large and cosmopolitan public. His books were translated into French, German, Italian, Spanish, Dutch, Russian, and the Scandinavian languages. Emerson, however, was of a completely different intellectual stature from Tupper, and gained the appreciation of a number of intelligent people. He was a friend of Thomas Carlyle, and Matthew Arnold bore witness to his influence. Probably his most popular books were his two volumes of *Essays*, published in 1841 and 1844. *GKC.*

11. This statement requires qualification. Gladstone formed his style from Aristotle's *Rhetoric*, a few lessons in voice production from Keate, Blair's lectures, and incessant practice in debate backed by an unusual range of reading. See British Library Add. MSS. 44808; G. M. Young, *Daylight and Champaign* (1948 edn.), pp. 54–9; *The Gladstone Diaries*, vol. i, ed. M. R. D. Foot (Oxford, 1968), pp. 31, 102. He did, however, for many years read to his family and servants a sermon on almost every Sunday he spent at home. The texts of those he wrote himself can be found in Add. MSS. 44779–81. See also Loren Reid, 'Gladstone's Essay on Public Speaking', *Quarterly Journal of Speech*, xxxix (1953), 265–72. *MRDF.*

12. See *The Times*, 23 Mar. 1877, p. 10c. *MRDF.*

13. See *Sir Robert Peel from his Private Papers*, ed. Charles Stuart Parker (3 vols., 1891–9), i. 10. *GKC.*

14. Daniel Defoe, *The Complete English Tradesman, in Familiar Letters: Directing him in all the several Parts and Progressions of Trade* (2 vols., 1725–7). *GKC.*

15. See Section XIII, note 3.

16. For Grote see Section II, note 9. Connop Thirlwall, Bishop of St. David's, published an eight-volume *History of Greece* between 1835 and 1847. Henry Hart Milman's major works were *The History of the Jews* (3 vols., 1829), *The History of Christianity from the Birth of Christ to the Abolition of Paganism in the Roman Empire* (3 vols., 1840), and a *History of Latin Christianity* (6 vols., 1854–5). The first volume of Macaulay's *History of England* appeared in 1848. Sir Charles Lyell's *Principles of Geology* was published in three volumes between 1830 and 1833, John Stuart Mill's *System of Logic* in 1843 and his *Principles of Political Economy* in 1848. Carlyle published *Past and Present* in 1843, but he had already produced *The French Revolution* (1837), *Sartor Resartus* (1838), *Chartism* (1840), and *On Heroes, Hero-Worship, and the Heroic in History* (1841). For Ruskin's *Modern Painters* see above, Section III, note 1. Tennyson's *In Memoriam A. H. H.* appeared in 1850. *GKC.*

17. This statement is misleading. The Minerva Press published sensational novels in the eighteenth and early nineteenth centuries, but Disraeli's first novels, *Vivian Grey* (1826) and *The Young Duke* (1831), belong in spirit to a later generation, and their most obvious models are the novels of fashionable life of the 'silver fork' school. See Dorothy Blakey, *The Minerva Press, 1790–1820* (1939). *GKC.*

18. This probably alludes to the work of Pierce Egan, the elder (1772–1849). His *Life in London; or, the Day and Night Scenes of Jerry Hawthorn, Esq., and his Elegant Friend, Corinthian Tom, accompanied by Bob Logic, the Oxonian, in their Rambles and Sprees through the Metropolis*, which began serial publication in 1821, enjoyed great success, and was widely pirated and copied. Doubtless when *The Pickwick Papers* first appeared in 1836 it was expected that Dickens would write comparable serial sketches around the sporting pictures of an artist, Robert Seymour. Dickens's genius naturally removed his own work from any resemblance to that model, and his intellectual descent should probably be traced from Smollett or Fielding. *GKC.*

19. cf. Douglas Jerrold's paper on 'The Factory Child', contributed to *Heads of the People: Or Portraits of the English*, drawn by Kenny Meadows (2 vols., 1840–1), i. 189:

> In some factories, the children whilst at work are allowed to sing; they may mingle voices in thanksgiving harmony. When we use the word thanksgiving, we wish to imply that no profane songs are permitted to be breathed, the children being rigidly restricted to the execution of hymns; which, as though they would utterly dumb-found their tyrant engine, they sing with a determination of piety that to some people would sound exceedingly gracious; the said good folks detecting no unpremeditated reproach and satire in the words sent forth. And yet there *are* men who, when the children of nine years old, doomed to work nine hours a-day for three shillings a-week, carol the following hymn, might be irresistibly compelled to contrast the condition with the verse of the singers:—
>
> > 'By cool Siloam's shady rill,
> > How sweet the lily grows!
> > How sweet the breath beneath the hill,
> > Of Sharon's dewy rose!'
>
> Who, beholding the reeking faces of the children in a temperature of ninety-eight degrees, but would feel the melancholy reproach in their almost unconscious aspiration for 'cool Siloam's shady rill'!

There is, however, no reference in this passage to 'A Frog He Would A'Wooing Go'. *JMC*.

20. Richard Oastler did in fact frequently impugn the morals of mill-owners in this period. See, e.g., his *Letter to . . . the Shareholders in the Bradford Observer* (Bradford, 1834), cited in J. T. Ward, *The Factory Movement, 1830–1855* (1962), pp. 126–7.

The case of the private tutor who beat a boy to death clearly refers to that of the proprietor of a school at Eastbourne, called Hopley, who killed a mentally deficient pupil, named Cancellor, in 1860, and was sentenced to four years' imprisonment for manslaughter. The case appears to have been fully reported in the contemporary press, and there is an account of it in the *Annual Register* (1860), Chronicle, pp. 58–60. It is necessary to question how much general significance should be attributed to a single outrageous incident.

The reference to Milton's comment on 'the City Man and his Religion' is presumably to the following passage of *Areopagitica*:

A wealthy man addicted to his pleasure and to his profits, finds Religion to be a traffick so entangl'd, and of so many piddling accounts, that of all mysteries he cannot skill to keep a stock going upon that trade. What should he doe? fain he would have the name to be religious, fain he would bear up with his neighbours in that. What does he therefore but resolvs to give over toyling, and to find himself out som factor, to whose care and credit he may commit the whole managing of his religious affairs; som Divine of note and estimation that must be. To him he adheres, resigns the whole ware-house of his religion, with all the locks and keyes into his custody; and indeed makes the very person of that man his religion; esteems his associating with him a sufficient evidence and commendatory of his own piety. So that a man may say his religion is now no more within himself, but is becom a dividuall movable, and goes and comes neer him, according as that good man frequents the house. He entertains him, gives him gifts, feasts him, lodges him; his religion comes home at night, praies, is liberally supt, and sumptuously laid to sleep, rises, is saluted, and after the malmsey, or some well spic't bruage, and better breakfasted then he whose morning appetite would have gladly fed on green figs between *Bethany* and *Jerusalem*, his Religion walks abroad at eight, and leavs his kind entertainer in the shop trading all day without his religion.

Complete Prose Works of John Milton, vol. ii, ed. Ernest Sirluck (New Haven, 1959), pp. 544–5. *JTW, GKC.*

21. See Coleridge's fourteenth lecture at Flower-de-Luce Court, Fetter Lane, 13 Mar. 1818 (*The Literary Remains of Samuel Taylor Coleridge*, ed. Henry Nelson Coleridge (4 vols., 1836–9), i. 238) and his *On the Constitution of the Church and State* (1830), pp. 47 ff. The word was formed from the German 'Klerisei' which has, however, a different meaning. *GKC.*

22. See Thomas Carlyle, *Chartism*, 2nd edn. (1840), pp. 98 ff.: 'Two things, great things, dwell, for the last ten years, in all thinking heads in England; and are hovering, of late, even on the tongues of not a few. . . . Universal Education is the first . . . general Emigration is the second.' *DRF.*

23. Since the works of Shelley seem to have been openly on sale in the shops of respectable booksellers in the 1830s and 1840s, it seems most improbable that by that time any attempt to condemn *Prometheus Unbound* as a blasphemous libel would have been effective. See next note. *GKC.*

24. The date given by Young is misleading. Shelley had *Queen Mab* printed privately, but in 1821, to his great annoyance, William Clarke, a struggling London bookseller, pirated an edition. In 1822 Clarke was indicted at the instigation of the Society for the Suppression of Vice, found guilty, and imprisoned for four months. After Shelley's death in the same year Richard Carlile bought up this edition and the remainder of the poet's own, and continued to sell it (William H. Wickwar, *The Struggle for the Freedom of the Press, 1819–1832* (1928), pp. 260–3). In 1840, after incessant pressure from Bishop Philpotts of Exeter, the Home Secretary instructed magistrates to search for blasphemous and seditious literature, and Hetherington, Cleave, and Heywood of Manchester were prosecuted for selling C. J. Haslam's *Letters to the Clergy of all Denominations* (*New Moral World*, 15 Aug. 1840). Hetherington brought counter-charges against three respectable booksellers, Moxon, Frazer, and Otley, for selling the works of Shelley, which by this date included *Queen Mab*. Moxon was found guilty on 23 June 1841, and it is this verdict to which Young alludes. It was, however, little more than a formality, as the court regarded the charge as frivolous, Moxon was not called up for judgement, the charges against Frazer and Otley were dropped, and the works of Shelley presumably remained on sale in their shops. See *Reports of State Trials*, N.S. iv. 694–722; Edward Royle, *Radical Politics, 1790–1900. Religion and Unbelief* (1971), pp. 44–5, 137; G. D. Nokes, *A History of the Crime of Blasphemy* (1928), p. 107. *ER, JAW.*

25. Milman did so in his *History of the Jews* (1829), which was violently attacked. See Arthur Milman, *Henry Hart Milman* (1900), pp. 83–93. *GKC.*

26. See the review of *Our Village* in the *Quarterly Review*, vol. xxxi (Dec. 1824 and Mar. 1825), pp. 167–8:

it is really provoking to find her studiously labouring to familiarize herself with the use, and to soil her pages by the introduction of such low and provincial corruptions of language as 'transmogrified', 'betweenity', 'dumpiness', 'rolypoly', 'kickshaws', 'hurry-scurry', 'scrap-dinners', 'pot luck', and similar flowers of diction . . .

However, the offending use of 'roly-poly' had nothing to do with a pudding, but occurred in Miss Mitford's description of two coursing bitches: 'There was a peculiar sort of innocent beauty about them, like that of a roly-poly child.' *BA, GKC.*

27. In 1838 Lord Holland said that he found Lords Howick and Morpeth so serious that he was 'afraid to talk before them' (Lord Broughton, *Recollections of a Long Life*, ed. Lady Dorchester (6 vols., 1909–11), v. 180). See David Spring, 'Aristocracy, Social Structure, and Religion in the Early Victorian Period', *Victorian Studies*, vi (1962–3), 263–80, which cites this among many examples of the same change. *GKC.*

28. The incident to which Young alludes has not been traced, but the words used were probably *minuere et contrahere pelvem* (see above, p. 51). It seems likely that it was rather a desire to use a technical medical term than a sense of decency which induced the Member of Parliament to resort to Latin. Lord Ashley was able to discuss the evils inflicted on pregnant women and young mothers by factory labour with reasonable freedom in the House of Commons. See *Hansard*, 3rd Ser. lxxiii. 1093–4 (15 Mar. 1844). *GKC.*

29. *The Times*, 3 June 1833, p. 2d, editorial on the Instructions issued by the Central Board of Factory Commissioners to the District and Medical Commissioners, 25 Apr. 1833. After commenting caustically on 'the curious pains which have been taken to *frustrate* the one and only honest aim of the commission', it went on:

The instructions contain a diversity of plans for inquiring into questions but remotely connected with that from which the establishment of the commission has arisen, and, indeed, not entirely compatible with that wholesome dread of ridicule and anxious love of decency which ought to characterize the proceedings of such a body. We subjoin, as a curiosity, some of the queries to be made of married women:—

'Was your first child born within one year of your marriage?
How many children have you had still-born?

How many miscarriages? In the first three months; in the next three months; in the last three months of pregnancy?

How many of these births were difficult cases; requiring instruments; not requiring instruments?'

This Central Board ought to be ashamed of itself; but Boards are insensible to all such laudable emotions.

Young is not quite accurate in citing the reaction of *The Times* as a manifestation of the 'drastic and vigilant censorship' with which he is dealing. It does, it is true, represent the traditionalists' dislike of Benthamite methods of collecting information; but it was also inspired by the widespread belief that the Commission had been appointed in order to whitewash the factory masters and to delay the pending Ten Hours Bill for the protection of factory children, which *The Times* supported. *JTW, DRF.*

30. There appears to be no passage in *The Economist* in 1847 to substantiate this statement. On 10 April it objected to Lord Morpeth's Bill on explicitly *laissez-faire* grounds (vol. v, pp. 411–12); but on 24 July it claimed to find no fault with Ministers for having brought forward the measure 'to comply with a great demand, and none for withdrawing it till it can be matured, and can carry with it the opinions of those most interested in its success, and of the functionaries who will have to work it' (vol. v, p. 834). On 20 November it observed that the approach of cholera lent 'an alarming importance' to the subject of sanitary reform (vol. v, p. 1335); and on 11 December, in an article on the Sanitary Commission, it seemed to approve of members of the upper classes concerning themselves with such matters as 'sewers and cesspools' (vol. v, pp. 1420–1).

However, on 20 May 1848 (vol. vi, pp. 564–6) it launched a violent attack, again from a *laissez-faire* point of view, on the Public Health Bill as reintroduced. One of its arguments was that water closets were more common in England than in France and Germany because there people had come to rely on public regulation rather than taking private initiative. It also criticized the details of the proposed regulations, and contended that it was impossible to control every closet, privy, ash-pit, and convenience. It continued:

What is offensive to write about and publicly to discuss, as this subject obviously is, cannot be a fit nor even decent subject for legislation;

and the depraved taste of the men habituated to dissecting rooms and close stools, who have led the legislature into meddling with these dirty matters, is quite as conspicuous as their want of wisdom.

This is probably the passage to which Young is referring. But it is noticeable that in fact the writer was prepared to discuss these matters, and this outburst reads like a sudden loss of temper induced by contemplation of the threatened interferences by the Government, and possibly by the thought of Chadwick and Southwood Smith. It does not seem to indicate a guilty conscience, for the writer apparently believed that 'with rare exceptions, there are not in the world such comfortable and splendid abodes for MILLIONS of people as in Great Britain', provided by the enterprise of individuals, unregulated and unchecked by the State. He acknowledged the suffering which disease brought to the poor, but hoped that the rich would be inspired to individual efforts to promote their welfare and elevation. The whole article is an interesting example of the passion which *laissez-faire* ideas excited in some people at that time, and has its counterpart in *The Economist*'s contemporary attitude to factory legislation. The editor in these years was James Wilson (1805–60), Walter Bagehot's father-in-law, who evidently wrote most of the paper. *GKC.*

SECTION IV

1. Harriet Martineau's *Illustrations of Political Economy* were apparently inspired in 1827 by Mrs. Marcet's *Conversations on Political Economy*, a work largely of popular education, first published in 1816 and reprinted in 1817, 1821, and 1824. The *Illustrations*, which appeared between 1832 and 1834, were an immediate success. The series began in February 1832 and by 10 February the first edition of 1,500 was nearly exhausted (*Harriet Martineau's Autobiography*, ed. Maria Weston Chapman (3 vols., 1877), i. 138–9, 160–81, 233–4).

Coningsby; or, The New Generation, by Benjamin Disraeli, was published in May 1844, and the first edition of 1,000 copies went off in a fortnight. 'Three considerable editions were sold in this country in three months; and it was largely circulated throughout the continent of Europe, and within a brief period more than 50,000 copies were required in the United States of America.' (Preface to 5th edn., quoted in Monypenny and Buckle, *Disraeli*, ii. 199.)

The English Constitution, by Walter Bagehot (see below, Section XXIV, note 5) first appeared serially from 15 May 1865 to 1 Jan. 1867 in the *Fortnightly Review*. For almost the whole of this period the *Fortnightly*, edited by George Henry Lewes, was not a financial success, and when Lewes handed over to John Morley in December 1866 its circulation was only 1,400 (F. W. Hirst, *Early Life and Letters of John Morley* (2 vols., 1927), i. 84). Since then Bagehot's *Constitution* has become a standard authority with a very wide circulation, but when first produced it must have reached a much smaller number of readers than either the *Illustrations* or *Coningsby*. Bagehot was therefore writing for a smaller, if more professional, public than either Miss Martineau or Disraeli. However, there is no reason to believe that Miss Martineau's public and Disraeli's readers were identical, and if Young's suggestion is that each of these books typified the ways of thought of different periods of the nineteenth century, account must be taken of the fact that each probably appealed to a different section of the reading public. *GKC, DRF.*

2. Young's statement is clearly drawn from three notes in Élie Halévy, *Histoire du peuple anglais au XIXe siècle* (6 vols., Paris, 1912–32), ii. 61 n. 3 (Radical); ii. 75 n. 1 (Liberal); iii. 61 n. 3 (Conservative). *GKC, JMC.*

3. John Goodwyn Barmby (1820–81) claimed to have coined the word Communism during a visit to Paris in 1840:

I . . . conversed with some of the most advanced minds of the French metropolis, and there, in the company of some disciples of Babœuf, then called Equalitarians, I first pronounced the name of Communism, which has since arisen in so many countries, and denominated so many different societies, until, through the French revolution, it has acquired that world-wide reputation, to prepare it for which we have so earnestly laboured, and which the calumnies of the British press have only increased.

Apostle and Chronicle of the Communist Church, 1 Aug. 1848. No earlier use of the term is recorded in the *O.E.D.* Barmby's Communism was a form of Christian Socialism drawing its inspiration from the early Church in Jerusalem, and in the 1840s he appears to have used the terms Communist and Communitarian interchangeably. In 1841, for example, he founded both the London Communist Propaganda Society and the Universal Communitarian Association. See the *O.E.D.* under these terms and the *D.N.B.* under Barmby for further references.

Mr. Baume, who planned a Communist University at Colney Hatch, was Pierre Henri Joseph Baume (1797–1875), on whom see the *D.N.B. GKC, JMC.*

4. The source of Mackintosh's remark has not been traced. *GKC.*

5. It is not clear from what source Young derived his figures on the French death-rate. Edwin Chadwick, on whom Young seems largely to have relied, gave figures of 1 in 30·02 for the year 1784 and 1 in 39·8 for the period 1816–31 (*Report on the Sanitary Condition of the Labouring Population* (1842), ed. M. W. Flinn (Edinburgh, 1965), p. 246). This represents a decrease from 33 to 25 per 1,000. *GKC, JMC.*

6. Young's comparison of the rates of infant mortality in London in 1730 and 1830 is probably drawn from a table compiled by T. R. Edmonds, printed in the *Lancet*, 1835–6, vol. i, p. 692, and reproduced in M. Dorothy George, *London Life in the XVIIIth Century* (1925), p. 406. Edmonds's researches showed that in the years 1730–49 the number of burials of children under five recorded in the Bills of Mortality amounted to 74·5 per cent of the number christened, whereas in the years 1810–29 the proportion had decreased to 31·8 per cent. This seems to give the basis for Young's statement. *GKC, JMC.*

7. For infant mortality in London in 1840 see the *Third Annual Report of the Registrar General*, H.C. (1841 Second Session) vi. 21. The figures there are not broken down into classes, but see below, Section IV, note 15, for comments on the validity of such breakdowns. The figures for Manchester and Leeds seem to come from Edwin Chadwick's *Report on the Sanitary Condition of the Labouring Population* (1842), ed. M. W. Flinn (Edinburgh, 1965), pp. 244–5: 'We have seen that in the lowest districts of Manchester of 1,000 children born, more than 570 will have died before they attain the fifth year of their age. In the lowest districts of Leeds the infant mortality is similar.' Young therefore presents statistics drawn from 'the lowest districts' of Manchester and Leeds to illustrate infant mortality in the two towns as a whole. *GKC, JMC.*

8. On the Irish immigration into England in the early nineteenth

century see the *Edinburgh Review*, vol. xlv (Dec. 1826 and Mar. 1827), p. 54:

> We are indeed firmly persuaded, that nothing so deeply injurious to the character and habits of our people has ever occurred as the late extraordinary influx of Irish labourers; and yet the system may be said to be only in its infancy. Previously to the increased facilities of conveyance afforded by means of steam navigation, the expense of the passage from Ireland to Britain, trifling as it was even then, formed a serious obstacle to the influx of Irish poor: But this expense has now been reduced to almost nothing; and it consists with our knowledge, that thousands of poor creatures have been landed from the steam-packets at Liverpool and Greenock within these two years, the cost of whose conveyance from Ireland did not exceed from 4d. to 6d. each!

OM.

9. For the statistics of the overseas corn trade see B. R. Mitchell and Phyllis Deane, *Abstract of British Historical Statistics* (Cambridge, 1962), pp. 94–5. In fact in the years between 1813 and 1837 'the schism between the commercial and landed interests' showed itself in the bitter discontent of the landed interest with policies which favoured commerce, such as the return to a gold-based currency which brought deflation and a fall in prices, and the failure to repeal the tax on malt, rather than in the discontent of the commercial interest with the imposition of a duty on imported corn. *GKC, BRM.*

10. In his youth, shocked by the prevalence of infanticide, Mill distributed tracts on contraception, was sentenced to fourteen days' imprisonment, but released before completing his sentence. For an account of the incident see John Robertson's letter of 23 May 1873 in *The Amberley Papers*, ed. Bertrand and Patricia Russell (2 vols., 1937), ii. 247–9, and for its repercussions see below, Section XXVI, note 5. *BA.*

11. It is difficult to interpret the discussion in John Wade's *History of the Middle and Working Classes* (1833) as suggesting that Trade Unions should give instruction in birth control. He believed that they should disseminate 'a knowledge of the true economical principles, which . . . have been shown to govern the rates of wages' (p. 294), and true economical principles would have included, among other things, a

knowledge of the danger to the working classes of an uncontrolled increase of population. This, however, might possibly have been kept under control by self-restraint and the postponement of marriage. Wade approached the question of contraception with great caution:

> The first condition of any preventive is, that it should be practicable; that is, consonant to the usages, feelings, and education of those for whom it is intended. Any suggestion of an opposite description, would be void of utility. For instance, to recommend infanticide, abortion, or any artifice to frustrate conception, might be positively mischievous (p. 327).

On the other hand he spoke of a class of philosophers 'who have sought to divest marriage of its impoverishing consequences', and gave quotations from Mill's *Elements of Political Economy*, from the *Supplement to the 4th, 5th, and 6th Editions of the Encyclopædia Britannica* on 'Banks for Savings', and on 'Colony', from Harriet Martineau's *Illustrations of Political Economy* and from *State of Society*, all of which seem to recommend artificial checks (pp. 337-9).

Of all the early nineteenth-century Radicals, Francis Place seems to have been the most ready openly to defend birth control. See Graham Wallas, *The Life of Francis Place 1771-1854*, revised edn. (1918), pp. 168-73.

'Croker's attack on Miss Martineau' presumably refers to the review of Harriet Martineau's *Illustrations of Political Economy* which appeared in the *Quarterly Review*, vol. xlix (Apr. and July 1833), pp. 136-52. The attack and its motivation are discussed in Vera Wheatley, *The Life and Work of Harriet Martineau* (1957), pp. 100-3. The article, though severe, is not as savage as has been suggested, and in any case it is now clear that it was written not by Croker but by G. Poulett Scrope. Croker did review Miss Martineau's *Morals and Manners* (*Quarterly Review*, vol. lxiii (Jan. and Mar. 1839), pp. 61-72), but this article contains no reference to contraception. See Myron F. Brightfield, *John Wilson Croker* (Berkeley, 1940), pp. 422-3, and *The Wellesley Index to Victorian Periodicals*, i. 713, 721. GKC.

12. Robert Dale Owen's *Moral Physiology*, published in America in 1830, was probably the first book to appear there on birth control, and was followed by Dr. Charles Knowlton's *Fruits of Philosophy* (1832), on contraception. Knowlton's book in various forms seems to have had some circulation in Britain, but the first important contribution to the

subject in this country, Dr. George Drysdale's *Physical, Sexual and Natural Religion*, was not published until 1854. Drysdale's book was a plea for sexual freedom, and also contained a chapter giving practical advice on contraception. The English version under the changed title of *The Elements of Social Science* sold in all 88,000 copies, but the only edition which gave the name of the author was the 35th published in 1905. However, a number of eminent men were becoming interested in the matter, and among them was Lord Amberley, the son and heir of Lord John Russell—see under 'Malthusianism' in the indices to *The Amberley Papers*, ed. Bertrand and Patricia Russell (2 vols., 1937). After a visit to America and the Oneida community this interest seems to have intensified, and in July 1868 when presiding over a meeting of the London Dialectical Society, Amberley expressed a wish that medical men should give their opinions on the best methods to restrict families without injury to health (*Amberley Papers*, ii. 168–73). For this he was violently attacked in the medical press, and abused during his unsuccessful parliamentary candidature for South Devon later in the year. Although these incidents ventilated it, the prejudice against open discussion of the subject remained very strong. Probably the turning point was the prosecution of Charles Bradlaugh and Mrs. Besant in 1877 for circulating Knowlton's *Fruits of Philosophy*. They were convicted, but the conviction was quashed on a technicality and after the trial the sales of Knowlton's book immediately increased until it was replaced by a more up-to-date pamphlet by Mrs. Besant. At this time, too, contraceptive appliances began to be produced commercially. Free discussion came in the twentieth century, but long before that the diffusion of knowledge must have been considerable. For the history of the subject see the first two chapters of John Peel and Malcolm Potts, *Textbook of Contraceptive Practice* (Cambridge, 1969); and for further comment see above, p. 157, and below, Section XXVII, note 11. *GKC.*

13. On the whole question of social provisions in the factory villages see Sidney Pollard, *The Genesis of Modern Management* (1965), pp. 197–205. Jedediah Strutt, followed by William and Joseph Strutt, developed large cotton mills at Belper and Milford, near Derby. See R. S. Fitton and A. P. Wadsworth, *The Strutts and the Arkwrights* (Manchester, 1958), especially pp. 224–60, and W. Felkin, *History of the Machine-wrought Hosiery and Lace Manufactures*, centenary edn. (Newton Abbot, 1967), pp. 100–1. Henry and Edmund Ashworth's mills were at Egerton, near Bolton. It is possible that Disraeli drew upon his know-

ledge of Egerton when describing the village controlled by Oswald Millbank, the father of Edith, in *Coningsby*, Book IV, Chapter 3. The possibility is discussed and the village is described in Rhodes Boyson, *The Ashworth Cotton Enterprise. The Rise and Fall of a Family Firm 1818–1880* (Oxford, 1970), pp. 115–40 and 257–9. The 'cosy houses and flourishing gardens' of South Hetton, a colliery in County Durham, were enthusiastically described by the Prussian visitor, Friedrich Von Raumer, who concluded that 'it is evident that this part of the population of England is better off, and enjoys a higher degree of prosperity than anywhere else' (*England in 1835* (3 vols., 1836), iii. 154–7). Price's Candle Works were at Battersea. The provision for the workers there is described in *The Victoria History of the County of Surrey*, vol. ii (1905), p. 408. Examples of many other paternalistic employers could be cited. Thomas Ashton of Hyde, for example, was much praised by J. P. Kay in *The Moral and Physical Condition of the Working Classes Employed in the Cotton Manufacture in Manchester*, 2nd edn. (1832), pp. 100–4. For another view of the philanthropy of Ashton and the Ashworths, however, see J. T. Ward, *The Factory Movement 1830–1855* (1962), p. 202. But it was Sir Titus Salt who created, after 1851, probably the most remarkable of all towns for workers in a particular factory—Saltaire, near Bradford. See James Stevens Curl, 'A Victorian Model Town', *Country Life*, 9 Mar. 1972 (vol. cli, 542–4).

Not all employers assumed any social responsibility for those who worked for them. In the questionnaire sent to manufacturers by the Factory Commission in 1833, question 65 ran: 'Do the workpeople live in the houses of their employers; and if so, is any control or superintendence exercised for their moral and social improvement, or any arrangements made to enforce domestic cleanliness; if so, specify their nature?' In many returns the question was either left unanswered, or answered in the negative. Strutt, however, reported that many of his workmen lived in houses provided by the firm, and the Ashworths not only provided cottages but also imposed a searching moral and social discipline (H.C. (1834) xx. 580, 762). *GKC, JMC.*

14. The Owenite fancy has not been identified. *GKC.*

15. These figures come from Section IV of Edwin Chadwick's *Report on the Sanitary Condition of the Labouring Population* (1842), ed. M. W. Flinn (Edinburgh, 1965), pp. 219–54. Chadwick relied for his evidence on the Registrar-General's reports, and on the work of various writers

describing conditions in their own localities. These seem to have based their attributions of death rates to different classes partly on the trades or professions of the deceased persons, partly on the localities in which the deceased persons lived or died, and partly on personal information gained by research. None of these tests was completely satisfactory. The evidence afforded by the localities in which the deceased persons lived was particularly unsatisfactory, since there were few localities in which any one class predominated. *GKC.*

16. *Madame Bovary* by Gustave Flaubert was first published in serial form in the *Revue de Paris*, 1856–7. Flaubert was prosecuted, together with the editor of the journal, for offences against public morals but acquitted after trial. *JMC.*

17. See Henry Crabb Robinson to his brother, Thomas, 3 June 1804: 'to express what we sho^d call puritanism in language And excess of delicacy in matters of physical love—the Word *Englanderei* has been invented ie an englishism.' (*Crabb Robinson in Germany 1800–1805. Extracts from his Correspondence*, ed. Edith J. Morley (1929), p. 147.) *GKC.*

18. See the imaginary dialogue between the poet and an uncle which forms the Epilogue to *Dipsychus*. To the uncle's criticism of the moral attitude developed by Dr. Arnold's teaching, the poet replies:

> The real cause of the evil you complain of, which to a certain extent I admit, was, I take it, the religious movement of the last century, beginning with Wesleyanism, and culminating at last in Puseyism. This over-excitation of the religious sense, resulting in this irrational, almost animal irritability of conscience, was, in many ways, as foreign to Arnold as it is proper to—[Here the uncle breaks in, and the dialogue comes to an end.]

The Poems of Arthur Hugh Clough, ed. A. L. P. Norrington (1968), p. 296. *GKC.*

19. The source of Treitschke's remark has not been traced. *GKC.*

20. See Shaftesbury's speech in the Lords in defence of the holding of religious service in theatres, 24 Feb. 1860:

The middle classes of the present day are much better informed than those of a former generation. They know that the safety of their lives and property, and the preservation of public order, depend on their having around them a peaceful, happy, and moral population; and they feel that the course now being pursued is one which, by the communication of Christian truth, will mainly conduce to that issue.

Speeches of the Earl of Shaftesbury upon Subjects Having Relation Chiefly to the Claims and Interests of the Labouring Class (1868), pp. 333–4. *AWS.*

21. District visiting 'with a register and account book' clearly refers to the practice described in *Shades of Character: or, Mental and Moral Delineations; Designed to Promote the Formation of the Female Character on the Basis of Christian Principle*, by Anne Woodrooffe (1766–1830), which went through seven editions between 1824 and 1855. See Mona Wilson, *Jane Austen and some Contemporaries* (1938), p. 111. For 'the Blush-to-the-Cheek-of-the-Young-Person business' see Mr. Podsnap's views as reported in Book I, Chapter 11 of *Our Mutual Friend* by Charles Dickens:

The question about everything was, would it bring a blush into the cheek of the young person [his only daughter]? And the inconvenience of the young person was that, according to Mr. Podsnap, she seemed always liable to burst into blushes when there was no need at all.

GKC, EJK.

22. cf. the opening paragraph of Charles Dickens, 'Our Parish', Chapter 6, 'The Ladies' Societies' in *Sketches by Boz*:

Our Parish is very prolific in ladies' charitable institutions. In winter, when wet feet are common, and colds not scarce, we have the ladies' soup distribution society, the ladies' coal distribution society, and the ladies' blanket distribution society . . . and all the year round we have the ladies' child's examination society, the ladies' bible and prayer-book circulation society, and the ladies' childbed-linen monthly loan society.

EJK.

SECTION V

1. Cholera reached England in 1831, not 1830. On its social impact see Section IX, note 2. *GKC.*

2. The Manchester Board of Health itself published no report. Young is no doubt referring to *The Moral and Physical Condition of the Working Classes Employed in the Cotton Manufacture in Manchester* (1832) by the secretary to the Board, J. P. Kay (afterwards Sir James Phillips Kay-Shuttleworth). Kay made it clear that most of the facts in his pamphlet came from inquiries made by the Board, but added that other facts had been obtained from the public offices of the town, or were the results of his own observation (pp. 5-6). The pamphlet contained 74 pages, not 30. *JMC.*

3. It seems probable that the maladministration of the Poor Law was not to any considerable extent the cause of distress in rural districts. However, Chadwick and those who thought like him had made up their minds that this was the main cause, and the Poor Law Commission reported accordingly. See Mark Blaug, 'The Myth of the Old Poor Law and the Making of the New', *Journal of Economic History*, xxiii (1963), 151-84, and 'The Poor Law Report Re-examined', ibid. xxiv (1964), 229-45. *GKC.*

4. The source of this quotation has not been traced. *GKC.*

5. It is not easy to accept Young's comment. Certainly the *O.E.D.* records that the word 'unemployment' was in common use only after 1895, and the first example given is from 1888. But the word 'unemployed', in the sense of a workman who has no job, has a longer history. The *O.E.D.* gives a quotation from Ruskin's *Unto This Last* (1860), iii. §54: 'The vexed question of the destinies of the unemployed workmen', and a seventeenth-century quotation from Yarranton, *England's Improvement* (1677), p. 61: 'Admit there be in England and Wales a hundred thousand poor people unimployed'. People in the early nineteenth century were naturally familiar with different types of unemployment in practice even if they had no abstract word to describe it. They were familiar with the seasonal unemployment of certain groups in a hard winter, with the technological unemployment

of such people as the handloom weavers, and the occasional unemployment of large groups of workers in bad times, as in the years 1838–42. It is true that in the minds of many the spectre of over-population loomed large, but they talked of a good many other possible causes for men being 'out of employment', such as the displacement of handicrafts by machines (this possibility troubled Sir Robert Peel), the vagaries of speculative capitalism and 'over-production', and, particularly between 1838 and 1845, the effects of the Corn Laws. Mr. E. P. Thompson has discovered instances of the word 'unemployment' in 'the trade union and Radical or Owenite writing of the 1820s and 1830s' (*The Making of the English Working Class* (1963), p. 776 n. 2). *GKC, JMC*.

6. The treatise in question is presumably William Thomas Thornton, *Over-Population and its Remedy; or, an Inquiry into the Extent and Causes of the Distress Prevailing among the Labouring Classes of the British Islands, and into the Means of Remedying it* (1846). Thornton defined over-population as '*a deficiency of employment for those who live by labour, or a redundancy of the labouring class above the number of persons that the fund applied to the remuneration of labour can maintain in comfort*' (p. 3). He approved of the teaching of Malthus and the actions of the Poor Law reformers, but found reasons for distress other than the increase in population, and recognized that 'A permanent deficiency of employment for the labouring class ... does not always proceed from an increase in the number of labourers, but may also originate in a diminished demand for labour' (p. 114). The remedies he suggested were the repeal of the Corn Laws, the provision of small holdings, emigration, education, improvements in housing, and factory legislation. He asserted that free trade would assure permanent prosperity and that better living conditions would prevent that increase in population which might prevent any policy from having beneficent results, for he believed that the increase in the birth rate was the result of social misery. The book certainly analysed some of the causes of unemployment, and did so advisedly, not in ignorance of the fact that unemployment might have causes other than an increase in population. In fact Thornton was completely conscious of the conception of unemployment and on occasion used the word 'unemployed'. *GKC*.

7. Rioting in the eighteenth century was endemic, and more serious than Young suggests, but it seems possible that it was not until the

threat of the French Revolution developed that it suggested to the authorities the possibility of general subversion. However, even before the French Revolution, the Gordon Riots in London, 2–13 June 1780, do seem to have excited apprehensions about the stability of society when confronted by the power of the mob. *GKC.*

8. See Kingsley's Preface addressed to the undergraduates of Cambridge, *Alton Locke*, new edn. (1862), p. viii. *GKC.*

9. Since this passage was written much work has been done on the electoral situation after the Reform Act, which can be studied in Norman Gash, *Politics in the Age of Peel* (1953), and elsewhere. Young's statements must therefore be questioned. He does not seem to realize how many nomination boroughs survived the Act; there is a list of some fifty of them in Gash, pp. 438–9. And his assertion that there was less rioting and less bribery after reform is misleading. For although many proprietary boroughs survived, the Corporation boroughs and many of the most absolute pocket boroughs, such as Old Sarum, disappeared. There were therefore more boroughs in which rival candidates could compete, and the Reform Act was followed by a period of lively party politics, during which there was much invasion of constituencies previously under the unquestioned control of one patron. The result was to extend the area in which bribery was used and rioting was likely to take place. *GKC.*

10. The tenants at will were enfranchised by a clause introduced into the Reform Bill by Lord Chandos, a Tory. See Gash, op. cit. pp. 91–4, and Michael Brock, *The Great Reform Act* (1973), pp. 227–9, 318. The clause was considered to have brought into the county franchise a group of voters who were peculiarly vulnerable to landlord pressure, and thus to have handed over the counties to Tory control. But this judgement should be questioned. First it should be remembered that by 1832 the value of a freeholder's qualification was very small, and that many who qualified as freeholders were likely to hold a great deal of their land as tenants at will, thus becoming equally vulnerable to the pressure of their landlords. Secondly, on issues connected with agriculture, tenants showed considerable independence between 1835 and 1846, and were largely responsible for the rejection of Peel as leader of the Conservative party when he turned against the Corn Laws. *GKC.*

11. It would be difficult to point to any but the most moderate Radical who was really satisfied with the Reform Act. It was followed in 1833 by the agitation against the assessed taxes which led to the riot in Coldbath Fields; and the constant theme of Radical politics in the next decade or so was that the Act had been a fraud and a betrayal on the part of the 'shopocracy'. *GKC.*

12. For the representative system created by the Reform Act of 1832 see Gash, op. cit. pp. 1–101, and Brock, op. cit. pp. 310–13, which should be used to correct Young's account. In particular it is misleading to suggest that the £10 householder was 'in effect a man with £150 a year and upward'. Regional variations were such that the social and economic status of the £10 householder varied from borough to borough (Gash, pp. 98–100). *GKC.*

13. The first use of 'electorate' as meaning the whole body of electors which the *O.E.D.* records is from 1879; previously it had normally meant the territory of an Elector in Germany. In 1831 'constituency' could mean all the electors in Great Britain. For instance on 1 March Lord John Russell, introducing the Reform Bill, said: 'It is my opinion, therefore, that the whole measure will add to the constituency of the Commons House of Parliament, about half a million of persons.' (*Hansard*, 3rd Ser. ii. 1083.) At the same date, however, it could also be used to describe an individual electoral district. On 30 May Macaulay described to his sister the following conversation with Lady Holland:

> I happened in speaking about the Reform bill to say, that I wished that it had been possible to form a few commercial constituencies, if the word constituency were admissible. 'I am glad you put that in,' said her Ladyship, 'I was just going to give it you. It is an odious word. Then there is *talented*, and *influential*, and *gentlemanly*. I never could break Sheridan of *gentlemanly*, though he allowed it to be wrong.'

The Letters of Thomas Babington Macaulay, ed. Thomas Pinney, vol. ii (Cambridge, 1974), p. 22. *GKC.*

14. For the history of the procedure of the House of Commons after 1832 see Josef Redlich, *The Procedure of the House of Commons* (3 vols., 1908), i. 73–132; Peter Fraser, 'The Growth of Ministerial Control in the Nineteenth-Century House of Commons', *English Historical*

Review, lxxv (1960), 444–63; Valerie Cromwell, 'The Losing of the Initiative by the House of Commons, 1780–1914', *Transactions of the Royal Historical Society*, 5th Ser. xviii (1968), 1–23. *GKC, JMC.*

15. Sir Thomas Dyke Acland, 10th Bt. (1787–1871), was elected to Parliament in 1812 in the Tory interest for the county of Devon, lost his seat in 1818 to Lord Ebrington, but was again returned in 1820 and 1826. In 1830 he joined his old opponent Lord Ebrington as a supporter of Parliamentary reform. 'By this time,' says the *D.N.B.* 'Sir Thomas Acland had spent, it was believed, over £80,000 in his parliamentary contests'; and his grandson later wrote that this statement was 'probably not far short of the mark' (*Memoir and Letters of Sir Thomas Dyke Acland* [11th Bt.], ed. Arthur H. D. Acland (1902), p. 290). The sum therefore is probably a general estimate or even a guess, and not the result of careful accounting. Acland was out of Parliament 1831–7, but represented North Devon 1837–57. He was an Evangelical and Sir Walter Scott noted in his diary on 19 Apr. 1828: 'He may be considered now as the head of the religious party in the House of Commons, a powerful body which Wilberforce long ago commanded.' (*The Journal of Sir Walter Scott*, ed. J. G. Tait and W. M. Parker (1950), p. 525.) On the cost of electioneering after the Reform Act see Norman Gash, *Politics in the Age of Peel* (1953), pp. 105–36. *GKC.*

16. Bribery, intimidation, and control of the votes of dependents were so prevalent that it is difficult to believe that impersonation could have been more common. Nor does it seem likely that Young had made any comprehensive calculation based on the facts of the situation when he made this statement. *GKC.*

17. See Prince Albert's memorandum, dated 20 Dec. 1845, on Lord John Russell's proposed arrangements had he been able to form a government on the resignation of Sir Robert Peel: 'The Vice-Presidency [of the Board of Trade] was to have been offered to his [Lord Clarendon's] brother, Mr Villiers, but finally, by his advice, to Mr Cobden!! (Lord Grey wanted Mr Cobden to be in the Cabinet!!!) This Lord John thought quite out of the question.' (*Letters of Queen Victoria*, 1st Ser. ii. 71.) *GKC.*

18. It is a mistake to believe that after 1832 the Lords were 'in equipoise with the Commons'. The lesson of the passage of the Reform Bill after

the creation of peers had been threatened was not forgotten, and it was realized by men like Sir Robert Peel and the Duke of Wellington that in the last resort the House of Lords must give way. This accounts for the passage of the English Municipal Reform Bill in 1835 and the repeal of the Corn Laws in 1846. *GKC.*

19. See Section V, note 14 for references to procedure. Young seems to have been mistaken in his statement about Lord John Russell's attempt to get a third night for Government business, through misreading the debate of 24 Nov. 1837 (*Hansard*, 3rd Ser. xxxix. 193–204). All that happened was that order days, two of which were already reserved for Government business and one for private Members, were given increased protection. *JMC.*

20. William Ewart represented Bletchingley 1828–30, Liverpool 1830–7, Wigan 1839–41, and Dumfries Burghs 1841–68. See W. A. Munford, *William Ewart, M.P. 1798–1869. Portrait of a Radical* (1960). *GKC, JMC.*

21. This paragraph will naturally call to mind Wordsworth's famous sonnet 'Composed upon Westminster Bridge'. It should, however, be remembered that the sonnet was written in 1802, and that in the next forty years the view which had inspired Wordsworth altered considerably. By the time this book must be held to start there would be more houses, more people, more traffic and, as a result of the development of industry and the railways, a greater probability of smoke at any hour of the morning. In due course new buildings and bridges would modify the prospect. Charing Cross railway bridge would block the view downstream from Westminster Bridge, while upstream there would appear, on one side St Thomas's Hospital, and on the other side the new Houses of Parliament, while the Thames itself would be hemmed in by embankments. For these changes see Francis Sheppard, *London 1808–1870: the Infernal Wen* (1971), pp. xv–xvi. *GKC.*

22. On the manners of the House of Commons in the thirties see Élie Halévy, *Histoire du peuple anglais au XIXᵉ siècle* (6 vols., Paris, 1912–32), iii. 60, and George Kitson Clark, *Peel and the Conservative Party* (1929), pp. 91–3. *GKC.*

23. See Lord John Russell's speech, 19 Feb. 1835 (*Hansard*, 3rd Ser. xxvi. 37–45). *GKC.*

24. On 11 June 1840 in the Committee on a Bill for the registration of voters in Ireland, O'Connell exclaimed: 'If you were ten times as beastly in your uproar and bellowing, I should still feel it to be my duty to interpose to prevent this injustice.' There was a sharp debate on O'Connell's use of the words 'beastly bellowing', which he declined to withdraw, saying that they were an accurate description of the noises made during his speech (*Hansard*, 3rd Ser. liv. 1093–9). The whole scene is described in Trevelyan, *Macaulay*, ii. 76–7, where it is placed in 1839, clearly owing to the misdating of an extract from Macaulay's journal. GKC.

25. See Charles and Frances Brookfield, *Mrs. Brookfield and Her Circle* (2 vols., 1905), ii. 356, describing a party given by Thackeray to Charlotte Brontë in 1849:

> The probable reason of the failure of the first party was perhaps Miss Brontë's own inability to fall in with the easy *badinage* of the well-bred people with whom she found herself surrounded.
>
> Alert minded and keen brained herself, she was accustomed only to the narrow literalness of her own circle, and could scarcely have understood the rapid give and take, or the easy conversational grace of these new friends. Also she may hardly have appreciated the charming conciseness with which they told their stories; for the members of this set were the first to break away from the pedantic ponderousness usual with all the great talkers, even those of their own time; and Miss Brontë, a square peg in a round hole, was doubtless, too, dismayed at anecdotes that gained in elegance as they lost in accuracy.

A dreadful example of Macaulay's methods in conversation appears in the same volume (p. 377). Asked by Mrs. Brookfield at dinner if he admired Jane Austen, he made no reply till there was a lull in the conversation when he said 'Mrs. Brookfield has asked me if I admire Jane Austen's novels, to which I reply'—and then launched into a lengthy set-piece ending with his thoughts by her grave. On Mrs. Carlyle's conversation see a reminiscence by Mrs. Brookfield: 'Mrs. Carlyle had the fatal propensity of telling her stories at extraordinary length. With her Scotch accent and her perseverance in finishing off every detail, those who were merely friendly acquaintances and not devotees sometimes longed for an abridgement, and perhaps also to have their own turn in the conversation.' (ibid. ii. 427.) Mrs. Brookfield's tone about

Mrs. Carlyle is often a little critical; her admiration and that of her husband seems to have gone more readily to Carlyle. *GKC*.

26. cf. G. W. E. Russell, *Collections and Recollections*, 7th edn. (1904), p. 139, on Gladstone's Budget speeches: ' "He talked shop," it was said, "like a tenth muse." ' *GKC*.

27. cf. Disraeli's account of the questions which men were asking about the possible nature of Peel's government after the dismissal of the Whigs in 1834:

> Was it to be a Tory government, or an enlightened-spirit-of-the-age, Liberal-moderate-reform government; was it to be a government of high philosophy or of low practice; of principle or of expediency; of great measures or of little men? A government of statesmen or of clerks? Of humbug or of humdrum?

Coningsby, Book II, Chapter 4, *GKC, EL*.

28. H.C. (1836) xxi. 103. *GKC*.

29. From 1769 the Treasury had employed to draft and settle its bills a Parliamentary Counsel, who had also helped other Government departments to prepare legislation. But on the death of the holder, William Harrison, in 1841 the office was discontinued, and in 1842 the task of drafting bills for the Treasury and some other departments was transferred to the Parliamentary Counsel to the Home Office, a position held by John Elliot Drinkwater Bethune 1837–48, Walter Coulson 1848–60, and Henry Thring 1861–9. Some departments, however, continued to use counsel of their own choice, who charged professional fees, and sometimes legislation was drafted by civil servants or ministers, with the result that costs were often unduly high, and the language and arrangement of statutes lacked uniformity and precision. To remedy these defects, Robert Lowe by a Treasury Minute dated 8 Feb. 1869 revived the office of Parliamentary Counsel to the Treasury. The holder was to have an assistant, neither was to engage in private practice, and they were to draft all Government legislation with the exception of Scottish and Irish bills. The then Home Office Counsel, Thring, was first appointed to the post, followed in 1886 by Sir Henry Jenkyns and in 1899 by Sir Courtenay Ilbert. On these developments see J. C. Sainty, *Office-Holders in Modern Britain*, vol. i *Treasury Officials*

1660–1870 (1972), pp. 99–100, and Henry Roseveare, *The Treasury. The Evolution of a British Institution* (1969), pp. 215–16.

Henry Thring (1818–1907) was educated at Shrewsbury School, when Benjamin Hall Kennedy, probably in his day the best teacher of classical scholarship in England, was Headmaster, and he always maintained that the training he received then had given him that feeling for the exact meaning of words which is necessary for good draftsmanship. He had started the work of drafting in 1850 by preparing a bill on colonial questions for Sir William Molesworth, and proved his skill by drafting the Succession Act of 1853 which formed an important part of Gladstone's Budget. In 1854, with the co-operation of Thomas Henry Farrer, he drew the Merchant Shipping Act, which must be one of the most comprehensive, and possibly one of the longest, pieces of legislation passed in the nineteenth century (see above, p. 112). Thring published his principles in 1878 in a small book entitled *Practical Legislation* (H.M.S.O.) which was republished in 1902 with a short autobiographical introduction. There is also an important article on Thring by Sir Courtenay Ilbert in the *D.N.B.* (Second Supplement). *GKC, JMC.*

30. On the first page of his *Statistical Account of the British Empire* (2 vols., 1837), J. R. McCulloch wrote: 'The British Empire, exclusive of its foreign dependencies, consists of the islands of Great Britain and Ireland, and of the smaller islands contiguous and subordinate to them.' Later he definitely stated that:

No work on the statistics of the British empire could have any pretensions to completeness that omitted to notice its colonies and dependencies. It would, however, be inconsistent alike with the objects and the limits of this work to enter into any detailed investigations, with respect to their statistics. Our object has been to exhibit the physical capabilities, the industry, wealth, and institutions of the British nation; and the statistics of our colonies and foreign dependencies are connected with our subject only in those respects in which they may be supposed to contribute to, or diminish, our wealth and prosperity. (i. 593–4.)

He did, in the pages that follow, deal with this last subject, but, given his declared object, it was perhaps natural that the allusions to Canada should cover fewer pages than were devoted to Oxford University in his chapter on English education. His use of the word 'Empire' seems to have been common in the eighteenth century. But the word was also used to imply overseas possessions. For instance in *The Wealth of Nations*, Book IV, Chapter 7, Part 3, Adam Smith wrote: 'To found a great Empire for the sole purpose of raising up a people of customers, may at first sight appear a project fit only for a nation of shopkeepers.' This use was known to McCulloch's contemporaries since G. R. Porter cited this quotation from Adam Smith in his *Progress of the Nation*, new edn. (1847), p. 730. In due course the modern usage of 'Empire', as describing an entity which necessarily included colonies and dependencies, became universal; but the older use of the word lingered on in the nineteenth century in a way that possibly affected the development of the meaning of the word 'Imperialism'. See Richard Koebner and Helmut Dan Schmidt, *Imperialism. The Story and Significance of A Political Word, 1840–1960* (Cambridge, 1964), particularly Chapter 2, 'The Name of the British Empire in the First Decades of Queen Victoria's Reign'. Young deals with the meaning of the word 'Imperialism' on pp. 174–5 above.

'Glad aspiring little burg' is from line 30 of the poem 'Pictor Ignotus' in Robert Browning's *Men and Women*. GKC.

31. The census reports in the early years of the nineteenth century were unreliable largely because there existed no satisfactory local machinery for gathering accurate information. For the first census in 1801 the task of enumeration was placed in the hands of the overseers of the poor who were incapable of performing it. It was not until the Municipal Reform Act of 1835 had produced reliable local officials in towns, and the Act of 1836 making provision for the civil registration of births, deaths, and marriages had led to the appointment of local registrars, that the work of enumeration could be carried out with reasonable accuracy. See J. A. Taylor, 'The Taking of the Census, 1801–1951', *British Medical Journal*, 1951, vol. i, pp. 715–22. The same difficulty applied to the calculation of the acreage of England in the census of 1831. Two estimates were given: 32,247,680 acres, which was at the time believed to be the actual area of England; and 31,770,615 acres, a figure obtained by adding together the acreages of the various counties which had themselves been obtained by adding together the acreages of the various parishes (H.C. (1833) xxxvii. 832). John Rickman who prepared the census report was aware of this discrepancy and drew attention to it (H.C. (1833) xxxvi, pp. xxii–xxiii). However, since the Ordnance Survey had not completed its work of surveying the country, all estimates of its area were likely to be inaccurate. In 1851 it was

possible to correct the figures with the help of surveys carried out under the Tithe Commutation Act, but there were still no maps based on the Ordnance Survey for Lancashire, Yorkshire, Westmorland, Cumberland, Northumberland, or Durham (H.C. (1852–3) lxxxv, pp. clvii–clxi). In 1861 the Ordnance Survey's figures for the areas of the northern counties were used, as far as they were available, and the acreage of England was given as 32,590,397 acres (H.C. (1863) liii (i), pp. 72, 79). However, there were still corrections to be made, and in the 1871 census the acreage was given as 32,597,398 acres (H.C. (1872) lxvi (i), p. vii).

On the subject of Official Values see *Guide to English Commercial Statistics 1696–1782* by G. N. Clark, with a catalogue of materials by Barbara M. Franks (1938); for the actual figures in aggregates see B. R. Mitchell and Phyllis Deane, *Abstract of British Historical Statistics* (Cambridge, 1962), pp. 279–92. On the foundation of the Statistical Department at the Board of Trade see Lucy Brown, *The Board of Trade and the Free-Trade Movement 1830–42* (Oxford, 1958), pp. 76–93; on the Registrar-General's Department see Section VI, note 25; and on the foundation of the Statistical Society of London, subsequently the Royal Statistical Society, see [H. W. Macrosty and J. Bonar], *Annals of the Royal Statistical Society, 1834–1934* (1934). In 1832 J. R. McCulloch published his *Dictionary of Commerce* and in 1837 his *Statistical Account of the British Empire*; in 1833 John Marshall published his *Digest of all the Accounts Relating to the Population etc. of the United Kingdom*, which was distributed to Members of Parliament; and in 1836 G. R. Porter, who was an official at the Board of Trade, and presided over the formation of the Statistical Department, began to publish his *Progress of the Nation. GKC, BRM.*

32. See Trevelyan, *Macaulay*, ii. 59. *GKC.*

33. The Prussian visitor was probably Friedrich Von Raumer, a Professor of History in the University of Berlin, who visited England in 1835 and published an account of his visit under the title of *England im Jahre 1835* (Leipsic, 1836). An English translation, *England in 1835* (3 vols., 1836), was prepared by Sarah Austin and H. E. Lloyd. Young may have derived his knowledge of Von Raumer from a statement by Élie Halévy (*Histoire du peuple anglais au XIXe siècle* (6 vols., Paris, 1912–32), iii. 93 n. 1) which was itself based on a review of Von Raumer's book in the *Quarterly Review*, vol. lvi (Apr. and July 1836), pp. 569–70. Von

Raumer believed that the Whigs were unconsciously working to erect a system comparable to that of 'happy Prussia', with its universal education, its liberal land law, and its general tolerance. Of the political conflict in England he wrote: 'The contest really is, whether England shall Germanize herself;—shall enter, at least in part, on the German career of civilization. This is the real point for which Whigs contend and which Tories resist;—though neither know enough of Germany to be aware of the fact.' (*England in 1835*, i. 219–20.) His account of the Poor Law and the Municipal Reform Act (ibid. i. 122–57, ii. 29–43) relied heavily on the reports of Royal Commissions, and he commended the part played by them in the English system as providing 'a second most efficient, salutary and popular parliament' in which a matter of importance could be thoroughly investigated and discussed so that 'public *opinion* rises to the dignity of public *conviction*'. In this, England, he believed, had an advantage over Prussia: 'The progress of legislation in Prussia . . . has been, in many respects, more summary, bolder, more consistent, better concatenated, more comprehensive; but it presents no monument of a people invited to deliberate with its government, and coming to a common understanding on its own affairs.' (ibid. i. 269–71.) *GKC, JMC.*

34. On the failure to produce statistics on agriculture, see G. R. Porter, 'Suggestions in Favour of the Systematic Collection of the Statistics of Agriculture', *Journal of the Statistical Society of London*, vol. ii (1839), pp. 291–6. *JMC.*

35. *Sybil* by Benjamin Disraeli was published in May 1845. He had paid two visits to the north in 1843 and 1844, and claimed in the advertisement that the descriptions were based upon his own observation, or the evidence received by Royal Commissions and Parliamentary Committees. For his indebtedness to the reports of the Royal Commission on Children's Employment, published in 1842 and 1843, see Sheila M. Smith, 'Willenhall and Wodgate: Disraeli's Use of Blue Book Evidence', *Review of English Studies*, N.S. xiii (1962), 368–84.

'The Cry of the Children' was published by Elizabeth Barrett, later Mrs. Browning, in August 1843 in *Blackwood's Magazine*, vol. liv, pp. 260–2. It was clearly inspired by the reports of the Children's Employment Commission, on which her friend and correspondent R. H. Horne served. He is referred to in a note attached in 1844 to the first four lines of the tenth verse:

A fact rendered pathetically historical by Mr. Horne's report of his Commission. The name of the poet of *Orion* and *Cosmo de Medici* [i.e. Horne] has, however, a change of associations, and comes in time to remind me that we have some noble poetic heat of literature still,—however open to the reproach of being somewhat gelid in our humanity.

The Poetical Works of Elizabeth Barrett Browning (1904), p. 233. GKC, JMC.

36. The Manchester Statistical Society was founded in 1833, a few months before the London Society. See T. S. Ashton, *Economic and Social Investigations in Manchester, 1833–1933* (1934). Further provincial societies were founded in Birmingham in 1835, in Bristol and Glasgow in 1836, and in Liverpool, Ulster, and Leeds in 1838. For the use of Rutland as a control experiment see 'Report on the Condition of the Population in Three Parishes in Rutlandshire, in March 1839. By the Statistical Society of Manchester', *Journal of the Statistical Society of London*, vol. ii (1839), pp. 297–302, and 'Report of a Committee of the Manchester Statistical Society on the State of Education in the County of Rutland in the year 1838', ibid. ii (1839), 303–15. For the Leeds investigation see E. P. Hennock, *Fit and Proper Persons. Ideal and Reality in Nineteenth-Century Urban Government* (1973), pp. 188–90. The first report of the Statistical Committee of the Council appeared in the *Journal of the Statistical Society of London*, vol. ii (1839), pp. 397–424. The inquiry cost £320 and occupied eleven months. GKC, JMC.

37. Douglas Jerrold's play *The Factory Girl* was first produced at Drury Lane on 6 Oct. 1832, condemned and performed only once more (Walter Jerrold, *Douglas Jerrold. Dramatist and Wit* (2 vols., [1914]), i. 211–13). To his paper on 'The Factory Child' contributed to *Heads of the People: Or, Portraits of the English*, drawn by Kenny Meadows (2 vols., 1840–1), i. 185–92, Jerrold attached the following note:

It is now six years since the writer of this paper essayed a drama, the purpose of which was an appeal to public sympathy in the cause of the Factory Children: the drama was very summarily condemned; cruelly maimed the first night, and mortally killed on its second representation. The subject of the piece 'was low—distressing.' The truth is, it was not then *la mode* to affect an interest for the 'coarse and vulgar' details of human life; and the author suffered because he was two or three years *before the fashion.*

JMC.

SECTION VI

1. For the fluctuations in trade after 1836 and their effects upon labour see R. C. O. Matthews, *A Study in Trade-Cycle History. Economic Fluctuations in Great Britain 1833–1842* (Cambridge, 1954), particularly pp. 137–48, 163–4, 209–17. GKC.

2. For 'Free Trade League' read 'Anti-Corn Law League'. GKC.

3. The argument that it was necessary for Britain to import corn from foreign countries to keep them in funds and thus enable them to pay for British manufactured articles played an important part in Cobden's case for the repeal of the Corn Laws, but the amount of raw cotton Lancashire imported from the United States was a point on the other side. GKC.

4. See Section III, note 28.

5. See Manners's speech on the second reading of the Factory Bill, 10 Feb. 1847:

> They were met by the assertion . . . that if they attempted to regulate the speed of manufacturing enterprise, they might destroy the springs by which it moved at all. Why, as well might they tell him, that—
>
> > 'when a horse
> > Full of high feeding, madly had broke loose,
> > And borne down all before him,'
>
> was subjected to the curb, and made to know his rider, his usefulness would be impaired, and his energy destroyed.

Hansard, 3rd Ser. lxxxix. 1109. Manners then gave figures to show that factory legislation had not impaired the energies of manufacturers. He protested on 3 Mar. against the kind of interpretation of his words which is suggested by Young (ibid. xc. 784), and the report of his speech of 10 Feb. supports his protest. *GKC.*

6. See Henry Ashworth's account of a meeting between a deputation from the Anti-Corn Law League and the Home Secretary, Sir James Graham, at the Colonial Office, 4 Aug. 1842: 'Mr. John Brooks, of Manchester, described the state of distress existing in that town, and spoke of the feverish discontent as evidently leading to political troubles. Sir James interrupted him, exclaiming, "Why, you are a Chartist!" ' Ashworth recorded that later in the discussion he told Graham:

> It could not therefore be wondered at, that the memorialists, who were themselves tax payers, and writhing under the pressure of the times, should take example from the landlords of a former period, or from the more recent example of the citizens of London, who in 1832, memorialised in like manner for the stoppage of supplies, until the Reform Bill had passed. Moreover, the industrious classes were beginning to feel their importance to the country, and could show the advantages to the community arising from their skill and labour; and they complained that whilst they were called upon to endure these grievous privations, the landlords were enjoying protection by law, with rents greatly increased in amount, and with comforts unknown and undreamt of by their forefathers. Sir James Graham assumed an air of indignant surprise and exclaimed, 'Why, you are a leveller,' and inquired if he was to understand that the labouring classes considered that they had some claim upon the landlord's estates?

Henry Ashworth, *Recollections of Richard Cobden, M.P. and the Anti-Corn-Law League* [1877], pp. 93–7. Ashworth's recollection of this incident may have been a little hazy as he records almost the same confrontation with Graham when describing a visit of deputies in March 1840 (ibid. pp. 41–3). Graham's state of mind is suggested by Ashworth's comment that he appeared 'captious and uneasy during the whole time of the conference'. The explanation of his outbursts was no doubt not that he wished to compromise the argument for repeal, but that he really did suspect the League leaders of planning direct action. His suspicions were mistaken, but they were partly justified by the extremely violent language of the League leaders, and their threats to stop their mills, or, if magistrates, not to oppose mob action if the Corn

Laws were not repealed. It should be realized that disturbances, which were later to be attributed to the League, were already starting. The miners were on strike in Staffordshire, and on the day after the interview turnouts began at Stalybridge. See G. Kitson Clark, 'Hunger and Politics in 1842', *Journal of Modern History*, xxv (1953), 355–74, GKC.

7. On 3 May 1842 Roebuck described O'Connor as 'the foolish, malignant, cowardly demagogue' (*Hansard*, 3rd Ser. lxiii. 54). *JTW.*

8. From 1800 until his retirement in 1829 Robert Owen (1771–1858) developed at mills in New Lanark a paternalistic system of factory management, which seemed to promise a beneficent future for industrialized society. His achievements and ideas, which contrasted with the attitudes of those who wished to return to a simpler more exclusively agricultural past or attacked industrialism without suggesting a practicable alternative, became famous both at home and abroad, and one of his most enthusiastic patrons was the Duke of Kent, Queen Victoria's father. However, from 1817 he began to shock many by his rejection of Christianity; between 1824 and 1828 he devoted himself to the development of a co-operative community in the United States; and as he grew older his schemes and pronouncements tended to become less intelligible and more impracticable. The Queen received him in 1840 and thereby caused an outcry since his irreligion and social views had become unacceptable to many of the upper classes. See the debates in the House of Lords, 24 Jan. and 4 Feb. 1840 (*Hansard*, 3rd Ser. li. 510–46, 1176–217). However, his influence on working-class movements in the days before Chartism and on the cause of co-operation was probably more important than Young appears to suggest. See J. F. C. Harrison, *Robert Owen and the Owenites in Britain and America* (1969). *GKC, JMC.*

9. See the Rev. William St. George Sargent's replies to questions 2528 and 2529 addressed to him by Viscount Ebrington and Mr. Rich from the Select Committee on Railway Labourers, 23 June 1846:

> You spoke of infidel opinions. Do you believe that many of them are Socialists?—Most of them in practice; though they appear to have wives, very few of them are married. Their infidel opinions lead them to doubt the authority of the Word of God, and very often to deny the existence of a First Cause.
>
> May not all that arise from ignorance, rather than the result of any

opinion?—I should rather think it does arise altogether from ignorance and from neglect. There are many of these men who as a matter of fact have been 10 and 11 years on the railway works, and have never been in a church, and perhaps never have been spoken to on the subject of religion during that time.

H.C. (1846) xiii. 606. *GKC*.

10. The term 'secularist' was suggested to Holyoake in June 1851 by W. Ashurst. Holyoake replied that he had already considered its use in an unpublished lecture on the 'Martineau and Atkinson Letters' (*Reasoner*, 25 June 1851). Thereafter the term was introduced gradually. In January 1852 Holyoake wrote: 'Secularity draws the line of demarcation between the things of time and the things of eternity. That is secular which pertains to this world—"the issues of which can be tested in this life."—*G. Combe*.' (*Reasoner*, 14 Jan. 1852.) Subsequently J. F. Adams stated that G. H. Lewes had suggested the word to Holyoake in 1849 (*National Reformer*, 27 Aug. 1865), but there is not sufficient evidence to confirm this. Of course the adjective 'secular' had been in use for some time, as in the phrase 'secular education'. *ER*.

11. The body of 'more intelligent workmen' who rejected Christianity must be distinguished from the railway navvies whom the Select Committee had under consideration. They were, if not 'belated', certainly persistent, rationalists. To them the works of Tom Paine were important, and so was phrenology, a system of thought and practice which derived from the belief that the various propensities and faculties of the human mind could be located in different parts of the brain. The innate strength and development of any of them in any particular human being could therefore be ascertained by examining the cranium to which the brain had given its form and shape. Phrenology was probably so popular because it seemed to offer a scientific approach to the problems of human personality. It was adopted and enthusiastically propagated by George Combe (1788–1858), an Edinburgh lawyer, who came to believe that it provided the key to all philosophical and social problems. His *Constitution of Man* was first published in 1828 and by 1839 over 50,000 copies had been sold in Britain alone. According to John Morley, 'it was seen on shelves where there was nothing else save the Bible and Pilgrim's Progress' (J. M. Robertson, *A History of Freethought in the Nineteenth Century* (1929), p. 70). One of the secularist Holyoake's

earliest public duties was to act as volunteer assistant to Combe when he came to lecture to the Birmingham Philosophical Institution (George Jacob Holyoake, *Sixty Years of an Agitator's Life*, 2nd edn. (2 vols., 1893), i. 60–5). On Cobden and phrenology see John Morley, *The Life of Richard Cobden* (2 vols., 1881), i. 93–4, 120–1. GKC.

12. It would be difficult to sum up with any accuracy the religious attitudes and origins of Chartism. It is probably true that the small group of working men who had become secularists were likely to become Chartists. But more were likely to be anti-clerical than secularist, against the Anglican clergy and the Nonconformist establishment, but not necessarily against Christianity. There is a certain amount of evidence that popular Methodism influenced Chartist organization and language. Chapels with working-class congregations became involved in Chartist agitations and J. R. Stephens, an eloquent minister who had broken with the main Methodist body, contributed greatly to the development of Chartism by the violence of his sermons on the wickedness of the new Poor Law.

There was certainly much public sympathy with the suffering of which Chartism was the symptom. Before 1841, and even afterwards, there was some sympathy between certain groups among the Tories and the Chartists. Many Tories supported factory reform which also appealed to Chartists; and in the general election of 1841 Tories and Chartists displayed a common fear and dislike of competitive capitalism. The potential alliance was, however, weakened when the Chartists realized that Peel and his Cabinet were not going to adopt the Ten Hours Bill and were going to maintain the new Poor Law, and when the Chartists undertook violent attacks on the established order of society. Nevertheless some Tories still remained factory reformers and opponents of the new Poor Law—attitudes which Disraeli and his friends were to romanticize, but not to originate.

A revolutionary movement with strong anti-clerical and some secularist tendencies was likely to be accused of either hostility to, or ignorance of, ordinary religious obligations; and that certainly happened to Chartism, whether or not the charge was justified. But the relationship between even the clergy of the Established Church and the Chartists was not necessarily one of hostility, as the career of W. F. Hook, the vicar of Leeds, demonstrates. The vestry was open, and Dissenting churchwardens were normally elected to prevent the levying of a Church Rate, but in 1842 they were replaced by Chartists. Hook very much approved of the change and said at the end of their term of office that 'they were the only churchwardens, since he came to Leeds, who had, as a body, conducted themselves in a thoroughly honourable, straightforward, and gentlemanly manner' (W. R. W. Stephens, *The Life and Letters of Walter Farquhar Hook*, new edn. (1880), pp. 350–2). Hook was an exceptional man, but it is probable that there were other West Riding and south Lancashire clergymen who continued to sympathize with the Chartists, as there had been a number of factory reformers among them. *ER, GKC*.

13. Count Chopski was identified by Graham Wallas as Count Czapski, a Polish officer who was put forward at the Birmingham Reform meeting on 7 May 1832 (*The Life of Francis Place 1771–1854*, revised edn. (1918), p. 302). There is nothing to connect him with Chartism, but other Poles, such as Major Beniowski who was active in London 1839–40, were involved in Chartist agitations. Francis Macerone, or Maceroni (1788–1846), was born in Manchester of an Italian father and an English mother. After an adventurous career during which he served as an aide-de-camp to Murat and as a brigadier-general in Colombia, he settled down in England as a company promoter and mechanical inventor. In 1832 he published *Defensive Instructions for the People, Containing the New and Improved Combination of Arms, Called Foot Lancers*. Maceroni has an entry in the *D.N.B.* and published his own memoirs in 1838. Again there is nothing to connect him directly with the Chartist movement, but his *Instructions* were undoubtedly reissued by the militant Chartists. See Napier's letters to S. M. Phillipps, 23 and 25 Apr. 1839 (Sir W. Napier, *The Life and Opinions of General Sir Charles James Napier* (4 vols., 1857), ii. 16, 18). It is unlikely that the long pikes and fowling pieces which Maceroni recommended would have been effective against muskets in the hands of disciplined troops, let alone against artillery. In general, Young exaggerates the danger of insurrection. There was much rhetoric and some preparation for violence but no clear revolutionary intention. The attempt on Newport in 1839 demonstrated with what ease a small disciplined force could put to flight a large body of Chartists, and although Chartists were involved in the disturbances of 1842, their origin was largely local and industrial (see G. Kitson Clark, 'Hunger and Politics in 1842', *Journal of Modern History*, xxv (1953), 355–74). The memoirs of Napier show how easily he could have contained any force that he would have been likely to encounter. The increases in the army only restored the

severe cuts made in the years immediately before 1839, and were partly dictated by overseas commitments. See F. C. Mather, *Public Order in the Age of the Chartists* (Manchester, 1959), pp. 159–61. The 'White Guard' must refer to unsuccessful attempts to form local associations in May 1839 (ibid. pp. 90–5). *FCM, GKC.*

14. On 16 July 1839 Wellington said in a debate on the Birmingham riots: 'I have been in many towns taken by storm, but never have such outrages occurred in them as were committed in this town only last night.' (*Hansard*, 3rd Ser. xlix. 374.) The Duke's opinion need not perhaps be taken very seriously. The Government itself had only learnt of what had happened from the Mayor of Birmingham at 12.30 a.m. and from the Superintendent of Police at 2.30 a.m. that morning—as Lord Lansdowne told the Duke in the debate (ibid. xlix. 382). The Duke could have had no access to official information, had certainly not been to Birmingham, and was merely relying on what he had picked up from unsupported newspaper reports. He was also old, in opposition, excitable, and given to over-emphatic statements.

For Shaftesbury's statement see the entry in his diary under 12 May 1866:

> Speaking at a meeting of Church Pastoral Aid Society, I denounced 'Ecce Homo' as a 'most pestilential book.' This expression I well recollect. The report adds 'ever vomited from the jaws of hell.' No doubt, then, I used the words. They have excited a good deal of wrath. Be it so. They were, perhaps, too strong for the *world*, but not too strong for the *truth*. It escaped, in the heat of declamation, justifiable and yet injudicious.

Hodder, *Shaftesbury*, iii. 164. It is probably fair to regard this, and other pronouncements by eminent Evangelicals, as typical of 'the melodramatic streak in the early Victorian temperament'. But it should be noted that the date at which the statement was made was not early Victorian. *GKC.*

15. On 30 Oct. 1831, after the rejection of the Reform Bill by the Lords, the mob in Bristol rose to protest against the advent to the city of the Tory Sir Charles Wetherell as Recorder. A large part of the city including the Bishop's Palace was burnt down. See Michael Brock, *The Great Reform Act* (1973), pp. 250–3. Charles Kingsley was a schoolboy at Clifton at the time, and never forgot what he saw. He described

it vividly in a lecture at Bristol in 1858 and on another occasion said that it had made him a Radical (*Charles Kingsley. His Letters and Memories of his Life*, ed. Mrs. Kingsley (2 vols., 1877), i. 20–2, 307–8). *GKC, JMC.*

16. See Young and Handcock, *English Historical Documents*, p. 612, referring to the evidence presented by the Royal Commission on Constabulary Forces (H.C. (1839) xix). *GKC.*

17. See Lord John Russell to Queen Victoria, 15 Aug. 1837, on the failure of Fox Maule in Perthshire and Hume in Middlesex at the general election occasioned by the Queen's accession:

> In this as in many other instances the superior organisation of the Tory party have enabled them to gain the appearance of a change of opinion, which has not in fact taken place.
> Lord John Russell is sorry to add that bribery, intimidation, and drunkenness have been very prevalent at the late elections, and that in many cases the disposition to riot has only been checked by the appearance of the Military, who have in all cases conducted themselves with great temper and judgment.

Letters of Queen Victoria, 1st Ser. i. 117. *GKC, JTW.*

18. On the emergency detachments of police provided for Manchester and Birmingham (and Bolton) in 1839 see F. C. Mather, *Public Order in the Age of the Chartists* (Manchester, 1959), pp. 119–27. On the Bradford incident see Section VI, note 22. *JMC.*

19. See L. Radzinowicz, *A History of English Criminal Law and its Administration from 1750*, vol. iv (1968), pp. 284–7; and Young and Handcock, *English Historical Documents*, p. 613, where he is incorrectly called 'McCarthy'. *GKC.*

20. On public expenditure see B. R. Mitchell and Phyllis Deane, *Abstract of British Historical Statistics* (Cambridge, 1962), pp. 396–7, 410–13, whose figures do not exactly correspond with those given by Young. *BRM.*

21. To understand the developments in the civil service described by Young, it is probably necessary to recognize that a change was taking

place in the theory of government. Originally all public servants were considered to be primarily servants of the Crown, and as such responsible alike to the King and Parliament. It is true that usually there were at the head of affairs a number of politicians whose influence and political aptitude enabled them to control Parliament, who might enter the King's service as a group and retire from it as a group; but, whatever were the political realities, they were considered to hold their places because they enjoyed the King's favour. In such circumstances there was little difference between one servant of the Crown and another, except in so far as one man was the official subordinate of another, or possessed greater political and social standing than another. It was therefore possible for a man to work up from a lowly clerical position to an important political post, and the fact of his becoming a Member of Parliament did not necessarily change him from a civil servant into a politician. J. C. Herries (1778–1855), for instance, entered the Treasury in 1798 as a copying clerk, became Secretary of the Treasury and a Member of Parliament in 1823, and Chancellor of the Exchequer in Goderich's Administration in 1827; but even after becoming Chancellor, he claimed that he was not a party politician, but merely the servant of the King. His Whig colleagues certainly objected to his appointment, but it would be difficult to determine whether in the complicated politics of that time they objected to him as 'a Tory clerk'. A quarrel between Herries and William Huskisson helped to bring down Goderich's Administration, and Huskisson himself had risen in much the same way as Herries.

The old system effectively came to an end in 1830, when Wellington's Ministry, although in full enjoyment of the King's favour, was defeated in the Commons, and succeeded by Grey's, which on many occasions during the next four years palpably did not retain office by the King's favour, but by virtue of the support of the Commons. Thereafter the conception that ministers were primarily the King's servants faded. An unusually large number of subordinate office holders resigned with the Duke in 1830. One of them was J. W. Croker, Secretary of the Admiralty since 1809, who wrote a letter of resignation to the incoming First Lord, saying that it was necessary for him to do this since 'there never has been an instance of the Secretary of the Admiralty being removed on a change of Ministry' (*The Correspondence and Diaries of John Wilson Croker*, ed. Louis J. Jennings (3 vols., 1884), ii. 74–5). The position of under-secretary thus came to be filled by men who were more completely politicians, and who would represent their office in the Commons and retire with the ministry. But at the same time the business of government increased rapidly, and as a result there developed a class of civil servants who were outside the political field altogether, but yet were much more than copying clerks. Edwin Chadwick, who became Secretary to the Poor Law Commission in 1834, is one example of this type; J. P. Kay (see Section VI, note 27) another. But similar developments were taking place in established offices, as the careers of Sir James Stephen at the Colonial Office, G. R. Porter and J. MacGregor at the Board of Trade, and Sir Charles Trevelyan at the Treasury show. Thus the service of the Crown was gradually split into two. On the one hand there were ministers with a special responsibility for the work of their offices to Parliament, and on the other civil servants who were permanent because they were outside politics, and could not present their case to Parliament. It was still possible, and it still is, for a politician to become a civil servant, or a civil servant a politician. G. C. Lewis (1806–63) was a Poor Law Commissioner from 1839 until 1847, when he resigned to enter Parliament and took a minor ministerial post. He was Chancellor of the Exchequer 1855–8, Home Secretary 1859–61 and Secretary for War 1861–3. Sir Benjamin Hawes (1797–1862), having been a Member of Parliament, resigned his seat in 1852 after becoming Deputy Secretary of the War Office, and in 1857 was appointed permanent Under Secretary, a position which he held until his death. William Blamire (1790–1862) made his reputation in Parliament by a speech on the Tithe Commutation Bill and retired from the House to become Chief Commissioner for bringing the Act into operation. This work lasted from 1836 until 1851, but he was also involved in the application of other statutes bearing on agricultural problems, and thus became a valuable civil servant although not holding a position in any public office. Although these changes of status are evidence of the flexibility of the mid-nineteenth-century governmental system, they should not be taken as evidence of the survival of the simple unitary system that had existed before 1830.

On the relation of the Crown to public servants see Sir Lewis Namier's Romanes Lecture of 1952, *Monarchy and the Party System*, reprinted in his *Personalities and Powers* (1955), pp. 13–38. See also below, Section IX, note 6. GKC.

22. 'Once they had to be protected with cavalry' is probably a reference to the experiences of the Assistant Poor Law Commissioner, Alfred

Power, in Bradford in October and November 1837. When he was assaulted by a mob, the civil force which consisted of two annual constables and three deputies showed no great desire to come to his assistance, and at his request six constables from the Metropolitan Police were sent to protect him. The magistrates, however, did not wish to swear them in and asked for military assistance. A troop of the 15th Hussars, subsequently reinforced by two companies of the 97th Foot and further troops of cavalry, were sent to Bradford by the Home Office. John Fielden did not ring his factory bells to drive assistant commissioners out of Todmorden but two constables from Halifax who were attempting to serve a warrant for distraint of goods on the overseers. On Bradford see *Fourth Annual Report of the Poor Law Commissioners* (H.C. (1837–8) xxviii. 263–78); on Todmorden *Fifth Annual Report* (H.C. (1839) xx. 23–4); and on both incidents Nicholas C. Edsall, *The Anti-Poor Law Movement 1834–44* (Manchester, 1971), pp. 109–12, 144–9, 157–60. *JTW, JMC, GKC.*

23. For the Northcote–Trevelyan Report on the Organisation of the Permanent Civil Service see H.C. (1854) xxvii. 3–23; an extract is printed in Young and Handcock, *English Historical Documents*, pp. 567–74. The practice of the Poor Law Commission is reflected in the paper on the reorganization of the civil service drawn up by Edwin Chadwick in 1854 (H.C. (1854–5) xx. 137–230); and that of the India Office in the evidence given in 1831 by James Mill to a Select Committee of the House of Commons (H.C. (1831–2) ix. 42–59). As early as 1823 when John Stuart Mill entered East India House, his father secured that, although he started at the bottom of the list of clerks, he should be employed from the beginning in preparing drafts of dispatches, so that he could be trained to succeed those who then filled the higher offices (J. S. Mill, *Autobiography* (1873), pp. 81–2). But James Mill's own appointment shows that even before his arrival it was realized that it was desirable to have abler men in the higher ranks of the service than could be found by promoting copying clerks; and in 1819 Mill himself, aged 46, Edward Strachey aged 45, formerly an Indian judge, and Thomas Love Peacock aged 34, already a literary man, were appointed from outside the service to undertake the important task of preparing dispatches (see C. H. Philips, *The East India Company 1784–1834* (Manchester, 1940), p. 18). But it should be remembered that direct appointment to a high and well remunerated post in the civil service could be a method of supplying a comfortable retreat to a political

adherent or relative, and the regulations which secured that newly appointed men should start at the bottom of the hierarchy prevented the intrusion of such unsuitable individuals into the upper posts. There were also those who believed that a civil servant should at the start of his career familiarize himself with the drudgery of those employed in the lowest ranks (see George Arbuthnot's criticism of the Northcote–Trevelyan Report, H.C. (1854–5) xx. 405–15, an extract from which is printed in H. J. Hanham, *The Nineteenth-Century Constitution 1815–1914. Documents and Commentary* (Cambridge, 1969), pp. 327–9).

There are two printed collections of the papers of Irish under-secretaries: *Mr. Gregory's Letter Box, 1813–1830*, ed. Lady Gregory (1898), and R. Barry O'Brien, *Thomas Drummond Under-Secretary in Ireland 1835–40. Life and Letters* (1889). Both show how important a role a man in that position could play. *GKC, GJ.*

24. The Poor Law School at Norwood was originally one of a number of privately owned establishments to which pauper children were sent under contract for their maintenance by the metropolitan vestries, since by Jonas Hanway's Act (7 Geo. III c. 39) it was not permitted to keep any child under the age of six in any workhouses within three miles of the Cities of London and Westminster. The Poor Law Amendment Act of 1834 did not interfere with these institutions, but in 1838 J. P. Kay, then an Assistant Poor Law Commissioner responsible for the London District, turned his attention to them. He singled out the establishment at Norwood because he was impressed by the character, methods, and willingness to adopt improvements of its proprietor, Aubin, gained the approval of the Guardians of the City of London Union to plans for its reorganization, and secured an annual grant of £500 for it from the Government. It thus became, although still privately owned, the Norwood District School of Industry. As an Assistant Commissioner in East Anglia, Kay had earlier become interested in a project for training children in workhouse schools to become pupil teachers, and arrangements were made to transfer to Norwood promising boys from other workhouse schools to be supported by private patrons. In 1840 boys from Norwood formed the nucleus of the training college at Battersea which Kay and his friend E. C. Tufnell, also an Assistant Commissioner, had started as a private venture in a house belonging to Kay, to fill a need which Government could not supply (see above, p. 74). Kay had become in 1839 the Secretary of the Committee of the Privy Council on Education and 'the new Education

Department' naturally continued the policy which he had initiated when working under the Poor Law Commission. The Norwood School was subsequently purchased by the Central London School District and removed to Hanwell, under Tufnell's management, with Aubin as Headmaster. See H.C. (1839) xx. 103-11, and Sir James Kay-Shuttleworth, *Four Periods of Public Education* (1862), pp. 287-92. GKC.

25. The Registration Act of 1836 which came into force in July 1837 (not 1838) provided a civil, rather than ecclesiastical, registration of births, deaths, and marriages, and was the culmination of a long campaign waged by Dissenters. The new registration districts were made coincident with the Poor Law Unions and Chadwick secured that not only the fact, but also the cause of death, should be reported. He also managed to obtain the appointment of William Farr as Assistant Registrar. The importance of the reform in establishing reliable vital statistics cannot be exaggerated. See Finer, *Chadwick*, pp. 124-6, 143, 154-5 and M. J. Cullen, 'The Making of the Civil Registration Act of 1836', *Journal of Ecclesiastical History*, xxv (1974), 39-59. GKC, JMC.

26. In 1838 the prevalence of disease in the East End, and the fact that Poor Law Guardians had no legal power to spend money on the removal of nuisances which might have contributed to distress, enabled Chadwick to persuade the Poor Law Commission to investigate the subject. Part of this task he assigned to Dr. Arnott, an old associate of Bentham, Dr. Kay (see next note), and Dr. Southwood Smith (see Section VI, note 29). On the whole episode see Finer, *Chadwick*, pp. 155-7. It has been held that this was the beginning of the course which led to the Public Health Act of 1848 and the appointment of the Board of Health. GKC.

27. Dr. J. P. Kay, subsequently Sir James Phillips Kay Shuttleworth (1804-77), was born at Rochdale. In 1824 he entered Edinburgh University where he worked as clinical assistant during an epidemic of typhus to W. P. Alison, a pioneer in the recognition of the relationship between destitution and disease. He then practised in Manchester and during the first cholera epidemic became Secretary to the Manchester Board of Health and published his notable report (see above, p. 43 and Section V, note 2). In 1835 he became an Assistant Poor Law Commissioner and in 1839 the first Secretary of the Committee of the Privy Council on Education. The educational system which Kay had to

administer was based on denominational schools, financed partly by the denominational societies and partly by grants from the Privy Council. To receive a Government grant, schools had to submit to inspection, and it has been held that the school inspectors, the factory and mines inspectors, and the assistant commissioners operating the new Poor Law were the sinews of the new regulating Welfare State. Kay retired, broken by overwork, in 1849. For further comments on his work see above, pp. 74 and 98, and Section VI, notes 24 and 26. *GKC.*

28. Leonard Horner (1785–1864) was the brother of Francis Horner, the economist. He himself was a geologist and mineralogist. One of the founders of the Edinburgh Academy and the London Institution, he became Warden of London University in 1827. After serving on the Factory Commission in 1833 he was appointed one of the inspectors under the Factory Act (1833) in which post he remained until 1859. He had an important influence on the development of factory regulations. See Bernice Martin, 'Leonard Horner: A Portrait of an Inspector of Factories', *International Review of Social History*, xiv (1969), 412–43.

Hugh Seymour Tremenheere (1804–93), a Fellow of New College, Oxford 1824–56, was called to the bar in 1834. After serving as a revising barrister, he entered the public service, becoming a School Inspector late in 1839. His first task was to investigate the state of education in South Wales after the Chartist rising in Newport. In 1842, owing to the severity of his criticisms of the schools run by the British and Foreign Society, it was deemed expedient to transfer him to the post of Inspector of Mines. He subsequently dealt with the conditions of children in bleaching works and other industries, and with the gang system in agriculture, and was an active member of the Commission on the Employment of Children and Women in Agriculture, which sat between 1867 and 1870. The fourteen Acts of Parliament to which his work gave rise in the period 1839–71 are listed in E. L. and O. P. Edmonds, *I Was There. The Memoirs of H. S. Tremenheere* (Eton, Windsor, 1965), pp. 114–15. They show, as do his memoirs, how much varied social legislation was attributable to his initiative, which was by no means always acknowledged at the time. See also R. K. Webb, 'A Whig Inspector', *Journal of Modern History*, xxvii (1955), 352–64. Men like Tremenheere and Edward Turner Boyd Twisleton (1809–74), on whom see the *D.N.B.*, are symptoms of the link that was to develop between the civil service and Oxford and Cambridge, after the first Benthamite impulse. *GKC.*

29. Thomas Southwood Smith (1788–1861) was born at Martock near Yeovil. His parents were extreme Calvinists and he was educated at the Baptist Academy at Bristol, but, partly under the influence of Coleridge, abandoned his Calvinism and became a Unitarian Minister. In 1816 he took his M.D. at Edinburgh and published *Illustrations of the Divine Government*, which went through several editions and excited the admiration of Byron, Moore, Wordsworth, and Crabbe. It probably owed its success to the fact that it lightened the burden which the Calvinist predestinarian conception of morality had imposed on Dissenter and Evangelical Churchman alike; and by rejecting the limitations on human capacity imposed by the Calvinistic conception of Divine Sovereignty it also predicted that human beings would develop an increasing power to mitigate the suffering and increase the happiness of others, particularly by the development of medical knowledge. This was the germ of the 'sanitary idea', the belief that social conditions could be indefinitely improved by the control of disease and the correction of the conditions which led to disease and degradation. It was the key idea behind the development of 'a Public Welfare Service' of which Young speaks on p. 57, and clearly owed much to the Medical School of Edinburgh, where J. P. Kay had also studied (see Section VI, note 27). Southwood Smith came to London in 1820, became a Licentiate and then a Fellow of the Royal College of Physicians, and in 1824 was appointed physician to the London Fever Hospital and subsequently to the Eastern Dispensary and the Jews' Hospital. He thus gained considerable knowledge of the areas of London which were the breeding grounds of fever, to which he introduced a number of eminent people, among them, in due course, Edwin Chadwick, and in 1830 published an important *Treatise on Fever*. He served on the Factory Commission in 1833 and the Commission on Children's Employment in 1842. With Kay and Arnott he was appointed by the Poor Law Commission in 1838 to report on the causes of fever in the East End of London (see Section VI, note 26), provided material for Chadwick's *Sanitary Report* in 1842, and from 1844 organized the Health of Towns Association to press for sanitary reform. In 1848 he became an unpaid, and in 1850 a salaried, Commissioner under the Public Health Act, a situation which he held until 1854.

Historians have seriously underestimated Southwood Smith's contribution to the development of the Welfare State. He has normally been eclipsed by Chadwick, but if any one man originated the 'sanitary idea' it was Southwood Smith, long before Chadwick was in the field. His relations with Bentham preceded Chadwick's by a number of years. He was one of the projectors of the *Westminster Review* to which he contributed important articles on medical subjects, and in all probability supplied much of the medical information which was used in the writing of Bentham's *Code*. He was given the macabre task of dissecting Bentham's body at a public demonstration after his death. After 1830 Chadwick's initiative as a public servant was all important, but Southwood Smith supplied medical knowledge which Chadwick did not possess, and his contribution has never been fairly assessed. There is a study of him by his granddaughter, Mrs. C. L. Lewes, *Dr. Southwood Smith: a retrospect* (1898), a full article in the *D.N.B.*, and an important contribution by F. N. L. Poynter, 'Thomas Southwood Smith—the Man', *Proceedings of the Royal Society of Medicine*, lv (1962), 381–92. GKC.

30. Sir John Simon (1816–1904) was the grandson of a Frenchman who lived in England for most of his life. He trained as a medical student at King's College Hospital and at St. Thomas's, becoming Senior Assistant Surgeon at King's in 1840, Lecturer in Pathology in 1847, and a full surgeon at St. Thomas's in 1853. In 1848 he was appointed Medical Officer of Health to the City of London, where his work and his reports were of considerable importance in developing the City's public health policy. The old Board of Health was dissolved in 1854 and in 1855 Simon became Medical Officer to the new Board, which was itself dissolved in 1858 when Simon became Medical Officer to the Privy Council. His annual reports on the sanitary state of the nation did much to prepare the way for the attempt to impose uniform standards in the Public Health Act of 1866, the first of an important series of statutes culminating in the consolidatory Act of 1875. The creation of the Local Government Board in 1871 (not 1870, as stated on p. 57) as the central authority in sanitary matters, placed Simon under its Permanent Secretary, John Lambert, formerly an Inspector of the Poor Law Board. This destroyed his independence and scope for initiative, and he retired prematurely in 1876. Without question Simon was one of the most important figures in the development of the machinery of State in this country. See Royston Lambert, *Sir John Simon 1816–1904 and English Social Administration* (1963). GKC.

31. Arthur Hill Hassall (1817–94), an M.D. of London University, specialized in the detection of the adulteration of food. His analytical

methods, particularly in the use of the microscope, were in advance of anything previously known. In 1850 Thomas Wakley, editor of the *Lancet*, instigated a campaign against adulteration and appointed two 'commissioners' to look into the matter—Hassall and Henry Letheby (1816–76), an expert on diet who succeeded Simon as Medical Officer to the City of London. Hassall made a series of startling revelations and published his findings in an important book, *Food and its Adulterations* (1855), which he followed with *Adulterations Detected* (1857). The subject was investigated by a Select Committee of the House of Commons in 1855 and 1856 before which Hassall gave evidence. As a result the first Food and Drugs Act was passed in 1860. The Act was, however, loosely administered and had to be drastically amended in 1872 when the appointment of analysts was made compulsory on the direction of the Local Government Board. The Food and Drugs Act of 1875 completed this period of legislative reform. See John Burnett, *Plenty and Want. A Social History of Diet in England from 1815 to the Present Day* (1966), pp. 190–213, and S. Squire Sprigge, *The Life and Times of Thomas Wakley* (1897), pp. 460–77, which gives full details of the adulterations which were practised. Hassall himself wrote *The Narrative of a Busy Life. An Autobiography* (1893). *GKC, JMC.*

SECTION VII

1. The sliding scale of 1828, by which the duty on imported corn was reduced as the price of corn rose, in fact slid too easily. By purchasing corn, speculators were able to drive the price up to the top of the scale, which reduced the duty to its lowest point. They then introduced a mass of corn which forced the price down and the duty up, and caught out their competitors and the British farmer bringing his corn to market. Peel inserted a stopping-point into the scale so that it could not be manipulated so easily. *GKC.*

2. Henry Pelham-Clinton, Earl of Lincoln (1811–64), later 5th Duke of Newcastle, was First Commissioner of Woods and Forests and briefly Chief Secretary for Ireland in Peel's Government. Charles John Canning (1812–62), later Earl Canning, third son of George Canning, was Under-Secretary for Foreign Affairs and subsequently First Commissioner of Woods and Forests. Sir James Andrew Broun-Ramsay (1812–

60), who succeeded as 2nd Baron Dalhousie in 1838, was Vice-President and later President of the Board of Trade. *GKC.*

3. Words attributed to an agricultural labourer at an anti-Corn Law meeting (Trevelyan, *Bright*, pp. 92–3). It would be desirable to know more about the identity and spontaneity of the speaker before accepting them as evidence, but without doubt the conditions of agricultural labourers in many districts were very bad, and their wages very low. Peel seems to have been aware of this fact, for on 27 Mar. 1846, in a debate on the repeal of the Corn Laws, he made the point that protection had not benefited the agricultural labourers, whose wages were lowest in those counties where there was no industry (*Hansard*, 3rd Ser. lxxxv. 237–44). *GKC.*

4. It is doubtful whether Peel had any clear plans for the future when news of the Irish potato famine broke. In the first half of 1845 he was preoccupied with the problems of Ireland and of rearmament, and he had not begun to consider his next budget when the news began to come in. He was, however, acutely conscious of the success of his tariff reductions, and aware that all was not well with agriculture. On 6 Feb. 1845 he conceded that there was considerable distress in certain districts, but attributed it to external causes, argued that it could not fairly be ascribed to his legislation, and stated that a restoration of the former protection was both irrelevant and impossible (*Hansard*, 3rd Ser. lxxvii. 205). He is reported to have found Cobden's speech of 13 Mar. 1845 on the injurious effects of protection on agriculture unanswerable (see Norman Gash, *Sir Robert Peel* (1972), pp. 470–1). His first year in office had impressed on him the disastrous social consequences of high prices (see his letter to J. W. Croker, 30 Oct. 1842, in *The Correspondence and Diaries of John Wilson Croker*, ed. Louis J. Jennings (3 vols., 1884), ii. 391–2), and on 10 June 1845 he openly repudiated the argument that a high price of corn would necessarily be accompanied by a high rate of wages (*Hansard*, 3rd Ser. lxxxi. 370). *GKC, DRF.*

5. For 'Peel's long-distance programme' see Prince Albert's memorandum, 25 Dec. 1845 (*Letters of Queen Victoria*, 1st Ser. ii. 76–9). It is true that Peel was not reconciled to the party system as it had developed after 1832, since his mind had been formed in a period when ministers were primarily servants of the Crown, not of a party (see above,

Section VI, note 21). He had also come to resent what he considered to be the unreasonable and often self-seeking claims of individual party politicians. Though probably one of the most efficient of all prime ministers both as an administrator and a framer of legislation, he was in no way a frigid man, but was in fact unusually sensitive and endowed with a naturally passionate nature, which he normally kept under very strict control. Possibly as a result of this tension his façade was apt to seem formidable, and he could indeed react disagreeably when approached. There is, however, no reason to believe that this fact caused his death. The horse which threw him had been carefully tested for his use by Mr. Beckett Denison, but had, unknown to him, a bad record for bucking and kicking. According to Goldwin Smith, it had been recognized when Peel was riding it by at least one man who knew its history: 'Our neighbour at Mortimer, Sir Paul Hunter, met Peel riding in the Park, recognised the horse, actually turned to warn him; but fearing to intrude, abstained.' (*Reminiscences* (New York, 1910), p. 175.) But there is nothing to suggest that this happened on the day of Peel's accident, and to judge from the route Peel probably took that day he could not have been said to have been riding in 'the Park'. Nor is it clear that Hunter's unfortunate diffidence had any other cause than a natural reluctance to volunteer such a statement to an eminent statesman, whom he may not have known well, if at all. For the circumstances of Peel's death see Gash, *Sir Robert Peel*, pp. 697–8.

The begging–letter writer has not been identified. Many were prosecuted by the Society for the Suppression of Mendicity, and Charles Dickens, an obvious target, was named in such a case on 22 May 1844 (*The Times*, 23 May 1844, pp. 6f–7a). There is no mention in that case of Peel or Queen Adelaide, and Peel appears neither in other contemporary cases nor in the books of the Mendicity Society for that year. The incident, however, is by no means improbable. Peel's papers show that he was very ready to give money even to beggars whose cases look very questionable. This inclination was characteristic of his compassionate nature. *NG, GKC.*

6. Thomas Drummond was Under-Secretary at Dublin Castle from July 1835 to April 1840. He reduced the corruption, inefficiency, and Protestant bias of the magistracy and police, and as a result the law was more equitably administered than it had ever previously been and the Executive gained a well deserved reputation for impartiality and efficiency. The 2nd Earl of Mulgrave, later 1st Marquess of Normanby,

was appointed Lord Lieutenant in April 1835, and played an important part in the development of this policy, the success of which influenced O'Connell's decision to drop momentarily his agitation for repeal of the Union. Normanby was succeeded in April 1839 by Viscount Ebrington, later 2nd Earl Fortescue, who held the post until the fall of the Whigs in 1841. He appears to have wished to pursue the same line, but the peaceful phase was drawing to a close. Drummond died in April 1840, and O'Connell, perceiving that the Whig ministry was nearing its end, founded his National Repeal Association. The name of Normanby would therefore have been more appropriate in this sentence than that of Ebrington. *GKC.*

7. Denman, speaking in the House of Lords, 4 Sept. 1844, on O'Connell's appeal, declared his intention of dealing with the challenge to the jury: 'it is of the most vital consequence that such a matter shall not be passed over without a due and sufficient remedy being provided, as otherwise a trial by jury, instead of being a protection to the party accused, would be a mockery, a snare and a delusion.' (*The Times*, 5 Sept. 1844, p. 6c.) He did not, therefore, use the words to describe what had happened at O'Connell's trial in Dublin; but the proceedings which he related in his speech would have justified his doing so. *GKC.*

8. The agitation for Repeal was renewed not in 1841 but in 1840, and not by Gavan Duffy but by O'Connell, who dominated it until his arrest in 1843. The role of Duffy, Thomas Davis, and others in this agitation was a subordinate one, but after 1843 they followed their own line and formed the group which came to be called 'Young Ireland'. Their policy was more militant than that of O'Connell and led to the events of 1848. Their newspaper, the *Nation*, initially supported O'Connell but later turned against him. The *United Irishman* was a far less important weekly paper founded in 1848 by John Mitchel, an intransigent nationalist. See Sir Charles Gavan Duffy, *Young Ireland. A Fragment of Irish History, 1840–45. Final Revision* (1896) and Denis Gwynn, *Young Ireland and 1848* (Cork, 1949). *GKC.*

9. For the Government's remedial measures see Kevin B. Nowlan, *The Politics of Repeal* (1965), pp. 80–92. For the Report of the Devon Commission on the Occupation of Land see H.C. (1845) xix–xxii. The Compensation to Tenants Bill which Lord Stanley introduced in 1845 and which was dropped would probably have been an ineffective

measure. Another Bill introduced by Lord Lincoln in 1846 was also abandoned. *GKC*.

10. The first report of the failure of the potato crop came from the Isle of Wight. The letter from the potato-dealer confirming the extent of the disease was received on 11 Aug. 1845 by Sir James Graham, who forwarded it to Peel. For this letter and Peel's subsequent inquiries into the scale of the disaster see *Memoirs by Sir Robert Peel*, ed. Lord Mahon and Edward Cardwell (2 vols., 1856–7), ii. 106–40 and Norman Gash, *Sir Robert Peel* (1972), pp. 531–7. *GKC*.

11. If the 'Cabinet paper' referred to is the memorandum printed in Peel's *Memoirs*, ii. 141–8 it does not bear out Young's remark. The word 'potato' is used quite naturally three times, and neither 'That Root' nor any other periphrasis is employed. *GKC*.

12. In July 1848 William Smith O'Brien (1803–64), M.P. for County Limerick, who had decided that force was the only solution for the problems of Ireland, toured the south-west of the country to recruit support. He gained little, but when he reached Mullinahone in Tipperary on 25 July he had the chapel bells rung to summon the people, news of the suspension of habeas corpus having convinced him that he must fight. A large body of peasants armed with pikes and firearms assembled, but many went away when O'Brien told them that he had no means of feeding them. Four days later O'Brien and the remainder attacked a body of forty-six armed policemen, who had taken possession of a house belonging to a woman known as the 'widow McCormack', in an attempt to secure their weapons. The attack failed, O'Brien's force faded away, and he was arrested on 5 August. *GKC*.

13. The Act to remove Doubts concerning the Transportation of Offenders under Judgement of Death to whom Mercy may be extended in *Ireland* (12 and 13 Vict. c. 27) received the royal assent on 26 June 1849. For the debates on it see *Hansard*, 3rd Ser. cvi. 283, 389–449, 784–800, 822–30. It would be interesting to know to what extent O'Brien believed that the Government were likely to carry out the sentence passed upon him. Certainly several of those who spoke in the debates seem to have regarded his move mainly as a way of upsetting the sentence of the court. He was transported to Van Diemen's Land in 1849, was allowed to return to Europe in 1854, received a free pardon in 1856, and returned to Ireland. *GKC*.

SECTION VIII

1. This is probably a reference to the opening address by William Newmarch (1820–82), banker, economist, and journalist, to the Economic Science and Statistics Section of the British Association at Manchester, 6 Sept. 1861:

> The experiment had wholly succeeded. . . . It had consolidated society in this part of the island, swept away a great mass of festering and growing discontent, placed the prosperity of the district on a broad, solid, and safe basis. . . . These results had flowed from the sagacious, persevering, and moral exertions of the advocates of the Ten Hours Bill.

The Times, 7 Sept. 1861, p. 7b. *JTW, DRF.*

2. See Section XXXI, note 3.

3. For Engels's sources see Friedrich Engels, *The Condition of the Working Class in England,* trans. and ed. W. O. Henderson and W. H. Chaloner (Oxford, 1958), pp. xi, xix–xxi. *GKC.*

4. The Act did not apply to all textile factories, and limited young persons to twelve, not ten hours. *JTW.*

5. To judge by Bentham's own words, the maxim should be cited as 'separate and (then) aggregate'. In the skeleton plan for the improved management of paupers which he produced in 1796 he emphasized the importance of 'separating' the various categories of those who required poor relief—the able-bodied, the aged, children, the sick, the blind, the insane, etc.—and 'aggregating' each category into a group which would receive appropriate treatment, accommodation, food, clothing, etc., and which would be called on to do appropriate work. The essence of the scheme was that the organization of poor relief should be taken over by a company which should make its profit from the work of paupers. Bentham later returned to the plan and expended much ingenuity in locating the various categories in very large pauper colonies, to be constructed on the panopticon principle of constant surveillance. See *The Works of Jeremy Bentham,* ed. John Bowring (11 vols., Edinburgh, 1843), viii. 362, 372–3 and J. R. Poynter, *Society and*

Pauperism (1969), pp. 122–44. The Report of the Royal Commission on the Poor Laws in 1834 accepted in principle the importance of separating the various categories of people requiring poor relief and aggregating them into groups for suitable treatment. The Commissioners recognized that this could not be done in a small workhouse with a limited district, but do not seem to have envisaged anything as large as Bentham's houses of industry. They did not revive much of Bentham's detail, nor his project for contracting the management of poor relief to a company. They believed that economies in administration would make their scheme no more expensive than existing arrangements, but what they envisaged seems to have been beyond the resources, or the administrative conceptions, of those who actually brought the New Poor Law into being. See H.C. (1834) xxvii. 170–6, from which an extract is printed in Young and Handcock, *English Historical Documents*, pp. 704–5. GKC.

6. On the failure to maintain the principle of refusing relief outside the workhouse see Michael E. Rose, 'The Allowance System under the New Poor Law', *Economic History Review*, 2nd Ser. xix (1966), 607–20; Young and Handcock, *English Historical Documents*, pp. 711–14. GKC.

7. 'Andover gristle' refers to a scandal which broke in 1845 when the paupers in the Andover workhouse were found to be so hungry that they ate the gristle in the bones which they had been given to crush for manure. See Ian Anstruther, *The Scandal of the Andover Workhouse* (1973); Finer, *Chadwick*, pp. 257–73; and the Report on the Andover Union (H.C. (1846) v and xxxvi. 201–10). Presumably the workhouse dietary cited by Young was for a week. For others see Young and Handcock, *English Historical Documents*, p. 710. GKC.

8. In his *Political Register*, 3 Oct. 1818, for example, Cobbett included among the advantages of America the fact that there were 'No Wilberforces. Think of that! No Wilberforces!' (Lewis Melville, *The Life and Letters of William Cobbett* (2 vols., 1913), ii. 107.) GKC.

9. This probably refers to Richard Hurrell Froude (1803–36), one of the leading figures of the Tractarian movement, who was in the West Indies when the Act emancipating the slaves was passed, and seems to have conceived an equal dislike for both the advocates and beneficiaries of the measure. For example, in a letter of 25 Sept. 1834 he wrote: 'I am

ashamed to say I cannot get over my prejudices against the niggers; every one I meet seems to me like an incarnation of the whole Anti-slavery Society, and Fowell Buxton at their head.' (*Remains of Richard Hurrell Froude* (2 vols., 1838), i. 377.) GKC.

10. On four occasions between 1832 and 1837 Sir Andrew Agnew, 7th Bt. (1793–1849), M.P. for Wigtownshire, introduced a Bill to forbid labour on Sundays, except for works of necessity and mercy. It was three times rejected on its second reading, in 1833 by 79 votes to 73, in 1834 by 161–125, and in 1836 by 75–43. On 4 May 1837 Agnew secured leave to introduce the Bill by 199 votes to 53, and the second reading was carried on 7 June by 110–66; but the dissolution necessitated by the death of William IV intervened, and as Agnew was not returned to the new House of Commons, the matter was dropped. In 1833 George Cruikshank attacked Agnew's Bill in a set of drawings entitled *Sunday in London*, with a text by J. Wight of the *Morning Herald*, but he does not appear to have reverted to the subject. See Albert M. Cohn, *George Cruikshank. A Catalogue Raisonné of the Work Executed During the Years 1806–1877* (1924), p. 240. In 1836 Dickens, writing under the name of 'Timothy Sparks', published an attack on the Bill, *Sunday Under Three Heads*, which is included in his *Reprinted Pieces*. The proposed legislation would certainly have penalized the working classes in many ways, but it must be remembered that the Sabbatarians were in favour of prohibiting factory work on Sundays and in some cases of granting a half-day on Saturdays. It is also interesting to note that the measure made significant progress for the first time *after* Dickens's attack. GKC, LGS.

11. cf. Charles Dickens, *Bleak House*, Chapter 8: 'I wants a end of these liberties took with my place.' EJK.

12. By clause 20 of the Act every child restricted to forty-eight hours labour in the week (i.e. from thirty months after its passage every child which had not completed its thirteenth year) had to attend a school chosen by the parents or guardian, or, failing them, the factory inspectors; and by clause 18 the latter were required to enforce school attendance. Clause 20 was easily evaded in a variety of ways. See Young and Handcock, *English Historical Documents*, pp. 951–2. GKC.

13. The Act of 1840, designed to protect the chimney-sweeping children, proved ineffective. Further legislation was needed, and effective

protection was not given to these children until 1875. See Hodder, *Shaftesbury*, iii. 151–8. Charles Kingsley's novel, *The Water Babies*, which is about a boy chimney-sweep, was published in 1863. GKC.

14. In 1840 on the motion of Lord Ashley a Royal Commission was appointed to investigate the conditions of employment of children in mines and collieries and other branches of trade and industry not covered by the Factory Acts. It reported on the conditions in mines in 1842 (H.C. (1842) xv–xvii) and the resultant outcry was so great that immediate legislation was demanded. On the effectiveness of this legislation see O. O. G. M. MacDonagh, 'Coal Mines Regulation: The First Decade, 1842–1852', in *Ideas and Institutions of Victorian Britain*, ed. Robert Robson (1967), pp. 58–86. GKC.

15. On 7 Mar. 1843 Sir James Graham introduced a Factory Bill which included proposals for the extension of the educational facilities for children under 13. Most Anglicans were at best lukewarm about these provisions, and the reaction of Dissenters of all shades was overwhelmingly hostile. Graham managed to secure further concessions from the Church and modified the Bill accordingly, but Nonconformist opposition continued, and the educational clauses were withdrawn on 15 June. See *Hansard*, 3rd Ser. lxvii. 422–4, 1411–77; lxviii. 39–40, 829–30, 1103–30; lxix. 1567–70; J. T. Ward, *The Factory Movement, 1830–1855* (1962), pp. 258–68; J. T. Ward and J. H. Treble, 'Religion and Education in 1843: Reaction to the "Factory Education Bill"', *Journal of Ecclesiastical History*, xx (1969), 79–110. For Brougham's comment see his letter to Graham of 21 Oct. 1841 (Charles Stuart Parker, *Life and Letters of Sir James Graham* (2 vols., 1907), i. 337). DRF, GKC.

16. Graham introduced the Bill, which proposed to reduce the hours of women's labour, not men's, to twelve, on 6 Feb. 1844 (*Hansard*, 3rd Ser. lxxii. 277–81). On 15 March Lord Ashley proposed to amend clause 2 so as to define 'night' as the period between 6 p.m. and 6 a.m., the effect of which, in conjunction with adjustments to clause 8, would have been to restrict the hours of young persons and females to ten. Graham, on behalf of the Government, firmly opposed the amendment (ibid. lxxiii. 1073–110). For Peel's rhetorical question, 18 March, and its sequel, in which the original proposition was defeated by 179 votes to 170, and Ashley's amendment carried by 161–153, see ibid. lxxiii. 1253–4, 1263–6, and Hodder, *Shaftesbury*, ii. 31. The Government

resolved to put the issue to the question once more on clause 8, which specified the hours of labour to be worked by women and young persons. Young's reference to 'a few nights later' is presumably to the events of 22 March when Ashley secured the defeat by 186–183 of their proposal that the hours should be twelve, but lost his ten hours amendment by 188–181 (*Hansard*, 3rd Ser. lxxiii. 1460–3). The Government withdrew the Bill and introduced a new one which retained the twelve hours provision. It was on 13 May 1844, in rejecting by 297 votes to 159 Ashley's proposed additional clause to limit the hours of young persons to eleven after 1 Oct. 1844 and to ten after 1 Oct. 1847, that the House actually reversed its decision of 18 March (ibid. lxxiv. 1104–7). See also Ward, *Factory Movement*, pp. 283–99; Robert Stewart, 'The Ten Hours and Sugar Crises of 1844: Government and the House of Commons in the Age of Reform', *Historical Journal*, xii (1969), 35–57. *DRF, JTW.*

17. For Macaulay on Southey and Mill see the *Edinburgh Review*, vol. xlix (Mar. and June 1829), pp. 159–89, 273–99; vol. l (Oct. 1829 and Jan. 1830), pp. 99–125, 528–65. For his criticism of Owen see p. 533 of the last article cited here. *JTW, DRF.*

18. Edmund Burke, *Thoughts and Details on Scarcity, originally presented to William Pitt, in the month of November, 1795* (1800), pp. 45–6. *DRF.*

19. See *Speeches of T. B. Macaulay* (1854), pp. 435–55. The first two sentences quoted by Young appear on p. 439, the next three on pp. 437–8, and the final three on p. 438. *JTW.*

20. For Dalhousie's policy on railway legislation see his speeches in the House of Lords, 11 July 1845 and 29 Jan. 1846 (*Hansard*, 3rd Ser. lxxxii. 388–90; lxxxiii. 353–8) and J. H. Clapham, *An Economic History of Modern Britain. The Early Railway Age, 1820–1850* (Cambridge, 1926), pp. 421–2, 527–8. *GKC.*

21. Macaulay's journal, 8 Apr. 1849: 'Hudson in a scrape. I never could bear him—a bloated, vulgar, insolent, purse proud, greedy, drunken blackguard. I used to say that when he swaggered up the House he looked like Mammon and Belial rolled into one.' (MS. Journal, Trinity College Library, Cambridge.) *FCM, RR.*

22. George Hudson (1800–71), the son of a Yorkshire farmer, started in business as a draper in York. His involvement in the promotion of railways began in 1837 and his activity, power, and prestige reached their peak in 1844–5. In 1847 the value of railway property fell rapidly, and the subsequent disclosure of the irregularities of Hudson's dealings ruined him and forced him to retreat to the Continent.

At a by-election for Sunderland in 1845 Hudson, standing as a Protectionist, beat Thomas Perronet Thompson, the veteran anti-Corn Law pamphleteer, by 627 votes to 498. See Norman McCord and P. A. Wood, 'The Sunderland Election of 1845', *Durham University Journal*, N.S. xxi (1959), 11–21. *The Times* received the result by a special train:

> By a special express, which left Sunderland at 17 minutes past 4 o'clock yesterday afternoon, and performed the distance (305 miles) from the committee-room in Bishopwearmouth in about eight hours, we have received the result of the . . . Sunderland election . . . The express was arranged by Mr. James Allport, of the Newcastle and Darlington Railway, who conveyed a special messenger with the intelligence to this office . . .

The Times, 15 Aug. 1845, p. 5e.

The origin of the story about Mrs. Hudson has not been established, but it was probably fabricated. She was an uneducated woman about whose blunders many malicious stories were circulated. On her, and Hudson's contacts with Prince Albert, which could hardly be interpreted as friendship, and with the Duke of Wellington see R. S. Lambert, *The Railway King, 1800–1871* (1934), pp. 176–81, 209–11, 228. GKC, DRF.

23. Jean Charles Léonard Simonde de Sismondi (1773–1842) was a distinguished historian and economist of Swiss–Italian origin. His relevant works on economic and allied subjects are *Nouveaux principes d'économie politique* (2 vols., Paris, 1819); *Études sur les constitutions des peuples libres* (Paris, 1836); and *Études sur l'économie politique* (2 vols., Paris, 1837–8). There is an article on him in the *Quarterly Review*, vol. lxxii (May and Sept. 1843), pp. 299–356 where, in an analysis of his economic views, it is pointed out that Sismondi attacked the belief, which he imputed to English economists, that national wealth was solely material, and declared that 'Whatever tends to loss of health or comfort, or deterioration of morals, in the main body of the nation, is not

wealth but poverty' (pp. 347–53). It seems that Peel read the *Quarterly*, and he may have drawn on this article for his speech; but to judge from contemporary library collections Sismondi's works had a fairly wide circulation in Britain and he may easily have gained his knowledge elsewhere. It should, however, be noted that he spoke of Italian economists, not of an Italian economist. See *Hansard*, 3rd Ser. xc. 812 (3 Mar. 1847).

Young's reference to the *Quarterly Review* of 1832 is probably to Poulett Scrope's review of Chalmers's *Political Economy* in the October issue of that year (vol. xlviii, pp. 36–69). In point of fact Peel had no need to go to this, or Sismondi, or Sadler, or Southey, or Young England to learn that the object of society ought to be to maximize welfare rather than wealth. That had always been his aim. He shrank from further restriction of the hours of labour in factories because he believed that the impediment to production would reduce the competitive power of British industry and produce the type of unemployment he had faced as Prime Minister in 1841–2. Such consequences would clearly reduce the welfare of the working classes. It is obvious from his speech that he realized that the English economists studied the conditions which they believed to contribute to the accumulation of material wealth because they thought that this was an important subject to investigate, not because they considered it to be the only object to be pursued in human affairs. GKC.

24. Good examples of the 'natural alliance' between the authoritative Tory and a Benthamite official can be seen in the close co-operation between Lord Shaftesbury and Chadwick on the Board of Health from 1848 to 1854, and in the practical support given to Chadwick's public health policy by Charles Blomfield, Bishop of London, and many of the parochial clergy. For the achievements of the 'alliance' in India see Eric Stokes, *The English Utilitarians and India* (Oxford, 1959), pp. 248 ff. GKC.

25. Mrs. Tonna (1790–1846) was an Evangelical who wrote under the name of 'Charlotte Elizabeth'. In 1841 she published *Helen Fleetwood: a tale of a factory girl*. On the origins of *The Perils of the Nation* see her widower's observations in Charlotte Elizabeth, *Personal Recollections*, 4th edn. (1854), pp. 408–9:

her acknowledged works do not comprise the whole or the most important of the labours of her pen. For, in the latter part of . . .

1842, the Committee of the Christian Influence Society, deeply impressed with a sense of the alarming state of the country, from the habitual grinding oppression to which the labouring classes were exposed, resolved upon the publication of a work to be expressly addressed to the Legislature and higher classes in the state, shewing on undoubted evidence of fact the existing evils, and on plain scriptural grounds the inevitable consequences of such a state of things. They proposed to her to undertake the work, with the understanding, that not only was the book to be published without a name, but that every precaution must be used to keep the authorship strictly secret; as it was not to be supposed that legislators and those for whose perusal it was intended, would pay much attention to a work on such a subject, from a woman's pen. She . . . commenced the work, and . . . completed the 'PERILS OF THE NATION', which was published at Easter in the year 1843.

The work attracted immediate attention, and even in the highest places in the land enquiries were made as to the authorship, but the secret, confined to a very few persons, was never divulged.

See also Mona Wilson, *Jane Austen and Some Contemporaries* (1938), pp. 202–4.

The Perils of the Nation was followed in 1844 by *Remedies Suggested for Some of the Evils which constitute 'The Perils of the Nation'*, also anonymous, but presumably also by Mrs. Tonna, the chief recommendation of which was apparently the provision of small-holdings. Both were published by Robert Benton Seeley (1798–1886), the Evangelical publisher, and author of *Memoirs of the Life and Writings of M. T. Sadler* (1842), which contained very severe strictures on what was held to be the creed of the political economists. Since *The Perils of the Nation* and its sequel were anonymous, they have sometimes been ascribed to Seeley and placed under his name in library catalogues.

Mrs. Tonna did not in fact attribute any advocacy of contraception to Harriet Martineau, nor did she call her names. She wrote:

The most horrifying abominations of Socialism, are avowedly reared on the foundation laid down in these pernicious little books [those on economic problems by Mrs. Marcet and Miss Martineau], which prepared the gross minds of the most ignorant classes for any practical application of the system that Satan might suggest. Very far, we are sure, from the purpose of the writers was it to pave the way for such hideous enormities; but when the bright lamp of truth is wilfully hidden, and man's shallow reasonings substituted for the infinite wisdom of God, who shall tell where it may end?

Perils of the Nation, p. 155. The 'enormities' in question might be the practice of contraception, but they might equally refer to abortion or even infanticide. *GKC, DRF.*

SECTION IX

1. Young's statement is partially substantiated by a table compiled by William Lawford, M.I.C.E., who was ordered by a Royal Commission on Railway Accidents to investigate the Continental situation and compare it with the British, which shows the number of accidents in Belgium, Germany, Switzerland, France, and England in 1874 (H.C. (1877) xlviii. 162). However, Lawford believed that no accurate comparison of relative safety could be established, since Continental traffic was slower and less extensive, and the statistics of Continental accidents normally derived from different methods of calculation. In particular, the total number of passengers was not usually given, making it difficult to ascertain the proportion of casualties, and in Prussia a death was not attributed to an accident unless it was recorded as having occurred within twenty-four hours (H.C. (1877) xlviii. 32–3, 142). No doubt these considerations must apply to any comparison made at an earlier date. At the same time, it seems clear that Continental railways came earlier under much stricter State control than the British, and this probably made for greater safety. See the evidence of Captain D. Galton before a Select Committee on Accidents on Railways (H.C. (1857–8) xiv. 613, answers to Questions 739–45). No comparison of the number of fatal accidents in England and Germany can be of much significance unless it is made clear over what period it is taken, what were the comparative sizes of the two railway systems at the time, and how the accident statistics were compiled. *GKC.*

2. For the review of Herbert Spencer's *Social Statics* see *Eliza Cook's Journal,* vol. v (Apr. and Oct. 1851), p. 390. The opinion stated here is in harmony with that expressed in other articles in the periodical. For instance, in March 1852 Samuel Smiles wrote a piece attacking local authorities for their failure to use the powers available to them under

the Public Health Act of 1848 (ibid. vol. vi, pp. 289–92). There is no reason, however, to believe that such views were necessarily generally entertained by a section of society which can reasonably be described as the 'lower middle class'. Indeed, it is significant that in 1875 Smiles still believed it to be necessary to repeat his attack on public indifference to important matters of common concern which were held to be 'nobody's business' (*Thrift* (1875), pp. 334–41). Possibly by 1851 Herbert Spencer's individualism ought to have been outdated, but his works continued to be widely accepted long afterwards and, what is more important, the ways of thought and social habits which enforced that individualism survived even longer.

The Nonconformist preacher was James Baldwin Brown (1820–84). In a lecture subsequently published as a pamphlet he observed: 'The decade, 1830–40, saw three things, very important indeed to the social welfare of England—the cholera, the London City Mission, and the works of Mr. Charles Dickens. It is a strange triad, but you will find that it is a triad.' (*The Cholera; How to Rob it of its Terror: or, the Mercies of Judgment* (1853), p. 7.)

The London City Mission was an interdenominational Evangelical institution founded in 1835 by a Scot, David Nasmith. Its primary objectives were religious, but the meetings which it promoted to gain support and its monthly *City Mission Magazine* drew attention to conditions in the slums of London. See John Matthias Weylland, *These Fifty Years. Being the Jubilee Volume of the London City Mission* [1885] and Kathleen Heasman, *Evangelicals in Action. An Appraisal of their Social Work in the Victorian Era* (1962), pp. 35–6. Its missionaries also played an important part in furthering the ragged school movement. See C. J. Montague, *Sixty Years in Waifdom* (1904), pp. 34–6.

The two novels which Dickens wrote after *The Pickwick Papers* and before 1840 were *Oliver Twist* (1837–9) and *Nicholas Nickleby* (1838–9). Baldwin Brown may have included in his view *The Old Curiosity Shop* and *Barnaby Rudge* which appeared in book form in 1841 or *A Christmas Carol* which was published in 1843, but he was probably thinking primarily of *Oliver Twist*.

On the influence of cholera on public opinion see Asa Briggs, 'Cholera and Society in the Nineteenth Century', *Past and Present*, xix (Apr. 1961), 76–96 and Norman Longmate, *King Cholera* (1966). In fact cholera was not the most common fatal disease in nineteenth-century England. It was epidemic and local, while typhus and other fevers were endemic, and few towns and villages were ever free from them. But of all diseases cholera was the most terrifying. In 1831–2 it was new and mysterious, and no one knew how it was propagated. When it reached a district it spread quickly, and the speed with which many of its victims passed from apparently perfect health to death in a peculiarly painful form was horrifying. It is therefore not surprising that it had a profound effect on public opinion and public policy. Unfortunately in many places the lessons it should have taught were either not received or not lasting. To many people, especially the poorer property owners, and most particularly shopkeepers, the possibility of cholera and the high probability of fever were less to be feared than the increase in the rates and the interference with private rights which were likely to result from sanitary reform. To take one example from many, Leeds suffered from serious visitations of cholera in 1832 and 1849, but for most of the century remained notoriously filthy; and during most of this period the town was controlled by the 'lower middle class'. See Royston Lambert, *Sir John Simon 1816–1904 and English Social Administration* (1963), pp. 433–4 and E. P. Hennock, *Fit and Proper Persons. Ideal and Reality in Nineteenth Century Urban Government* (1973), pp. 179–291. *GKC, JMC.*

3. The relevant articles in Bentham's *Constitutional Code* are Chapter XXIX, on 'Sublegislatures', and Chapter XXX, on 'Sublegislation Ministers'. See *The Works of Jeremy Bentham*, ed. John Bowring (11 vols., Edinburgh, 1843), ix. 640–3. *GKC.*

4. George Alfred Walker (1807–84) was a physician practising in London. As a boy in Nottingham he had been struck by the state of its densely packed cemeteries, and as a medical student in Paris he visited the cemeteries, and recognized the evils of intramural interment. He later explored, at great risk to his health, the graveyards which surrounded his surgery at 101 Drury Lane, and published his findings in his first book, *Gatherings from Graveyards*, in 1839. The following year he gave evidence before a Select Committee of the House of Commons on the Health of Towns (H.C. (1840) xi. 513–20). Other publications followed, and it was partly as a result of his agitation that the Act controlling intramural interment was passed in 1850. See the *D.N.B.* for further details. The matter is touched on by Dickens in Chapter 16 of *Bleak House*. *GKC.*

5. For Chadwick's activities see Finer, *Chadwick*, pp. 154–63, 212–42,

293–482. For the Report see Edwin Chadwick, *Report on the Sanitary Condition of the Labouring Population* (1842), ed. M. W. Flinn (Edinburgh, 1965). *GKC.*

6. See Palmerston to Queen Victoria, 25 Feb. 1838 (*Letters of Queen Victoria*, 1st Ser. i. 136–8). The interest of the letter lies not only in its extremely early use of the word 'bureaucratic', but also in Palmerston's assertion that it was essentially a Continental phenomenon, which contrasted with the English system in two main ways. Whereas in England ministerial heads of department might have to defend themselves in Parliament, and had therefore to be minutely acquainted with the business of their departments, ministers of state in Europe were unlikely to be accountable in this way, and consequently could afford to delegate more to subordinates. In England, too, a change of government entailed the departure from office not only of heads of departments, but also of the majority of the under-secretaries, and therefore, with one or two exceptions, no under-secretary possessed sufficient superior experience or knowledge to enable him 'to overrule the opinion, or to guide the judgement, of his superior'. On the Continent, however, there were men who had spent most of their working lives in their offices. These factors encouraged the development on the Continent of a system of control by the subordinates in public offices, or, in modern jargon, 'bureaucracy'.

This opinion should be considered in relation to the development described in Section VI, note 21. While Palmerston recognized the significance of ministerial responsibility, he did not realize the importance of the expansion of the powers of government which had already begun. That no one did so is revealed by the shape which that expansion was allowed to assume, for considerable administrative discretion was conceded to men who were not sufficiently under ministerial control and for whom no minister was answerable in Parliament. As Young states, in 1834 the Poor Law Commission, though endowed with great independent power, was not placed under effective ministerial control. In 1847 it was brought within the sphere of ministerial responsibility; but so little had men learned their lesson that in 1848 a Board of Health was created in which the Minister could be outvoted. It was, indeed, as a result of this lack of awareness that the bureaucracy which Palmerston described as essentially Continental emerged in England under the impact of necessity. This impercipience had important consequences in the development of the English State. For further details see G. Kitson Clark, ' "Statesmen in Disguise": Reflexions on the History of the Neutrality of the Civil Service', *Historical Journal*, ii (1959), 19–39 and *An Expanding Society* (Cambridge and Melbourne, 1967), pp. 126–83. GKC.

7. I have been unable to find evidence of the operations of the Private Enterprise Society in 1849, Its origins are obscure, but in Finer, *Chadwick*, p. 466 n. 3 it is suggested that it came into existence in 1854, as the creation of the gas and water companies opposed to Chadwick.

Two Years Ago, written by Charles Kingsley in 1856 and published in 1857, gives a convincing picture, which is confirmed by many local records, of the torpor and self-interest which hampered the operation of the Act of 1848, and of the inability of the Board of Health to interfere until a catastrophe had occurred, and not always even then. It is doubtful, however, that Kingsley's account was based on the Mevagissey outbreak which took place in 1849 and not in 1854. Nor is there any reflection in *Two Years Ago* of its most striking episode. A local doctor obtained tents from the Board of Ordnance and set up a camp, to which he persuaded a large section of the town's population to migrate. None who did so caught the disease, which killed many of those who remained behind. See Norman Longmate, *King Cholera* (1966), p. 176. GKC.

8. Young has mistaken the date of this circular. On 31 Jan. 1837 an 'Instructional letter addressed to various Boards of Guardians, on their formation', signed by Edwin Chadwick on behalf of the Poor Law Commissioners, was sent out. In section 46 it is stated that in the selection of local officers the disqualifications mentioned by Young are 'regarded by the Commissioners as presumptive evidence of unfitness' (H.C. (1837) xxxi. 181). In 1854 Chadwick submitted this portion of the letter as an appendix to his paper on the reorganization of the civil service (H.C. (1854–5) xx. 224). JMC.

9. It is not clear whence Young drew this statement, but it seems probable that what these 'returning exiles' saw was at best a temporary phenomenon. The operation of the Act (16 and 17 Vict. c. 128) was impeded by legal technicalities, and the problem was probably unmanageable in terms of the resources of the nineteenth-century State. During the rest of the century there are certainly a number of descriptions of the smoke which London factory chimneys emitted, and of the

contribution which factories and domestic fires continued to make to London fogs. For the provisions of the Act and the case law on the subject see John Hunt, *London Local Government* (2 vols., 1897), i. 294–7. HJD, GKC.

10. In 1825 Dr. John Russell, Headmaster of Charterhouse, having 480 boys in the school and only eight masters, adopted the monitorial system. It seems, however, to have militated against the popularity of the school, and the number of pupils had fallen to 137 by 1832. See E. M. Jameson, *Charterhouse* (1937), p. 20. GKC.

11. Dr. Andrew Bell (1753–1832) was a clergyman of the Church of England who had been a chaplain at Madras, as a result of which his was often called 'the Madras system'. Joseph Lancaster (1778–1838) was a Quaker. Each claimed to have invented the monitorial system. Lancaster believed in non-sectarian education and in 1808 the British and Foreign School Society was founded to maintain schools in his principles. Bell believed that popular education should be in the hands of the Church of England, and he became Superintendent of the National Society for Promoting the Education of the Poor in the Principles of the Established Church, formed in 1811 and incorporated by royal charter in 1817. GKC.

12. See Charles Dickens, *Great Expectations*, Chapter 7. GKC.

13. There were in fact two major public inquiries into elementary education in the 1830s, a Select Committee appointed on the motion of Lord Kerry in the House of Commons in May 1833 (H.C. (1834) ix. 1–261 and H.C. (1835) vii. 765–1003), and a Select Committee on the Education of the Poorer Classes set up in 1837 (H.C. (1837–8) vii. 157–343). The second drew extensively on the findings of the investigations of a number of private societies, including the Statistical Societies of Manchester, Birmingham, and London, of which the most significant were probably the reports of the Manchester Society. Their paid investigator, J. R. Wood, contributed some of the most important evidence laid before the 1837 Committee, when called on to confirm the findings of his report (H.C. (1837–8) vii. 273–301). It is from the interrogation of Wood that Young's reference to the Dame who objected to the counting of children on religious grounds is taken (Question 1104):

Do you remember one who had conscientious scruples, and said, 'It would be a flat flying in the face of Providence. "No, no," said she, "you shan't catch me counting; see what a pretty mess David made of it when he counted the children of Israel" '?—Yes, I remember that very well; I ran the risk of counting the scholars during a further conversation with her.

However, the examples specified by Young are by no means all taken from the Report of this Select Committee, and probably come from the Manchester reports. For further details see T. S. Ashton, *Economic and Social Investigations in Manchester, 1833–1933* (1934), pp. 13–15, 141 ff.; R. K. Webb, 'Working Class Readers in Early Victorian England', *English Historical Review*, lxv (1950), 333–51; E. G. West, 'Resource Allocation and Growth in Early Nineteenth-Century British Education', *Economic History Review*, 2nd Ser. xxiii (1970), 68–95; J. S. Hurt, 'Professor West on Early Nineteenth-Century Education', ibid. xxiv (1971), 624–32; and E. G. West, 'The Interpretation of Early Nineteenth-Century Education Statistics', ibid. xxiv (1971), 633–42. *GKC.*

14. Sir Antony Panizzi (1797–1879) was born in the Duchy of Modena, but fell foul of the authorities through his involvement with the Carbonari, and fled to England in 1822. He became friendly with Brougham who, as Lord Chancellor, secured him an appointment as an Assistant Librarian at the British Museum in 1831. He became Keeper of Printed Books in 1837, Principal Librarian in 1856, and retired in 1866. His services to the British Museum Library played a very important part in its development. He was largely responsible for drawing up the catalogue, obtained an increased grant for the Library and membership of the Civil Service for its staff, and planned and oversaw the erection of the Reading Room. See the *D.N.B.*; Edward Miller, *Prince of Librarians. The Life and Times of Antonio Panizzi of the British Museum* (1967) and *That Noble Cabinet. A History of the British Museum* (1973). *GKC.*

15. On the origins, development, and social composition of Mechanics' Institutes see Thomas Kelly, *George Birkbeck, Pioneer of Adult Education* (Liverpool, 1957). *GKC.*

16. This is presumably a reference to the proposals made by Joseph Hume, 21 June 1836 and 20 and 21 Aug. 1839 (*Hansard*, 3rd Ser. xxxiv. 680–93; l. 465–6, 471–3). *GKC.*

17. For details see Finer, *Chadwick*, pp. 92–3. GKC.

18. See the speech of J. A. Roebuck, 30 July 1833 (*Hansard*, 3rd Ser. xx. 139–66). Enlarging on the public tranquillity which he expected to result from a general understanding of the laws of political economy, he argued that every man

> should be made acquainted with the circumstances on which his happiness as a member of society is necessarily dependent; and also he should know the general principles of the Government under which he lives. For example, for the well-being of the mass of labourers it is essential that each should know what circumstances govern the rate of wages.

Ibid. xx. 158–9. GKC.

19. It was intended to institute a 'model' or 'normal' school where schoolmasters might be trained and the best methods of teaching introduced, but the scheme broke down owing to the religious difficulty. See the official letter from Lord John Russell to Lord Lansdowne, Lord President of the Council, 4 Feb. 1839 (H.C. (1839) xli. 255–7, printed in Young and Handcock, *English Historical Documents*, pp. 851–4). On Kay's personal initiatives see above, Section VI, note 24. The intervention on behalf of the Church of Scotland was perfectly reasonable and legitimate. The Education Committee of the General Assembly wished to know whether the proposed system of school inspection was to be extended to schools maintained by the Church of Scotland, what were to be the purposes of inspection, and how the inspectors were to be nominated. They suggested that the proposed system might be incorporated into their own existing one. The minutes of the Privy Council were sent to them to show that it was intended to respect the claims of religious bodies. See H.C. (1840) xl. 385–7. GKC.

20. The minutes of the Education Committee of the Privy Council, August and December 1846 (H.C. (1847) xlv. 1, 5–6, printed in Young and Handcock, *English Historical Documents*, pp. 866–9) regulated the appointment of pupil teachers, grants to normal schools and to teachers trained under this system, and contained arrangements for the payment of pensions to efficient teachers who became incapacitated by age or disability. Their representatives maintained that these pro-

visions gave the teachers an equitable claim to a pension, but this interpretation was resisted by the Education Department, and on 6 Aug.
1851 a further minute regulated the allocation of pensions and restricted the sum to be granted for the purpose in England and Scotland
(and presumably Wales) in any one year to £6,500. In 1862, with the
acceptance of the Revised Code, all provisions for future pensions
were abandoned, but they were replaced by a minute of 1875, by which
special preference was given to those appointed between 1846 and
1851, who alone were considered to have claims not limited by the
ruling of 1851 (H.C. (1875) lviii. 79–83). In 1884 another minute
extended these arrangements to teachers in employment in 1862
(H.C. (1884) xxiv. 123). It was, however, always explicitly denied
that any teacher had a legal right to a pension, and the sum allocated
for the purpose was always inadequate. A statutory system of teachers'
superannuation was established in 1898. For a general account of the
history of the matter see the evidence given by G. W. Kekewich, 1
Apr. 1892, to a Select Committee of the House of Commons (H.C.
(1892) xii. 280–9). *GKC*.

21. See Charles Dickens, *Our Mutual Friend*, Chapter 18. *GKC*.

22. See Thomas Hardy, *Jude the Obscure*, Chapters 19–21. *GKC*.

23. See *Hansard*, 3rd Ser. xci. 1006–26 (19 Apr. 1847); *Speeches of
T. B. Macaulay* (1854), pp. 466–91. *GKC*.

24. This statement is inaccurate. Until 1866 the Congregational Union
asserted that the State had no educational responsibilities 'except towards those whom destitution, vagrancy, or crime casts upon its
hands'. See, e.g., the views of a minority on the Newcastle Commission (H.C. (1861) xxi (i), p. 298). *GKC*.

SECTION X

1. This is presumably a reference to Froude's passage on the Church on
the eve of the Oxford Movement in Letter I on 'The Oxford Counter-
Reformation', in *Short Studies on Great Subjects*, 4th Ser. new edn.
(1883), pp. 237–43. It should be compared with R. W. Church, *The*

Oxford Movement (1891), pp. 1–19. Their assessments, though made from different angles, have much in common. At the same time, there was another side to the picture of the Church as portrayed by Froude, and another, harsher, side to his own father as his unhappy childhood amply testifies. *GKC.*

2. Thomas Whately (1773–1864), an elder brother of Richard Whately, Archbishop of Dublin. As Vicar of Cookham, near Maidenhead, he was listed among clergymen who had depauperized their parishes in the Report of the Royal Commission on the Poor Law. At the request of the ratepayers he had assumed management of poor relief and had used his control of the select vestry to remove its objectionable features, make reliance on the parish the least attractive proposition for the able-bodied, and apply the workhouse test to the potentially fraudulent, while providing more ample relief for the infirm and impotent. The parish also boasted a friendly society, a savings bank, a lying-in charity, arrangements to provide a new suit of clothes for anyone going into service, and three schools. Chadwick, who visited Cookham while collecting evidence for the Commission, was impressed by what he found and by the attitude of Whately, whose work was warmly commended in the Report, where it was stated that both the rates and grants in kind had been greatly reduced, pauperism had virtually disappeared, and cases of bastardy fallen to negligible proportions. Consequently the inhabitants were prosperous and contented, and although the parish contained not only threshing machines but a paper mill with machinery, there had been no manifestation of the recent agricultural disturbances. Moreover, 'the last census shows that the new system is giving a wholesome check on redundant procreation'. See H.C. (1834) xxvii. 134–48 and H.C. (1834) xxix. 274–82. From 1837 to his death Whately was Rector of Chetwynd in Shropshire. *GKC.*

3. For Tozer's comment see *Vacation Tourists and Notes of Travel in 1860*, ed. Francis Galton (Cambridge and London, 1861), p. 384. Philip Gilbert Hamerton (1834–94) was an artist, and the editor of *Portfolio*. In his *French and English* (1889), p. 155, he observed that 'in England, you may live in the upper classes for a lifetime without having once been inside a dissenter's house, or seen a dissenter eat'. See also his *Human Intercourse* (1884), pp. 242–3. *DRF, GKC.*

4. The source of this estimate has not been found. It is unlikely to have any satisfactory statistical basis as there do not seem to be any reliable figures available. *GKC.*

5. Speaking in defence of Church Rates in the House of Commons, 8 Feb. 1860, Lord Robert Montagu, Conservative M.P. for Huntingdonshire, divided the country into those who were hostile and those who were favourable to them. He reckoned that $16\frac{1}{2}$ per cent of the population, consisting of six sects of Baptists ($2\frac{1}{2}$ per cent), the Independents ($7\frac{1}{4}$ per cent), Jews, Mormons, and other sects ($6\frac{3}{4}$ per cent) were opposed. On the other hand, the Roman Catholics ($3\frac{1}{2}$ per cent) and seven sects of Wesleyans (13 per cent) were not against them, comprising a total of 16 per cent of the population, to which must be added the church-going members of the Church of England (42 per cent) and 'the irreligious poor' (25 per cent). He claimed to have derived these figures from an unspecified document of later date than the Religious Census of 1851 (*Hansard*, 3rd Ser. clvi. 649). By that Census it was calculated that 7,261,032 attended some service on 30 Mar. 1851, that 5,288,294 could have done so but did not, and that of every 100 worshippers, 52 went to Church of England services, and 48 elsewhere. While these statistics are by no means entirely satisfactory, they were the result of an attempt actually to count heads on a particular day, and it is difficult to believe that Montagu's figures were anything more than unsupported guesses. In the debate in the House of Lords on the holding of divine service in theatres, 24 Feb. 1860, Shaftesbury said: 'I believe I may state without fear of contradiction, as the statement is founded on minute inquiry, that not two per cent. of the working men in London attend any place of worship whatever.' (*Speeches of the Earl of Shaftesbury, K.G. upon Subjects Having Relation Chiefly to the Claims and Interests of the Labouring Class* (1868), p. 318.) His estimate was explicitly confined to London. For the Religious Census of 1851 see H.C. (1852–3) lxxxix; K. S. Inglis, 'Patterns of Religious Worship in 1851', *Journal of Ecclesiastical History*, xi (1960), 74–86; D. M. Thompson, 'The 1851 Religious Census: Problems and Possibilities', *Victorian Studies*, xi (1967–8), 87–97. *GKC.*

6. Borrioboola-Gha was the settlement in Africa which monopolized the philanthropic activities of Mrs. Jellyby, to the neglect of her duties at home. See Charles Dickens, *Bleak House*, Chapter 4. *GKC.*

7. For the task to which the Churches had to address themselves in the great cities see G. Kitson Clark, *The Making of Victorian England* (1962), pp. 163–76. GKC.

8. The Unitarians were certainly the most cultivated and liberal of the Dissenting bodies, and the least inhibited by the old Puritan prohibitions. However, even among Independents and Congregationalists the taboo on the theatre was not uniform. Quite early in the century there were Independents who did not object to a man going to the theatre, provided he did not talk about it. See Richard Garnett, *The Life of W. J. Fox* (1910), pp. 26–8. GKC.

9. Mr. Stiggins appears in *The Pickwick Papers*; Mr. Chadband in *Bleak House*. DRF.

10. See *Athenaeum*, 21 Sept. 1878 (no. 2656, pp. 369–70). GKC.

11. Jabez Bunting (1779–1858) was probably the most prominent Methodist minister of the first half of the nineteenth century. He was elected Secretary of the Conference, the Methodists' governing body, in 1814, and was President in 1820, 1828, 1836, and 1844. He was more than anyone else responsible for the organization of the Methodist Church as a body independent of the Church of England. GKC.

12. For a statistical analysis of Wesleyan voting behaviour in a number of constituencies at the 1841 general election see J. R. Vincent, *Pollbooks: How Victorians Voted* (Cambridge, 1967), pp. 69–70. JMC.

13. In his *Life of Jabez Bunting* (2 vols., 1859–87), ii. 112, Thomas Percival Bunting, discussing the social disturbances of 1816 and 1817, wrote: 'There is a sense in which my father's memorable saying, some years afterwards, may be amply vindicated, as there is a sense in which it may not: "Methodism is as much opposed to democracy as to sin." ' No precise date is given for the observation. In Élie Halévy, *Histoire du peuple anglais au XIXᵉ siècle* (6 vols., Paris, 1912–32), iii. 145, it is associated with a series of quotations from Bunting's statements to the Methodist Conference in 1831, 1832, and 1833, given to demonstrate his determination to prevent the Methodists from becoming involved in the popular unrest of that time; but since the only reference supplied

is to the passage cited above, it is probable that Halévy had no definite reason for assigning the remark to this period. *ERT, GKC.*

14. 'Mark Rutherford' was William Hale White (1831–1913), civil servant, literary critic, novelist, journalist, and philosopher. The qualities of the Nonconformity which he described can be judged from *The Autobiography of Mark Rutherford* (1881), *Mark Rutherford's Deliverance* (1885), and *The Revolution in Tanner's Lane* (1887). Although they look back to the time of W. Daniell, they are actually the products of a far more sophisticated period. Daniell's *Warminster Common*, published in 1850, is a largely autobiographical account, based partly on a diary, of the spiritual history of a neglected area of Wiltshire, which Methodist missionaries had penetrated. It is not only very attractive in its general tone, but a historical record of considerable importance. The account of the first 'tea-fight' is on pp. 33–4, that of the meeting at Christmas 1829 on p. 160. Young has omitted a sentence to the effect that the latter was attended by 107 people, of whom about fifty were children. Throughout the book there are records of Daniell's cures, effected by 'medical electricity'. *GKC.*

15. It is unlikely that such a belief was very widespread. The common Conservative view was that the Government had encouraged popular excitement and then, owing either to incapacity or to criminal complaisance, had failed to control it when it degenerated into riots at Derby, Nottingham, and Bristol. See, e.g., the speech of J. W. Croker, 16 Dec. 1831 (*Hansard*, 3rd Ser. ix. 392–418). For the current suspicion of the Whigs' designs on the Church see, e.g., *Letters and Correspondence of John Henry Newman*, ed. Anne Mozley (2 vols., 1891), i. 236–7, 247, 276. *GKC.*

16. For further details of Mill's scheme for Church reform, which appeared in the *London Review* in July 1835, see Alexander Bain, *James Mill. A Biography* (1882), pp. 381–9. *GKC.*

17. On 6 Feb. 1834 a petition against alterations in the Church, signed by 7,000 clergymen, was presented to the Archbishop of Canterbury. See Owen Chadwick, *The Victorian Church*, Part I, 2nd edn. (1970), pp. 75–7. On 27 May 1834 a declaration in support of the Church, signed by over 230,000 laymen, 'for the most part substantial householders and heads of families, and all of them persons of mature age',

was presented to the King. See *Annual Register* (1834), Chronicle, pp. 71–2. For the Dissenters who were lukewarm about or did not desire the separation of Church and State see Élie Halévy, *Histoire du peuple anglais au XIXe siècle* (6 vols., Paris, 1912–32), iii. 147–8. GKC.

18. Charles James Blomfield (1786–1857), Bishop of Chester, 1824–8, of London, 1828–56, and a distinguished classical scholar, was the dominant figure in the Ecclesiastical Commission from its establishment in 1836, and the leading spirit in the development of King's College, London. Sir Charles Lyell, the geologist, wrote to Dr. Fleming, 1 May 1833:

> Since I launched my work, I have been busy lecturing. The King's College governors determined this year that ladies should not enter my lecture-room, because it diverted the attention of the young students, of whom I had *two* in number from the College last year, and *two* this. My class being thus cut down to fifteen, I gave them a short course. . . . The Royal Institution invited me very warmly to lecture in their theatre, and I consented to seven lectures, which have been attended by 250 persons (scarce ever less), about a hundred of them men. . . . I regret that the bishops cut short my career at King's College, as I should have had a splendid class this year, and thrice as profitable as at the Royal Institution, but there seems no way of having a large audience but by one of two methods—an academical class, or one open to women as well as men.

Life, Letters and Journals of Sir Charles Lyell, ed. Mrs. Lyell (2 vols., 1881), i. 396–7. MJSR, GKC.

19. The critic in question was John Stuart Mill (*Dissertations and Discussions*, vol. i (1859), pp. 330–2, 393–7). For the exchange between Coleridge and Miss Martineau see *Harriet Martineau's Autobiography*, ed. Maria Weston Chapman (3 vols., 1877), i. 397–8:

> He told me that he (the last person whom I should have suspected) read my tales as they came out on the first of the month; and, after paying some compliments, he avowed that there were points on which we differed: (I was full of wonder that there were any on which we agreed:) 'for instance', said he, 'you appear to consider that society is an aggregate of individuals!' I replied that I certainly did: whereupon he went off on one of the several metaphysical

interpretations which may be put upon the many-sided fact of an organized human society, subject to natural laws in virtue of its aggregate character and organization together. After a long flight in survey of society from his own balloon in his own current, he came down again to some considerations of individuals, and at length to some special biographical topics, ending with criticisms on old biographers, whose venerable works he brought down from the shelf. No one else spoke, of course, except when I once or twice put a question; and when his monologue came to what seemed a natural stop, I rose to go.

In her view, Coleridge was 'constitutionally defective in will, in conscientiousness and in apprehension of the real and true, while gifted or cursed with inordinate reflective and analogical faculties, as well as prodigious word power.' (ibid. i. 398–9.) *GKC.*

20. This sentence underestimates the significance of the High Church tradition, and should be contrasted with Young's analysis of the problem on p. 123 above. *GKC.*

21. Young's statement that 'in the eye of his critics' Arnold 'was not much better than an infidel' cannot be accepted. In fact, Arnold's view of Newman and his associates was a good deal harsher than theirs of him, and his article on 'The Oxford Malignants and Dr. Hampden' in the *Edinburgh Review*, vol. lxiii (Apr. and July 1836), pp. 225–39, accused the critics of Hampden's Professorship of serious moral evil. Newman was much more temperate. The two men met in 1828 when Newman obliged Arnold by disputing with him for the B.D. degree, and he did not entirely disapprove of Arnold's published sermons in 1830, although he naturally reacted sharply against his plan of Church reform. While Newman considered that Arnold's thought lacked consistency and depth of understanding, he admired his work at Rugby. He summarized his attitude to Arnold, with whom he had a rather strained meeting at Oriel in 1842, in a letter of 31 Oct. 1844: 'He is a man whom I have always separated from the people he was with, always respected, often defended, though from an accident he got a notion, I believe, that I was a firebrand, and particularly hostile to him.' See *Letters and Correspondence of John Henry Newman*, ed. Anne Mozley (2 vols., 1891), i. 180, 220, 374–5; ii. 401, 434, 440–2.

Young makes unfair use of the quotation from Newman, who explained the remark in his *Apologia*:

At this time [1833] I was specially annoyed with Dr. Arnold though it did not last into later years. Some one, I think, asked, in conversation at Rome, whether a certain interpretation of Scripture was Christian? it was answered that Dr. Arnold took it; I interposed, 'But is *he* a Christian?' The subject went out of my head at once; when afterwards I was taxed with it, I could say no more in explanation, than (what I believe was the fact) that I must have had in mind some free views of Dr. Arnold about the Old Testament:—I thought I must have meant, 'Arnold answers for the interpretation, but who is to answer for Arnold?'

John Henry Cardinal Newman, *Apologia Pro Vita Sua*, ed. Martin J. Svaglic (Oxford, 1967), p. 42. *GKC*.

22. The reference to Milman is a mistake. The story was told of himself by Tom Mozley, editor of the *British Critic* from 1841 to 1843. One day, while waiting to deliver proofs and manuscripts in Bell Yard in the Temple, he was accosted by two men, one of them a journeyman tailor, who asked him this question and argued the point. See Rev. T. Mozley, *Reminiscences, chiefly of Oriel College and the Oxford Movement* (2 vols., 1882), ii. 221–2. *OC, GKC*.

23. It is not clear on what source Young based this statement. On 16 Dec. 1846 Lyell described to his father an after-dinner conversation at Bowood, Lord Lansdowne's house, during which the geologists' time-scale and that traditionally derived from Scripture were compared (*Life, Letters and Journals of Sir Charles Lyell*, ed. Mrs. Lyell (2 vols., 1881), ii. 116–17). He did not say what views he himself had expressed, but it is impossible to believe that he could have given so short a span as 50,000 years as the age of the world. Nor had he any aversion to his views reaching a larger public. In the previous September, at the meeting of the British Association, he had given a public lecture in which he said that the alluvial matter in the Mississippi delta must have been deposited over a period of 67,000 years, and that in the plain above over 33,500 years, but that these 100,000 years were insignificant from a geological point of view (*Report of the Sixteenth Meeting of the British Association for the Advancement of Science held at Southampton in September 1846* (1847), Transactions of the Sections, pp. 118–19). This lecture was reported in the press (see, e.g., *The Times*, 16 Sept. 1846, p. 5e); but Lyell's views can have caused no surprise, for the

processes described in his *Principles of Geology*, published between 1830 and 1833, implied a time-scale far longer than that which any form of biblical fundamentalism could allow. GKC.

24. See Lyell to George Ticknor, 7 Feb. 1849:

> I had an argument with Macaulay about the atrocious crimes which he says God commanded the Israelites to perpetrate. All that he could say was that he was on 'the orthodox' side, and that according to my view 'the God of the Old Testament differed from the God of the New,' and that if I merely thought that the Israelites *believed* they were acting under God's special command when they hewed Agag in pieces, and that they were mistaken, I should be obliged to renounce their history and the prophets.
>
> That he himself believed it he neither said nor the contrary, but certainly he need not have written that passage about the Puritans in such strong terms.

Lyell, *Life, Letters and Journals*, ii. 154.

Lyell was referring to the passage in Chapter I of Macaulay's *History of England* in which, discussing the inspiration drawn by the Elizabethan Puritans from the Old Testament, he observed that it 'contained the history of a race selected by God to be witnesses of his unity and ministers of his vengeance, and specially commanded by him to do many things which, if done without his special command, would have been atrocious crimes'. The relevant passage of Butler is presumably that in his *Analogy of Religion*, Part II, Chapter III, Section 27 (see *The Works of Joseph Butler*, ed. W. E. Gladstone (3 vols., 1896), i. 239). That Macaulay was influenced by Butler's arguments is confirmed by his journal, 17 Feb. 1849, which also illuminates his own view of the problem:

> Lyell came to me with a strange criticism. He told me that many people had taken offence at what I said of the Old Testament Massacres and assassinations. I asked what he would have me say. It seems that he would have had me take the high neological ground, and deny the truth of the narrative. A pretty nest of hornets I should have brought about my ears. And after all Butler's arguments, which I have taken, are quite unanswerable on the hypothesis of an extraordinary interference of the Deity. Lyell seemed to think that the case was analogous to a case with which he is more familiar. Grave divines, he said, give up the geology of the Old Testament;

and he seemed to infer that they would as easily give up its morality. But surely there is all the difference in the world. Religion has nothing to do with the order of strata and the motions of the stars. But it has a great deal to do with the relations of men to each other and to God.

MS. Journal, Trinity College Library, Cambridge. *GKC, RR.*

25. See *The Life and Letters of Charles Darwin*, ed. Francis Darwin (3 vols., 1887), ii. 326: 'Writing on July 22 to Dr. Asa Gray my father thus refers to Lyell's position:—"Considering his age, his former views and position in society, I think his conduct has been heroic on this subject." ' Darwin was alluding to a review by Samuel Wilberforce, Bishop of Oxford, in the July 1860 number of the *Quarterly Review* (vol. cviii, pp. 263-4):

> That Mr. Darwin should have wandered . . . into the jungle of fanciful assumptions is no small evil. We trust that he is mistaken in believing that he may count Sir C. Lyell as one of his converts. We know indeed the strength of the temptations which he can bring to bear upon his geological brother. . . . Yet no man has been more distinct and more logical in the denial of the transmutation of species than Sir C. Lyell. . . . We trust that Sir C. Lyell abides still by these truly philosophical principles; and that with his help and with that of his brethren this flimsy speculation may be . . . completely put down . . .

Darwin remarked to J. D. Hooker: 'The concluding pages will make Lyell shake in his shoes. By Jove, if he sticks to us, he will be a real hero. Good night. Your well-quizzed, but not sorrowful, and affectionate friend.' Darwin was apparently amused by the article and, advising his own clergyman to get it, observed that 'the Bishop of Oxford has made such capital fun of me and my grandfather'. (Darwin, *Life and Letters*, ii. 324-5.) Perhaps Darwin did not take the matter as seriously as Young suggests. *GKC, JWB.*

26. Perhaps the best account of Arnold's principles of exegesis can be found in a letter from Bonamy Price to Arthur Penrhyn Stanley in the latter's *Life and Correspondence of Thomas Arnold* (2 vols., 1844), i. 195-201. Price wrote that Arnold had developed a method which he himself had not had sufficient opportunity to apply, but which would be of inestimable value in the future:

He had a very remarkable, I should rather say (if I might) wonderful discernment for the divine, as incorporated in the human element of Scripture; and the recognition of these two separate and most distinct elements,—the careful separation of the two, so that each shall be subject to its own laws, and determined on its own principles,—was the foundation, the grand characteristic principle of his Exegesis. . . . he approached the human side of the Bible in the same real historical spirit, with the same methods, rules, and principles, as he did Thucydides.

Subject to the limitations imposed by linguistic and historical criticism, he also acknowledged in the Bible the work of God and, additionally:

the Christian prophet and interpreter had in his eyes a still more exalted office. God's dealings with any particular generation of men are but the application of the eternal truths of His Providence to their particular circumstances, and the form of that application has at different times greatly varied. . . . Thus, he vindicated God's command to Abraham to sacrifice his son, and to the Jews to exterminate the nations of Canaan, by explaining the principles on which these commands were given, and their reference to the moral state of those to whom they were addressed; thereby educing light out of darkness, unravelling the thread of God's religious education of the human race, from its earliest infancy down to the fulness of times, and holding up God's marvellous counsels to the devout wonder and meditation of the thoughtful believer.

GKC.

27. It has not been possible to identify this quotation, but Matthew Arnold made the same point in a letter to his mother, 18 Nov. 1865: 'papa's greatness consists in his bringing such a torrent of freshness into English religion by placing history and politics in connexion with it' (*Letters of Matthew Arnold 1848–1888*, ed. George W. E. Russell (2 vols., 1895), i. 311). GKC, JMC.

28. *Oakfield; or Fellowship in the East* (1853), by William Delafield Arnold, second son of Thomas Arnold, is about Anglo-Indian society. It has been reprinted, with an introduction by Kenneth Allott, in the 'Victorian Library' series (Leicester, 1973). GKC.

SECTION XI

1. See Section II, note 23.

2. Walter Farquhar Hook (1798–1875) was incumbent of Holy Trinity, Coventry 1828–37, and Vicar of Leeds 1837–59. See W. R. W. Stephens, *The Life and Letters of Walter Farquhar Hook*, new edn. (1880). He was a pre-Tractarian High Churchman and a friend of Pusey, a warm supporter of the movement for the protection of factory children and anxious to promote popular education (see Section XIX, note 5). Young's comment about the 'well-bred impatience' with which High Churchmen shook off 'humanitarian professions' is not borne out by the tone of Pusey's own letters and sermons, nor does it seem fair to a movement which inspired the ritualistic slum priests and the women in religious orders who distinguished themselves by nursing poor cholera patients and provided nurses for Florence Nightingale. Manning as a High Church clergyman was interested in popular education, as were Gladstone and his friends as High Church laymen. High Churchmen were also to be associated in various ways with social reform in the later nineteenth century. *GKC.*

3. It is not easy to accept Young's group of 'Arnoldians' as a clearly identifiable entity. The term was in use as early as the 1830s: A. P. Stanley, who came into residence at Oxford in 1834, declared three years later that he would not be elected into a fellowship at Balliol because member after member of the society 'has given in to the overwhelming terror of the outcry against Balliol as an heretical and Arnoldian college' (Rowland E. Prothero, *The Life and Correspondence of Arthur Penrhyn Stanley* (2 vols., 1893), i. 191). Few people were as profoundly influenced by Arnold as Stanley, but Young seems to have been thinking of a slightly later, more secular-minded generation, perhaps the generation of Clough and Matthew Arnold, whose ways of thought are vividly presented in *The Correspondence of Arthur Hugh Clough*, ed. Frederick L. Mulhauser (2 vols., Oxford, 1957). Another typical figure might be Tom Hughes, the author of *Tom Brown's Schooldays*. A keen Rugbeian, a devoted Christian Socialist and follower of F. D. Maurice, he did in fact make himself conspicuous by smoking in the streets (see *Early Victorian England*, ed. G. M. Young (2 vols., 1934), i. 99). It is possible that the group Young had in mind were the

'Socialists' whom Hughes described in *Tom Brown at Oxford*, Chapter 42, the sequel to the earlier book, published in 1861 and dedicated to F. D. Maurice. The strong social conscience which Arnold developed in his boys can also be seen in Rugbeians who went to Cambridge, such as the Christian Socialist D. J. Vaughan, or F. J. A. Hort, whose letters supply a clear picture of the way in which in the late forties and early fifties the social challenge affected an intelligent young man with a Rugby training. The results of Arnold's influence may also be discerned in the achievements of another Cambridge Rugbeian, Richard Assheton Cross (see above p. 128). But the development of the state of mind which Young ascribes to his 'Arnoldians' seems to have been part of a more general and gradual process. As the letters of Frederick Temple show, the social as opposed to the theological challenge of the times affected young men who were at Oxford during the period of the Oxford Movement, but who were not noticeably influenced by Arnold; and the history of the Cambridge Apostles and of F. D. Maurice shows that it affected men in no way influenced by Arnold at a date before the Oxford Movement began. *GKC.*

4. See Macaulay's speech on the sugar duties, 26 Feb. 1845:

> What can be more immoral than to bring ridicule on the very name of morality, by drawing distinctions where there are no differences? Is it not enough that this dishonest casuistry has already poisoned our theology? Is it not enough that a set of quibbles has been devised, under cover of which a divine may hold the worst doctrines of the Church of Rome, and may hold with them the best benefice of the Church of England? Let us at least keep the debates of this House free from the sophistry of Tract Number Ninety.

The Works of Lord Macaulay, ed. Lady Trevelyan (8 vols., 1866), viii. 299. *AWS.*

5. On the Hampden and Gorham controversies see Owen Chadwick, *The Victorian Church*, Part I, 2nd edn. (1970), pp. 237–71. *DRF.*

6. See Rajah Brooke's letter to his mother written in 1842:

> Though you may know that I have a great deal to do, yet I continue most of my lazy habits, and I generally compress a good deal of work into a short compass. I read daily and nightly several hours,

and my studies are very theological. I have now gone so far as to write a treatise against Article 90 of the 'Oxford Tracts', which is a Jesuitical performance.

Gertrude L. Jacob, *The Raja of Saráwak* (2 vols., 1876), i. 215. *GKC.*

7. The Princess Royal's christening took place at Buckingham Palace on 10 Feb. 1841. The painting by C. R. Leslie, who was invited to be present to make preliminary sketches, shows the 'sham altar loaded with the family plate' and two candles can be seen behind Archbishop Howley. It was exhibited to the public and much praised at the time, and is now in the possession of the Queen. See Leslie's *Autobiographical Recollections*, ed. Tom Taylor (2 vols., 1860), i. 171, and the catalogue to the exhibition of Victorian Church Art held at the Victoria and Albert Museum, Nov. 1971–Jan. 1972, pp. 4–5. *GKC.*

8. See Charles Dickens, *Bleak House*, Chapter 12, describing the house party at Sir Leicester Dedlock's home, Chesney Wold:

> Dandyism? There is no King George the Fourth now (more's the pity) to set the dandy fashion. . . . But is there Dandyism . . . notwithstanding, Dandyism of a more mischievous sort . . .?
>
> Why, yes. It cannot be disguised. There *are*, at Chesney Wold this January week, some ladies and gentlemen of the newest fashion, who have set up a Dandyism—in Religion, for instance.

There follows a description of Puseyism, as Dickens saw it. The dating of the action of *Bleak House* is inconsistent (see Humphry House, *The Dickens World* (1941), pp. 30–3), but its satirical butts belong to the early 1850s. It should be remembered that Dickens was writing about a movement which he disliked and never came near to understanding; and that in *Loss and Gain*, written in the winter of 1847, two years after his reception into the Roman Catholic Church, Newman was satirizing a party he had abandoned and wished to ridicule (see Wilfrid Ward, *The Life of John Henry Cardinal Newman* (2 vols., 1912), i. 259–60). *PAWC, GKC.*

9. For the final judgement in the stone altar case, Faulkner *v.* Litchfield and Stearn, given on an appeal to the Court of Arches, see the *Annual Register* (1845), Chronicle, pp. 345–54. The case related to the restoration of the Church of the Holy Sepulchre at Cambridge where a stone

altar had been introduced in place of a communion table. *The Restora-*
tion of Churches is the Restoration of Popery was the title of a sermon
preached by the Rev. Francis Close, Vicar of Cheltenham, on 5 Nov.
1844, and subsequently produced as a pamphlet. On the whole episode
see Elliot Rose, 'The Stone Table in the Round Church and the Crisis
of the Cambridge Camden Society', *Victorian Studies*, x (1966–7),
119–44. *GKC, JMC.*

10. In the Book of Common Prayer the only place provided for a sermon is after the Creed in the Communion Service. But clearly the
practice had grown up of having a sermon at both Morning and
Evening Prayer. This was not illegal since it was outside the service,
and was recognized by the Act of Uniformity Amendment Act (1872).
Since it was outside the service, it was natural for a preacher to change
from his surplice. However, a morning service could consist of Morning Prayer, Litany, and Ante-Communion, i.e. the Communion
Service down to the Creed. The sermon would then take place in the
place provided for it in the Book of Common Prayer. Of course if the
service continued after the sermon, the priest would have to resume
his surplice, but the rubric would enjoin him to move towards the
table, and in many churches those members of the congregation who
wished to partake would either then or at the exhortation go into the
chancel and kneel at the rail or table. There would therefore be a break
during which the priest would put on his surplice. It is difficult to see
why the Ante-Communion prayers should have been taken after the
sermon unless the whole of the service was to have been said. Certainly
preaching in the surplice was a High Church practice and caused curiously great offence, but fairly early in the ritualist controversies, there
was trouble about ornaments. *GKC.*

11. See Mrs. Brookfield's description of an expedition to St. Barnabas
on the evening of 18 June:

> We arrived there at twenty minutes to seven and found the whole
> street crowded, quite mobbed with well-dressed people; . . . but
> not a chance of getting into the Church! . . . Mr. Thackeray appeared
> in the crowd (he had heard the day before that we meant to be
> there) and joined us just as the procession appeared, and I fear he
> scandalised some of the crowd by remarks more humorous than
> reverent, 'Oh, my dear fellow countrymen of the nineteenth cen-

tury, are we gone back to this?' but he and Harry and all the men took off their hats as the door opened to admit the procession, and the Altar was revealed to view, a blaze of lights, twenty or thirty little tapers exactly like those at the Oratory.

It was quite the Hippopotamus excitement over again, and would form a good pendant to it in the next *Punch*. Some of the people in the crowd called out 'Just like the Catholics, there's the Saint.'

Charles and Frances Brookfield, *Mrs. Brookfield and her Circle* (2 vols., 1905), ii. 309. *GKC*

12. On 21 Aug. 1859 and subsequent Sundays there were violent riots in the London Church of St. George's-in-the-East. They were alleged to be in protest against the ritualistic practices of the incumbent, Bryan King, and the mission of Anglo-Catholic priests, including C. F. Lowder and A. H. Mackonochie, whom he had called in to help him with the parish. No doubt some of the rioters were single-minded Protestant fanatics, but many of them came from outside the ordinary congregation and were attracted by the prospect of a riot. Moreover, it seems probable that more sinister elements, disturbed by an increase in pastoral activity, were involved. The predominant power in the parish lay in the tavern keepers, who were also in many cases keepers of brothels. Lowder stated that at one time the publican interest was so strong that for years one at least of the churchwardens was a publican. (*Twenty-One Years in S. George's Mission* (1877), p. 33.) There is some evidence that such men were behind the disturbances. See William Crouch, *Bryan King and the Riots at St. George's-in-the-East* (1904). *GKC*.

13. After his reception into the Roman Catholic Church, Newman's position had been obscure and his motives and ways of thought suspect, as far as ordinary Englishmen were concerned. But in the January 1864 number of *Macmillan's Magazine*, in a review of the seventh and eighth volumes of J. A. Froude's *History of England*, Kingsley wrote: 'Truth, for its own sake, had never been a virtue with the Roman clergy. Father Newman informs us that it need not, and on the whole ought not to be' (vol. ix, p. 217). The resultant controversy led to the publication of Newman's *Apologia* which was acclaimed by Hutton of the *Spectator*, by the *Saturday Review* and *The Times*, thus giving Newman a public position he had not hitherto enjoyed. *GKC*.

NOTES TO PAGE 85

14. The phrase was Newman's:

Experience proves surely that the Bible does not answer a purpose for which it was never intended. It may be accidentally the means of the conversion of individuals; but a book, after all, cannot make a stand against the wild living intellect of man, and in this day it begins to testify, as regards its own structure and contents, to the power of that universal solvent, which is so successfully acting upon religious establishments.

John Henry Cardinal Newman, *Apologia Pro Vita Sua*, ed. Martin J. Svaglic (Oxford, 1967), p. 219. *GKC, JMC.*

15. The geologist has not been identified. *GKC.*

16. J. B. Lightfoot (1828–89) became a Fellow of Trinity College, Cambridge in 1852, Hulsean Professor of Divinity in 1861, Lady Margaret Professor of Divinity in 1875, and was Bishop of Durham from 1879 until his death. With him must be associated B. F. Westcott (1825–1901), and F. J. A. Hort (1828–92), whose edition of the New Testament appeared in 1881. This Cambridge school was no doubt equal to the scholarship of Germany, and Lightfoot was certainly capable of dealing with the scholarly points on which the Tübingen school had rested their case. To meet the general issues about the historicity of the Bible which the nineteenth century raised, and in particular the problems suggested by the Old Testament such as those mentioned on p. 81 above, which seem to have troubled a large number of people, a more radical approach in due course became necessary. The pioneer in Old Testament studies seems to have been T. K. Cheyne (1841–1915), and the most important contributor S. R. Driver (1846–1914); and the pioneer in New Testament Studies E. Hatch (1835–89). But it may be doubted whether these scholars made much impact on the educated public. *GKC.*

17. *Vestiges of the Natural History of Creation* was published anonymously in 1844; it was republished in 1969 by Leicester University Press in their 'Victorian Library', with an introduction by Sir Gavin de Beer. Its author was Robert Chambers, a member with his brother William of the Edinburgh firm of booksellers and publishers. According to the *D.N.B.* he took extraordinary precautions to escape identification in order not to compromise himself and his firm. The publishing arrange-

ments were conducted through Alexander Ireland of Manchester who received the proofs from London, sent them under fresh covers to Chambers, then in St. Andrews, and again acted as intermediary on their return to London. The book was apparently ascribed to many different people including Sir Charles Lyell and Prince Albert. *GKC.*

18. Young seems to have been mistaken if he was suggesting that Tennyson drew some of the evolutionist passages of *In Memoriam* from Chambers's *Vestiges*. See his letter to the bookseller Edward Moxon, dated November 1844:

> I want you to get me a book which I see advertised in the *Examiner*: it seems to contain many speculations with which I have been familiar for years, and on which I have written more than one poem. The book is called *Vestiges of the Natural History of Creation*, and published by J. Churchill, Princes St. Soho; the price 7s. 6d., but you can get it cheaper.

The Life and Works of Alfred Lord Tennyson (12 vols., 1898–9), i. 288. In a note to the letter his son Hallam Tennyson definitely states that the sections of *In Memoriam* about evolution had been read by Tennyson's friends some years before the publication of *Vestiges*. *GKC.*

19. The most important study of Newman's *Essay on the Development of Christian Doctrine* (1845) is to be found in Owen Chadwick, *From Bossuet to Newman. The Idea of Doctrinal Development* (Cambridge, 1957); see especially the discussion of the relation of the *Essay* to contemporary thought, pp. 96–119. Milman's criticism appeared in the *Quarterly Review*, March 1846, and was reprinted in his *Savonarola, Erasmus, and other Essays* (1870), pp. 296–373. The possibility that Newman was a pioneer in suggesting the ideas of development and evolution is dismissed by Young with some contempt, but it is supported by quite weighty authority. Acton said that the *Essay* did more than any other book of the time to make the English 'think historically, to watch the process as well as the result', and Mark Pattison wrote to Newman, 5 Apr. 1878:

> Is it not a remarkable thing that you should have first started the idea—and the word—Development, as the key to the history of church doctrine, and since then it has gradually become the dominant idea of all history, biology, physics, and in short has metamorphosed our view of every science, and of all knowledge?

Chadwick, op. cit. pp. ix–x. It need not be said that both Acton and, Pattison had read the *Essay* and probably Milman's criticism. However, no claim to primacy with the idea of development can be sustained. It was in the air. It had been detected in one of his critics. Milman, for example, in his criticism, wrote 'We, too, . . . have our theory of development' (*Savonarola*, p. 366), and Newman had attacked Milman's *History of Christianity* (1840) for putting forward the notion that Christianity was 'an idea which had developed itself' in response to circumstances (Chadwick, op. cit. p. 100). GKC.

20. This 'childlike craving for certitude', for established and unchanging dogma in either religion or science, seems to be most satisfactorily explained not so much in the terms of Young's formula as in the inability of men in the nineteenth century to grasp the conception advanced by Alfred North Whitehead in *Science and the Modern World* (Cambridge, 1926). In Chapter XII on 'Religion and Science' he makes the case that from long before the nineteenth century the content of both religion and science had constantly been changed without the truths which underlay them necessarily being affected. He says (p. 255):

> We are told by logicians that a proposition must be either true or false, and that there is no middle term. But in practice, we may know that a proposition expresses an important truth, but that it is subject to limitations and qualifications which at present remain undiscovered. It is a general feature of our knowledge, that we are insistently aware of important truth; and yet that the only formulations of these truths which we are able to make presuppose a general standpoint of conceptions which may have to be modified.

Neither current biblical scholarship, nor perhaps the current philosophy of science, prepared men's minds to accept this. cf. Section XVII, note 19. GKC.

21. It is clearly impossible to summarize with any certainty what, at any point in the century, 'most educated men' believed. There were certainly many educated men who retained their belief in Christ's divinity until the end of the century, as there were those who from the beginning of the century had never believed in it. Young probably had in mind a particular group connected with Oxford and Cambridge,

including J. A. Froude, Francis Newman, Matthew Arnold, and Mark Pattison. But the process was rather slower than this passage implies. The histories of Henry Sidgwick and W. K. Clifford in Cambridge and of T. H. Green and R. L. Nettleship in Oxford suggest that the critical period for many was the late sixties and early seventies. *GKC.*

22. See Clough's 'Review of Mr. Newman's "The Soul" ':

> You have found out God, have you? The vessel goes on its way: how? You conclude there is someone somewhere working these wheels, these pistons, these strong and exquisitely-adapted means. Oh, my friends! and if in a dark room, under the main deck, you have hunted out a smudgy personage with a sub-intelligent look about the eyes, is that so great a gospel for me?

The Poems and Prose Remains of Arthur Hugh Clough, ed. Mrs. Clough (2 vols., 1869), i. 301. *PG.*

23. It is difficult to accept the statement that this was Ruskin's *final* assurance. He seems to have been troubled with religious doubts from early in the 1850s, and in 1858 he experienced what he called a process of 'unconversion', which caused him to leave not only the narrow Protestantism of his childhood but Christianity as well (see E. T. Cook, *The Life of John Ruskin* (2 vols., 1911), i. 521–2). During the next period of his life he accepted the 'religion of humanity', with which the statement in the text is probably compatible. In 1874, how-ever, while working on the frescoes of Giotto at Assissi, he began to move back towards his own form of Christianity (ibid. ii. 253–5). The statement is also incompatible with much that he said in his later writ-ings, such as *Fors Clavigera* (1871–84), the *Bible of Amiens* (1884), and *Præterita* (1885–9). *GKC.*

24. Young says that 'Introspection within a closed circle of experience was the trouble.' But was it? Or was it the main trouble? Another weak-ness of both Romanticism and Evangelicalism was the tendency to con-centrate on the emotion which the Evangelical or the Romantic enter-tained, and not on the object to which the emotion was supposed to be directed and which gave the emotion its reason and justification, for example on the importance of being in love and the ecstasies and des-pairs of the lover, rather than on union with the beloved. It is an

attitude which may tempt a man to entertain an emotion for the sake
of emotion and for no other reason. See Newman's comments on the
errors of those who preach justification by Faith only:

> True faith is what may be called colourless, like air or water; it
> is but the medium through which the soul sees Christ; and the soul
> as little really rests upon it and contemplates it, as the eye can see the
> air. When, then, men are bent on holding it (as it were) in their
> hands, curiously inspecting, analyzing, and so aiming at it, they are
> obliged to colour and thicken it, that it may be seen and touched.
> That is, they substituted for it, something or other, a feeling, notion,
> sentiment, conviction, or act of reason, which they may hang over,
> and doat upon. They rather aim at experiences (as they are called)
> within them, than at Him that is without them. They are led to en-
> large upon the signs of conversion, the variations of their feelings,
> their aspirations and longings, and to tell all this to others . . .

John Henry Newman, *Lectures on Justification* (1838), p. 385. Compare
the completely independent testimony of a Churchman of a very
different school, Chenevix Trench, in a letter to the Rev. J. C. Hare,
28 Nov. 1836, about a sick lady whom Trench had been attending:

> She is a little perplexed, and her perfect peace in some slight degree
> hindered through the mischievous consequence of the system which
> turns attention to the quality of the faith rather than to Christ, the
> Object of the faith, the Centre out of ourselves, but in the main is
> finding strength and strong consolation in God. I often feel in deal-
> ing with the sick how injurious this perversion of the Gospel is, how
> needful it is we should understand ourselves better on the matter
> of Justification; but here we come again upon the question of
> Baptism . . .

Richard Chenevix Trench Archbishop. Letters and Memorials, [ed. Maria
Trench] (2 vols., 1888), i. 218. *GKC.*

25. It is possible that Samuel Wilberforce used the word 'introverted'
of Peel, for he certainly used the word 'introvertive' of Newman in
1864 (*Essays Contributed to the 'Quarterly Review'* (2 vols., 1874), i. 358).
But the word is older than Young suggests. In the *O.E.D.* the first
example of the use of the word is from 1669, and other examples of a
later date are cited from Cowper (1781), Hazlitt (1822), and Emerson
(1847). *GKC, JMC.*

26. *Dipsychus* was composed by A. H. Clough in 1850, *Stanzas in Memory of the Author of 'Obermann'* by Matthew Arnold in 1849, and *Obermann Once More* probably between 1865 and 1867. *The City of Dreadful Night* was contributed by James Thomson (1834-82) to the *National Reformer* from March to May 1874. It was published with other poems in 1880. GKC.

27. Kingsley's attitude to women is very well exemplified by his ideals for Argemone Lavington, the heroine of *Yeast*, as described in a letter to J. M. Ludlow written in November or December 1849 (*Charles Kingsley. His Letters and Memories of his Life*, ed. Mrs. Kingsley (2 vols., 1877), i. 219-20). See also his letter to an unspecified correspondent on marriage written in 1848 (ibid. i. 186-91). Kingsley's being 'on the one hand silenced as an advocate of socialism, on the other denounced as a propagator of impurity' refers to two incidents in 1851. He was inhibited by Bishop Blomfield from preaching in London because he was considered a possible source of disturbance; the inhibition only lasted for a fortnight (ibid. i. 288-91). He was also attacked in the Church newspaper the *Guardian* for implying in *Yeast* that 'a certain amount of youthful profligacy does no real and permanent harm to the character, perhaps strengthens it for a useful and even religious life'. Kingsley answered in a sharp letter in which he said to the author of the attack, apparently the first Lord Coleridge, in words drawn from Pascal's *Provincial Letters*, 'Mentiris impudentissime' ['You lie most shamelessly'] (ibid. i. 282-4; G. M. Young, *Daylight and Champaign* (1948 edn.), pp. 101-2). GKC.

SECTION XII

1. See Gladstone's speech proposing the second reading of the Representation of the People Bill, 12 Apr. 1866 (*Hansard*, 3rd Ser. clxxxii. 1132). MRDF.

2. These general statements should be viewed with caution. Certainly an increase in real wages and improvements in living conditions in the second half of the nineteenth century brought greater prosperity to sections of the working class, but it remains uncertain how far this prosperity extended and how secure it was. Unemployment in a bad

year, or as the result of the collapse of a particular trade or industry, could cancel the prosperity of entire groups of working men, while illness or old age could strike with devastating effect at individuals. It is also probable that behaviour became more orderly, but it would be difficult to prove this by reference to criminal statistics, which are notoriously deceptive and difficult to interpret. They are subject to local variants and adventitious circumstances, such as the variable policy of the courts, different definitions of offences by successive statutes, and the varying efficiency of local police forces, which have nothing to do with the general incidence of crime at any one time. See J. J. Tobias *Crime and Industrial Society in the 19th Century* (1967), pp. 14–21. Similar considerations apply to the problem of drunkenness. There are certainly signs of greater sobriety in the later nineteenth century, and of the development of popular forms of amusement and the use of non-alcoholic liquors, but it is not easy to be sure how far this extended, and again the statistics do not help. Indeed there seems to have been an actual increase in the second half of the century in the per capita consumption of alcohol, which oscillated with the state of trade. The statistics of arrests for drunkenness are subject to the same difficulties as all criminal statistics. It seems probable, however, that a general decrease in drunkenness is a twentieth- rather than a nineteenth-century phenomenon. See Brian Harrison *Drink and the Victorians* (1971), pp. 297–318. *GKC.*

3. The source of Delacroix's observation has not been traced. Another French visitor, Hippolyte Taine, noted:

The climate is very dirty, things have to be changed and replaced frequently. Every newspaper carries the advertisements of dealers who will come to your house and buy your part-worn clothes. Immaculate appearance is obligatory for a gentleman: his suits, once past their best, go to a man of the lower classes and end up in rags on the back of a pauper. Hence one's clothes are a badge of social rank. In nothing is the distance between classes so clearly indicated as in a man's appearance. Imagine a dandy's evening suit, or a lady's pink, flowered hat: the one you will see again on some poor wretch huddled on the steps leading down to the Thames, the other at Shadwell on the head of an old hag sorting rags and rubbish.

Taine's Notes on England, trans. Edward Hyams (1957), pp. 18–19. However, many pictures and descriptions make it clear that large sections of the working classes dressed not in the cast-off clothes of the upper classes, but in distinctive styles of their own. *JMC, GKC.*

4. See *The Greville Memoirs* under 13 Apr. 1848, describing the preparations made in the Privy Council Office: 'our office was fortified, a barricade of Council Registers was erected in the accessible room on the ground-floor, and all our guns were taken down to be used in defence of the building.' On 9 Apr. Frederic Rogers, then a Commissioner at the Colonial Land and Emigration Board, wrote to the Rev. James Mozley:

> we are all expected to appear at nine o'clock to-morrow, and to stay the night—dying at our posts if necessary. Guns are to be had on application at the Treasury, but only in case of special need (in which event of course not a soul would be able to get out of the house), and with a distinct charge that no one is to be trusted with a gun who does not know how to load and fire it—or who is likely to be in a very great fright. . . . Downing Street preparing its mind for bloodshed, and for accepting assistance from the Emigration Office . . . in case they should 'lose any men!' Everybody is a special constable; and constabular rank is regulated by official rank—rather a fantastic notion. . . . Some of the fat messengers and skinny copyists who are put in requisition, and whom I saw swearing to do their duty 'without favour or partiality, ill will or malice' (they say nothing about fear), pass ludicrousness.

Letters of Frederic Lord Blachford, ed. George Eden Marindin (1896), p. 135. *JMC, GKC.*

5. Henry Mayhew reported that the coal whippers 'were extremely proud of their having turned out to a man on the 10th of April, 1848, and become special constables for the maintenance of law and order' and that they 'were, I believe, the first class of persons who spontaneously offered their services as special constables' (*London Labour and the London Poor* (4 vols., 1861–2), iii. 233, 237). There is nothing in his report about supporting the Duke of Wellington or marching from Wapping, and it is not known where those details came from. The coal whippers unloaded coal from ships in the Pool of London. In 1843 a coal whippers' office had been created by statute to organize their pay and employment, and had led to a great improvement in their standards and self-respect. It is possible that it was in recognition of

the value of the Act that they behaved as they did in 1848. But Chartism was not particularly strong among the riverside trades, and, although Irish labourers were often involved, the London movement seems to have been dominated by artisans not of the top rank, such as shoemakers, tailors, plasterers, carpenters, and masons. *GJC.*

6. In the opening chapter of his *History of England* Macaulay, after discussing the failures of Britain in America and Ireland, wrote:

> Yet, unless I greatly deceive myself, the general effect of this chequered narrative will be to excite thankfulness in all religious minds, and hope in the breasts of all patriots. For the history of our country during the last hundred and sixty years is eminently the history of physical, of moral, and of intellectual improvement.

And at the end of Chapter 10, which was written in November 1848, after reviewing the fate which had overtaken other nations in Europe, he said:

> Meanwhile in our island the regular course of government has never been for a day interrupted. The few bad men who longed for license and plunder have not had the courage to confront for one moment the strength of a loyal nation, rallied in firm array round a parental throne. And, if it be asked what has made us to differ from others, the answer is that we never lost what others are wildly and blindly seeking to regain. It is because we had a preserving revolution in the seventeenth century that we have not had a destroying revolution in the nineteenth.

GKC.

7. It was in July 1840, not 1848, that Thackeray wrote 'I'm not a Chartist, only a republican. I would like to see all men equal, and this bloated aristocracy blasted to the wings of all the winds. . . . but no physical force—the bigotry of that and of the present Chartist leaders is greater than the bigotry we suffer under.' (*The Letters and Private Papers of William Makepeace Thackeray*, ed. Gordon N. Ray (4 vols., 1945–6), i. 458.) In the 1840s he supported the Anti-Corn Law League and believed that power should pass into the hands of the middle class (ibid. ii. 129, 216). He also wrote for *Punch* which was a Radical paper, and satirized upper-class society in his *Book of Snobs*. He did not, however, wholly dissociate himself from that society, did not share the

more extreme Radicalism of Douglas Jerrold and Charles Dickens, and succeeded in modifying the attitude of *Punch*, particularly towards the clergy (ibid. ii. 274–5). After *Vanity Fair*, published in monthly numbers 1847–8, had begun to be successful he was prepared to mix with high society to an extent that annoyed part of the literary world (Gordon N. Ray, *Thackeray. The Age of Wisdom 1847–1863* (1958), pp. 25–57). In 1848 he pitied the poor, wished for social change and was angry with fashionable people for their complaisance, but he condemned the socialism of Louis Blanc and universal suffrage, and feared the results of violence (*Letters and Private Papers*, ii. 355–7, 364–5). To judge by his reports of Chartist meetings, he does not seem to have feared Chartism but rather to have viewed the activities of the Chartists with some contempt (*William Makepeace Thackeray. Contributions to the Morning Chronicle now First Reprinted*, ed. Gordon N. Ray (Urbana, 1955), pp. 192–201). In 1851 he published a 'May Day Ode' to celebrate the royal opening of the Great Exhibition (*The Times*, 30 Apr. 1851, p. 5c). His mood seems to have been echoed by other writers in *Punch*, who, however, viewed with distaste the spectacle of the officers of the Court walking backwards before the Queen (*Punch*, vol. xx (Jan.–June 1851), pp. 189, 190), a distaste which Thackeray apparently shared. In 1855, after a period of trying to be a 'Whig and Quietist', he was plunged into Radicalism again by his anger at the mismanagement of the Crimean War, and at what he called the 'Pococurantism' of the Whigs in appointing aristocrats to places in Lord Palmerston's government. This drew him into closer alliance with Dickens from whom he had been separated partly by personal feelings and partly by his sympathy, however critical, for the upper classes. In this period Thackeray became an administrative reformer, stood for Parliament at Oxford, and wrote his *Four Georges* with its praise of the middle-class gentleman and its severe polemic against George IV (see Ray, *Age of Wisdom*, pp. 250–90). After 1858 his mind seems to have been occupied by his personal feud with Dickens precipitated by the libel produced by Edmund Yates. *GKC*.

8. It is very difficult to know how extensive or effective Queen Victoria's popularity in Ireland was. She was initially well received in political circles. O'Connell credited her with liberal views and a regular theme of his was that if only she would act as she should, repeal would be carried. On the other hand the younger politicians who followed O'Connell tended to be republicans and to be attracted by the more

extreme republicans in France in 1848. The Queen did not visit Ireland until 1849. She had not been very enthusiastic about going, and though her visit was satisfactory, it does not seem to have had any important political consequences. See Kevin B. Nowlan, *The Politics of Repeal* (1965), p. 229. *KBN, GKC.*

9. Lady Flora Hastings was a Lady of the Bedchamber to the Duchess of Kent, Queen Victoria's mother. In 1839 she was suffering from a tumour on the liver, but was suspected by the Queen and other members of her household of being pregnant. After Lady Flora had submitted to a medical examination, the Queen asked her forgiveness, but by then her family had taken up the matter and the scandal had become public. Lady Flora died in July. The incident demonstrated that the Queen could be partisan, and hasty and harsh in her judgement, but not that she was heartless. Her remorse seems to have been perfectly genuine; and it should be remembered that she was not yet twenty, that the whole matter was entangled by her unhappy relations with her mother and Sir John Conroy (the Comptroller of her mother's household), and that the influence of Lord Melbourne was unfortunate. The scandal certainly made her unpopular, particularly with those members of the public who objected to her close identification with her Whig ministers. After Peel's attempt to form a government in May was foiled by the Queen's refusal to change any of her Whig Ladies of the Bedchamber, this feeling became stronger and she was on occasion hissed when she appeared in public. The diarist Greville recorded, when the scandal about Lady Flora broke: 'the whole proceeding is looked upon by society at large as to the last degree disgusting and disgraceful. It is really an exemplification of the saying, that "les Rois et les Valets" are made of the refuse clay of creation'; and 'nobody cares for the Queen, her popularity has sunk to zero, and loyalty is a dead letter' (*The Greville Memoirs* under 2 and 25 Mar. 1839). The best account of this phase in the Queen's life is to be found in Elizabeth Longford, *Victoria R.I.* (1964). Several of the critical documents appeared in the *Annual Register* (1839), Chronicle, pp. 463–72, and show how damaging were the revelations made in the public press. *GKC.*

10. This refers to an incident on 1 Feb. 1842 when Elizabeth Fry acted as guide to the King of Prussia on his visit to Newgate. Apparently only

Elizabeth Fry actually knelt down and prayed. See Susanna Corder, *Life of Elizabeth Fry* (1853), pp. 573-4. *GKC.*

11. Lord Stanley, subsequently 14th Earl of Derby, was the acknowledged leader of the Conservative party after the break with Peel in 1846. Disraeli, although the foremost debater, did not even gain the sole lead in the Commons until the winter of 1851-2. See Robert Blake, *Disraeli* (1966), pp. 247-69. *JMC.*

12. cf. J. L. Motley, *The Rise of the Dutch Republic* (3 vols., 1855), iii. 627, on the death of William the Silent: 'when he died the little children cried in the streets'. See also Lord Rosebery's account of Peel's death: 'On the night of his resignation a silent multitude awaited him as he left the House of Commons, and, with bared heads, escorted him home. As he lay dying, a sadder crowd surrounded that home day and night, waiting breathlessly for the tidings of the father of their country.' (*Sir Robert Peel* (1899), p. 95.) There is a picture of this crowd in the *Illustrated London News*, vol. xvii (July–Dec. 1850), p. 9. *EJK, GKC.*

13. See the memorandum by Prince Albert, dated 3 Mar. 1850, on an interview between the Queen and Lord John Russell, who, reporting a conversation he had held with Palmerston, stated:

> Lord Palmerston said that he could not have helped to have become aware that he had forfeited the Queen's confidence, but he thought this had not been on *personal* grounds, but merely on account of his line of policy, with which the Queen disagreed. (The Queen interrupted Lord John by remarking that she distrusted him on *personal* grounds also, but I remarked that Lord Palmerston had so far at least seen rightly; that he had become disagreeable to the Queen, not on account of his person, but of his political doings, to which the Queen assented.)

Letters of Queen Victoria, 1st Ser. ii. 279-80. *RB, GKC.*

14. Introducing his Bill for Parliamentary Reform on 12 Mar. 1866, Gladstone claimed that it was not like the Trojan horse and, quoting from *Aeneid*, ii. 242-3, that it could not be said of it that

Scandit fatalis machina muros,
Foeta armis: mediaeque minans illabitur urbi

('The fateful engine climbs our walls teeming with arms, and glides threateningly into the midst of the city'). Lowe replied:

this is now the fifth Reform Bill that has been brought in since 1851. Now, just attend to the sequel of the passage quoted by the right hon. Gentleman. I am no believer in *sortes Virgilianae*, and the House will see why in a moment—

'O Divum domus Ilium, et inclyta bello
Moenia Dardanidum! Quater ipso in limina [sic] portae
Substitit, atque utero sonitum quater arma dedere.'

But that is not all—

'Instamus tamen immemores, caecique furore,
Et monstrum infelix sacrata sistimus arce.'

Well, I abominate the presage contained in the last two lines; but I mix my confidence with fear.

Hansard, 3rd Ser. clxxxii. 59, 164. The passage quoted by Lowe may be rendered 'Oh Ilium home of Gods, and you Dardan battlements renowned in war! Four times at the very threshold of the gates it halted, and four times arms clashed from its belly. Yet we press on heedless and blind with frenzy, and set the ill-omened monster in our hallowed citadel.' Disraeli described Lowe as an 'inspired schoolboy' in the House of Commons, 15 July 1867 (*Hansard*, 3rd Ser. clxxxviii. 1612).

Gladstone's 'via prima salutis' speech drew on *Aeneid*, vi. 96–7 ('Your path of safety shall first, little as you deem it, be opened up from a Grecian city') and was made in presenting the budget on 10 Feb. 1860 (*Hansard*, 3rd Ser. clvi. 815). It had possibly been used before since Sir George Rose stated on 22 Mar. 1832 that Pitt had quoted it when Fox obtained a seat for a Scotch burgh in 1784 (ibid. 3rd Ser. xi. 679).

Speaking very early in the morning, on 3 Apr. 1792, in support of Wilberforce's motion for the abolition of the slave trade, Pitt said:

Then also will Europe, participating in her [Africa's] improvement and prosperity, receive an ample recompense for the tardy kindness (if kindness it can be called), of no longer hindering that continent from extricating herself out of the darkness which, in other more fortunate regions, has been so much more speedily dispelled—

Nos primus equis oriens afflavit anhelis;
Illic sera rubens accendit lumina Vesper.

Parliamentary History, xxix. 1157. The passage is from *Georgics*, i. 250–1 ('When on us the rising sun first breathes with panting steeds, there glowing Vesper is kindling his evening rays'). GKC.

15. From 1856 until his death in 1892 Thomas Cooper lectured on Christian evidences; William Newton of the Amalgamated Society of Engineers, William Allan of the Iron Workers, and Thomas Mottershead, a silk weaver, were all old Chartists who were active in the organization of trade unions; W. J. Linton, Ernest Jones, and G. J. Harney could all be considered as old republicans who were 'shouting for war' in 1853–4; an old pacifist who in the same period no doubt declaimed to empty halls was Joseph Sturge who denounced the Crimean War, as did John Bright. *FBS, GKC.*

16. In 1857 the steamer *Cagliari*, whose owner was Piedmontese and the nationality of which was generally agreed to be Piedmontese, was seized when on a voyage between Genoa, Sardinia, and Tunis by revolutionaries and used to land Pisacane's expedition in Sicily. It was then captured by the Neapolitan navy outside Neapolitan waters and towed into Naples where its crew, which included two British engineers Watt and Park, were imprisoned and badly treated. The Piedmontese government pressed for the restitution of ship and crew, and there was some excitement in Britain about the two engineers. The expedient which Roebuck believed to be suitable was to send a battleship:

> A three-decker in the Bay of Naples within cannon-shot of the Royal palace—that is what I would have sent. The right hon. Gentleman talks about using amiable language. Sir, the 'amiable language' that I would have spoken would have been cannon-shot.

Hansard, 3rd Ser. cxlix. 94 (12 Mar. 1858). The engineers were recovered without recourse to drastic methods.

In early life Sir John Bowring (1792–1872) was closely associated with Jeremy Bentham and was one of the first editors of the *Westminster Review*. He also produced what was for long the standard English edition of Bentham's works. He was a friend of Cobden and one of the founders of the Anti-Corn Law League. After performing various services for government and serving as a Radical Member of Parliament 1835–7, 1841–9, his financial position made it necessary for him to seek from Palmerston the position of Consul at Canton. In 1854 he became British Plenipotentiary to China and Governor of Hong Kong. In 1856 the Chinese boarded the lorcha *Arrow* in search of two pirates and removed eight of its crew. The *Arrow* had once had British registration, and may have been flying the British flag. It was claimed that this was only the culmination of a number of incidents. Because he did not get the reparation he thought necessary, Bowring ordered Admiral Seymour to enter the harbour of Canton where he destroyed the forts and sank a large number of junks. Bowring's action was rather hastily endorsed by Palmerston's government, but a motion condemning it was carried in the House of Commons. Palmerston appealed to the country and was victorious in a general election. Bowring had further adventures including a voyage to the Philippines on the return from which he was wrecked and spent three days on a coral reef. He seems to have been rather a pedantic man and was known at one time as Dr. Boring. *DEDB, GKC.*

17. See the report in *The Times*, 12 June 1865, p. 9c, on the opening of the Langham Hotel:

> It is scarcely more than four years since the hotel accommodation of London was an unpleasant byword, a something which inferred little more than the comforts of a public house, and little less than the expenses of a palace. . . . The costly discomfort of these batches of private houses made to do this duty has naturally led to reaction. The Great Western, the Westminster Palace, and the Grosvenor were the first improvements. Now we have the Charing-cross and the Langham.

The rest of the article is mainly journalistic puff, and the Prince's remark to the manager that 'the new hotel was even finer in its arrangements and general scheme of accommodation than the specimen hotel of New York—the Fifth Avenue' an obvious commonplace. The descriptions do not indicate that either the Langham or the railway hotels were the scene of a brilliant social life. *PAB.*

18. The third chapter of Macaulay's *History of England* was written in 1848, and in 1857 he added a note:

> During the interval which has elapsed since this chapter was written, England has continued to advance rapidly in material prosperity. I have left my text nearly as it originally stood; but I have added a

few notes which may enable the reader to form some notion of the progress which has been made during the last nine years; and, in general, I would desire him to remember that there is scarcely a district which is not more populous, or a source of wealth which is not more productive, at present than in 1848.

These notes include statistics showing increases in the quantity of coal brought into London, in the population of Leeds, Sheffield, Birmingham, and Liverpool, in the tonnage of steamers in the port of London, and in the number of letters carried by the post office. *GKC*.

19. cf. Shakespeare, *The Passionate Pilgrim*, xiii:

> Crabbed age and youth cannot live together:
> Youth is full of pleasance, age is full of care.

EJK.

20. See Section V, note 18.

21. On the general position of agriculture see Lord Ernle, *English Farming Past and Present*, ed. Sir A. D. Hall (1936), pp. 374-5. On the history of rent in the nineteenth century see the paper read by R. J. Thompson on 17 Dec. 1907, *Journal of the Royal Statistical Society*, lxx (1907), 587-624. For the acreage under wheat and the yield per acre see Michael G. Mulhall, *The Dictionary of Statistics*, 4th edn. (1899), pp. 13-18. The area under wheat between 1871 and 1875 seems to have been 3,740,000 acres, but it seems unlikely that the average yield of bushels per acre was more than 28. *BRM, GKC*.

22. cf. an entry in Macaulay's journal under 4 Nov. 1849, describing a visit to Lord Hatherton:

> After dinner we had evening prayers which occupied no very long time. There are prayers every morning at nine, but I have not finished dressing in time to attend. To my surprise Lord H. said that there were only 3 land-owners of £500 a year in all Staffordshire who had not morning family prayers. I cannot help thinking that unless the Staffordshire Lords and gentlemen are a race apart, many of them must lead such lives that their prayers must give more scandal than their vices.

MS. Journal, Trinity College Library, Cambridge. *RR*.

23. For Mr. Podsnap and Mr. Twemlow see *Our Mutual Friend* by Charles Dickens. Mr. Twemlow's sole claim to distinction was that he was the first cousin of Lord Snigsworth. Presumably the one decision Mr. Podsnap had to take was to break off relations with Mr. and Mrs. Lammle who had been trying to engineer a marriage between his daughter and the scoundrel Fledgeby in return for a payment of one thousand pounds (Book III, Chapter 1). Since Podsnap had been told of the plot his action does not seem to merit much praise. It is not easy to see why Young calls him 'a belated and sterile type'. Many of the Philistines attacked by Matthew Arnold must have been like him; Sir Pompey Bedell in Du Maurier's pictures in *Punch* in the eighties had much in common with him, especially in his estimation of foreigners; and the type reappears in some of Bernard Shaw's plays. Sir Leicester Dedlock was the large landowner in Dickens's *Bleak House* and the Iron-master, the successful manufacturer who was the son of his housekeeper, Mrs. Rouncewell. *GKC.*

24. The source of Gladstone's phrase 'a sneaking kindness for a lord' has not been traced. In November 1877 in an article on the county franchise in the *Nineteenth Century*, he wrote: 'Call this love of inequality by what name you please, the complement of the love of freedom, or its negative pole, or the shadow which the love of freedom casts, or the reverberation of its voice in the halls of the constitution; it is an acting, living, and life-giving power' (*Gleanings of Past Years* (7 vols., 1879), i. 150). He had, however, been more direct earlier in the article: 'It is not love of equality which has carried into every corner of the country the distinct undeniable popular preference, whenever other things are substantially equal, for a man who is a lord over a man who is not.' (ibid. i. 148.) cf. G. M. Young, *Today and Yesterday* (1948), pp. 36–7. *JMC, HCGM, AWS.*

25. The increase in public business and the increased activity of Members after the First Reform Act had made it necessary to impose new rules upon the procedure of the House (see above p. 47 and Section V, note 14). But they left all Members many opportunities not only to debate matters which Ministers brought before the House, but also to raise issues and propose legislation on their own initiative. It has not been possible to identify the fortnight to which Young refers, but any volume of *Hansard* for the middle of the nineteenth century will reveal the variety of issues discussed by the House. Whether its capacity

to dispatch public business was as satisfactory is open to question. The matter was investigated by two Select Committees which suggested changes (H.C. (1847–8) xvi. 139–93; (1854) vii. 11–103). But the procedure of the House continued to give dissatisfaction to a number of Members and another Select Committee was proposed in 1861 (*Hansard*, 3rd Ser. clxi. 153–79). For its report see H.C. (1861) xi. 431–511. In all the debates on the matter Ministers showed deep respect for the wishes of the House. *GKC*.

26. See Gladstone's memorandum, dated 14 Aug. 1845, of a conversation with Peel on 12 July (*The Prime Ministers' Papers: W. E. Gladstone*, vol. ii, *Autobiographical Memoranda 1832–1845*, ed. John Brooke and Mary Sorensen (1972), pp. 279–80). In Morley, *Gladstone*, i. 297–300 the same passage is printed as part of a memorandum dated 24 July 1846. *GKC*.

SECTION XIII

1. The second chapter of Edwin Paxton Hood, *The Age and its Architects: Ten Chapters on the English People in Relation to the Times* (1850) was entitled 'The Victorian Commonwealth', which he described as 'the most wonderful picture on the face of the earth, perhaps on no other spot of ground has heaven ever grouped so bright a constellation of its best mercies' (p. 71). No use of the word 'Victorian' as early as this is recorded in the *O.E.D.* cf. Asa Briggs, *The Age of Improvement 1783–1867* (1959), p. 446. *JMC*.

2. See Bagehot's essay 'Mr. Gladstone', published in 1860: 'During the discussion on the Budget [of 1860], an old Whig who did not approve of it, but who had to vote for it, muttered to its author, "Ah, Oxford on the surface, *but* Liverpool below." ' Later in the essay Bagehot himself commented: 'Underneath the scholastic polish of his Oxford education, he has the speculative hardihood, the eager industry of a Lancashire merchant.' (*Biographical Studies*, ed. Richard Holt Hutton (1881), pp. 86, 89.) *JMC, GKC*.

3. This passage should be read in conjunction with those on pp. 109–10 and 117–19 above. The notes to those pages deal with most of the in-

dividuals Young mentions. Arnold Toynbee became a Tutor in Econ-omics at Balliol College, Oxford in 1878. His lectures were remarkable for their insights into economic history, and his rejection of the old eco-nomic orthodoxies. See G. Kitson Clark, *Churchmen and the Condition of England 1832–1885* (1973), pp. 279–89, and for his work in the East End, Section XXIX, note 7. The neglect of Ruskin must refer to the rejection between 1860 and about 1875 of his economic teaching, not of his work as an art critic; the rejection of the poetry of Browning was more absolute until about 1868. In fact, although the narrowness of outlook which prevailed in the earlier years of the century and had been enforced by the values of Evangelical religion, was probably relaxing after 1850, the hold on the public mind of what were held to be the principles of political economy continued for much longer, as Ruskin's experience shows. *GKC.*

4. Bagehot's comment on Enoch Arden in his essay on 'Wordsworth, Tennyson, and Browning', published in 1864 (*Literary Studies*, ed. Richard Holt Hutton (3 vols., 1905–7), ii. 364). *GKC.*

5. See Brougham's speech, 7 Oct. 1831, on the second reading of the Reform Bill in the House of Lords (*Hansard*, 3rd Ser. viii. 265). *GKC, JMC.*

6. *A Plea for the Middle Classes* (1848) was written by the Rev. Nathaniel Woodard and was the first stage of the plan which developed into the Woodard schools. See Brian Heeney, *Mission to the Middle Classes. The Woodard Schools 1848–1891* (1969). *GKC.*

7. 'Barbarians', 'Philistines', and 'Populace' were the terms used by Matthew Arnold in the third chapter of *Culture and Anarchy* (1869) to describe the aristocratic, middle, and working classes. *JMC.*

8. These were the calculations of the Newcastle Commission published in 1861 (H.C. (1861) xxi (i), p. 293). They seem to have been based on a complete miscalculation of the education available to children in the towns, and especially in the great cities. This was exposed by an inquiry in 1866 into the state of education in Manchester, the results of which were endorsed by further inquiries in Liverpool, Birmingham, and Leeds. These revelations provided the background to Forster's Educa-tion Act of 1870 (see above pp. 121–2). *GKC.*

9. For the doubts expressed in 1858 on the value of the education financed by public grant see the debate in the House of Commons on 21 June (*Hansard*, 3rd Ser. cli. 135–53). GKC.

10. Robert Lowe, introducing the Revised Code on 13 Feb. 1862, said:

> I cannot promise the House that this system will be an economical one, and I cannot promise that it will be an efficient one, but I can promise that it shall be either one or the other. If it is not cheap it shall be efficient; if it is not efficient it shall be cheap. The present system is neither one nor the other.

Hansard, 3rd Ser. clxv. 229. GKC.

11. See Section VI, note 27.

12. There seems to be little doubt that Dr. Strong's school described in Chapters 16 and 17 of *David Copperfield* represented to Dickens what he felt had been lacking in his own boyhood, and since the school was placed at Canterbury it has been natural to identify it with the King's School. There is, however, no documentary evidence to support this identification, and it seems much more likely that Dr. Strong's school was simply a creation of Dickens's imagination and was not modelled on any existing institution. See Philip Collins, *Dickens and Education* (1963), pp. 117–20. GKC, JMC.

13. The Taunton Commission was appointed on 28 Dec. 1864 to inquire into those schools which had not been considered by the Newcastle Commission on popular education or the Clarendon Commission on the public schools. Its results were published in 17 parts in H.C. (1867–8) xxviii. An extract from the Report is printed in Young and Handcock, *English Historical Documents*, pp. 905–11. GKC.

14. On *The Governess* by Marguerite, Countess of Blessington (1789–1849), which appeared in 2 volumes in 1839 see Michael Sadleir, *Blessington–D'Orsay. A Masquerade* (1933), pp. 274–7. Lady Blessington herself gave an account of her motives in writing the book in a letter dated 30 Nov. 1839 to her niece Mrs. Fairlie. 'It was my anxious wish,' she said, 'to point attention and excite sympathy towards a class from which [more is] expected and to whom less is accorded, than to any other.' And she went on to describe the responsibilities and sufferings of

governesses (ibid. p. 275). This was not, however, the first appearance of a governess in English literature. In Jane Austen's *Emma*, Miss Taylor, who married Mr. Weston, had been Emma's happy and well-respected governess; and in the same book it was said of Jane Fairfax, who was preparing to be a governess, that: 'With the fortitude of a devoted noviciate, she had resolved at one-and-twenty to complete the sacrifice, and retire from all the pleasures of life, of rational intercourse, equal society, peace and hope, to penance and mortification for ever.' (Book II, Chapter 2.) *East Lynne* by Mrs. Henry Wood (1814–87) appeared in parts in the *New Monthly Magazine* from January 1861, and in book form later in the year. It achieved great popularity, went through a number of editions, and was dramatized in several versions which became the staple of many touring companies until well after the end of the century. *GKC, JMC.*

15. The school kept by Louisa Browning and her sister was at 4 Dartmouth Row, Blackheath. There is a description of the school and its curriculum in Jo Manton, *Elizabeth Garrett Anderson* (1965), pp. 33–6. George Eliot's school was kept by Mary and Rebecca Franklin in Warwick Row, Coventry. There is a description of it in Gordon S. Haight, *George Eliot. A Biography* (Oxford, 1968), pp. 10–21. *GKC.*

16. See Section I, note 12. The term 'ministering angel' was used by Shakespeare, *Hamlet*, Act V, Scene i: 'A ministering angel shall my sister be'; and by Sir Walter Scott, *Marmion*, Canto VI, Verse 30:

> When pain and anguish wring the brow,
> A ministering angel thou!

WAL, JMC.

17. For Queen Victoria's view of the movement towards equality of the sexes see her letter to Sir Theodore Martin, 29 May 1870:

> The Queen is most anxious to enlist any one who can speak and write . . . [against] this *mad, wicked folly* of 'woman's rights' with *all* the attendant horrors on which her poor feeble sex seems bent, viz: in forgetting every sense of womanly feeling and propriety. Lady Amberley ought to get a good whipping. It is a subject which makes the queen so furious that she cannot contain herself. God created man and woman different and let each remain in their position. Tennyson

has some beautiful lines on the difference of man and woman in 'The Princess'. Woman would become the most hateful, heartless—and disgusting of human beings were she allowed to unsex herself! Where would be the protection which man was intended to give to the weaker sex? Pray try and get some good writing against it. The *Times* has written extremely well about it, and there is an excellent article on Lady Amberley's folly in yesterday's *Times*.

Royal Archives, Windsor Y 168/69. The letter is published by the gracious permission of Her Majesty the Queen.

In May 1870 the Queen was also writing to Gladstone to express her horror at the attempt of women to enter the same professions as men, the occasion being the attempt by Miss Jex Blake and her companions to qualify for medical practice through Edinburgh. See Philip Guedalla, *The Queen and Mr. Gladstone* (2 vols., 1933), i. 227–9. *GKC, EL.*

18. For Bella Rokesmith's comment see Charles Dickens, *Our Mutual Friend*, Book IV, Chapter 5. In Act III of Henrik Ibsen's play *A Doll's House*, Nora says: 'But our home has been nothing but a playroom. I have been your doll-wife, just as at home I was papa's doll-child; and here the children have been my dolls.' *LGS, GKC.*

19. The doctrine of the 'two spheres' asserted that each sex had a sphere which was its natural domain—for men business, politics, or war; for women the building and care of the home, the nurture of children, the tending of the sick, and possibly religion. Each had the psychological equipment which suited them for what they had to do; each should be educated in such a way as to fit them for their natural sphere. For a woman to try to do what was outside the ambience of her natural sphere was wrong and would lead to disaster. This doctrine was challenged by the feminists, and some of the problems it presented were reflected in Tennyson's *Princess* (1847), but it was widely held in the second half of the nineteenth century even by intelligent writers who had the interests of women at heart. For instance the novelist Charlotte M. Yonge, in a selection of articles serialized in the *Monthly Packet*, 1874–7, and republished under the title *Womankind* in 1887, accepted it, together with the corollary that woman was in certain respects naturally inferior to man. But it is clear that the problem was much on her mind, and she constantly returned to aspects of it in her novels: in *The Daisy Chain* (serialized 1853–5), *The Clever Woman of the Family* (1865), *The*

Three Brides (serialized 1874–6), and *Magnum Bonum* (serialized 1877–9). Probably the most eloquent exposition of the doctrine was in §§ 67 and 68 of John Ruskin's *Sesame and Lilies*, first published in 1865 and apparently his most popular book. He wrote:

> We are foolish, and without excuse foolish, in speaking of the 'superiority' of one sex to the other, as if they could be compared in similar things. Each has what the other has not . . . and the happiness and perfection of both depends on each asking and receiving from the other what the other only can give.

The Works of John Ruskin, ed. E. T. Cook and Alexander Wedderburn (39 vols., 1903–12), xviii. 121. Although the doctrine could be held by enlightened people it could be put to very unenlightened use, and result in the ruthless sacrifice of the lives of women to the convenience of the inhabitants of the 'home' and the denial to women of education and opportunities which were held to be irrelevant to the requirements of their natural 'sphere'. *AMHC, GKC.*

20. In Thackeray's *Vanity Fair* Miss Pinkerton's academy for young ladies, at which Amelia Sedley and Becky Sharp were educated, was on Chiswick Mall; in *Edwin Drood* by Charles Dickens Miss Twinkleton's Seminary for Young Ladies was in the Nuns' House at Cloisterham. Dora Spenlow was David Copperfield's first wife. *GKC.*

21. The Hon. Amelia Murray (1795–1884), daughter of Lord George Murray, Bishop of St. David's, was nominated Maid of Honour to Queen Victoria in 1837. One of the most intelligent and advanced women of her time, she became interested in education and collected money for a women's college. On learning that the Governesses' Benevolent Institution, with the support of F. D. Maurice and other professors of King's College, intended to open such a college in 1848, she decided to contribute the money to their scheme. It is believed that it was Miss Murray who persuaded Queen Victoria to allow the college to be called Queen's, although there seems to be no documentary proof of this. Information about the early history of Queen's College has been very kindly supplied by Miss C. Oliver.

King's College, London, had an early association with both Queen's College and Bedford College. Later, lectures for ladies in connection with King's were organized in Richmond and Twickenham in 1871, in Kensington Vestry Hall in 1878, and finally in King's College itself in

1882. See F. J. C. Hearnshaw, *The Centenary History of King's College London 1828–1928* (1929), pp. 312–18, 489–509. But see above, Section X, note 18, on the attitude of the Governors in 1833 to young ladies attending Lyell's lectures on geology. GKC.

22. Dorothea Beale (1831–1906) and Frances Mary Buss (1827–94) were among the earliest pupils of Queen's College. In 1849 Miss Beale was appointed mathematical tutor at the College, and in 1854 head teacher of a school attached to it. She became head teacher of the Clergy Daughters' School, Casterton, in 1857 but resigned within a year and in 1858 was appointed Principal of the Ladies' College at Cheltenham, the first proprietary school for girls in England. She developed it into a large and flourishing institution and paid particular attention to the development of facilities for the training of teachers. Before Miss Buss entered Queen's College she had kept a school with her mother, and after leaving Queen's ran this family school in various places. It was reconstituted in 1870–1 as the North London Collegiate School for Girls where she remained Headmistress until her death. In 1864 as the result of a petition promoted by Miss Emily Davies, girls' schools were included among the subjects of inquiry by the Taunton Commission. Miss Beale, Miss Buss, and Miss Davies all gave evidence (see H.C. (1867–8) xxviii). In 1865 a committee of which Miss Davies was secretary persuaded Cambridge University to admit girls to its junior and senior Local Examinations. Admission to these examinations and the Report of the Taunton Commission were turning points in the modernization of girls' schools, but there was a long way to go before the right of women to higher education was generally recognized. GKC.

SECTION XIV

1. See Macaulay to T. F. Ellis, 29 May 1835: 'As for myself, I rejoice that I am out of the present storm. "Suave mari magno;" or, as your new Premier, if he still be Premier, construes, "It is a source of melancholy satisfaction." ' (Trevelyan, *Macaulay*, i. 439.) But cf. Charles Stuart Parker's note to G. R. Dawson's account of Peel's examination: 'To this glowing eulogy one may afford to append an Oxford tradition, that in the famous passage of Lucretius beginning, "Suave, mari magno

turbantibus æquora ventis," ["It is sweet, when on the great sea the winds are buffeting the waters"] Peel construed *suave*, "It is a source of gratification."' (*Sir Robert Peel from his Private Papers* (3 vols., 1891-9), i. 23.) Parker derived the story from Goldwin Smith. The text Peel was set to construe was the opening passage of the second book of Lucretius, *De Rerum Natura*. See also *The Letters of Thomas Babington Macaulay*, ed. Thomas Pinney, vol. iii (Cambridge, 1976), p. 140 n. 3. *GKC, RR.*

2. At Oxford the New Examination Statute established the honours examination in 1802 and in 1807 a School of Mathematics and Physics separate from the School of *Literae Humaniores* was instituted. In both Schools classes were introduced; the examination was largely oral. In 1808 Robert Peel established a record with a first in both mathematics and classics. See Charles Edward Mallet, *A History of the University of Oxford* (3 vols., 1924-7), iii. 167-9. At Cambridge the Senate House Examination gradually developed during the eighteenth century as part of the procedure which led to a degree. It was exclusively a test of mathematical ability. The Classical Tripos was not established until 1822 but in men like Richard Porson (1759-1808), Peter Paul Dobree (1782-1825), and Charles James Blomfield (1786-1857) classical scholarship at Cambridge had before that date achieved great distinction. See D. A. Winstanley, *Early Victorian Cambridge* (Cambridge, 1940), pp. 65-71, 149-52, 157-60. *GKC, JMC.*

3. It is probable that Sir Robert Peel, whose interest in the subject was considerable, could have talked science with Prince Albert. *GKC.*

4. On Grote see Section II, note 24. The elder Mill is no doubt called 'the most exacting classical tutor of the age' because of the severity with which he trained his children. John Stuart Mill when three years old was set to learn 'vocables' or lists of Greek words with English meanings. By his eighth year he had read Aesop's *Fables*, the whole of Herodotus, parts of Xenophon, Diogenes Laertius, Lucan and Isocrates, and the first six *Dialogues* of Plato (J. S. Mill, *Autobiography* (1873), p. 5). *GKC.*

5. Bagehot went to University College in October 1842 and graduated in 1846. Richard Holt Hutton's memories of college life appear in his prefatory memoir to Bagehot's *Literary Studies* (3 vols., 1905-7), i. pp. xii-xix. He wrote:

But of this, at least, I am sure, that Gower Street, and Oxford Street, and the New Road, and the dreary chain of squares from Euston to Bloomsbury, were the scenes of discussions as eager and as abstract as ever were the sedate cloisters or the flowery river-meadows of Cambridge or Oxford. Once, I remember, in the vehemence of our argument as to whether the so-called logical principle of identity (A is A) were entitled to rank as 'a law of thought' or only as a postulate of language, Bagehot and I wandered up and down Regent Street for something like two hours in the vain attempt to find Oxford Street (p. xiii).

GKC.

6. The number of students at Owens College, Manchester, sank from 62 in 1851 to 33 in 1856–7 and 34 in 1857–8, and Manchester newspapers talked of the College as a failure. Thereafter the numbers rose steadily from 40 in 1858–9 to 108 in 1862–3 and 327 in 1871–2. The increase may have been partly due to the replacement in 1857 of the Professor of Chemistry, Edward Frankland, by Henry Enfield Roscoe (1833–1915). See under Roscoe in the *D.N.B.* (1912–21); *The Owens College, Manchester*, ed. P. J. Hartog (Manchester, 1900), p. 22; and Sir J. J. Thomson, *Recollections and Reflections* (1936), pp. 10–33. Despite the development of universities in the great cities, however, the social prestige of Oxford and Cambridge tended to make rich manufacturers send their sons to the older universities. Disraeli, explaining to Queen Victoria the models which had contributed to his characterization of the Thornberry family in his novel *Endymion*, wrote on 10 Feb. 1881: 'the catastrophe of the family occurred literally to Mr. Potter, the Socinian Mayor of Manchester, and M.P., who, having made his fortune, sent his two sons to Oxford to make them gentlemen; but they only became Roman Catholics.' (*Letters of Queen Victoria*, 2nd Ser. iii. 195.) *GKC.*

7. See Freeman on University Extension, in answer (25 Oct. 1853) to questions circulated by the Committee of the Oxford Tutors' Association:

the University is not merely, or even primarily, a place of clerical education, but one where the youthful intellect of England in general should be subjected to its sound teaching and wholesome discipline. At present, besides the clergy, we get only a portion, I believe a diminishing portion, of men designed for the bar, and the usual allowance of young men of rank and fortune. A lay member of the University not coming under one of these two heads is something quite exceptional. A father has two sons, one designed to be a clergyman or barrister, the other to be a banker, merchant, surgeon, or solicitor; the first goes to the University, he never thinks of sending the second. Even such highly intellectual professions as those of medicine, architecture, and engineering, are all but exclusively filled with non-academical members.

Papers published by the Tutors' Association, Oxford, 1853. 1854 (Oxford, 1854), Part II, p. 147. The whole paper is of interest. DRF.

8. 'You are ignorant of everything but horses and dogs, yet know nothing of horses and dogs.' The source of the quotation is unknown, but its language suggests that it was composed in the nineteenth or twentieth century. FHS.

9. Connop Thirlwall (1797–1875) left Cambridge in 1834 after publishing a pamphlet on the admission of Dissenters to university degrees in which he cast doubts on the spiritual value of religious services in college chapels. Thereafter he does not appear to have taken a leading part in university reform. A. C. Tait (1811–82), afterwards Archbishop of Canterbury, was a Fellow of Balliol College, Oxford 1834–42. He studied conditions in German universities and as a College Tutor made suggestions for reform, but in 1842 he left to become Headmaster of Rugby. He was an active member of the Royal Commission on Oxford, but it can hardly be said that he was acting from 'within the gates'. Benjamin Jowett (1817–93), a Tutor at Balliol 1842–70, and Master 1870–93, was the only one of the three men mentioned by Young who was resident at his university during the whole period of reform. It is impossible to determine how far either university would have reformed itself had there been no pressure from without. On the forces working for and against reform see D. A. Winstanley, *Early Victorian Cambridge* (Cambridge, 1940); W. R. Ward, *Victorian Oxford* (1965); E. G. W. Bill and J. F. A. Mason, *Christ Church and Reform, 1850–1867* (Oxford, 1970); and E. G. W. Bill, *University Reform in Nineteenth-Century Oxford. A Study of Henry Halford Vaughan* (Oxford, 1973). The Chancellor of Cambridge University was Prince Albert. For the part he played in reform see Winstanley, op. cit. especially pp. 198–213. GKC.

10. Temple Grove was founded by Dr. Pearson, a clergyman, who in 1810 purchased Sheen Grove, a house and estate of twenty acres between Mortlake and Richmond Park. Since the estate had belonged to Lord Palmerston, it was renamed Temple Grove after his family name. In 1817 Pearson handed the school over to another clergyman, Dr. Pinckney, who was Headmaster until 1835 when the school numbered 120 boys. He was succeeded as Headmaster by Thompson and Rowden until in 1860 Ottiwell Charles Waterfield took over the school when it became a very notable training ground, particularly for Eton. There are several accounts of life at Temple Grove in its early years, for example in Henry J. Coke, *Tracks of a Rolling Stone* (1905), pp. 9–13, and Christabel Maxwell, *Mrs. Gatty and Mrs. Ewing* (1949), pp. 58–60, although it has not been possible to trace the origin of all the stories mentioned by Young. The accounts do not describe a happy place, but rather a school where boys were under-fed, severely flogged, and taught a very narrow range of subjects, and where personal cleanliness was impossible. The use of sulphur and treacle is not an importation from *Nicholas Nickleby*, Chapter 8, but comes from Coke, op. cit. p. 9. Information about the school has been very kindly supplied by Mr. A. A. M. Batchelor, formerly Headmaster of Temple Grove. *GKC*.

11. The most easily available account of conditions in College at Eton before the reforms of E. C. Hawtrey, Headmaster 1834–52 and Provost 1852–62, and F. Hodgson, Provost 1840–52, could take effect, is in George R. Parkin, *Edward Thring. Life, Diary and Letters* (2 vols., 1898), i. 21–6. *GKC*.

12. See Cowper's letter to the Rev. John Newton, 27 Nov. 1784, where he said of *Tirocinium* which he had just written:

> It treats of the scandalous relaxation of discipline, that obtains in almost all schools universally, but especially in the largest, which are so negligent in the article of morals, that boys are debauched in general the moment they are capable of being so. It recommends the office of tutor to the father, where there is no real impediment; the expedient of a domestic tutor, where there is; and the disposal of boys into the hands of a respectable country clergyman, who limits his attention to two, in all cases where they cannot be conveniently educated at home.

Letters of William Cowper, ed. J. G. Frazer (2 vols., 1912), i. 326–7. *GKC*.

13. For the schools run by the family of Rowland Hill see Sir Rowland Hill and George Birkbeck Hill, *The Life of Sir Rowland Hill and the History of Penny Postage* (2 vols., 1880), i. 47–215. George Edmondson (1798–1863) was a Quaker educationalist who after a visit to Russia as tutor to the children of a fellow Quaker settled there for some time. On his return he founded schools at Blackburn in 1830, and shortly afterwards at Tulketh Hall near Preston. In 1847 he moved his school to Queenwood Hall in Hampshire, which had previously been an Owenite co-operative colony. See the *D.N.B. GKC.*

14. See the evidence given by Faraday to the Clarendon Commission (H.C. (1864) xxi. 911–18). He did not make the remark attributed to him by Young, but something of its purport appears in his answers to Questions 22, 40–1, and 52–4. *GKC.*

15. The 'Public Schools' were named in the schedule to the Public Schools Act, 1864 (27 and 28 Vict. c. 92). They were Eton, Winchester, Westminster, Charterhouse, St. Paul's, Merchant Taylors (in London), Harrow, Rugby, and Shrewsbury. The object of the Act was to enable Parliament to make changes in their governing bodies. *GKC.*

16. See G. Kitson Clark, *The Making of Victorian England* (1962), pp. 266–7. *GKC.*

17. To place the Headmaster of Eton's reply in its proper context it is desirable to read Questions 3548–55 addressed to him by the Clarendon Commission (H.C. (1864) xxi. 116–17). *GKC.*

18. For the claims of the Headmaster of Westminster see his replies to Questions 1320–4 addressed to him by the Clarendon Commission (H.C. (1864) xxi. 443). For Queen Victoria's fears about the effect of education on the health of the upper classes see the entry in her journal under 30 July 1886 (*Letters of Queen Victoria*, 3rd Ser. i. 168). The account of Sedbergh in the fifties comes from *James M. Wilson: an Autobiography 1836–1931* (1932), p. 29:

> It was part of the tradition of the place that everyone should have read Homer, Thucydides and Sophocles before he went up, and a good many other books too, such as Virgil, Horace, Catullus, Euripides and even Lucan were regarded as necessities. I felt degenerate

because there were two books of Thucydides I had not read, and about 6 or 8 books of the *Iliad*, and 3 or 4 of the *Aeneid*.

GKC, HCGM, JMC.

19. See the Duke of Wellington to Lord Fitzroy, 8 Dec. 1845, commenting on suggestions made by Sidney Herbert as Secretary at War for rewards for good service for non-commissioned officers:

> in my opinion it is a great mistake to suppose that the conduct or character of the British Army is to be attributed to the non-commissioned officers! It is to the officer exclusively! the man of education, manners, honour, and other qualities acquired by the education which English gentlemen receive.
>
> This is *the man* to whom all look in moments of difficulty and danger—more particularly if his conduct in general should be such as that of a gentleman ought to be! It is quite astonishing what they do, not only in presence of an enemy in the field, but in every situation in which their duty places them. In their insulated cantonments, in South Wales or in Ireland, accident or mistake is never heard of. Then look at a youth from 16 to 18 years of age, just from school possibly, embarked in a transport with a non-commissioned officer, and from fifteen to twenty men in charge of hundreds of felons to convey them in safety to the Antipodes—a voyage which takes months; and I cannot say that I recollect an instance of an accident of any description, or of blame imputed to any officer.
>
> Then observe, that these are not the officers of one or two regiments, but those of all. Each regiment in its turn has this duty to perform.
>
> I know them well; their faults as well as their merits! But I declare that there is no greater mistake than to suppose that the service performed by the British Army could be carried on by any other description of man excepting one educated as is an English gentleman!

Lord Stanmore, *Sidney Herbert Lord Herbert of Lea. A Memoir* (2 vols., 1906), i. 75–6. cf. G. Kitson Clark, *The Making of Victorian England* (1962), p. 266. GKC.

20. 'For there is a sun and a cheerful light for us alone who are initiated and who lived our lives in a reverent fashion towards both the foreigners and the common man.' (Aristophanes, *Frogs*, 454–9.) The word here

translated as 'reverent' presents difficulties as it implies respect both for the gods and the rights of men, and there is some doubt about the meaning of the word here translated as 'common man'. *FHS.*

21. For a description of Kelmscott Manor, the house on the Upper Thames occupied by William Morris, see J. W. Mackail, *The Life of William Morris* (2 vols., 1899), i. 224–39. *GKC.*

SECTION XV

1. See Section XXI, note 2.

2. For details and references see J. R. Poynter, *Society and Pauperism* (1969), pp. 303–4. *GKC.*

3. cf. Homer, *Odyssey*, x. 81 ff. *EJK.*

4. In an almost identical sentence in his essay on 'Victorian History' in *Selected Modern English Essays*, 2nd Ser., ed. Humphrey Milford (1932), p. 270, Young named Mark Rutherford as the commentator he had in mind. He was presumably referring to the concluding passages of *The Early Life of Mark Rutherford* (1913), pp. 89–91:

> The greater part of my life has been passed in what it is now usual to contemn as the Victorian age. Whatever may be the justice of the scorn poured out upon it by the superior persons of the present generation, this Victorian age was distinguished by an enthusiasm which can only be compared to a religious revival. . . . The excitement of those years between 1848 and 1890 was, as I have said, something like that of a religious revival, but it was reasonable.

DRF.

5. cf. John, Viscount Morley, *Recollections* (2 vols., 1917), i. 14:

> Critics today are wont to speak contemptuously of the mid-Victorian age. They should now and then pause to bethink themselves. Darwin's famous book appeared in 1859. Buckle's *History of Civilisation* caught lively public attention the year before, and whatever may be

decided on his worth either as philosopher or scholar, his system with its panoply of detail must . . . have powerfully appealed to something or other in the public mind, or told something or other very important that people wanted to know. This something or other in the public mind was, in truth, a common readiness to extend an excited welcome to explanation whether of species or social phenomena by general laws, at the expense of special providence.

DRF.

6. Torben Christensen, *Origin and History of Christian Socialism* (Aarhus, 1962) is probably the best work on the subject. For a brief account with references to further reading see G. Kitson Clark, *Churchmen and the Condition of England, 1832–1885* (1973), pp. 303–13. For the literature on the Pre-Raphaelites see William E. Fredeman, *Pre-Raphaelitism: A Bibliocritical Study* (Cambridge, Mass., 1965). There is a useful survey in Timothy Hilton, *The Pre-Raphaelites* (1970). *GKC.*

7. This paragraph brings to an end the essay which Young wrote to conclude his edition of *Early Victorian England* (2 vols., 1934). He clearly felt that an important intellectual change took place at about this time. As presented here, the critical years would seem to be 1859 and 1860, when much appeared that was to mould or typify the mood of the period that followed. The 'last of the Augustans' was Macaulay, who died on 28 Dec. 1859, but was not in fact buried in Westminster Abbey until 9 Jan. 1860 (*RR, DEDB*). In 1859 Philip Webb (1831–1915), who had just set up on his own as an architect, began to build for William Morris the Red House at Upton in Kent, which was to mark a new departure in house and furniture design (see below, Section XVIII, note 2). In June 1860 John Ruskin began in the *Cornhill Magazine*, recently started under the editorship of Thackeray, a series of attacks on current conceptions of social morality and economics, which provoked such an uproar that they were stopped after the fourth article. The decision came not from Thackeray, as Young implies, but from the proprietors of the magazine. Ruskin published the four essays in 1862 as *Unto This Last*, which in due course had a profound influence on the social thought of all classes. In 1859 Charles Darwin published *The Origin of Species*, J. S. Mill *On Liberty*, Edward Fitzgerald his translation of *The Rubaiyat of Omar Khayyam*, and George Meredith *The Ordeal of Richard Feverel*. The following year seven Broad Churchmen

published a volume of essays on religious subjects entitled *Essays and Reviews*. Their tone was liberal and they caused an outcry, though from any modern point of view they appear for the most part very innocuous. By demonstrating the inability of the ecclesiastical courts to check heresy, the incident led to greater freedom from dogmatic control (see below, Section XX, notes 8 and 9). Meredith's *Modern Love* was published in 1862, J. R. Seeley's *Ecce Homo*, a humanizing portrayal of Christ, anonymously in 1865. Swinburne's *Poems and Ballads* appeared in 1865, and the following year Walter Pater began to write for the *Westminster Review* (see below, Section XVIII, note 2). GKC.

SECTION XVI

1. These suggestions should be viewed with scepticism. Morier was the favourite of the Crown Princess of Prussia, then at bitter enmity with Bismarck, and it was she who alleged, 26 May 1864, that it was Hammond's antagonism to him that restricted his influence (*Letters of Queen Victoria*, 2nd Ser. i. 205). In 1867 the Queen suggested that he should be appointed Secretary to the Embassy at Berlin; but, evidently on the decision of the Foreign Secretary, Lord Stanley, he was passed over because he was unacceptable to Bismarck and had become a violent partisan in German politics (ibid. i. 461–2). The Foreign Office was certainly ill-informed in July 1870, and the British Ambassador in Berlin, Lord Augustus Loftus, was unusually defective. Lord Granville, who described him in November 1870 as 'wanting in tact, and a great bore', became anxious to move him, though he found it difficult to decide where he might be placed (ibid. ii. 85, 130). He was sent to St. Petersburg, but during the crisis over the Eastern Question in 1876 Lord Beaconsfield found him useless: 'He was absurd in quiet times, but now that there is real business, he is not only absurd; he is mischievous.' (ibid. ii. 477–8.) He was subsequently sent out, like Hilaire Belloc's imaginary Lord Lundy, to 'govern New South Wales'. Yet it is difficult to see how even proper representation would have enabled Britain to counteract the results of Bismarck's intrigues and Napoleon III's folly. GKC.

2. See Granville's statement in the House of Lords, 11 July, in answer to Lord Malmesbury's request for information on the Government's

awareness of and attitude towards the sudden threat to European peace:

> I had the honour of receiving the seals of the Foreign Office last Wednesday [6 July]. On the previous day I had an unofficial communication with the able and experienced Under Secretary, Mr. Hammond, at the Foreign Office, and he told me . . . that with the exception of the sad and painful subject about to be discussed [the murder of British subjects by Greek brigands], he had never during his long experience known so great a lull in foreign affairs, and that he was not aware of any important question that I should have to deal with. At 6 o'clock that evening . . . I received a telegram informing me of the choice which had been made by the Provisional Government of Spain of Prince Leopold of Hohenzollern, and of his acceptance of the offer.

Hansard, 3rd Ser. cciii. 3. See also Lord Edmond Fitzmaurice, *The Life of Granville George Leveson Gower, Second Earl Granville* (2 vols., 1905), ii. 32–3. *DRF.*

3. Postscript to a letter from John Morley to Frederic Harrison, 22 Feb. 1871: 'Sir H. Bulwer says: "Europe has lost a mistress, and gained a master." Neat.' (F. W. Hirst, *Early Life and Letters of John Morley* (2 vols., 1927), i. 179.) *GKC.*

4. The source of this quotation has not been traced. *GKC.*

5. Contrary to Young's statement, it seems probable that the Prussian victory reduced the danger of a successful invasion of England by a foreign power. Before 1870 the French army, apparently the strongest in Europe, had been supported by the second most powerful navy, based on ports within striking distance of this country; but afterwards the strongest army, now the German, was backed by a relatively weak navy based on ports remote from Britain. That the significance of this situation was realized at the time is shown by the speech of H. C. E. Childers, a former First Lord of the Admiralty, on 30 Apr. 1874 (*Hansard*, 3rd Ser. ccxviii. 1417–46).

H.M.S. *Captain*, a fully rigged ship with a very low free-board, built in response to the prolonged agitation of Captain Cowper Coles for battleships with guns in turrets rather than in broadside, capsized and sank on 7 Sept. 1870, with the loss of most of her company. On the commemorative plaque in St. Paul's is inscribed what purports to be 'the official account of the disaster', which appears to blame those who accepted the design of the ship, those who built it, and those who permitted it to go into service and neglected to send its captain essential information. It is not, however, an 'official account', but merely a series of selections from the conclusions of the subsequent court martial, at which important interests were not represented, and against whose findings Childers, as First Lord, published a minute. Responsibility for the calamity probably rested with the politicians who accepted the design of the ship against the advice of Admiralty experts, but the circumstances of the case were so exceptional that it is not a reliable indication of the general efficiency of the navy in the 1870s. The cases of the *Agincourt* or the *Megaera* may be more relevant; but the balance of evidence suggests that the navy was a sufficiently effective instrument to have been able to prevent a cross-Channel invasion unsupported by naval force. For an understanding of the technical problems of the period and an indication of the effectiveness of the navy in 1870 see the series of articles by Admiral G. A. Ballard on British battleships of the 1870s in *Mariner's Mirror*, xv (1929), 101–23, 391–407; xvi (1930), 48–67, 168–86, 212–38; xvii (1931), 113–34, 244–69. The last of these articles is on the *Captain*. See also Arthur Hawkey, *H.M.S. Captain* (1963).

The fact that the navy was probably efficient enough vitiates the cogency of the conjectural account by Sir George Tomkyns Chesney (1830–95), a soldier with engineering experience, of an invasion of England by a German-speaking army, which appeared under the title of 'The Battle of Dorking' in *Blackwood's Magazine* in May 1871 (vol. cix, pp. 539–72). Intended to influence public opinion, it excited great interest and was reprinted as a pamphlet and translated into a number of foreign languages. Though it is an able piece of work, its treatment of the possible role of the fleet, which is removed by a diversion and the use of a mysterious machine, is perfunctory. It also assumes that preparations for an invasion could be concealed.

Even had Bismarck wanted to attack Britain, which does not seem to have been the case, it is by no means clear that he would have been able to do so effectively. *GKC*.

6. A new interest in the army probably began with the Crimean War and the Mutiny, and certainly with the raising of the Volunteers in 1859. The first of the Volunteers' annual Easter Monday field man-

œuvres took place at Brighton in 1861, and thereafter they were repeated each year. To judge by the press, they immediately attracted public attention. See the *Illustrated London News*, vol. xxxviii (Jan.– June 1861), pp. 343–55. The 1871 army manœuvres were described and illustrated ibid., vol. lix (July–Dec. 1871), pp. 275–6, 293, 300–3, 318– 19. Sir James Hope Grant (1808–75), after a distinguished career of some 20 years in China and India, was made Quarter-Master-General at the Horse Guards in 1865, and appointed to the command of the Aldershot camp in 1870. According to the *D.N.B.*:

> His tenure of this post marks the beginning of almost a new phase of military instruction throughout the British army. Hitherto the Prussian system of manœuvring troops as two opposing forces had been angrily denounced by most of our military authorities as child- ish, and even pernicious. Grant held a different opinion, persisted in spite of all opposition, and finally succeeded in bringing to pass the autumn manœuvres of 1871–2–3, the value of which has been so fully recognised that the practice thereof has been continued up to the present day.

On the other hand, Sir Robert Biddulph, *Lord Cardwell at the War Office* (1904), pp. 189–90 seems to ascribe the initiation of field man- œuvres in 1871 to Edward Cardwell, Secretary for War 1868–74. However the credit for their initiation is apportioned, it is clear that the training they supplied was badly needed by the regular army. Lord Wolseley (1833–1913), a protégé of Grant, was present at the manœuvres of 1871 as a field officer; and in Sir F. Maurice and Sir George Arthur, *The Life of Lord Wolseley* (1924), pp. 59–60, it is stated: 'the need of systematic training was painfully apparent. The troops . . . were given their tents, but hardly any one knew how to pitch them. They were handed their field cooking utensils, but few knew how to prepare food in them.' In 1871 an Act was passed to facilitate man- œuvres in the autumn in Berkshire, and parts of Hampshire and Surrey. In 1872 they were repeated in Wiltshire and Dorset, and in 1873 on Dartmoor, on Cannock Chase, and at the Curragh. The estimates for 1874 contained provision for manœuvres but none took place, and thereafter none were held on a large scale until 1898. *GKC, DRF.*

SECTION XVII

1. See Morley, *Gladstone*, ii. 146, on Gladstone's electoral speech at Manchester, 18 July 1865: 'In the fine hall that stands upon the site made historic by the militant free-traders, he used a memorable phrase. "At last, my friends," he began, "I am come among you, and I am come among you 'unmuzzled.' " ' *JMC*.

2. The Reform Bill introduced by Earl Russell's Government in March 1866 was defeated on 18 June and the Government resigned. The Earl of Derby formed an administration, with Benjamin Disraeli as Chancellor of the Exchequer and leader of the House of Commons. On 23 July 1866 there was a clash between the police and a crowd intent on holding a reform meeting in Hyde Park, entry to which had been denied to them. Ill-health forced Derby to retire in February 1868 when he was succeeded as Prime Minister by Disraeli, who resigned following the defeat of the Conservatives in a general election at the end of the year.

In 1867 the Derby Government passed the second Reform Act by which the vote, given by the Act of 1832 to the occupiers in boroughs of any land or tenement of an annual rateable value of £10 (see above, p. 45), was extended to all householders. Votes were also given to lodgers. In the counties the occupiers of land or tenements of an annual rateable value of £12 joined the forty-shilling freeholders in enjoying the right to vote. However, under both Acts there were other qualifications for the franchise in the counties. For details of the Act of 1867 see Young and Handcock, *English Historical Documents*, pp. 123, 181–4. Its effects are discussed in F. B. Smith, *The Making of the Second Reform Bill* (Cambridge, 1966), pp. 236–41; and the changes in politics which ensued are dealt with in H. J. Hanham, *Elections and Party Management* (1959). *GKC*.

3. It had been made possible for Dissenters to qualify for a degree at Oxford in 1854 and at Cambridge in 1856. The University Tests Act of 1871 threw open to men of all creeds all lay posts both in the Colleges and the University at Oxford and Cambridge. *GKC*.

4. The Supreme Court of Judicature Act of 1873 (36 and 37 Vict. c. 66) set up one Supreme Court of Judicature in England in which the

Common Law Courts (Queen's Bench, Common Pleas, Exchequer, the High Court of Chancery as a Court of Equity, and other Courts) were merged, thereafter to administer the same law. *GKC.*

5. The source of this remark has not been traced. *GKC.*

6. A procession of match-makers to Parliament to protest against the tax on matches included in Robert Lowe's budget of 1871 degenerated, largely as a result of police mismanagement, into a minor riot. The tax was withdrawn, along with the proposed succession duty, and twopence was placed on the income tax. *GKC.*

7. In 1870 the Tsar took advantage of the defeat of France by Prussia to repudiate those clauses of the Treaty of Paris of 1856 which provided for the neutralization of the Black Sea. In 1872 an international tribunal awarded the United States the sum of 15,500,000 dollars in gold as compensation for damage inflicted during the American Civil War by the *Alabama* and other Confederate cruisers fitted out in Britain. *GKC.*

8. This probably refers to Gladstone's appointments of Mr. Harvey to the living at Ewelme and Sir Robert Collier to the Judicial Committee of the Privy Council. In each case he evaded regulations by a transparent formality, and got himself into trouble. See *Annual Register* (1871), History, pp. 123–5, Chronicle, pp. 133–4; ibid. (1872), History, pp. 17–19, 26–36. *GKC.*

9. This probably refers to the discovery in 1873 that almost £1,000,000, partly from the Post Office, partly from the Post Office Savings Bank, had been applied to the extension of the telegraph system instead of being paid into the Consolidated Fund. It was not a case of the malversation of public money into private hands, but merely into the wrong public fund. See *Annual Register* (1873), History, p. 80. *GKC.*

10. Instead of exercising its forestal rights to prevent the scheme of the lords of various manors in Epping Forest to enclose their land in order to sell it for building lots, the Crown elected to sell its rights at a few pounds an acre. As the Forest was much valued as an open space near London, the matter was taken up in the House of Commons, an inquiry forced, and a motion carried against the Government. See

Annual Register (1871), History, pp. 90–1; *Hansard*, 3rd Ser. ccv. 1852–71. GKC.

11. On 13 Feb. 1873 Gladstone proposed a scheme to extend and reorganize university education in Ireland. It failed to satisfy either Catholics or Protestants and was defeated on its second reading, 11 Mar. 1873, by 287 votes to 284. Gladstone resigned, but resumed office a week later. See *Hansard*, 3rd Ser. ccxiv. 377–429, 1186–277, 1398–513, 1617–713, 1741–868; Morley, *Gladstone*, ii. 434–56. GKC.

12. John Hanning Speke (1827–64) set out in 1856 with Richard Francis Burton (1821–90) on a mission to discover the source of the Nile. In 1858 they separated, and in August Speke discovered the lake which he named Victoria Nyanza and claimed to be the source of the Nile. A dispute with Burton over the validity of the claim led to their estrangement. Speke returned in 1860 with James Augustus Grant (1827–92) to confirm his discovery. On 28 July 1862 he reached the place where the Nile leaves Victoria Nyanza, which he named the Ripon Falls. It was therefore in 1862 that Speke saw the waters of the Nile flowing north. GKC.

13. There is a mistake here. Henslow visited Abbeville and Amiens in 1860, but was not convinced that the flint instruments were of the antiquity claimed for them. He announced his views in two letters to the *Athenaeum*, 20 Oct. 1860 (no. 1721, p. 516) and 3 Nov. 1860 (no. 1723, pp. 592–3), in the second of which he concluded:

> We have cast off old prejudices erroneously deduced from the letter of the Scriptures, in regard to the age of the earth; but we cannot cast off our received opinions in regard to the time man has inhabited the earth, without first feeling assured that these hatchet-bearing gravels must be several thousand years older than the Pyramids of Egypt.

It is possible that he revised his opinion before his death in 1861, but the evidence is inconclusive. See the Rev. Leonard Jenyns, *Memoir of the Rev. John Stevens Henslow* (1862), pp. 214–19. On the other hand, in 1859 Sir Charles Lyell examined the discoveries and announced his conviction of their authenticity to the annual meeting of the British Association (*Report of the Twenty-Ninth Meeting of the British Association for the Advancement of Science held at Aberdeen in September 1859* (1860), Transactions of the Sections, pp. 93–5); and Joseph Prestwich described the discoveries to the Royal Society (*Proceedings of the Royal Society of London*, x (1859–60), 50–9). Presumably the educated layman learnt of the matter through Lyell's *Geological Evidences of the Antiquity of Man*, published in 1863. For many people it must have entailed a revolution in their conceptions of human history. Although Boucher de Perthes had published his claims in 1847, Prestwich declared in 1864 that it was doubtful whether before 1858 and 1859 'there were twenty men of science in Europe who would have admitted the possibility of the contemporaneity of man and of the extinct mammalia' (*Proceedings of the Royal Institution of Great Britain*, iv (Apr. 1864), 213–22). On the development of anthropology in this period see J. W. Burrow, *Evolution and Society* (Cambridge, 1966). *GKC.*

14. The Articles read as follows:

XX. *Of the Authority of the Church.*
The Church hath power to decree Rites or Ceremonies, and authority in Controversies of Faith: And yet it is not lawful for the Church to ordain any thing that is contrary to God's Word written, neither may it so expound one place of Scripture, that it be repugnant to another. Wherefore, although the Church be a witness and a keeper of holy Writ, yet, as it ought not to decree any thing against the same, so besides the same ought it not to enforce any thing to be believed for necessity of Salvation.

XXI. *Of the Authority of General Councils.*
General Councils may not be gathered together without the commandment and will of Princes. And when they be gathered together, (forasmuch as they be an assembly of men, whereof all be not governed with the Spirit and Word of God,) they may err, and sometimes have erred, even in things pertaining unto God. Wherefore things ordained by them as necessary to salvation have neither strength nor authority, unless it may be declared that they be taken out of holy Scripture.

GKC.

15. See his address in the Sheldonian Theatre, Oxford, 25 Nov. 1864: 'instead of believing that the age of faith has passed, I hold that the characteristic of the present age is a craving credulity.' (Monypenny and Buckle, *Disraeli*, iv. 371.) *GKC.*

16. William Sanday (1843–1920) was Ireland Professor of the Exegesis of Holy Scripture from 1882 and Lady Margaret Professor of Divinity from 1895 to 1919. His main achievement was to convey to English scholars an appreciation of the extensive Continental work on biblical criticism, but it is possible that in singling him out Young overestimates his importance. See Section XI, note 16. *GKC.*

17. The *Speaker's Commentary* was a commentary on the Bible undertaken in about 1864 at the suggestion of John Evelyn Denison, Speaker of the House of Commons, to answer questions raised by *Essays and Reviews* and Colenso. A Commission was formed and the Bible was divided into eight sections, each assigned to a different editor. Canon Frederic Charles Cook, assisted by the Archbishop of York and the Regius Professors of Theology at Oxford and Cambridge, was in charge of the whole project. The first volume, on Genesis and Exodus, appeared in 1871 and the fourth, on the New Testament, in 1881. See the *D.N.B.* (Supplement) under F. C. Cook.

Natural Law in the Spiritual World was published in 1883 by Henry Drummond (1851–97), a Scottish Free Church divine, prominent in the Sankey and Moody revival in 1875. He was for a time Lecturer in Natural Sciences at the Free Church College, Glasgow, and in 1879 he accompanied Sir Archibald Geikie on a geological expedition to the United States. In his book, according to the *D.N.B.*, he contended that 'the scientific principle of continuity extended from the physical universe to the spiritual world. The thesis was based upon a series of brilliant figures of speech rather than upon a chain of reasoning.' Although its fallacies were pointed out at the time, the work was enthusiastically reviewed, and within five years 70,000 copies had been sold. Drummond subsequently did important scientific and geological work in Africa.

'Pusey on Daniel' refers to the Rev. E. B. Pusey, *Daniel the Prophet. Nine Lectures, delivered in the Divinity School of the University of Oxford* (Oxford and London, 1864). In the Preface, where he wrote that the lectures represented a 'contribution against that tide of scepticism, which the publication of the "Essays and Reviews" let loose upon the young and uninstructed', Pusey reproduced and adapted from a French Professor at Turin a curious argument. He contended that starting from the received chronology of the Flood (2348 B.C.) with six people, 'and taking as the annual increase 1/227, a number not far from that which represents the annual increase of the population of France', one would arrive at a figure very close to that of the known population of the earth (pp. xxii–xxiii). He considered this to be a fact for which science had to account.

In 1890 in *The Impregnable Rock of Holy Scripture* Gladstone attacked some remarks by Huxley on the story of the Gadarene swine, published in the *Nineteenth Century* in February 1889 (vol. xxv, p. 172). Huxley replied in the *Nineteenth Century* in December 1890 (vol. xxviii, p. 967–79). Gladstone replied in the *Nineteenth Century* in February 1891 (vol. xxix, pp. 339–58) and added a note to the later editions of *The Impregnable Rock*. For his original comment and the note see the revised and enlarged edition of 1891, pp. 171–81, 302–6. Huxley replied in the *Nineteenth Century* in March 1891 (vol. xxix, pp. 455–67). The dispute largely turned on whether the owners of the swine were Hebrews. GKC.

18. This quotation has not been found. If it does come from the *Edinburgh Review* the author would not have been Bishop Wilberforce, who wrote for the *Quarterly*. GKC.

19. The concept of 'Being as Process' presents a significant ethical ambiguity. Process may be conceived as a method by which values which have already been accepted are vindicated, realized, and, perhaps, extended, as in Tennyson's *In Memoriam*, Shelley's *Prometheus Unbound*, and Miss Martineau's letter (see below, Section XVIII, note 4). On the other hand, it may be taken to mean a development which has no ethical significance, as in Hardy's *Dynasts* and, possibly, Meredith's *Woods of Westermain*. If the survival of the fittest means only the survival of those fittest to survive in any given circumstances, the process of evolution is likely to be morally neutral. The following extracts from the three works cited here by Young illustrate his point:

The last stanza of *In Memoriam* (1850):

> That God, which ever lives and loves,
> One God, one law, one element,
> And one far-off divine event,
> To which the whole creation moves.

Section IV of *The Woods of Westermain* (1883):

> Then you touch the nerve of Change,
> Then of earth you have the clue;

Then her two-sexed meanings melt
Through you, wed the thought and felt.
Sameness locks no scurfy pond
Here for Custom, crazy-fond:
Change is on the wing to bud
Rose in brain from rose in blood.

The Fore Scene of *The Dynasts* (1903):

Shade of the Earth:
   What of the Immanent Will and Its designs?
Spirit of the Years:
   It works unconsciously, as heretofore,
   Eternal artistries in Circumstance,
   Whose patterns, wrought by rapt aesthetic rote,
   Seem in themselves Its single listless aim,
   And not their consequence.

Probably the best philosophical discussion of the concept is in A. N. Whitehead, *Process and Reality* (New York, 1929). *GKC.*

SECTION XVIII

1. This account of Henry Fawcett's views, especially when taken with Young's comment on his 'complacency' (see above p. 120), might lead to a serious misunderstanding of them. After discussing the problems created by Chinese emigration to California he wrote:

we should ask ourselves, What will England do, and what would be the effect on our country, if the Chinese at some future day show the same anxiety to come to us, as they have shown to settle in Australia and California? The contingency may be thought too improbable and too remote to be worthy of consideration, yet such speculations may possess interest and importance, if we desire to reflect upon the aspect which progressive civilization may in future ages assume. Probably, in every community, there must be always 'hewers of wood and drawers of water;' and if a whole nation like our own should advance as greatly in wealth, intelligence, and happiness, as we could desire, an inferior race may perhaps come amongst us, to perform the comparatively menial duties which industry requires.

Increasing enlightenment and humanity would prevent such a race being treated with injustice, indignity and cruelty; liberty and all the rights of property would be secured to them, and thus the lot of the whole human race might be improved, if inferior races were gradually enlightened and elevated, by bringing them into contact with the ideas and institutions of a high civilization.

The Economic Position of the British Labourer (1865), pp. 225–6. This was Fawcett's only observation on the prospect described by Young; and, as can be seen, it was only suggested as a remote speculation. On the other hand, he clearly had few illusions about the condition of many of the working class in his own day, and the very small advantages that economic progress seemed to have brought to them. He noted that 'in close contiguity' to growing wealth 'there are still the same miserable homes of the poor', and asked: 'How is it that this vast production of wealth does not lead to a happier distribution? How is it that the rich seem to be constantly growing richer, whilst the poverty of the poor is not perceptibly diminished?' (ibid. pp. 6–7.) He entreated 'commercial men' 'no longer to estimate the prosperity of the country by the amount of wealth which is produced', and to 'inquire how that wealth is distributed', and dwelt on the poverty of the agricultural labourers, the miners, and of the labourers who built the docks, railways, and canals (ibid. pp. 237–9). His remedy was apparently some form of co-operation, and possibly emigration. *GKC.*

2. The group to which Young refers in this paragraph typify the characteristics of those who were on the late Victorian side of the 'frontier' of which he writes on p. 110 above. He apparently conceived his early Victorian study as ending in 1865, but it would be wrong to fix the frontier at any particular date. T. H. Huxley coined the word 'agnostic' in 1869; but some of these people were active rather earlier. After a period at Oxford John Morley (1838–1923) began to work as a journalist in London in 1860, and in 1863 joined the *Saturday Review*. He found its High Church politics uncongenial and became friendly with J. S. Mill and George Eliot. From 1867 to 1882 he was editor of the *Fortnightly Review*, which represented the advanced thought of the day, and was particularly critical of orthodox Christianity. Morley continued the tradition and in 1869 published Huxley's important article on 'The Physical Basis of Life'. Leslie Stephen (1832–1904), son of the prominent Evangelical and civil servant, Sir James

Stephen, became a Fellow of Trinity Hall in 1854 and a Tutor in 1856. As was natural at that time for a man in his position, he was ordained in 1855, but a change in his religious views led him to give up his Tutorship in 1862. Two years later he went to London to work as a journalist and through his articles in the *Fortnightly* and *Fraser's* he became one of the most effective exponents of agnostic thought. A collection of these articles goes to make up his *Agnostic's Apology* (1893).

William Morris (1834–96), the son of wealthy parents, was educated at Marlborough and Exeter College, Oxford, where he formed his lifelong alliance with Edward Coley Burne-Jones (1833–98), son of a Birmingham businessman. At first they were romantically High Church and planned to found a monastery; but in 1854 their religious position became unsettled and, after almost becoming Roman Catholics, they turned to the study of the aesthetic and social significance of art. In 1856 Morris was articled to the architect, George Edmund Street (1824–81), in whose office he formed his association with Philip Webb (see above, Section XV, note 7). Meanwhile Burne-Jones had left Oxford and was studying painting under Rossetti, with whom he persuaded Morris to abandon architecture for painting. Morris's attention later turned to interior and furniture design and in 1861 he founded his firm, with Webb and Burne-Jones as partners. He became an active Social Democrat in the 1880s and was in Trafalgar Square on 'Bloody Sunday' in 1887. He published *News from Nowhere* in 1891. Algernon Charles Swinburne (1837–1909), son of an admiral, was educated at Eton and Balliol. In 1857 he abandoned his High Church views and became a religious nihilist and a republican. At the same time he made the acquaintance of Rossetti, Morris, and Burne-Jones. His reputation began to extend beyond his own circle in 1865 with the publication of *Atalanta in Calydon* and he achieved fame and notoriety in 1866 with his *Poems and Ballads*, which he dedicated to Burne-Jones.

Walter Horatio Pater (1839–94), son of a London physician, entered Queen's College, Oxford, in 1858 and in 1864 became a Fellow of Brasenose, where he remained for the rest of his life. He too was an associate of the Pre-Raphaelites and Swinburne, and wrote for the *Fortnightly*. Young's reference to the *Renaissance* is to Pater's *Studies in the History of the Renaissance* (1873), in which were republished some of his early articles for the *Westminster*. The emergence of Pater, who shared Ruskin's strong feeling for beauty, without his stern moral tone, in some ways represented the beginning of the aesthetic movement. George Meredith (1828–1909), grandson of a prosperous Portsmouth tailor, was articled to a solicitor in London in 1845, but in 1847 he turned to journalism and became a publisher's reader. After 1860 his reputation as a poet and novelist was established. He met and befriended Morley in 1863 and Stephen in 1866. His *Ordeal of Richard Feverel* brought him into touch with Swinburne and the Pre-Raphaelites, and he briefly had a room in the house occupied by Swinburne and Rossetti, but he found their way of life not to his liking. The *Essay on Comedy* referred to by Young is Meredith's work, *An Essay on Comedy and the Uses of the Comic Spirit* (1897), originally produced as a lecture in 1877.

The intellectual and spiritual histories of these people seem to confirm Young's view that round about 1860 there was a change in nineteenth-century culture, after which traditional beliefs and loyalties became less generally acceptable and were rejected by men who earlier would have been unlikely to question them. At the same time, they also confirm his suggestion on pp. 117–18 above, that there was an extensive and significant overlap in the influence of men and women whose intellectual history went much further back. This was true not only of the influence of Mill and George Eliot on the 'agnostics', but also of that of Tennyson, Ruskin, and Rossetti on the 'romantics'. This overlap had important results. Not only was there a less drastic change in nineteenth-century culture at this point than the concept of a 'frontier' might suggest, but even those who were unquestionably on the later nineteenth-century side of the dividing line were not necessarily suitably equipped to handle the problems of the future. The individualism of Morley would not supply an answer to the political problems of the twentieth century, nor the Pre-Raphaelitism of Morris a policy for its Socialism. See above, pp. 170–1. GKC.

3. This surely alludes to F. W. H. Myers's famous reminiscence of George Eliot in *Essays Classical and Modern* (1883), pp. 268–9:

I remember how, at Cambridge, I walked with her once in the Fellows' Garden of Trinity, on an evening of rainy May; and she, stirred somewhat beyond her wont, and taking as her text the three words which have been used so often as the inspiring trumpet-calls of men,— the words *God, Immortality, Duty,*—pronounced with terrible earnestness, how inconceivable was the *first*, how unbelievable the *second*, and yet how peremptory and absolute the *third*. Never, perhaps, have sterner accents affirmed the sovereignty of impersonal and un-recompensing law. I listened, and night fell; her grave, majestic countenance turned towards me like a Sibyl's in the gloom; it was as though she withdrew from my grasp, one by one, the scrolls of promise, and left me the third scroll only, awful with inevitable fates. And when we stood at length and parted, amid that columnar circuit of the forest-trees, beneath the last twilight of the starless skies, I seemed to be gazing, like Titus at Jerusalem, on vacant seats and empty halls,—on a sanctuary with no Presence to hallow it, and heaven left lonely of a God.

That Young was familiar with at least part of this passage is clear from *Daylight and Champaign* (1948 edn.), p. 226. GKC.

4. The 'answers' which Young suggests are perhaps those embodied in the following quotations:

The last stanza of Shelley's *Prometheus*:

> To suffer woes which Hope thinks infinite;
> To forgive wrongs darker than death or night;
>   To defy Power, which seems omnipotent;
> To love, and bear; to hope till Hope creates
> From its own wreck the thing it contemplates;
>   Neither to change, nor falter, nor repent;
> This, like thy glory, Titan, is to be
> Good, great and joyous, beautiful and free;
> This is alone Life, Joy, Empire, and Victory.

Henry George Atkinson and Harriet Martineau, *Letters on the Laws of Man's Nature and Development* (1851), pp. 284–5:

> If we feel a contentment in our own lot which must be sound because it is derived from no special administration of our affairs, but from the impartial and necessary operations of Nature, we cannot but feel, for the same reasons, a new exhilaration on account of the unborn multitudes who will, ages hence, enter upon existence on better terms than those on which we hold it,— contented as we are with our share of the good and evil of human life.—It is a pleasant thing to have a daily purpose of raising and disciplining ourselves for no end of selfish purpose or ransom, but

from the instinctive tendency to mental and moral health. It is a pleasant thing to be free from all arbitrary restraint in ministering to the good—great or small,—of any who are about us. But what a thing it is to have, over and above all this, the conception of a future time, when all discipline will consist in a sweet and joyful surrender to Nature, and all the forces of the universe will combine to lift Man above his sorrows, to expand his old faculties, and elicit new, and to endow him at once with all the good obtained by former generations, together with new accessions far beyond the compass of our thought!

The Epilogue of *In Memoriam*:

> A soul shall draw out from the vast
> And strike his being into bounds,

> And, moved thro' life of lower phase,
> Result in man, be born and think,
> And act and love, a closer link
> Betwixt us and the crowning race

> Of those that, eye to eye, shall look
> On knowledge; under whose command
> Is Earth and Earth's, and in their hand
> Is Nature like an open book;

> No longer half-akin to brute,
> For all we thought and loved and did,
> And hoped, and suffer'd, is but seed
> Of what in them is flower and fruit.

See also above, Section XVII, note 19. GKC.

5. The sentence from Dante, *Monarchia*, ii. 9 may be translated as 'That people which, when all around were contending like athletes for the Empire of the world, prevailed, prevailed by virtue of the judgement of God.' The other Latin phrases in the note may be rendered as follows: *apti nati ad principari*: 'by birth fitted to rule'; *apti ad subiici*: 'fitted to become subjects'; *subiiciendo sibi orbem, bonum publicum intendit*: 'in subjecting the world to its rule, aimed at the common good'; *natura locum et gentem disposuit ad universaliter principandum*: 'nature adopted both the place and the race for universal dominion'; *certamina*: 'contests'; *duella*: 'wars'. The connection suggested by Young between

'the principles laid down in i. 14' and those of the Statute of Westminster of 1931 seems to be fanciful. *GKC.*

6. Charles Wentworth Dilke, *Greater Britain: A Record of Travel
in English-Speaking Countries during 1866 and 1867* (2 vols., 1868).
Far from being a mere 'travel book', it is the expression of an idea, out-
lined in the Preface:

> In 1866 and 1867, I followed England round the world: everywhere
> I was in English-speaking, or in English-governed lands. If I re-
> marked that climate, soil, manners of life, that mixture with other
> peoples had modified the blood, I saw, too, that in essentials the
> race was always one.
>
> The idea which in all the length of my travels has been at once my
> fellow and my guide—a key wherewith to unlock the hidden things
> of strange new lands—is a conception, however imperfect, of the
> grandeur of our race, already girdling the earth, which it is destined,
> perhaps, eventually to overspread.
>
> In America, the peoples of the world are being fused together, but
> they are run into an English mould: Alfred's laws and Chaucer's
> tongue are theirs whether they would or no. There are men who say
> that Britain in her age will claim the glory of having planted
> greater Englands across the seas. They fail to perceive that she has
> done more than found plantations of her own—that she has imposed
> her institutions upon the offshoots of Germany, of Ireland, of Scan-
> dinavia, and of Spain. Through America, England is speaking to
> the world.
>
> Sketches of Saxondom may be of interest even upon humbler
> grounds: the development of the England of Elizabeth is to be
> found not in the Britain of Victoria, but in half the habitable globe.
> If two small islands are by courtesy styled 'Great', America, Aus-
> tralia, India, must form a Greater Britain.

GKC.

SECTION XIX

1. The primary cause of exceptional suffering in East London in 1866 was the failure of industries which had previously provided employment there. The silk-weaving industry had been declining for some time, and a final blow had been given to it by the commercial treaty which Cobden negotiated with France in 1860. The financial crisis which followed the failure of Overend and Gurney had fatal results for the Thames-side shipbuilding industry and its auxiliary trades, and also caused a slump in the building industry and in railway construction. In addition, from July to December 1866 there was a cholera epidemic which claimed 3,909 lives in East London. The harvest was disastrous and the winter of 1866-7 exceptionally severe; and conditions on the Thames dislocated the work of the docks and produced further unemployment. See Gareth Stedman Jones, *Outcast London. A Study in the Relationship between Classes in Victorian Society* (Oxford, 1971), pp. 100-4. The distress in East London in 1866 was highlighted by the fact that in the first half of the year there was an influential movement of protest against the inadequacy of the local Poor Law authorities, particularly in their treatment of the sick poor. In the second half of the year news of the cholera filled the newspapers, and £70,000 was distributed in charity. The epidemic was the occasion for the heroic activities of Mrs. Gladstone both in the London Hospital and in the succour of the children of those who had died. See Norman Longmate, *King Cholera* (1966), pp. 215-22. However, even before 1866 socially conscious men and women had been kept aware by journalists, by the reports of charitable organizations, and by government inquiries of the suffering that was endemic in the East End (see G. Kitson Clark, *Churchmen and the Condition of England, 1832-1885* (1973), pp. 68-70); just as before 1865 Fawcett was fully aware of the poverty that existed in such places as Glasgow and Liverpool (see above, Section XVIII, note 1). *JMC, GKC.*

2. The privilege of limited liability for the shareholders of joint stock companies, whereby the shareholder's liability for the debts of the company was limited to the nominal value of the shares he held and did not involve his whole estate, was gradually extended in the nineteenth century by a series of laws culminating in the Companies Act of 1862 (25 and 26 Vict. c. 89). This clearly afforded a much greater

variety of opportunities for the private investor. In the 1850s the practice invaded the money market and in 1865 the important firm of Overend and Gurney became a limited company. This attracted large public subscriptions but made it necessary for them to publish their accounts and reveal the extent of their indebtedness; and in Walter Bagehot's view it was largely as a result of this that they became bankrupt in 1866 (*Lombard Street* (1873), pp. 273–5). The consequence was a severe panic and financial crisis; but it is as well to compare Young's estimate of its effects with that of Sir Albert Feavearyear, who believed that while it lasted it was the most severe of all nineteenth-century crises, with the possible exception of that of 1825. He contended that there was little or no public panic in 1847 and that in 1857 it was confined to Glasgow and Lancashire, whereas in 1866 it extended to the whole country. However, he held that the position had been more fundamentally serious on the previous occasions, when a number of important banking houses were in danger, while in 1866 most banks were safe, the prestige and resources of the joint stock banks had increased, and banking technique had generally improved. It therefore seems doubtful whether serious permanent consequences can be attributed to this crisis. See Sir Albert Feavearyear, *The Pound Sterling*, 2nd edn., ed. E. Victor Morgan (Oxford, 1963), pp. 301–5. *GKC*, *BRM*.

3. See Cobden's pamphlet on *England, Ireland, and America* (1835) from which significant extracts are quoted in John Morley, *The Life of Richard Cobden* (2 vols., 1881), i. 107–8. *GKC*.

4. Speech on the introduction of the Education Bill, 17 Feb. 1870 (*Hansard*, 3rd Ser. cxcix. 465–6). For the situation which led to Forster's Act see above, pp. 97–8. *GKC*.

5. On Hook see Section XI, note 2. For his educational proposals of 1838 see W. R. W. Stephens, *The Life and Letters of Walter Farquhar Hook*, new edn. (1880), pp. 248–50. *GKC*.

6. Gladstone's memorandum: 'But he was a very impracticable man placed in a position of great responsibility.' (Morley, *Gladstone*, iii. 49.) The comment, written long after 1870, was in fact made on Forster's conduct as Chief Secretary in Ireland in 1880. *GKC*.

7. This statement is questionable. The private lives of many Englishmen had come into contact with the administrative State through the New Poor Law of 1834, through regulations embodied in the Factory Acts, the Public Health Act of 1848, or local Health and Police Acts, particularly since the Public Health Act of 1866 had made a common standard of inspection and regulation in sanitary matters compulsory. In such other matters as the emission of fumes from factory chimneys, or the vaccination of children, regulations imposed by the State had interfered with the lives and free actions of Englishmen. *GKC.*

8. cf. Sir Arthur Conan Doyle, 'The Adventures of Sherlock Holmes. XXIII.—The Adventure of the Naval Treaty', *Strand Magazine*, vol. vi (July–Dec. 1893), p. 401, describing a train journey made by Holmes and Watson:

> Holmes was sunk in profound thought, and hardly opened his mouth until we had passed Clapham Junction.
>
> 'It's a very cheering thing to come into London by any of these lines which run high and allow you to look down upon the houses like this.'
>
> I thought he was joking, for the view was sordid enough, but he soon explained himself.
>
> 'Look at those big, isolated clumps of building rising up above the slates, like brick islands in a lead-coloured sea.'
>
> 'The Board Schools.'
>
> 'Lighthouses, my boy! Beacons of the future! Capsules, with hundreds of bright little seeds in each, out of which will spring the wiser, better England of the future. I suppose that man Phelps does not drink?'

On the development of school architecture in the nineteenth century and the principles adopted in the design of the London Board schools see E. R. Robson, *School Architecture*, with an introduction by Malcolm Seaborne (Leicester, 1972). *GKC.*

SECTION XX

1. See Disraeli's letter to the Queen, 23 Mar. 1868, in which he referred to Gladstone's having raised the question of the disestablishment of the Irish Church: 'It is, perhaps, providential, that this religious controversy should have arisen to give a colour to the character, and a form to the action, of the newly enfranchised constituencies.' (*Letters of Queen Victoria*, 2nd Ser. i. 518.) GKC.

2. See Richard Hooker, *Of the Laws of Ecclesiastical Polity*, Book V, Chapter LXVII, Section 6:

> 'This is my body', and 'This is my blood', being words of promise, sith we all agree that by the sacrament Christ doth really and truly in us perform his promise, why do we vainly trouble ourselves with so fierce contentions whether by consubstantiation, or else by trans-substantiation, the sacrament itself be first possessed with Christ, or no?

GKC.

3. See John William Colenso, Bishop of Natal, *The Pentateuch and Book of Joshua critically examined* (7 parts, 1862-79), the Preface of which takes the form of a letter, dated 4 Oct. 1862, which Colenso said he had addressed to a Professor of Divinity in an English University, but had not forwarded. In it he confessed that as a young man some questions about religion had caused him uneasiness, but that he had contented himself with the 'specious explanations' in the biblical commentaries, and had lost sight of them in parochial work. However, he remained troubled by the stories of the Creation and the Flood:

> But, on the whole, I found so much of Divine Light and Life in these and other parts of the Sacred Book, so much wherewith to feed my own soul and the souls of others, that I was content to take all this for granted, as being true in the main, however wonderful, and as being at least capable, in an extreme case, of *some* sufficient explanation.
> Here, however, as I have said, amidst my work in this land, I have been brought face to face with the very questions I then put by. While translating the story of the Flood, I have had a simple-minded, but intelligent, native,—one with the docility of a child, but the reasoning powers of mature age,—look up, and ask, 'Is all that true?

Do you really believe that all this happened thus,—that all the beasts, and birds, and creeping things, upon the earth, large and small, from hot countries and cold, came thus by pairs, and entered into the ark with Noah? And did Noah gather food for them *all*, for the beasts and birds of prey, as well as the rest?' My heart answered in the words of the Prophet, 'Shall a man speak lies in the Name of the Lord?'

As a matter of fact, Colenso had had problems in teaching in England before he went to Zululand, and had experienced difficulties in imparting to a girl of five the doctrine of eternal punishment. See P. O. G. White, 'The Colenso Controversy', *Theology*, lxv (1962), 402–8. *GKC.*

4. Young almost certainly exaggerates the probability of disbelief in the Gospels and Creed by these three men, particularly Thirlwall and Stanley. The Clerical Subscription Act of 1865 (28 and 29 Vict. c. 122) was passed to put into effect the recommendations of a Royal Commission. The declaration required of a man on ordination was:

> I assent to the Thirty-nine Articles of Religion, and to the Book of Common Prayer and of the ordering of bishops, priests and deacons. I believe the doctrine of the United Church of England and Ireland, as therein set forth, to be agreeable to the Word of God; and in public prayer and the administration of the sacraments I will use the form in the said book prescribed, and none other, except so far as shall be ordered by lawful authority.

J. R. Seeley's *Ecce Homo* excited the wrath of Lord Shaftesbury (see above, Section VI, note 14), but it was nearer to orthodox Christianity than anything in Matthew Arnold's work, and was probably more generally acceptable to believers. *GKC.*

5. See Gladstone to Queen Victoria, 22 Jan. 1874, in reply to her letter suggesting legislation to deal with ritualism. He deprecated legislation, but recognized the fears expressed by ecclesiastical authorities about the future of the Church:

> Mr. Gladstone feels no surprise at these alarms, and is not himself wholly free from them. More than thirty years ago, he was very greatly under their influence. Now, with advancing years, not usually more sanguine, he is even more deeply struck with the tenacious vitality of the Church of England (which Dr. Döllinger, in a masterly survey, declares to be the most powerful National Church in

Christendom) than with its serious dangers, and its unquestionably great and grievous scandals.

He went on to speak of the extremists and of the use he had made of the patronage of the Crown, but concluded:

Amidst the pain and apprehension caused by these extremes, which engender and exasperate one another, he has often to remind himself, and even presumes to remind your Majesty, by way of consolation, of that which he believes to be as indisputable as it is creditable. For centuries past there has not been a time of so much practical and hearty work, so much earnest preaching, so much instruction and consolation given, so much affectionate care for the poor and for the young.

Letters of Queen Victoria, 2nd Ser. ii. 306–10. GKC.

6. See Section XI, note 5.

7. See 'Baptismal Regeneration. A Sermon delivered on Sunday Morning, June 5th, 1864, by the Rev. C. H. Spurgeon, at the Metropolitan Tabernacle, Newington', *Metropolitan Tabernacle Pulpit*, x (1865), 313–28. DRF.

8. The Judicial Committee of the Privy Council decided that:

Our province is, on the one hand, to ascertain the true construction of those Articles of Religion and Formularies referred to in each charge, according to the legal rules for the interpretation of statutes and written instruments; and, on the other hand, to ascertain the plain grammatical meaning of the passages which are charged as being contrary to or inconsistent with the doctrine of the Church, ascertained in the manner we have described. It is obvious that there may be matters of doctrine on which the Church has not given any definite rule or standard of faith or opinion; there may be matters of religious belief on which the requisition of the Church may be less than Scripture may seem to warrant; there may be very many matters of religious speculation and inquiry on which the Church may have refrained from pronouncing any opinion at all. On matters on which the Church has prescribed no rule, there is so far freedom of opinion that they may be discussed without penal consequences. . . . The proposition or assertion that every part of the

Scriptures was written under the inspiration of the Holy Spirit is not to be found either in the Articles or in any of the Formularies of the Church.

See *Annual Register* (1860), Chronicle, pp. 241–6. GKC.

9. The quotation, the last clause of which should read 'and this trust was his righteousness', is taken from the article by Professor Rowland Williams (1817–70), Vice-Principal of St. David's College, Lampeter, on 'Bunsen's Biblical Researches' in *Essays and Reviews*, 4th edn. (1861), p. 61. It is in fact an account of Bunsen's opinions. Young's comment on the Victorian mind reflects Dr. Johnson's observation on 'the anfractuosities of the human mind', meaning its involutions, intricacies, and obliquities (see Boswell's *Life of Johnson* under 1780). Thirlwall's opinions at this time can be assessed from his charge to the clergy of St. David's, delivered in 1857, in which he discussed Williams's sermon on 'Rational Godliness', and from the subsequent published correspondence between the two men. While generally critical of Williams's views, he refuted the more extreme accusations levelled against him and conceded much the same freedom of interpretation of the Bible as was later granted by the Privy Council (*A Charge delivered to the Clergy of the Diocese of St. David's, by Connop Thirlwall, D.D. Bishop of St. David's, at his Sixth Visitation, October 1857* (1857), pp. 61–88). In 1861 Thirlwall, with the other Liberal Bishops, Tait of London and Hampden of Hereford, joined the Bishops as a whole in issuing a general statement which effectively condemned *Essays and Reviews*. According to Archdeacon Denison, he also expressed a strong opinion in favour of the Church resorting to Synodical action in Convocation (George Anthony Denison, *Notes of My Life, 1805–1878* (1878), pp. 291–2). In his important diocesan charge of 1863 he analysed a number of passages in *Essays and Reviews* which appeared to him to be incompatible with the claims of Christianity as a revealed religion and which, though they would have been unremarkable had they been produced by laymen, seemed to him to require condemnation as the work of clergymen of a Christian Church. He seems, however, to have changed his mind as to the appropriate action to be taken, and to have come to doubt the desirability of Convocation intervening in such matters (*A Charge delivered by Connop Thirlwall at his Eighth Visitation* (1863), pp. 98 ff.). Thirlwall also opposed the condemnation of Colenso. His biographer believed that in 1861 he was persuaded to

act as he did by Bishop Wilberforce, but that he later fell under the influence of Dean Stanley (John Connop Thirlwall, *Connop Thirlwall, Historian and Theologian* (1936), pp. 225-44). It seems more likely that he came personally to distrust Convocation as a potential arbiter on such questions, and he does not appear at any time to have favoured resorting to the Church Courts, where proceedings were initiated against Williams by Walter Kerr Hamilton, Bishop of Salisbury. GKC.

10. Charles Voysey (1828-1912), Vicar of Healaugh, Tadcaster, was found guilty of publishing heretical writings by the Chancery Court of the Diocese of York in December 1869. He appealed to the Privy Council and conducted his own defence, but their judgement of 11 Feb. 1871 sustained the previous decision, and pronounced sentence of deprivation, with costs, against him. In summing up its decision, the Privy Council declared:

> We have not been unmindful of the latitude wisely allowed by the Articles of Religion to the clergy. . . . Neither have we omitted to notice the previous decisions of the Ecclesiastical Courts, and especially the judgements of this tribunal, by which interpretations of the Articles of Religion which by any reasonable allowance for the variety of human opinion can be reconciled with their language, have been held to be consistent with a due obedience to the laws ecclesiastical, even though the interpretation in question might not be that which the tribunal itself would have assigned to the Article.

See *Annual Register* (1871), Chronicle, pp. 166-87. GKC.

11. Letter to the *Globe*, July 1862, refuting a suggestion that he intended to return to the Church of England: 'I do hereby profess *ex animo* with an absolute internal assent and consent, that Protestantism is the dreariest of possible religions; that the thought of the Anglican service makes me shiver, and the thought of the Thirty-nine Articles makes me shudder.' (Wilfrid Ward, *The Life of John Henry Cardinal Newman* (2 vols., 1912), i. 581.) GKC.

12. For the Commission on Ritual see H.C. (1867) xx. 719-896 and H.C. (1867-8) xxxviii. The evidence it collected gives an account of the ritualistic practices of the day and also some idea of what was common in more normal churches. It also gives an estimate of the size of congregations and attempts to analyse their social composition.

The practice of 'rubbing black powder on the faces of the people' probably refers to that whereby devout members of the congregation burnt the previous year's Palm Sunday cross on Ash Wednesday and sprinkled the ashes on their foreheads. Sprinkling holy water on candles on particular occasions is practised by quite moderate churches and might seem to be at the least innocuous. Giving an acolyte a decanter to hold was probably to enable him to provide water, either for the mixed chalice, at this date a source of controversy, or for use in the ablutions after Communion. *GKC.*

13. The decrees of the Twentieth Ecumenical Council which met in Rome in 1869–70 and established the infallibility of the Pope as a dogma. Perhaps some idea of the reaction they provoked in this country can be gathered from Gladstone's pamphlet, *The Vatican Decrees in their bearing on Civil Allegiance: A Political Expostulation* (1874), and its reception. The matter is discussed in E. R. Norman, *Anti-Catholicism in Victorian England* (1968), pp. 80–104. *GKC.*

14. The phrase was used by Disraeli in the House of Commons, 15 July 1874 (*Hansard*, 3rd Ser. ccxxi. 80). *GKC.*

SECTION XXI

1. See the Report presented to the Trades Union Commissioners by the examiners appointed to investigate trade union malpractice in Sheffield (H.C. (1867) xxxii. 397–866). It has been reprinted as *The Sheffield Outrages*, with an introduction by Sidney Pollard (Bath, 1971). *DRF.*

2. Disraeli wrote the greater part of *Endymion*, his last complete novel, between 1870 and 1873, before he became Prime Minister for the second time; but he did compose at least the last fifth of the book while in office, between 1878 and 1880. Young's implication that the social legislation of his second ministry represented the fulfilment of the concept of paternalistic Tory democracy adumbrated by him when in opposition to Peel in the 1840s can no longer be accepted. See Robert Blake, *Disraeli* (1966), pp. 552–6, 732–9; Paul Smith, *Disraelian Conservatism and Social Reform* (1967), pp. 198–325; below, Section XXII, note 2.

For Young's references to Cross, see G. W. E. Russell, *Collections and Recollections*, 7th edn. (1904), p. 222: 'the statesman once characteristically described by Lord Beaconsfield as "Mr. Secretary Cross, whom I can never remember to call Sir Richard" '; and p. 328: 'Lord Cross, when the House laughed at his memorable speech in favour of Spiritual Peers, exclaimed, in solemn remonstrance, "I hear a smile." ' *GKC, RR.*

3. Translation of a jingle current in Prussia at the time of Palmerston's dismissal from office in 1851:

> Hat der Teufel einen Sohn
> So ist er sicher Palmerston.

See the *D.N.B. JPTB.*

4. See *The Times*, 30 Jan. 1864, p. 5c. It is pertinent to note that the period of extreme economy in corporate expenditure in Birmingham had begun to draw to a close in 1859. *GKC.*

5. For the history and statistics of public health in Birmingham, and the Corporation's treatment of the Medical Officer, see John Thackray Bunce, *History of the Corporation of Birmingham* (3 vols., Birmingham, 1878–1902), ii. 95–151; Conrad Gill, *History of Birmingham*, vol. i (1952), pp. 346–73, 410–30; Asa Briggs, *History of Birmingham*, vol. ii (1952), pp. 67–82. For the general development of municipal government in the town see E. P. Hennock, *Fit and Proper Persons. Ideal and Reality in Nineteenth-Century Urban Government* (1973), pp. 17–176. *GKC.*

SECTION XXII

1. On his defeat in 1874 Gladstone determined to retire from the leadership of the Liberal party, and thereafter attended the House of Commons intermittently. He did not, however, formally retire till just before the Parliamentary session of 1875, when the Marquis of Hartington was elected in his place. *GKC.*

2. The 'two Trade Union Bills' were the Conspiracy and Protection of Property Act (38 and 39 Vict. c. 86), which amended the law of conspiracy to free the non-criminal activities of trade unions from

prosecution, and repealed the Criminal Law Amendment Act of 1871 (34 and 35 Vict. c. 32) which had made even peaceful pickets liable to prosecution, and the Employers and Workmen Act (c. 90), which ameliorated the inequities of the laws relating to masters and servants. The Sale of Food and Drugs Act is 38 and 39 Vict. c. 63, the Public Health Act c. 55 (Scotland, c. 74), and the Artisans' Dwellings Act c. 36 (Scotland, c. 49). The Merchant Shipping Act (c. 88) failed to provide adequate protection to seamen against being sent to sea in over-insured, unseaworthy ships, and Samuel Plimsoll, who had agitated the issue, was provoked into making a scene in the House. Although a more comprehensive and effective Act was passed in 1876, further legislation remained necessary. The problem was taken up by Joseph Chamberlain as President of the Board of Trade, 1880–5, and while he failed to get his Bill of 1884 through Parliament, a Royal Commission was appointed in the same year and reported in H.C. (1884–5) xxxv and H.C. (1887) xliii. A series of Acts, culminating in the code enacted in 1894, were passed in the following seven years.

The Acts of the 1875 session seem to owe less to ideas and principles peculiar to Disraeli's Government than to the factors customarily responsible for the promotion of nineteenth-century social reform: agitation on specific issues, inquiries by Royal Commissions and Select Committees of Parliament, the views of civil servants, the accumulated experience of successive administrations, and the common stock of ideas of politicians of all parties.

Queen Victoria's refusal to become a patron of the Metropolitan Artisans' and Labourers' Dwellings Association, of whose objects she approved, was based on her general principle of declining to lend her name to financial undertakings, in this case a joint stock company. See Sir Thomas Biddulph to Disraeli, 1 July 1875 (*Letters of Queen Victoria*, 2nd Ser. ii. 411). Swindlehurst, a fellow director, and an auctioneer were imprisoned for their involvement in the purchase of land and its subsequent sale to the Association at an enhanced price. See the *Annual Register* (1877), Chronicle, pp. 107, 186–91.

The Public Entertainments Act of 1875 (38 and 39 Vict. c. 21) amended the provision of an Act of 1752 (25 Geo. II c. 36) whereby no house or garden in London or Westminster, even though licensed, could open for public entertainment before 5 p.m., so as to permit opening from twelve noon. *GKC.*

3. Sir Walter Scott, *Marmion*, Introduction to Canto First. *GKC.*

4. See Palmerston to Clarendon, 14 May 1855 (Evelyn Ashley, *The Life and Correspondence of Henry John Temple, Viscount Palmerston* (2 vols., 1879), ii. 313). *DRF.*

5. In November 1876 Tsar Alexander had a conversation with Lord Augustus Loftus, the British Ambassador in Russia, in which he claimed to have no designs on Constantinople and no desire to go to war with Britain. This led to an amicable exchange of telegrams between the Tsar and Queen Victoria on 4 and 6 November (*Letters of Queen Victoria*, 2nd Ser. ii. 494). However, on 9 November Lord Beaconsfield made a speech at the Lord Mayor's inaugural banquet in the Guildhall in which he seemed to speak of the possibility of war (*The Times*, 10 Nov. 1876, p. 8c). *GKC.*

6. See *The Times*, 9 Dec. 1876, pp. 7a–8d. The speakers included the Duke of Westminster, Anthony Trollope, the Bishop of Oxford, George Howell, Lord Shaftesbury, E. A. Freeman, James Bryce, Henry Fawcett, and Gladstone. Although there was talk of applying force to Turkey, and one speaker envisaged seizure of her navy by the British fleet, it is difficult to discern in the speeches any proposal to embark on the precisely conceived military adventure described by Young. The general view seems to have been that force would be brought to bear on Turkey by Russia, or that moral pressure would be exerted by the Concert of Europe; and there was a general anxiety to persuade Turkey that she could not rely on Britain for protection. Many speakers expressed a wish to strengthen Lord Salisbury's hand, while Fawcett and Gladstone attacked the Government with great bitterness. On this meeting and its sequels see R. T. Shannon, *Gladstone and the Bulgarian Agitation, 1876* (1963), pp. 258–64. *GKC.*

7. Young has misquoted Gladstone's letter to Bright, 14 July 1882: 'The act of Tuesday was a solemn and painful one, for which I feel myself to be highly responsible' (Morley, *Gladstone*, iii. 84). *GKC.*

SECTION XXIII

1. This presumably refers to Bright's speech in the House of Commons, 17 Feb. 1866 (*Hansard*, 3rd Ser. clxxxi. 689–90). See also Trevelyan, *Bright*, pp. 347–9. *GKC.*

2. Both Cobden and Bright became interested in Irish land reform in the late 1840s, and wished to transfer control of their lands to a significant number of Irish farmers, by first giving them security of tenure, and then facilitating land purchase. See Bright's speech in Dublin, 30 Oct. 1866 (*Speeches on Questions of Public Policy by John Bright*, ed. James E. Thorold Rogers (2 vols., 1868), i. 372-4). The 'Bright Clause' in Gladstone's Land Act of 1870 provided that tenants could borrow two-thirds of the purchase price of their holdings on a 5 per cent annuity for thirty-five years. Although little used, this provision, and the purchase clause in the Disestablishment Act of 1869, provided precedents for more effective arrangements made by subsequent legislation. To that extent Young's claim for Bright is justified. For his views on land purchase in 1886 see Trevelyan, *Bright*, p. 447. *KBN*, *GKC*.

3. See John Stuart Mill, *Principles of Political Economy*, 3rd edn. (2 vols., 1852), i. 399:

> There is no necessity for depriving the landlords of one farthing of the pecuniary value of their legal rights; but justice requires that the actual cultivators should be enabled to become in Ireland what they will become in America—proprietors of the soil which they cultivate.
>
> Good policy requires it no less. Those who, knowing neither Ireland nor any foreign country, take as their sole standard of social and economical excellence English practice, propose as the single remedy for Irish wretchedness, the transformation of the cottiers into hired labourers. But this is rather a scheme for the improvement of Irish agriculture, than of the condition of the Irish people. The status of a day labourer has no charm for infusing forethought, frugality, or self-restraint, into a people devoid of them.

These passages, from Book II, Chapter X, date from this edition of the book. *GKC*.

4. See above, p. 60.

5. On 27 Feb. 1865, in a debate on the state of Ireland, Palmerston said: 'As to tenant-right, I may be allowed to say that I think it is equivalent to landlords' wrong.' (*Hansard*, 3rd Ser. clxxvii. 823.) He

also believed that land reform would be of little benefit to Ireland as the country's most urgent need was an influx of capital. *GKC.*

6. See Gladstone to Queen Victoria, 23 May 1885 (*Letters of Queen Victoria,* 2nd Ser. iii. 652–5). *GKC.*

7. The Central Irish Board, or Council, proposed by Joseph Chamberlain in 1885 in the mistaken belief that it would satisfy Parnell, was to be an elected, or representative, body which would have the widest possible control over Irish local affairs, but not the powers of a separate legislature. The Cabinet rejected the scheme on 9 May and thus ended the attempts of Chamberlain and Dilke to solve the Irish question in that government. See C. H. D. Howard, 'Documents relating to the Irish "Central Board" Scheme, 1884–5', and 'Joseph Chamberlain, Parnell and the Irish "Central Board" Scheme, 1884–5', *Irish Historical Studies,* viii (1952–3), 237–63, 324–61. *GKC.*

8. See Bright's letters to Chamberlain of 15 Dec. 1885 and 4 Feb. 1886 (Trevelyan, *Bright,* p. 446). Bright had, however, spoken of 'Irish rebels' in 1883 (Morley, *Gladstone,* iii. 111–12), and in his address to his constituents in 1886 he said: 'My six years' experience of the Irish party, of their language in the House of Commons, and of their deeds in Ireland makes it impossible for me to consent to hand over to them the property and the rights of four millions of the Queen's subjects, our countrymen in Ireland.' (*Annual Register* (1886), History, p. 232.) *GKC.*

9. See the diary of Queen Victoria under 12 Jan. 1840: 'Stockmar's saying Albert had no idea how high parties ran here; of its being worse within these last 2 years, and that I was sure it couldn't go on so. "Oh! it will,—it'll lumber along," Lord M. answered.' (*The Girlhood of Queen Victoria. A Selection from Her Majesty's Diaries between the Years 1832 and 1840,* ed. Viscount Esher (2 vols., 1912), ii. 295.) *GKC.*

10. See Walter L. Arnstein, *The Bradlaugh Case; a Study in Late Victorian Opinion and Politics* (Oxford, 1965). *GKC.*

11. On the changes in procedure described in the preceding two paragraphs see Josef Redlich, *The Procedure of the House of Commons* (3 vols., 1908), i. 133–85, and Edward Hughes, 'The Changes in Parliamentary

Procedure, 1880–1882', in *Essays Presented to Sir Lewis Namier*, ed. Richard Pares and A. J. P. Taylor (1956), pp. 289–319. *GKC, JMC.*

12. Young may be referring to the views expressed by Salisbury in his speech to the Middlesex Conservatives in June 1875 (F. S. Pulling, *The Life and Speeches of the Marquis of Salisbury* (2 vols., 1885), i. 216–17), but what he said then should be compared with his remarks on legislation in the House of Lords, 16 Apr. 1875 (*Hansard*, 3rd Ser. ccxxiii. 1089–90). Salisbury's general view seems to have been that contentious and coercive legislation should only be resorted to infrequently and when it was clear that persuasion had failed. It is relevant to add that he was a member of a government which in 1875 and 1876 carried into law one of the most fruitful legislative programmes of the century (see above, p. 128). *GKC.*

13. For Disraeli's promise see his election address to the county of Buckingham, 24 Jan. 1874 (*The Times*, 26 Jan. 1874, p. 8a). For Gladstone's accusation see his election manifesto in 1880 (Morley, *Gladstone*, ii. 607). *GKC, JMC.*

14. The 'Unauthorized Programme' was a description of the measures supported by Chamberlain in the general election of 1885, which were believed to go beyond those authorized by the official leaders of the Liberal party. The title of 'the supplemental or unauthorized programme' was given to them, in criticism, by a moderate Liberal, G. J. Goschen, in a speech at Glasgow on 14 October, reported in *The Times*, 15 Oct. 1885, p. 8a. Since they were those measures which seemed to Chamberlain to be practical politics at the moment, it is important to distinguish between those on which Chamberlain was prepared to insist at that election and those which he may have promoted before it took place, or was to press in January 1886. Because he fails to do this, and indeed inserts measures for which he has no authority, the list which J. L. Garvin gives in *The Life of Joseph Chamberlain*, vol. ii (1933), pp. 75–6, is not to be trusted. In fact it seems that in the election of 1885 Chamberlain pressed only two measures as being essential if he were to join a Liberal government—what he called 'free education', that is education for which the recipients had not to pay anything; and compulsory land purchase, that is the compulsory acquisition of land by democratically elected local authorities in order to provide a large number of small-holdings for labourers. He did, however,

envisage other measures, which he would develop when the times were more propitious, such as the adoption of a system of discriminatory taxation, the disestablishment of the Church of England and the Church of Scotland, and a system of district councils which might include Ireland. Free education was effectively conceded in 1891. Land purchase never took place in England or Scotland in the form and on the scale which Chamberlain had envisaged. The best account of Chamberlain's programme is C. H. D. Howard, 'Joseph Chamberlain and the "Unauthorized Programme"', *English Historical Review,* lxv (1950), 477–91. *GKC.*

15. The eight dailies may have been *The Times, Daily Telegraph, Daily News, Daily Chronicle, Standard, Morning Post, Morning Advertiser,* and either the *Pall Mall Gazette* or the *St. James's Gazette.* For the London and provincial press at this period see H. R. Fox Bourne, *English Newspapers* (2 vols., 1887), ii. 326–66. *GKC.*

16. 'Limehouse' refers to the type of oratory which Lloyd George directed at the Lords in 1909–10 in speeches at Limehouse and elsewhere; 'Lord Randolph' refers to the popular speeches of Lord Randolph Churchill, probably in particular those aimed at Gladstone. *GKC.*

17. When judging Gladstone's display of apparently excessive emotion on the details of Irish affairs, it is necessary to remember that Lord Frederick Cavendish had been almost a fifth son to him and that after 6 May 1882 he could never think of Ireland without remembering his murder. *MRDF.*

18. The League of Cambrai, a coalition of European powers formed in 1508, was aimed at the destruction of the republic of Venice. The two Irishmen were Shaw and Wilde, but Galsworthy and Wells, although not Irish, were equally critical of contemporary English society. *GKC.*

SECTION XXIV

1. For '1885' read '1884'. *GKC.*

2. The Corrupt and Illegal Practices Act of 1883 had already made a considerable difference to election techniques before the legislation of 1885. It effectively reduced expenses and seems to have put an end to many traditional abuses, although it did not eliminate bribery from really corrupt constituencies. See H. J. Hanham, *Elections and Party Management* (1959), pp. 262–83, and Cornelius O'Leary, *The Elimination of Corrupt Practices in British Elections 1868–1911* (Oxford, 1962), pp. 159–78. *GKC.*

3. Auberon Herbert (1838–1906), 3rd son of the 3rd Earl of Carnarvon, was returned as a Radical for Nottingham in 1870. He attempted to support Dilke's motion for an inquiry into the civil list, 19 Mar. 1872, but was continually interrupted before the House was cleared of strangers. In the course of his speech he affirmed that 'he considered the Republican form of government a better and a more reasonable form of government than the Monarchical'. Dilke, however, was allowed to address the House at considerable length, although he had given offence by appearing to attack the Queen in a speech at Newcastle. Gladstone's 'invective' in reply to Dilke came in the same debate (*Hansard*, 3rd Ser. ccx. 251–317). The vote on the grant to Prince Arthur, Duke of Connaught, took place on 31 July 1871. There was in fact more than one division. The government's proposal that an annuity of £15,000 be paid out of the Consolidated Fund to the Prince from his coming of age, in addition to the moneys granted to the Crown under the civil list, was opposed by P. A. Taylor of Leicester; and G. Dixon of Birmingham moved an amendment to reduce the grant to £10,000. 51 Members supported the amendment and 289 opposed it. Then 276 Members voted in favour of the original motion and 11 against it, that is, presumably, against granting any annuity at all (ibid. 3rd Ser. ccviii. 570–90). *GKC.*

4. See Boswell's *Life of Johnson* under 9 May 1772: 'He [Johnson] said, "Walpole was a minister given by the King to the people: Pitt was a minister given by the people to the King,—as an adjunct." ' *GKC.*

5. Bagehot really described the constitution as it existed *before* the Reform Act of 1867, and in the introduction to the second edition of *The English Constitution* (1872), p. vi, he said his book 'describes the English Constitution as it stood in the years 1865 and 1866. Roughly speaking, it describes its working as it was in the time of Lord Palmerston; and since that time there have been many changes, some of spirit and some of detail. In so short a period there have rarely been more changes.' I do not think he would have claimed that there had been changes or the signs of future change on the points on which Young comments; but it is important to remember that he himself considered that his work had dated very quickly. *GKC.*

6. Queen Victoria to Earl Granville, 8 Aug. 1880:

A *Democratic Monarchy* (as described by Mr. Briggs in his address to that Communistic French Ambassador M. Challemel-Lacour, which proceedings she thinks *very objectionable*) she will not *consent to belong to. Others* must be found *if* that is to be, and she *thinks* we are on a dangerous and doubtful slope which may become too rapid for us to stop, when it is too late.

Letters of Queen Victoria, 2nd Ser. iii. 131. *GKC.*

7. The Marquis of Salisbury to Queen Victoria, 9 July 1889, on the individuals to be nominated for the Committee on Royal Grants: 'There are *no* Moderate Liberals in the present day. The old judicial type of Member, who sat rather loose to his Party and could be trusted to be fair on an occasion of this kind, has disappeared. They are all partisans, and will vote as the Radicals tell them.' (*Letters of Queen Victoria*, 3rd Ser. i. 510.) *RR.*

8. Queen Victoria to Sir Henry Ponsonby, 23 July 1892, on the change of government which she viewed with 'utter disgust': 'As for the trouble and fatigue to the Queen, which she feels particularly unfit for, not one of these greedy place-seekers . . . care a straw for what their old Sovereign suffers. This is a very bitter feeling.' (*Letters of Queen Victoria*, 3rd Ser. ii. 132.) *GKC.*

SECTION XXV

1. See the tables in Michael G. Mulhall, *The Dictionary of Statistics*, 4th edn. (1899), pp. 13–18, and Chart V in Christabel S. Orwin and Edith H. Whetham, *History of British Agriculture 1846–1914* (1964), p. 391. GKC.

2. These lines come from different verses of Tennyson's 'Prefatory Poem to my Brother's Sonnets', written in 1879. From verse I:

> The cuckoo of a joyless June
> Is calling out of doors . . .

and from verse III:

> The cuckoo of a worse July
> Is calling thro' the dark . . .

GKC.

3. Albert Grant (1830–99) is said to have been the pioneer of modern company promoting. By collecting lists of clergymen, widows, and the like he discovered a large body of small investors who were anxious for profit, incautious and inexperienced. The considerable sums he obtained from these sources tempted him to embark on a large number of ambitious schemes without proper investigation, and he was able to raise about £24,000,000 in capital for projects in which he was interested, of which £20,000,000, on the market value of the shares, was lost. He, of course, received considerable rewards for promotion. In 1865 he was elected Member for Kidderminster and was again elected in 1874 although his election was declared void on petition; and in 1868 King Victor Emmanuel gave him the title of Baron Grant for services in connection with the Galleria Vittorio Emanuele in Milan. In 1873 he purchased a large area near Kensington Palace, demolished the slum property and built a large house upon it, and in 1873–4 purchased Leicester Fields in Leicester Square, and handed them over to the public. Soon after this, however, he had to face a series of proceedings in the bankruptcy court which continued nearly until his death, and in 1876 he was charged by a shareholder with fraudulent promotion. The house in Kensington, used only once for the Bachelors' Ball in July 1880, was demolished in 1883 and the site seized by his

creditors. Grant died in comparative poverty in 1899. See the *D.N.B.* (Supplement). The source of the couplet quoted by Young has not been traced.

In 1873 Trollope started to write *The Way We Live Now*, 'instigated', as he said in his *Autobiography*, 'by what I conceived to be the commercial profligacy of the age'. The career of his character Melmotte was in many ways not unlike that of Baron Grant. Trollope believed that:

> a certain class of dishonesty, dishonesty magnificent in its proportions, and climbing into high places, has become at the same time so rampant and so splendid that there seems to be reason for fearing that men and women will be taught to feel that dishonesty, if it can become splendid, will cease to be abominable. If dishonesty can live in a gorgeous palace with pictures on all its walls, and gems in all its cupboards, with marble and ivory in all its corners, and can give Apician dinners, and get into Parliament, and deal in millions, then dishonesty is not disgraceful, and the man dishonest after such a fashion is not a low scoundrel.

Anthony Trollope, *An Autobiography* (2 vols., 1883) ii. 209–11. GKC.

4. In the period 1888–90 £446,000,000 of capital was called up in London, and in 1890 Barings had to report to the Bank of England that they had underwritten a mass of South American and other securities which the public had not taken off their hands before their own liability became due. The Bank took over the burden and liquidated Barings. See J. H. Clapham, *An Economic History of Modern Britain. Machines and National Rivalries (1887–1914)* (Cambridge, 1938), pp. 7–8. GKC.

5. Between 1832 and 1840 the 6th Duke of Devonshire constructed at Chatsworth, under the superintendence of his gardener Joseph Paxton, the stove, greenhouse, arboretum, and the great conservatory, 300 feet long, 145 feet wide, and 60 feet high. In 1849 Paxton was successful in flowering there the *Victoria regia*, the giant South American water-lily, for the first time in Europe. He subsequently submitted the winning design for the buildings of the Great Exhibition of 1851.

Whittaker Wright was born in 1845 in the north of England. After a period in the United States, where he speculated in mining ventures, he returned to England in 1889 and took up company promoting. His main interest was in mining shares, but he also promoted the unsuccessful Baker Street and Waterloo Railway. His large house and estate at Lea Park, Witley, four miles from Godalming, had an observatory, a private theatre, and, what excited most interest at the time, a billiard room under a stretch of water. Financial difficulties developed towards the end of the century, and on 28 Dec. 1900 two of his companies went into liquidation. In due course Wright was prosecuted under the Larceny Act of 1861 for making false statements in the balance sheets and reports of the London and Globe Finance Corporation, fled to New York, but was extradited. After a long trial in 1904 he was convicted and received the sentence of seven years penal servitude, but took poison and died immediately after sentence. The case was conducted at a time when there was considerable public anxiety about financial frauds and the adequacy of the law to prevent them. See *D.N.B.* (2nd Supplement); *Annual Register* (1903), History, pp. 24–5; ibid. (1904), History, p. 17; Derek Walker-Smith, *Lord Reading and his Cases* (1934), pp. 133–54. *GKC.*

6. It would be difficult to find authority for the universality of this rule, but by the middle of the century a number of landowners were reflecting that they were getting a lower rate of return from their land than from capital invested in Government stock. See F. M. L. Thompson, *English Landed Society in the Nineteenth Century* (1963), p. 290. *GKC.*

7. In 1890 the London County Council promoted the London (Strand) Improvement Bill which embodied the principle that a higher rate should be levied on property deriving a distinct and direct advantage from an improvement such as the Council had effected on the Aldwych site. Since the betterment clauses were struck out in committee it was decided not to proceed with the measure. In 1895, however, parliamentary recognition for the principle was obtained. See A. G. Gardiner, *John Benn and the Progressive Movement* (1925), p. 106. *GKC.*

8. Arnold's attitude to railways seems to have been ambivalent. On the one hand he regarded them and their construction camps as a symbol of the 'homeless, unsocial, herding' which was 'in the main the lot of every population who are brought to live in a place only because they are employed to work in it'. This he contrasted with an earlier form of society, when men and women lived where they had roots and there was a more balanced distribution of the various classes. See his letter to the *Hertford Reformer*, 29 Dec. 1838 (*The Miscellaneous Works of Thomas*

Arnold (1845), pp. 457–61). On the other hand, when the railway came to Rugby he is reported to have said: ' "I rejoice to see it, and think that Feudality is gone for ever. It is so great a blessing to think that any one evil is really extinct. Bunyan thought that the giant Pope was disabled for ever,—and how greatly was he mistaken." ' (Arthur Penrhyn Stanley, *The Life and Correspondence of Thomas Arnold* (2 vols., 1844), ii. 388.)

Shaw's views on the effects of dynamite on capitalism can be found in a lecture delivered to the Liberal and Social Union, 26 Feb. 1885. After discussing the activities of dynamiters in Russia, Austria, and Ireland, he said: 'Now, if Socialism be not made respectable and formidable by the support of *our* class—if it be left entirely to the poor, then the proprietors will attempt to suppress it by such measures as they have already taken in Austria and Ireland. Dynamite will follow. Terror will follow dynamite. Cruelty will follow terror. More dynamite will follow cruelty.' (Bernard Shaw, *Platform and Pulpit*, ed. Dan H. Laurence (1962), p. 11.)

Sir Frederick Bramwell's prophecy was made in the course of a communication 'On some of the Developments of Mechanical Engineering during the last half-century'. Discussing changes in the use of fuel, he remarked: 'however much the Mechanical Section of the British Association may to-day contemplate with regret even the mere distant prospect of the steam-engine becoming a thing of the past, I very much doubt whether those who meet here fifty years hence will then speak of that motor except in the character of a curiosity to be found in a museum.' (*Report of the Fifty-First Meeting of the British Association for the Advancement of Science held at York in August and September 1881* (1882), p. 505.)

In 1914 there were still 'a dozen or more' bullock teams at work on Sussex farms. The last of these was given up in 1929, but in 1931 there was still one team at work in Cirencester (T. Hennell, *Change in the Farm* (Cambridge, 1934), pp. 23–6). *GKC, JMC.*

9. This note clearly refers to Sir George Elliot's scheme for amalgamating the coal industry, discussed in *The Times*, 20 Sept. 1893, p. 4c. Its occasion was the violent series of strikes by coal miners which had begun in 1892, and were partly caused by the fall in the price of coal brought about by competitive price-cutting. Sir George, who had worked as a miner before becoming a coal owner, knew the problems of the industry well, and proposed that it should be controlled by a

semi-public company. See J. H. Clapham, *An Economic History of Modern Britain. Machines and National Rivalries (1887–1914)* (Cambridge, 1938), p. 220. GKC.

10. No instance of Chamberlain's actually calling himself a Socialist has been found, but it was an accusation frequently made against him. See Queen Victoria's Journal, 8 Feb. 1885, reporting a conversation with Hartington: 'He and others of the Cabinet had been very much annoyed at Mr. Chamberlain's language, amongst other things, with reference to taxation, which almost amounted to socialism.' (*Letters of Queen Victoria*, 2nd Ser. iii. 604.) But at this time the term could be attached to either Liberals or Conservatives. On 30 Sept. 1885, for example, Gladstone told the Duke of Argyll: 'I deeply deplore the oblivion into which public economy has fallen . . . and the leaning of both parties to socialism, which I radically disapprove.' (Morley, *Gladstone*, iii. 221.) See above, p. 169, for further references. GKC, JMC.

11. From 1890 onwards, because of the growing volume of departmental legislation, it was deemed necessary to publish *Statutory Rules and Orders* in annual volumes under expert editorship. From the late seventies, owing to the increasing pressure of foreign competition and the palpable success of protectionist Germany, the dogmas of free trade were questioned by a number of people and in 1881 a 'Fair Trade League' was formed. In response to the Franco-Prussian War an agitation for compulsory military service developed which was fiercely opposed by Liberals like John Morley. See F. W. Hirst, *Early Life and Letters of John Morley* (2 vols., 1927), i. 170–5. Colonel Charles Chesney, a Professor of Military History at Sandhurst and the brother of the author of *The Battle of Dorking* (see Section XVI, note 5), was one of those who favoured compulsory service. Forster's phrase comes from his speech introducing the Education Bill in 1870 (see above, p. 121). GKC.

SECTION XXVI

1. The prentices marching through London in 1821 were supporting Queen Caroline in her contest with George IV. The great bell of St. Paul's sounded in 1901 to announce the death of Queen Victoria. The guns defending London were in this case doing so against air attack in the First World War. *GKC.*

2. The phrase 'monogamic idealism about sex' is from C. S. Lewis, *The Allegory of Love* (Oxford, 1936), p. 360. See G. M. Young, *Daylight and Champaign* (1948 edn.), p. 156. *RR.*

3. See Walter Bagehot, *The English Constitution*, 2nd edn. (1872), p. 286: 'The material necessities of this age require a strong executive: a nation destitute of it cannot be clean, or healthy, or vigorous like a nation possessing it.' *GKC.*

4. On the reorganization of local government see J. P. D. Dunbabin, 'The Politics of the Establishment of County Councils', *Historical Journal*, vi (1963), 226–52, and 'Expectations of the New County Councils and their Realization', ibid. viii (1965), 353–79. *JMC.*

5. For Mill's youthful Malthusian activities see Section IV, note 10. The incident was obliquely referred to in a hostile obituary article in *The Times*, by Abraham Hayward, who wrote:

> He must have been a boy in years when a foolish scheme for carrying out the Malthusian principle brought him under the lash of the satirist. In Moore's *Ode to the Goddess Ceres* we find:
>
> > 'There are two Mr. Mills, too, whom those who like reading
> > What's vastly unreadable, call very clever;
> > And whereas Mill senior makes war on *good* breeding,
> > Mill junior makes war on all *breeding* whatever.'

The Times, 10 May 1873, p. 5d. When the Rev. Stopford Brooke reproached him in a sermon on the following Sunday, Hayward replied in a letter to Brooke, which he privately circulated to the influential figures of the day, giving further details of the youthful incident and of Mill's later views on birth control. Mill was defended by, among others, W. D. Christie in a pamphlet entitled *John Stuart Mill and Mr.*

Abraham Hayward, Q.C. As a result of the ensuing public controversy, Gladstone withdrew his subscription to Mill's memorial, although such men as the Duke of Argyll, Lord Salisbury, and Lord Derby all subscribed (Morley, *Gladstone*, ii. 543–4). See Norman E. Himes, 'John Stuart Mill's Attitude Toward Neo-Malthusianism', *Economic History*, i (1926–9), 457–84. GKC, JMC.

6. 'It was thus that Etruria grew strong, and thus, assuredly, that Rome became the fairest of all things.' (Virgil, *Georgics*, ii. 533–4.) GKC.

7. See G. M. Young, *Daylight and Champaign* (1948 edn.), p. 62:

> Speaking of Bellamy's *Looking Backward*, Morris warns his readers that every Utopia must be regarded as the expression of the writer's temperament, and very shrewdly he observes, of reformers of another brand, that they aimed at turning the working classes into middle classes. Perhaps he was thinking of Fawcett, who seriously looked forward to a time, not far distant, when they would all be so respectable that we should have to import negroes and Chinese to do the dirty work.

On Fawcett see Section XVIII, note 1. cf. J. W. Mackail, *The Life of William Morris* (2 vols., 1899), ii. 243–5. GKC.

8. cf. J. S. Mill, *Autobiography* (1873), p. 232:

> The social problem of the future we [Mill and his wife] considered to be, how to unite the greatest individual liberty of action, with a common ownership in the raw material of the globe, and an equal participation of all in the benefits of combined labour. We had not the presumption to suppose that we could already foresee, by what precise form of institutions these objects could most effectually be attained, or at how near or how distant a period they would become practicable. We saw clearly that to render any such social transformation either possible or desirable, an equivalent change of character must take place both in the uncultivated herd who now compose the labouring masses, and in the immense majority of their employers. Both these classes must learn by practice to labour and combine for generous, or at all events for public and social purposes, and not, as hitherto, solely for narrowly interested ones.

GKC.

9. There is a significant difference in both date and background between the first two and the last three books. *Praeterita*, the reminiscences of John Ruskin published 1885–9, and *David Copperfield*, written by Dickens in monthly parts 1849–50, are about pre-Victorian children in unusual circumstances. Ruskin was born in 1819 and spent a peculiarly isolated and regimented childhood. *David Copperfield*, the imaginative work of a creative genius, reflected Dickens's memories of an impoverished and at times bitterly unhappy boyhood which was effectively over by 1827. Juliana Horatia Ewing's novel *Six to Sixteen* was first published in *Aunt Judy's Magazine* in 1872. While partly based on memories of her father's vicarage in the forties and fifties, it drew largely on her experiences as the wife of an army officer after 1867. *A Book with Seven Seals* appeared anonymously in 1928 and was republished under the name of Agnes Maud Davies in 1974. The authoress, born in 1858, was the daughter of the incumbent of Chelsea Old Church and her narrative extended into the seventies. Mary Vivian Hughes, the daughter of a London stockbroker, published *A London Child of the Seventies* in 1934. GKC.

SECTION XXVII

1. Lewis Carroll's *Alice's Adventures in Wonderland* (1865) and *Through the Looking-Glass* (1871), Mrs. Ewing's stories such as *Mrs. Overtheway's Remembrances* (1866–8) or *A Flat Iron for a Farthing* (1870–1), Mrs. Molesworth's novels such as *The Cuckoo Clock* (1877), and Du Maurier's drawings in *Punch* after 1864, certainly contrast with much of the pietistic homiletic literature produced for children in the first half of the century. But the change was neither as simple nor as complete as Young suggests. Fairy stories without moral overtones, such as William Roscoe's *The Butterfly's Ball and the Grasshopper's Feast* (1807), were written from the beginning of the century; Edward Lear's *Book of Nonsense* was published in 1846; and Catherine Sinclair's *Holiday House* (1839), for example, did not take a pietistic view of children. On the other hand, realistic and sympathetic as Mrs. Ewing's books undoubtedly were, she did from time to time feel it to be her duty to inculcate moral lessons; and pietistic books continued to be published, and read, throughout the century. Maria Louisa Charlesworth's *Ministering Children* (1854) was followed, apparently on request, by a sequel in

1862; and *Jessica's First Prayer*, which seems to have been popular, was published anonymously by the Religious Tract Society in 1867. GKC.

2. See 'Juvenile Literature', *British Quarterly Review*, vol. xlvii (Jan. and Apr. 1868), pp. 128-49. GKC.

3. See the description of Mr. Veneering's dinner table in Book I, Chapter 2 of Charles Dickens, *Our Mutual Friend*: 'a caravan of camels take charge of the fruits and flowers and candles, and kneel down to be loaded with the salt'. GKC.

4. Bulstrode is the banker in *Middlemarch*, by George Eliot. The crime of which he is guilty, and the moral evasions and dilemmas which led him to it and which resulted from it, are discussed in Chapter 61. For an account of the reasons for the failure of the marriage of Dorothea and Casaubon see Chapter 48. GKC.

5. Henry Sidgwick (1838-1900), Fellow of Trinity College and Knightbridge Professor of Moral Philosophy, was an important pioneer in the development of women's education at Cambridge, and played a critical part both in the opening of lectures and courses and in the foundation of Newnham College. In 1876 he married the sister of A. J. Balfour, who co-operated with him in his work on psychical research, for which he held that she had a special aptitude. She subsequently became Vice-President, and in 1892 Principal, of Newnham College where she and Sidgwick resided until his death. GKC.

6. Sidgwick's choice, Rose Jocelyn, appeared in *Evan Harrington* by George Meredith published in 1861; Swinburne's choice, Violet North, in *Madcap Violet* by William Black (1841-98) published in 1876. The D.N.B. (Supplement) says that both in this book and in *A Princess of Thule* and *A Daughter of Heth*, 'the delineation of female character was an especial charm'. The occasion of neither Sidgwick's nor Swinburne's choice has been discovered. George Saintsbury's selection came from his introduction to *Pride and Prejudice*, written in 1894 and reprinted in his *Prefaces and Essays* (1933), pp. 208-9:

In the novels of the last hundred years there are vast numbers of young ladies with whom it might be a pleasure to fall in love; there are at least five with whom, as it seems to me, no man of taste and spirit can help doing so. Their names are, in chronological order, Elizabeth Bennet, Diana Vernon, Argemone Lavington, Beatrix Esmond, and Barbara Grant. I should have been most in love with Beatrix and Argemone; I should, I think, for mere occasional companionship, have preferred Diana and Barbara. But to live with and to marry, I do not know that any one of the four can come into competition with Elizabeth.

Elizabeth Bennet appeared in *Pride and Prejudice* (1813) by Jane Austen; Diana Vernon in *Rob Roy* (1818) by Sir Walter Scott; Argemone Lavington in *Yeast* (1851) by Charles Kingsley; Beatrix Esmond in *The History of Henry Esmond* (1852) by Thackeray; and Barbara Grant in *Catriona* (1893) by Robert Louis Stevenson. GKC, JMC.

7. See George Meredith, *An Essay on Comedy and the Uses of the Comic Spirit* (1897), p. 61:

But where women are on the road to an equal footing with men, in attainments and in liberty—in what they have won for themselves, and what has been granted them by a fair civilization—there, and only waiting to be transplanted from life to the stage, or the novel, or the poem, pure Comedy flourishes, and is, as it would help them to be, the sweetest of diversions, the wisest of delightful companions.

GKC.

8. The Contagious Diseases Acts passed between 1864 and 1869 enabled the police to enforce medical inspection and treatment on prostitutes and suspected prostitutes in certain specified military areas. Florence Nightingale and Harriet Martineau had begun the attack on the Acts before Josephine Butler entered the field, although she had previously worked among prostitutes, receiving them into her house with the full consent of her husband Canon Butler. The campaign may be said to have started in earnest in January 1870 with the ladies' appeal and the formation of a national association. The Acts were not repealed until 1886. The Government candidate whom the opponents of the Acts managed to defeat was Sir Henry Knight Storks, a general who was being brought into Parliament to help Cardwell. He had previously been Governor of Malta where he was said to have enforced the Acts with particular severity, and indeed to have expressed a wish to extend them to soldiers' wives. When he put out an address at Newark they

conducted so sharp an agitation that he was unable to stand, and when in November 1870 he stood for Colchester, one of the areas under the Acts, Dr. Baxter Langley was put up to split the Liberal vote. Mrs. Butler herself intervened at considerable physical risk, and he was defeated by the Conservative candidate, but in 1871 came in for the pocket borough of Ripon. At Pontefract in 1872 they unsuccessfully attacked Childers who, having been First Lord of the Admiralty until 1871, had been concerned with the administration of the Acts. The references to Mill and Fawcett are misleading. Mill did little to encourage the movement (see *The Later Letters of John Stuart Mill 1849–1873*, ed. Francis E. Mineka and Dwight N. Lindley (4 vols., Toronto, 1972), under 'Contagious Diseases Acts'); and it seems probable that Fawcett did not sympathize with it (Mill to G. C. Robertson, 6 Nov. 1871, ibid. iv. 1850).

There is a considerable literature on the subject. Josephine Butler herself contributed *Personal Reminiscences of a Great Crusade* (1896), *Recollections of George Butler* [n.d.], and *An Autobiographical Memoir*, ed. George W. and Lucy A. Johnson (1909). For a recent assessment see F. B. Smith, 'Ethics and Disease in the Later Nineteenth Century: the Contagious Diseases Acts', *Historical Studies*, xv (1971–3), 118–35. GKC, JMC.

9. On 20 May 1867 J. S. Mill moved an amendment to the Reform Bill then before the Commons which would have extended the occupation franchise in the counties to women. He was defeated by 196 votes to 73, both Bright and Labouchere voting with him (*Hansard*, 3rd Ser. clxxxvii. 817–45). From then until the end of the century proposals for granting parliamentary votes to women were repeatedly brought before the House. The government normally granted a free vote, although when an attempt was made to amend the Representation of the People Bill in 1884, Gladstone officially opposed it on the grounds that it would endanger the passage of the Bill (ibid. 3rd Ser. cclxxxviii. 1957–64). His arguments were more reasonable and compelling than Young suggests. The various proposals were supported and opposed by men from both parties. Of the Conservatives, Lord John Manners spoke in favour in 1884 (ibid. 3rd Ser. cclxxxix. 92–101), George Wyndham did so in 1897 (ibid. 4th Ser. xlx. 1216–19), and Balfour and Gorst voted in favour. Indeed in 1884, 98 Conservatives voted for the proposal (*Annual Register* (1884), History, p. 135) and there was a Conservative majority in the House when a bill to enfranchise women passed its

second reading in 1897 (*Hansard*, 4th Ser. xlv. 1173–238). The promoters were generally Liberal, although Gladstone was ambiguous. In the early stages Henry James, subsequently Lord James of Hereford, was a determined opponent. He spoke effectively in 1871 in opposition to Jacob Bright's proposal (ibid. 3rd Ser. ccvi. 107–13), but did not speak on the amendment of 1884, although according to the *Annual Register* (1884), History, p. 132, he 'had over and over again expressed his scorn and dislike of the "fad" '. James, although unmarried, was a close friend and adviser of Sir Charles Dilke in the divorce proceedings of 1886, but it may be questioned whether his experience 'of an exceptional breadth' was anything more than vicarious. There were other eminent Liberals among the opponents of the enfranchisement of women, such as Labouchere, Sir William Vernon Harcourt, and ultimately Asquith; and John Bright must be numbered among them. In contradiction to Young's statement, he explicitly stated in a public letter to Theodore Stanton, 21 Oct. 1882, that he had never changed his mind on the subject. He said that he had voted in 1867 rather for Mill than for his measure, and then with great doubt and reluctance; that he had subsequently deeply regretted what he had done and had fully explained his opposition to the measure in the House (*The Public Letters of John Bright*, ed. H. J. Leech, 2nd edn. (1895), pp. 234–5). Bright's explanation is supported by Labouchere, who claimed to have been in Bright's company at the time of the vote in 1867, and said that all who voted for the amendment, except for Mill himself, did so 'as a huge joke' (*Hansard*, 4th Ser. xlv. 1201). Bright's arguments against enfranchisement seem to have been the common ones. His attitude to women is summed up in John Vincent, *The Formation of the Liberal Party 1857–1868* (1966), pp. 209–10, where an extremely revealing letter from his sister is quoted.

A review of the debates suggests that the proposals never had sufficient force to change the law. It took a bitter battle to repeal the Contagious Diseases Acts, a purely technical issue. Over the franchise, masculine, and in some cases feminine, prejudice was more massive and deep seated. The measure had dedicated supporters, such as J. S. Mill, Henry Fawcett, Sir Charles Dilke, L. H. Courtney, and Lord Denman, but the debates suggest that its opponents did not take it seriously. *GKC*.

10. Mary Wollstonecraft to William Godwin, 27 Jan. 1797 (C. Kegan Paul, *William Godwin: his Friends and Contemporaries* (2 vols., 1876), i. 242). On Mary Wollstonecraft see Section I, note 13. *RR*.

11. The fall in the birth-rate among the provident and educated classes after 1875 was no doubt partly due to the greater use of contraceptive measures (see Section IV, note 12), but it was also no doubt due to the postponement of marriage, or greater restraint within marriage. A revolution in attitude on this point is foreshadowed in Montague Cookson, 'The Morality of Married Life', *Fortnightly Review*, N.S. vol. xii (July–Dec. 1872), pp. 397–412. The motive behind the restriction of families may have been the increasing expense of the standard of life which the middle class had come to think was necessary. See J. A. Banks, *Prosperity and Parenthood* (1954). It may also have derived from an increasing recognition of the rights of women as individuals, and not simply as wives and mothers, which is signalized by the passage in 1882 of the Married Women's Property Act after a prolonged campaign, and the steps that were being taken to provide university education for women. But see J. A. and Olive Banks, *Feminism and Family Planning in Victorian England* (Liverpool, 1964). *GKC.*

SECTION XXVIII

1. It is not clear what date Young had in mind in this paragraph. Charles Darwin had died in 1882, Carlyle in 1881, and George Eliot in 1880. Robert Browning died in 1889, Cardinal Newman in 1890 and Tennyson in 1892. Rudyard Kipling came to London in 1889 and within the next year achieved great notoriety. If the date suggested is about 1890, it is perhaps worth remembering that the tendencies discussed on pp. 160–1, and 163 had begun at a much earlier date, and continued after 1890. *GKC.*

2. Plato, *Republic*, x. 619. *GKC.*

3. These strictures cannot be applied to the whole public-school system. In 'College' at Winchester or Eton, at St Paul's, Rugby, and elsewhere, flexible intellectual training of a very high standard was given, and men were produced who, particularly if they passed through Balliol, or some of the other colleges at Oxford and Cambridge, played a very important part in building up and maintaining the administrative system of Great Britain and the British Empire. *GKC.*

4. 'I can tell they are boys from my old school.' The inscription beneath the statue of Sir Philip Sidney on the memorial to the members of Shrewsbury School who were killed in the First World War. Sidney had been a Salopian. *GKC*.

5. Thackeray was the first editor of the *Cornhill Magazine*, 1859–62, and in its heyday made £600 a month out of it. The first number sold 120,000 copies, and the average per number during Thackeray's editorship was 85,000. See Gordon N. Ray, *Thackeray. The Age of Wisdom 1847–1863* (1958), pp. 291–321. The best account of the *Athenæum* is by Leslie A. Marchand, *The Athenæum. A Mirror of Victorian Culture* (Chapel Hill, 1941). He quotes (p. 81) a letter written in 1855 by Beresford Hope, one of the founders of the *Saturday Review*, to the effect that the profits of the *Athenæum* cleared for its proprietor, Charles Wentworth Dilke, £5,000 a year. *GKC, JMC*.

6. For Robert Giffen's address on 'The Recent Rate of Material Progress in England' see *Report of the Fifty-Seventh Meeting of the British Association for the Advancement of Science held at Manchester in August and September 1887* (1888), pp. 808–26. In addition to F. Koenig, *Die Lage der englischen Landwirtschaft unter dem Drucke der internationalen Konkurrenz der Gegenwart* (Jena, 1896), it would be desirable to consult more modern works such as Christabel S. Orwin and Edith H. Whetham, *History of British Agriculture 1846–1914* (1964), and F. M. L. Thompson, *English Landed Society in the Nineteenth Century* (1963). Young's explanation of the troubles of London in the eighties is not a convincing one. Falling income from agricultural rents must have been offset by rising gross rental income from, for example, urban property and mining royalties, and the luxury trades were not as badly hit by the depression as the docks and the sweated trades. Moreover those who suffered unemployment or underemployment do not appear to have been very largely recruited from recent immigration from the countryside. *GKC, BRM*.

7. No doubt there is some truth in what Young says, but he greatly exaggerates the contrast between the last thirty or forty years of the nineteenth century and the period preceding it. Inventions of worldwide importance continued to be made in England and by Englishmen: Sir Henry Bessemer's improvements in the making of steel came into practical use in Sheffield in 1859 and were ultimately perfected by

S. G. Thomas in 1879; the invention of the pneumatic tyre by J. B. Dunlop in 1887 was all-important for the development of motor cars and bicycles; and in the years after 1884 Sir Charles Parsons developed the steam turbine, first for generating electricity and then for propelling ships. Nor did the Victorian reading public disappear in the way Young suggests, for the serious periodicals continued and their contents do not suggest a narrowing of interest. No doubt there was more specialization as science and scholarship became more professional, and fewer scientists were clergymen after Oxford and Cambridge had been to a large extent laicized; but it was still possible for men holding important positions in commerce to complete distinguished scholarly work. Between 1879 and 1899 Thomas Hodgkin (1831–1913), a banker in Newcastle, produced *Italy and her Invaders*, a work of some importance, and in 1906 *A History of England from the Earliest Times to the Norman Conquest*. Another banker, Walter Leaf (1852–1927), after obtaining high academic distinction at Cambridge, entered his family business. His career, which culminated in his becoming Chairman of the London and Westminster Bank and in 1919 Chairman of the Institute of Bankers, did not prevent his co-operating in 1882 in a translation of the *Iliad*, nor from producing between 1886 and 1888 an important edition which he subsequently revised with the collation of new manuscripts. It may be said that Hodgkin and Leaf were exceptional men, but so in their day were Roscoe and Grote. Perhaps in neither case were their activities typical of the society in which they lived, but it cannot be said that such careers were impossible in the late nineteenth century. *GKC*.

8. John Austin (1790–1859), at one time Professor of Jurisprudence in the University of London, lived in Germany 1841–3, and in Paris 1844–8. He maintained his connection with Germany, and his wife Sarah edited and translated a number of German works including those of Ranke (see Section I, note 7). J. S. Mill's relations with De Tocqueville were close, and Mr. and Mrs. Grote's relations with France can be studied in her life of her husband. Mazzini lived in England for a considerable period. *GKC*.

9. It would be difficult positively to identify the 'living critic', since it is a commonplace that Trollope offended contemporary opinion by the account of his mechanical methods of composition in his *Autobiography*, posthumously published in 1883. The matter is effectively discussed by

Donald Smalley in *Trollope. The Critical Heritage* (1969), pp. 6–10. The statements in the *Autobiography* confirmed and emphasized what many critics had been saying about Trollope for a considerable time, and his reputation and popularity would probably have declined anyway. GKC.

10. This rather mysterious statement may refer to Stevenson's reputation for conscious artistry in the choice of the right word. See Walter Raleigh, *Robert Louis Stevenson* (1895), pp. 31–45. GKC.

11. It may be questioned how far the influence of French naturalism was really responsible for the situation in the eighties and nineties. The interest in that aspect of French culture was not new. From the days of George Sand onwards an important section of the intelligent reading public had been interested in French novels, if others had rejected them as immoral, over-sophisticated, and perhaps politically dangerous (see Kathleen Tillotson, *Novels of the Eighteen-forties* (Oxford, 1954), pp. 7–9). What on the whole was new was the development of 'the notion of art as an enclosed world, obedient to its own laws only'. The emergence of that view and the growing division between popular and sophisticated taste must have had a deeper cause than the infusion of French naturalism.

'The intervention of the police' may refer to the prosecution of Oscar Wilde in 1895. 'To bards and painters a certain limited eccentricity had always been permitted' reflects Horace, *Ars Poetica*, 9–10. LGS, GKC, EJK.

12. The 'Shepherd's Chief Mourner' was painted by Edwin Landseer (knighted in 1850) in 1837. His pictures were in general extremely popular, and other pictures by him, such as 'Bolton Abbey in the Olden Time' (1834) or 'The Monarch of the Glen' (1851), appear as frequently. Algernon Graves in his *Catalogue of the Works of the late Sir Edwin Landseer* [1875] listed 434 of his works from which engravings had been made by 1875. No less than 126 engravers had been employed upon them. The 'Meeting of Wellington and Blucher', a fresco painted by Daniel Maclise for the Royal Gallery in the House of Lords, was started in 1857 and completed in 1861. The cartoon for it was bought by the Royal Academy after Maclise's death. The companion picture in the House of Lords was 'The Death of Nelson'. Engravings and lithographs of Maclise's historical paintings were issued by the Art Union of

London. The popular culture of which Young speaks was probably in part created by improvements in the processes of printing and engraving, which made relatively cheap mass production possible. *GKC, LGS.*

13. The source of Morley's remark has not been traced. *GKC.*

14. cf. G. M. Young, *Daylight and Champaign* (1948 edn.), pp. 163–4:

There is in Tennyson's literary character a well-marked strain of journalistic adaptability. From the rick-burners of 1830 to the Krakatoa sunsets of 1883, all was copy that came to his muse. In *Maud*, the hero learns 'to feel with his native land'; and Tennyson had learnt to feel about Company Promoting and Industrial Insurance as the Christian Socialists felt: about the Northern Anarch and John Bright as a warlike electorate felt.

The topical allusions in Tennyson's poetry cited by Young are as follows.

Chancery Procedure—from *Edwin Morris; or the Lake*:

<blockquote>

But for me,
They set an ancient creditor to work:
It seems I broke a close with force and arms:
There came a mystic token from the King
To greet the Sheriff, needless courtesy!
I read, and fled by night . . .
</blockquote>

Company Promoting—from *Maud*, Part I, verse 3:

<blockquote>
Did he fling himself down? who knows? for a vast speculation
had failed,
And ever he muttered and maddened, and ever wanned with
despair,
And out he walked when the wind like a broken worldling wailed,
And the flying gold of the ruined woodlands drove through the
air . . .
</blockquote>

Industrial Insurance—from *Maud*, Part I, verse 12:

<blockquote>
When a Mammonite mother kills her babe for a burial fee,
And Timour-Mammon grins on a pile of children's bones . . .
</blockquote>

Coaling Stations—from 'The Fleet', published in *Tiresias* (1886), with
as a note a quotation from a speech by Sir Graham Berry at the Colonial
Institute, 9 Nov. 1886, on the need for coaling stations:

> Her dauntless army scattered, and so small,
> Her island-myriads fed from alien lands . . .

GKC, JG.

15. 'To burn always with this hard gem-like flame, to maintain this
ecstacy, is success in life.' (Walter H. Pater, *Studies in the History of the
Renaissance* (1873), p. 210.) *GKC.*

16. Utamaro (1753–1806) was a Japanese painter; Benvenuto Cellini
(1500–71) the Renaissance artist of whose autobiography John Adding-
ton Symonds published a translation in 1887; José-Maria de Heredia
(1803–39) a Cuban poet; and Narcisse Virgilio Diaz (1808–76) a
French painter. *FBS, GKC.*

17. 'John Henry' is John Henry Newman. The quotation is from his
essay on St. Gundleus, the hermit saint: 'their deeds and sufferings
belong to countries far away, and the report of them comes musical and
low over the broad sea.' (*The Lives of the English Saints*, ed. Arthur
Wollaston Hutton (6 vols., 1900–1), iii. 8.) It seems rather extravagant
to call James Garbett 'the grandfather of aestheticism'. An Evangelical
and a strong opponent of the Oxford Movement, he was elected Professor of Poetry in 1842 in opposition to the Tractarian Isaac Williams.
Dean Church described him as 'an accomplished gentleman of high
culture, believed to have an acquaintance, not common then in Oxford,
with foreign literature, whose qualifications stood high in the opinion
of his University friends, but who had given no evidence to the public
of his claims to the office' (R. W. Church, *The Oxford Movement* (1891),
p. 274). The source of his remark at a viva has not been traced. *Guy
Livingstone* by G. A. Lawrence was published anonymously in 1857, but
no 'old Irish story' appears there. *GKC, JMC.*

18. 'Efficiency' was the key word of a movement promoted at the
beginning of the twentieth century by those who were shocked by the
exposures of inefficiency in the Boer War, and afraid of the dangers to
Britain of the competition of such nations as Germany and Japan. Lord
Rosebery was not the only one to give the word currency: in 1901, for

example, a journalist named Arnold White published a book called *Efficiency and Empire*. Nor was the word new: in 1859 J. S. Mill had prescribed as an ideal for government 'the greatest dissemination of power consistent with efficiency' (*On Liberty* (1859), p. 204), and there are earlier instances of its use. See G. R. Searle, *The Quest for National Efficiency* (Oxford, 1971). GKC.

19. See, for example, the case of George Cottar, the hero of Rudyard Kipling's story 'The Brushwood Boy' published in *The Day's Work* (1898):

> It dawned on him, that a regiment in India was nearer the chance of active service than he had conceived, and that a man might as well study his profession. A major of the new school backed this idea with enthusiasm, and he and Cottar accumulated a library of military works, and read and argued and disputed far into the nights. But the adjutant said the old thing: 'Get to know your men, young 'un, and they'll follow you anywhere. That's all you want—know your men.'

GKC.

20. Tyndall's speech was made at a banquet held in his honour, 29 June 1887, on his retirement from the Chair of Natural Philosophy in the Royal Institution. He said that in Europe governments had given large sums to science and scientific education:

> In England we had nothing of this kind, and to establish an equivalent state of things we had to appeal, not to the Government, but to the people. They have been roused by making the most recondite discoveries of science the property of the community at large. And as a result of this stirring of the national pulse—this development of self-reliance—we see schools, colleges, and universities now rising in our midst, which promise by and by to rival those of Germany in number and importance.

The Times, 30 June 1887, p. 10d.

Sir William de Wiveleslie Abney (1843–1920) was an officer in the Royal Engineers, who in 1877 joined the Science and Art Department at South Kensington as Inspector of Science Schools. In 1884 he became Assistant Director for Science, in 1893 Director and in 1899 Principal Assistant Secretary to the Board of Education. He retired in 1903. It is stated in the *D.N.B.* (1912–21) that in 1877 there were not half a dozen practical laboratories connected with the Science and Art Department which were suitable for teaching purposes, but that at the end of seven years more than a hundred were in existence, and that by 1903 there were, owing to Abney's initiative, more than a thousand chemical or physical laboratories, besides laboratories for mechanics, metallurgy, and biology. *GKC*.

21. The School Inspector is Matthew Arnold. 'Porro unum est necessarium' ('But one thing is needful') comes from Luke, 10:42, where it characterizes Mary's choice while Martha was 'troubled about many things'. Arnold used the phrase as the title of an essay on the importance of organizing the secondary education of the country (*Mixed Essays*, 2nd edn. (1880), pp. 143-79). But in *Culture and Anarchy* (1869), pp. 174-5, he attacked the Puritans for believing that in their religion they possessed the 'one thing needful', and that therefore they did not need to bother whether they encouraged 'vulgarity, hideousness, ignorance, violence'. He said: 'The real *unum necessarium* for us is to come to our best at all points.' *GKC*.

SECTION XXIX

1. The Union Chargeability Act of 1865 (28 and 29 Vict. c. 79) transferred the expenses of the Poor Law from the parish to the much larger area of the Poor Law Union. The parish authorities had therefore no longer any occasion to remove anyone requiring relief to the parish in which he had his 'settlement' and which consequently had a financial responsibility to relieve him, and such removals were discouraged. This put an end to the practice whereby parish authorities endeavoured to prevent anyone who might possibly come on the rates from stopping long enough in the parish to acquire a settlement; and this in turn made it much easier for a labourer to move from his home to a place where he could find work.

For the destruction of rural society and the exodus of the farm labourers from the countryside see Thomas Hardy's article on 'The Dorsetshire Labourer' in *Longman's Magazine*, vol. ii (1883), pp. 252-69; H. Rider Haggard, *A Farmer's Year, being his Commonplace Book for 1898* (1899), pp. 73, 170-1, 203, 338-9, 408-9, 457-69, and *Rural England* (2 vols., 1902). While neither was precise about dates, Hardy saw the decline as having begun some twenty years earlier, and Rider Haggard in about 1870. In *Rural England*, i. 282-6 the latter cited Hardy's article with approval and printed a long letter from Hardy describing the change. *GKC*.

2. The Warwickshire Agricultural Labourers' Union was formed by Joseph Arch (1826-1919) in 1872, not 1870. The 'Reform of 1885' presumably refers to the third Reform Act, which enfranchised the agricultural labourer, and was in fact passed in 1884. *GKC*.

3. See Section XXVIII, note 6.

4. The orderliness of Victorian London and of Victorian England in general is easily exaggerated, as the history of the Salvation Army, the relations of the Irish with their neighbours, and elections demonstrate. See Donald Richter, 'The Rôle of Mob Riot in Victorian Elections, 1865-1885', *Victorian Studies*, xv (1971-2), 19-28. *GKC*.

5. On 7 Feb. 1886 a meeting in Trafalgar Square led to disorder, and windows were broken in Pall Mall. See *Annual Register* (1886), Chronicle, p. 6. On 13 Nov. 1887, 'Bloody Sunday', an attempt to hold a meeting which had been forbidden the use of the Square resulted in a battle between the crowd and the police. Eventually the Square was cleared by the military. There were over one hundred casualties and two of the crowd died of their injuries. See ibid. (1887), Chronicle, p. 54. *GKC*.

6. There seems to be little doubt that the dynamite outrages were in general the work of Irish Fenians, and the result of an organized, if futile, campaign of terrorism largely financed from America. The most serious incidents took place in 1883, 1884, and 1885, but there was a threat of recrudescence as late as 1896. One incident, however, must be attributed to foreign anarchists. On 15 Feb. 1894 Martial Bourdin, a French tailor of known anarchistic views, blew himself up in Greenwich Park near to the Royal Observatory. What he was doing or intended to do is obscure, but the police theory was that he had planned to blow up the Observatory. The episode was made the subject of Joseph Conrad's novel *The Secret Agent* (1907). It is discussed in Eloise Knapp Hay, *The Political Novels of Joseph Conrad* (Chicago and London, 1963), pp. 219-63. *GKC*.

7. Edward Denison (1840–70) was the son of Edward Denison, Bishop of Salisbury. While acting as an almoner for the Society for the Relief of Distress in the District of Stepney he became dissatisfied with a form of charity which seemed to have as its only end the distribution of doles, and in 1867 he went to live in Philpot Street, off the Mile End Road, in order to study conditions at first hand. After eight months he left to stand for Parliament and was returned for Newark in 1868, but his health broke down soon after he took his seat. He went to Australia, partly to study emigration routes, partly to regain his health, but he died at Melbourne soon after his arrival. His views can be studied in *Letters and Other Writings of the late Edward Denison*, ed. Sir Baldwyn Leighton (1872), and there is an article on him in the *D.N.B.*

In 1875 Samuel (1844–1913) and Henrietta Barnett (1851–1936) made contact with Arnold Toynbee and others of his group at Oxford and interested them in the conditions prevailing in Barnett's parish in Whitechapel. Several of them visited the area and Toynbee passed several vacations in lodgings in the Commercial Road. He died in 1883 and the following year, on the motion of Barnett, Toynbee Hall, a settlement in Whitechapel where University men lived at the beginning of their careers, was founded as a memorial to him. A number of distinguished men were among the residents, and much of the social policy of the twentieth century originated there. See Dame Henrietta Barnett, *Canon Barnett. His Life, Work, and Friends* (2 vols., 1918); Werner Picht, *Toynbee Hall and the English Settlement Movement*, trans. Lilian A. Cowell (1914).

Alfred, later Lord, Milner (1854–1925) formed a close friendship with Toynbee at Balliol. In 1884, after a period devoted to journalism and educational work in the East End in association with Toynbee and the Barnetts, he became private secretary to G. J. Goschen. He unsuccessfully contested Harrow at the 1885 general election. In 1886 he was very active in the establishment of the Liberal Unionist Association, and when Goschen became Chancellor of the Exchequer at the end of the year Milner was appointed his official Private Secretary. In 1889 he was sent to Egypt as Director-General of Accounts, and the following year was promoted to Under-Secretary in the Egyptian Finance Ministry. In 1892 he was recalled to assume the Chairmanship of the Board of Inland Revenue. Chamberlain appointed him High Commissioner to South Africa in 1897, and in 1901 Milner began to recruit a group of able young men, largely from Oxford or Toynbee Hall, to assist him in the work of reorganization and social reform after the Boer War.

They later became famous as 'Milner's Kindergarten'. See Walter Nimocks, *Milner's Young Men* (1970). GKC.

8. The 'forgotten' novel is *De Profundis. A Tale of the Social Deposits* (1864), by William Gilbert (1804–90), who also wrote *Dives and Lazarus; or the Adventures of an Obscure Medical Man in a Low Neighbourhood* (1858) and other, less relevant, novels. See the *D.N.B.* (Supplement). *Sybil*, by Benjamin Disraeli, was published in 1845; *Alton Locke*, by Charles Kingsley, in 1850; *All Sorts and Conditions of Men*, by Walter Besant, in 1882; and *Esther Waters*, by George Moore, in 1894. See P. J. Keating, *The Working Classes in Victorian Fiction* (1971). GKC.

9. From 1834 until the end of the century there was no law to control alien immigration. The Special Branch at Scotland Yard, established in 1884 to meet the threat of Fenian outrages, later came to deal with foreign anarchists and to exercise some supervision over potentially undesirable aliens. See W. Cunningham, *Alien Immigrants to England* (1897) and Bernard Gainer, *The Alien Invasion* (1972). GKC.

10. In 1869 W. T. Thornton published a treatise entitled *On Labour; Its Wrongful Claims and Rightful Dues; Its Actual Present and Possible Future*, attacking the conception of the wage fund, which he had previously criticized in the *Fortnightly Review*. For Mill's acceptance of his arguments see John Stuart Mill, *Dissertations and Discussions*, vol. iv (1875), p. 43. GKC.

11. See Macaulay's journal, 28 July 1850:

> I brought home, and read, the 'Prelude.' It is a poorer 'Excursion;' . . . The story of the French Revolution, and of its influence on the character of a young enthusiast, is told again at greater length, and with less force and pathos, than in the Excursion. The poem is to the last degree Jacobinical, indeed Socialist. I understand perfectly why Wordsworth did not choose to publish it in his lifetime.

Trevelyan, *Macaulay*, ii. 280. When describing the crowds in the streets at the time of the Great Exhibition, 1 May 1851, Macaulay noted: 'I was struck by the number of foreigners in the streets. All, however, were respectable and decent people. I saw none of the men of action with whom the Socialists were threatening us.' (ibid. ii. 293.) He also

recorded in his journal, 12 Aug. 1854: 'I read Dickens's "Hard Times."
One excessively touching, heart-breaking passage, and the rest sullen
socialism. The evils which he attacks he caricatures grossly, and with
little humour.' (ibid. ii. 383.) *GKC.*

12. For '1885' read '1884'. *GKC.*

13. For William Morris see Section XVIII, note 2. Robert Bontine
Cunninghame Graham (1852–1936), a romantic figure with the
appearance and manner of a Spanish grandee, was returned for North-
West Lanarkshire in 1886 as a Liberal but, profoundly moved by
injustice and popular distress, he became an ardent Socialist. He was
deeply devoted to Morris, with whom he was in Trafalgar Square on
'Bloody Sunday', when he was seriously wounded by a policeman.
GKC.

14. Charles Gore (1853–1932), a prominent High Churchman, and
Bishop successively of Worcester, Birmingham, and Oxford, was a
leading member of the Christian Social Union, founded in 1889.
Robert William Radclyffe Dolling (1851–1902), a prominent Ritualist
and social reformer, was Vicar of the Winchester College Mission at
St. Agatha's, Landport, 1885–95, and recorded his experiences in a
well-known book, *Ten Years in a Portsmouth Slum* (1896). He was Vicar
of St. Saviour's, Poplar, 1898–1901, at a time of great distress and
suffering. *GKC.*

15. This probably refers to Macdonald's speech to his constituents at
Stafford, 13 Jan. 1879. According to *The Times*, 15 Jan. 1879, p. 10c, he
declared that 'he was not strongly hostile to the views of the Government, and he thought they had had enough of Whig rule. When he
entered Parliament they had gained more from the Conservatives in
respect to matters affecting the working men than the Liberals would
ever have granted.' He added, however, that he opposed the Government's Russophobe policy, and condemned their conduct in Afghanistan. In Monypenny and Buckle, *Disraeli*, v. 369 there is a quotation
from a speech by Macdonald to his constituents in 1879 with almost the
same wording as that used by Young. It seems probable that it is from
the same speech, possibly from an independent report of it. *GKC.*

16. The Local Government Act of 1888, for which the Conservatives
were responsible, created county councils, including the London

County Council, which enabled the Fabians to promote a policy of 'municipal Socialism' in London. This policy had, however, already been partially adopted for practical reasons elsewhere; and before it was developed in London 170 towns owned their own gas works, thirty-one their own trams, and an advanced housing policy had been initiated in Liverpool, Greenock, and Glasgow. On the other hand, the Fabians were unable to effect some of their more ambitious ideas. See A. M. McBriar, *Fabian Socialism and English Politics, 1884–1918* (Cambridge, 1962), pp. 187–233. *GKC*.

17. For the concept that only good men could produce good buildings see Kenneth Clark, *The Gothic Revival*, 3rd edn. (1962), pp. 159–60. *GKC*.

18. These ideals are largely those reflected in the writings of William Morris, particularly in his *News from Nowhere* (1891). *GKC*.

19. Gerald Massey (1828–1907), son of a poor canal boatman, had only a rudimentary education and began work as an errand boy at the age of eight. He educated himself, read widely, became a Chartist in 1848 and the editor of the *Spirit of Freedom*, a paper largely written by working men, in 1849. He was attracted by the Christian Socialists, became Secretary to their Board, and wrote for their journal. Massey later earned his living as a poet, journalist, and popular lecturer, and is held to have contributed to the portrayal of George Eliot's character, Felix Holt. See the *D.N.B.* (2nd Supplement). The refrain of the poem cited by Young, 'The Chivalry of Labour Exhorted to the Worship of Beauty', is, with minor variations:

> Come let us worship Beauty with the knightly faith of old,
> O Chivalry of Labour toiling for the Age of Gold.

(*The Poetical Works of Gerald Massey*, new edn. (1861), pp. 387–90.) The poem 'On a Jacobin of Paris', by George Smythe, 7th Viscount Strangford (1818–57), appears in his *Historic Fancies* (1844), pp. 182–8, as one of a number of diverse character sketches. Smythe was one of the 'Young England' group associated with Disraeli, and is reckoned to have been the original of the hero of the latter's novel, *Coningsby*. Massey's earlier works were poems of revolt, but he composed a number of patriotic verses on the Crimean War, entitled *War Waits*, and his poem 'Sea Kings' is held to have anticipated Kipling's 'Song of the Dead' in *The Seven Seas* (1896). *GKC*.

20. This probably refers to Bradlaugh's speech of 24 Feb. 1890, in opposition to an amendment to the Address moved by Cunninghame Graham (*Hansard*, 3rd Ser. cccxli. 1100–11). *GKC.*

21. The source of this anecdote has not been traced. *GKC.*

SECTION XXX

1. The Newcastle Programme was the comprehensive series of proposals which was adopted in October 1891 by the Council of the National Liberal Federation as the official programme of the Liberal party. The adherent who described it as 'a Blooming Plant' has not been identified. The programme did not include a proposal to restrict the hours of labour in industry to eight, although this had long been an ideal cherished by large sections of the population and had become one of the primary objectives of most labour groups. However, in his speech at Newcastle on 2 Oct. 1891 Gladstone cautioned the working classes against committing themselves to any policy in regard to the hours of labour which would interfere with private liberty, and personally declined to pass any absolute judgement on a problem which he did not consider to have been adequately investigated (*Annual Register* (1891), History, p. 184). In 1893 and 1894 a Bill restricting miners' hours to eight was proposed in a House of Commons in which the Liberals were in a majority. The Government declared itself to be neutral and left the question to a free vote. The Bill did not receive sufficient Parliamentary time to pass into law, but on two occasions, 3 May 1893 and 25 Apr. 1894, it was supported after a full debate by a majority of the House. It is, however, clear from the debates and the division lists that Liberals voted on both sides, as did the Conservatives. See *Hansard*, 4th Ser. xi. 1841–1900; xxiii. 1329–83. *GKC.*

2. See Acton's introduction to Niccolò Machiavelli, *Il Principe*, ed. L. Arthur Burd (Oxford, 1891), p. xl: Machiavelli 'is more rationally intelligible when illustrated by lights falling not only from the century he wrote in, but from our own, which has seen the course of its history twenty-five times diverted by actual or attempted crime'. *GKC.*

3. The career of Sir Charles Dilke, whom Young believed to have

been the man to supply the leadership which Liberalism lacked, was frustrated by the accusations levelled at him in the divorce proceedings of Donald Crawford against his wife in 1885-6, as was that of Parnell by his being cited as co-respondent in the divorce case of Captain O'Shea against his wife in 1890. *GKC.*

4. The 'Melian debate' is that which Thucydides put into the mouths of the envoys of an Athenian force which invaded the Island of Melos in 416 B.C., who argued that the only course open to the Melians was to submit to overwhelming strength 'since justice only enters where there is equal power to enforce it', and the authorities of Melos, who resolved to resist (*History of the Peloponnesian War*, v. 84-116). The Athenians took the Island, killed all the men of military age, and sold the women and children into slavery. In the same year they were contemplating their fatal expedition against Syracuse. Young clearly saw an analogy between the wanton aggression of the Athenians in these two cases and the attitude of Britain towards the Boer Republics at the time of the South African War. Some resemblance might be traced between the arguments on Imperialism attributed by Young to the Conservatives (see above, pp. 174-5) and the line taken by the Athenians in the Melian debate; but to the rest of Young's imaginary debate the latter has no relevance.

Gilbert Murray (1866-1957), Professor of Greek at Glasgow University, 1889-99, and Regius Professor of Greek at Oxford, 1908-36, appears in Bernard Shaw's play, *Major Barbara* (1905), as Adolphus Cusins, a Professor of Greek, who is engaged to the heroine. As he is working on an edition of Euripides (as did Murray) he is called 'Euripides' by Barbara's father, Sir Andrew Undershaft. In 1900 Murray denounced nationalism but in 1914 he decided that Germany's bid for power must be met by force. After the war he devoted much of his life to promoting the cause of the League of Nations as an effective organization to prevent conflict. In *Major Barbara* Cusins becomes a manufacturer of armaments. *GKC.*

5. For an example of the old use of the word 'Imperialism' see Charles Kingsley to John Bullar, 26 Nov. 1857:

Tired of the helplessness of *laissez-faire*, educated men are revolting fast to Imperialism; and when once the commercial classes shall have discovered, as France has done already, that a Despotism need not interfere in any wise with the selfish state of society, but that 'XXXX and son' and 'XXXX and brothers,' can make money as fast under a Napoleon as under Christ, Manchester will not lift a finger to save the liberties of England.

Charles Kingsley. His Letters and Memories of his Life, ed. Mrs. Kingsley (2 vols., 1877), ii. 37.

After 1870 'Imperialism' is equated with 'Bonapartism' in the *Punch* cartoons depicting the competitors for power in France. See, however, Section V, note 30. *GKC.*

6. Tupper used the phrase 'Empress of India' in a sonnet published in 1860. See Martin Farquhar Tupper, *My Life as an Author* (1886), p. 221. *GKC.*

7. For Dilke's ideas see Section XVIII, note 6.

8. Henry Howard Molyneux Herbert, 4th Earl of Carnarvon (1831–90), was Under-Secretary for the Colonies from February 1858 to June 1859, and Colonial Secretary from June 1866 to March 1867, when he was responsible for the Act which confederated the British North American Provinces. In the House of Lords, 14 Feb. 1870, he spoke of the urgent need 'to knit up the different portions of the Empire once more into closer bonds one with another' (*Hansard*, 3rd Ser. cxcix. 193–213). He became Colonial Secretary in Disraeli's Government in 1874 and devoted most of his energy to a scheme to confederate the states of South Africa, but was only able to secure the passage of a permissive Act in 1877, which enabled such of the states as were willing to unite under one authority. He resigned from the Cabinet in January 1878 in protest against Lord Beaconsfield's policy of intervention against Russia in the Russo-Turkish war. As Lord Lieutenant of Ireland from June 1885 to February 1886 he favoured conceding to Ireland home rule status similar to that enjoyed by a Canadian province within the Dominion. In his address on 'Imperial Administration' to the Edinburgh Philosophical Society, 5 Nov. 1878, Carnarvon distinguished 'true Imperialism' from false, that is aggressive and materialistic Imperialism, with an obvious reference to the policy of Beaconsfield's Government (*The Times*, 6 Nov. 1878, p. 6c). *GKC, DRF.*

9. That is, between the 'true Imperialism' as defined, according to Young, by Lord Carnarvon and the two meanings which he quotes

from the *O.E.D.*, where other definitions of the word, with which Young is not concerned, are in fact given. *GKC*.

10. See, e.g., the concluding paragraphs of *Past and Present* for such passages as the following:

> But it is to you, ye Workers, who do already work, and are as grown men, noble and honourable in a sort, that the whole world calls for new work and new nobleness. Subdue mutiny, discord, wide-spread despair, by manfulness, justice, mercy and wisdom. Chaos is dark, deep as Hell; let light be, and there is instead a green flowery World. O, it is great, and there is no other greatness. To make some nook of God's Creation a little fruitfuler, better, more worthy of God; to make some human hearts a little wiser, manfuler, happier,—more blessed, less accursed! It is work for a God.

Thomas Carlyle, *Past and Present* (1843), p. 398. *GKC*.

11. For Macaulay's minute of 2 Feb. 1835 see Trevelyan, *Macaulay*, i. 405–7; John Clive, *Thomas Babington Macaulay: The Shaping of the Historian* (1973), pp. 342–426. While a number of influential men in the early nineteenth century believed it was desirable to employ more natives in the administration of India, James Mill did not in fact share their view. He thought that the main concern of the people of India was that the business of government should be efficiently and cheaply performed, that it was of little consequence to them who executed it, that to encourage any people to believe that 'the grand source of elevation' was to become a government employee was far from desirable, and that the appointment of Indians to government posts could have only a very limited effect. See his evidence before a Select Committee of the House of Commons on the Affairs of the East India Company in 1831 (H.C. (1831) v. 396, especially his answer to Question 4194) and Eric Stokes, *The English Utilitarians and India* (Oxford, 1959), pp. 63–6. Section 87 of the Charter Act of 1833 laid down that 'no native of the said territories, nor any natural-born subject of His Majesty resident therein, shall by reason only of his religion, place of birth, descent, colour, or any of them, be disabled from holding any place, office, or employment under the said Company'; but the explanatory memorandum sent out with the Act reiterated Mill's opinion.

The Queen's Proclamation of 1858 promised that 'our subjects, of whatever race or creed, may be freely and impartially admitted to office in our service, the duties of which they may be qualified, by their education, ability and integrity, duly to discharge'. However, in 1853 the Indian Civil Service had been opened to competitive examination in which, as it was held in London, it was extremely difficult for an Indian to compete successfully. Victoria inclined to believe that the rule of the Indian Civil Service was harsh and unpopular, a view probably derived from her Indian servants. See her memorandum of 2 May 1891 (*Letters of Queen Victoria*, 3rd Ser. ii. 25–6). The works of Herbert Spencer were at one time held in high esteem among Indian Nationalists, one of whom founded a Herbert Spencer Lectureship at Oxford. GKC.

12. Leonard Trelawny Hobhouse (1864–1929) was educated at Oxford, became an Assistant Tutor of Corpus Christi College in 1890 and a Fellow in 1894. In 1897 he joined the staff of the *Manchester Guardian*, with which he retained a connection until 1925, and he was political editor of the *Tribune*, 1906–7. He continued his work on philosophy and sociology and in 1907 was appointed the first Professor of Sociology at London University. The 'old Chartist' who rebuked him has not been identified, but he might have been George Jacob Holyoake (1817–1906). Few Chartists survived into the reign of Edward VII, and Holyoake and Hobhouse's uncle, Arthur Hobhouse, were in correspondence on the state of the press in 1904. Such a rebuke is also in accordance with Holyoake's pedantic habit of mind. *GKC, ER.*

13. On 9 Aug. 1880 General Sir Frederick Roberts set out from Kabul with an army of 10,000 men and marched through the mountains of Afghanistan to relieve the British garrison at Kandahar, which they entered on 31 August. In 1883 William Hicks ('Hicks Pasha'), an English officer in the Egyptian service, was dispatched with an Egyptian force into the Sudan to suppress the Mahdi, the 'false prophet' from 'the wastes beyond Wady Halfa'. After an initial success he and his men were ambushed and massacred at El Obeid. Lhassa, the seat of the Dalai Lama, the most powerful ruler in Tibet, was in fact visited by European Capuchins and Jesuits in the eighteenth century, and by an Englishman, Thomas Manning, in 1811–12. For most of the nineteenth century, however, European travellers were prevented from reaching it, but in 1903 a British mission led by General Younghusband entered Tibet with a military escort under Sir J. R. L. Macdonald. Lhassa was entered on 3 Aug. 1904 and a treaty was obtained. The journey to Khiva was

accomplished by Frederick Burnaby, an officer in the Household Cavalry and an enterprising traveller who, on learning that the Russians were preventing foreigners from entering Central Asia, set out on 30 Nov. 1875 with the intention of travelling to Bokhara. When he reached Khiva he was recalled by the Duke of Cambridge, at the request of the Russian Government. On his return he wrote *A Ride to Khiva* (1876), which achieved great success and reached its 11th edition in 1877. *King Solomon's Mines*, the famous romantic novel published by Henry Rider Haggard in 1885, was partly based on knowledge of the Zulus and Matabele acquired while he was on the staff of Sir Theophilus Shepstone in Zululand in 1877–8. *GKC.*

14. Contemporary distaste for Sir Henry Morton Stanley (1841–1904), the explorer, stemmed partly from the belief that he treated Africans more roughly than did Livingstone, that he was too ready to use fire-arms, and that he had abandoned his rearguard to its fate on his expedition to rescue Emin Pasha. However, it was probably intensified by the fact that he was of a very ambiguous origin and achieved, under the sponsorship of an American paper, something which Englishmen had failed to do, by finding Livingstone. *GKC.*

15. On 3 Jan. 1896 the Kaiser sent a telegram of congratulation to President Kruger on his repulsion of the Jameson Raid (see Section XXX, note 20) without appealing for the help of friendly powers. On 17 Dec. 1895 Grover Cleveland, President of the United States, invited Congress to inquire into the dispute between Venezuela and Great Britain over the border of British Guiana, and declared that it would be the duty of the United States to resist by all means in its power, as a wilful aggression on its rights and interests, the appropriation by Great Britain of any lands which were determined by the investigation rightfully to belong to Venezuela. Count George Leo von Caprivi was Chancellor of Germany from 1890 to 1894. Although it was a period of tension in colonial affairs Caprivi was himself responsible for the Anglo-German agreement of 1 July 1890 whereby Britain exchanged Heligoland for Zanzibar and a predominant influence in Uganda. Chamberlain did not become Colonial Secretary until 1895, and his most serious 'exchanges' occurred in 1901 and 1902 with von Bülow, German Chancellor from 1900 to 1908. It was possibly these which Young had in mind. Immediately prior to these incidents Chamberlain had been

working for an alliance with Germany. See Julian Amery, *The Life of Joseph Chamberlain*, vol. iv (1951), pp. 135–78. GKC.

16. Richard Olney, the American Secretary of State, intervened at the request of Venezuela in her border dispute with British Guiana. In a note of 20 July 1895 he cited the Monroe Doctrine as the justification for American involvement. He expressed the objection of the United States to any European state maintaining a permanent relationship with any part of the American continent and asserted: 'That distance and three thousand miles of intervening ocean make any permanent political union between an European and an American State unnatural and inexpedient will hardly be denied.' (*Speeches and Documents in American History*, ed. Robert Birley (4 vols., 1942–4), iii. 208.) GKC.

17. On this literature see I. F. Clarke, *Voices Prophesying War, 1763–1984* (1966), pp. 64–161. The source of the quotation has not been identified. GKC.

18. William Banting was an undertaker afflicted by corpulence. Before he was 60 he became incapable of tying his shoes. In 1862, at the age of 65, after trying exercise, Turkish baths, and medicines without success, he consulted William Harvey, who put him on a diet consisting chiefly of meat, fish, and dry toast. As a result Banting lost over three stones in weight, and enjoyed such improved health that he described his experiences in a *Letter on Corpulence, addressed to the Public* (1863), which gained great attention and introduced the process of 'banting' and the verb 'to bant' into the language, and thus into the *O.E.D.* As he died in 1878, the Banting of the 1887 Jubilee must have been a descendant.

Questions were asked in Parliament about the brown wash applied to the Coronation Chair, which was apparently done to tone it down to what was considered to be a suitable shade. D. R. Plunket, the First Commissioner of Works, accepted responsibility, and said that the wash could easily be removed, and that the Dean of Westminster and the President of the Society of Antiquaries were satisfied that no harm had been done. See *Hansard*, 3rd Ser. cccxvi. 934, 1785–6 (24 June and 5 July 1887). This view has not been endorsed by those who have taken an interest in the antiquities of the Abbey. GKC.

19. See *Annual Register* (1887), History, pp. 145–6; *Hansard*, 3rd Ser. cccxvi. 1491–4, 1610, 1782–5, 1796–1830; cccxvii. 76–8, 789–90, 1769–

72, 1888; cccxviii. 551, 1153-4, 1715-16; cccxix. 70; cccxx. 464-5. *GKC*.

20. On 29 Dec. 1895 Dr. Leander Jameson (1853-1917), using a force composed partly of the servants of the British South African Company and partly of the Bechuanaland police, invaded the Transvaal to support a projected rebellion by the foreigners in Johannesburg. It did not take place and Jameson and his force were captured by the Boers and returned to England for punishment. The question of the authorship of the raid was referred to a Select Committee of the House of Commons. Their inquiry cannot be said to have ended 'abruptly' as it continued for five months; but of a series of fifty-one telegrams which had passed between England and South Africa before the raid seven were withheld from the Committee. It was suggested that these contained proof that Joseph Chamberlain, Colonial Secretary at the time, had known and approved of the raid beforehand, an implication possibly desired by those who had withheld the telegrams, who were the friends of Rhodes. The telegrams have since been published and do not appear to substantiate the charge. Nor was the contemporary suspicion as general as Young's words might suggest. Two of Chamberlain's Liberal opponents, Sir William Vernon Harcourt and Sir Henry Campbell-Bannerman, were members of the Committee and both acquitted him of any responsibility for the raid. See J. L. Garvin, *The Life of Joseph Chamberlain*, vol. iii (1934), pp. 85-125. *GKC*.

21. Alfred Beit (1853-1906), Solomon Barnato Joel (1865-1931), and Barnett Isaacs Barnato (1852-97) were financiers associated with Rhodes who made fortunes in South Africa. They were all of Jewish origin, Beit from Hamburg, Joel and Barnato from London; and were suspected, rightly or wrongly, of using financial methods which many people found distasteful. *GKC*.

22. Something of the anxiety which was felt about the change in English morals at this time can be sampled in Hilaire Belloc's novel *Emmanuel Burden*, published in 1904. *GKC*.

23. This song has not been identified. *GKC*.

24. For '1905' read '1906'. This passage refers to the result of the general election of January that year, when 400 Liberals, 83 Irish Nationalists

and 30 Members who had accepted the nomination of the Labour Representation Committee were returned, as against only 157 Conservatives. The 'small, vigorous, and disconcerting auxiliary' was of course the group of Labour Members. *GKC.*

25. See Stephen Gwynn and Gertrude M. Tuckwell, *The Life of Sir Charles W. Dilke* (2 vols., 1917), ii. 502, quoting from 'the fragment of commentary in which Sir Charles dealt with the change of Sovereigns':

> The Accession Council after the Queen's death was a curious comment on history. History will tell that Victoria's death plunged the Empire into mourning, and that favourable opinion is more general of her than of her successor. Yet the Accession Council, attended almost solely by those who had reached power under her reign, was a meeting of men with a load off them. Had the King died in 1902, the Accession Council of his successor would not have been thus gay; there would have been real sorrow.

It seems probable that Dilke was attributing his own feelings to others *JMC.*

SECTION XXXI

1. See Spencer Walpole, *The Life of Lord John Russell* (2 vols., 1889), ii. 446–9. *GKC.*

2. Gerard Manley Hopkins, 'The Wreck of the Deutschland'. *GKC.*

3. Edward Gibbon, *Essay on the Study of Literature*, Section XLIX:

> Among the great multitude of facts, there are some, and these are the greatest number, which prove nothing beyond their own existence. Some, again, may be very properly cited for a partial conclusion, from which the philosopher may judge of the motives of an action, or a trait in a character; they disclose one link of a chain. Those which prevail in the general system, which are intimately connected with it, and which move its interior springs, are very rare; and it is a still rarer thing to find minds who can distinguish them among the vast chaos of events, and can draw them from hence pure and unmixed.

The Miscellaneous Works of Edward Gibbon, ed. John, Lord Sheffield (1837 edn.), p. 655. *GKC.*

4. See Constable's fourth lecture at the Royal Institution, Albemarle Street, 16 June 1836: 'Painting is a science, and should be pursued as an inquiry into the laws of nature. Why, then, may not landscape painting be considered as a branch of natural philosophy, of which pictures are but the experiments?' (C. R. Leslie, *Memoirs of the Life of John Constable,* ed. Jonathan Mayne (1951), p. 323.) *GKC.*

5. Young later recanted the notion of the 'objective mind'. See *Daylight and Champaign* (1948 edn.), pp. 172, 175, 271-7. *RR, GKC.*

6. The source of this quotation has not been traced. *GKC.*

7. cf. Thomas Hobbes, *Leviathan,* Part IV, Chapter 47: 'the Papacy is no other than the *ghost* of the deceased *Roman empire,* sitting crowned upon the grave thereof.' *EJK.*

8. Gerard Manley Hopkins, 'The Loss of the Eurydice'. *RR, DEDB.*

INDEX

INDEX